TAXING DEMOCRACY

In memory of
Leslie Whittington
(1955-2001)

Taxing Democracy

Understanding Tax Avoidance and Evasion

Edited by

VALERIE BRAITHWAITE

The Australian National University, Canberra

ASHGATE

Published by
Ashgate Publishing Limited
Gower House
Croft Road
Aldershot
Hants GU11 3HR
England

Ashgate Publishing Company
Suite 420
101 Cherry Street
Burlington, VT 05401-4405
USA

Ashgate website: http://www.ashgate.com

British Library Cataloguing in Publication Data
Taxing democracy : understanding tax avoidance and evasion
1.Taxation - Australia 2.Tax collection - Australia
3.Taxpayer compliance - Australia
I.Braithwaite, V. A. (Valerie A.), 1951-
336.2'05'0994

Library of Congress Cataloging-in-Publication Data
Taxing democracy : understanding tax avoidance and evasion / edited by Valerie Braithwaite.
p. cm.
Includes bibliographical references and index.
ISBN 0-7546-2243-6
1. Taxation--Australia. 2. Tax evasion--Australia. I. Braithwaite, V. A. (Valerie A.), 1951-

HJ3091.T39 2003
336.2'06'0994--dc21

2002036105

ISBN 0 7546 2243 6

Reprinted 2004

Printed in Great Britain by Antony Rowe Ltd, Chippenham, Wiltshire

Contents

Chapter 1

A New Approach to Tax Compliance

Valerie Braithwaite

In the late 1990s, the Australian Taxation Office (ATO) underwent a series of reforms that set the stage for a new proactive role in building a voluntary taxpaying culture. The evaluation of these measures is being undertaken rather more systematically than reforms in other countries, with results that have implications for all nations' tax regimes. This process of reform is built on the premise that although legislation is one of the basic building blocks for compliance, it is far from sufficient. Tax law is contestable; it is also complex; and it is not beyond the initiative of taxpayers to avoid and evade tax in ways that are costly, both in terms of revenue that will never be collected and enforcement that is resource intensive. The traditional tax infrastructure of law, auditors, penalties, debt collectors, and court cases needs to be supplemented by measures that boost taxpayers' commitment to paying tax with or without the tax authority watching over their shoulders.

At the heart of the reform strategies of the late 1990s was the building of a relationship with the Australian community in which the tax office was to be (a) professional, responsive, fair, open, and accountable in helping taxpayers comply with their tax obligations; as well as (b) effective in bringing to account those who intentionally avoided their obligations. Through adopting such practices, the intent was that the tax office earn (c) the trust, support and respect of the community (Australian Taxation Office, 1997).

The first initiative toward building this relationship was the Taxpayers' Charter (Australian Taxation Office, 1997). The Charter articulated 12 rights of taxpayers and committed tax officers to treating taxpayers fairly and reasonably, to explain decisions, assist with questions, and provide reliable information, to respect taxpayer privacy, to keep the taxpayers' compliance costs to a minimum, and to be accountable, if necessary, through independent review. The taxpayers' obligations, articulated also in the Charter document, were four-fold and involved being truthful in dealings with the tax office, keeping records in accordance with the law, taking reasonable care in preparing tax information, and lodging tax returns and required documents by the due date.

Bringing the Charter to life was no small challenge for the Australian Taxation Office. The traditional regulatory style of the ATO has been heavily weighted toward command and control with the automatic application of penalties for various forms of non-compliance (see Chapter 6). At the same time, the authority has not always used its prosecutorial powers effectively, with a history of slap-on-the-wrist prosecutions that rarely touch major evaders or avoiders (Grabosky and

Braithwaite, 1986). In order for the tax office to change course, it was necessary to show fairness and reasonableness to those who were willing to cooperate, and focus enforcement capacity on those flagrantly ignoring their tax obligations. The companion reform that addressed this issue and enabled the Charter to be mainstreamed in ATO operations was the ATO Compliance Model. Originating in the Cash Economy Task Force (1998),[1] the Compliance Model drew on the work of regulatory scholars at the Australian National University as well as on the vast research literature on tax compliance. Consistent with this literature (see Coleman and Freeman, 1997, for example), the Task Force urged the ATO to better understand not only the business profiles of taxpayers (which auditors traditionally, if partially, do), but also the nature of the industry they belong to, the economic factors that impinge on that industry and society more broadly, and the psychological and sociological factors that frame taxpayers' decisions or non-decisions about the actions they will take to meet their tax obligations. In the words of the Task Force:

> none of these factors stand alone as the sole reason for a taxpayer's behaviour, and equally, it is not possible to identify which factors in combination may influence the behaviour of any one particular person. However, it is possible to identify a combination of factors that is more likely to influence behaviour for certain categories of taxpayers (Cash Economy Task Force, 1998, p. 20).

Better understanding of the complexity and interrelationships of factors shaping taxpayer actions was accompanied by an implicit distinction in the Cash Economy Task Force Report (1998) between the detection of non-compliance and the management of non-compliance. The detection problem involved identifying those among us who will be non-compliant. The human management problem involved nudging those of us who are non-compliant toward compliance, 'without adversely affecting compliant taxpayers' (p. 22). The Cash Economy Compliance Model was constructed to provide a methodology for addressing the human management problem, while providing better intelligence to improve detection. The development of the detection problem was followed up more systematically by the Large Business and International line of the ATO. In adapting the ATO Compliance Model to their needs, Large Business introduced a sophisticated risk management component (Australian Taxation Office, 2000).

The core of the ATO Compliance Model, as developed by the Cash Economy Task Force, is presented diagrammatically in Figure 1.1.

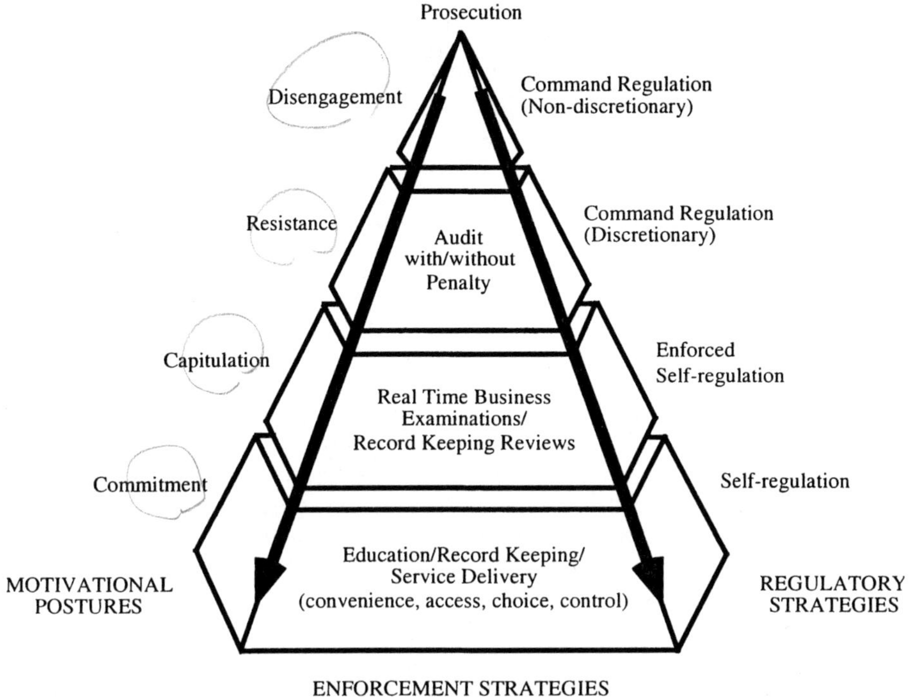

Figure 1.1 Example of regulatory practice with ATO Compliance Model

On the left hand side of the model are the motivational postures. These are the stances that taxpayers openly express in their relationships with the tax authority. These postures were identified in earlier regulatory work (Braithwaite, Braithwaite, Gibson and Makkai, 1994; Braithwaite, 1995) to describe the way in which taxpayers controlled the amount of social distance they placed between themselves and the tax office. When taxpayers were open to admitting wrongdoing, correcting their mistakes, and getting on with meeting the law's expectations, they were likely to be displaying the postures of commitment or capitulation (see Chapter 2 for a more detailed description of the postures). The tax official's task is relatively straightforward in such circumstances. Their authority will be taken seriously, and compliance will follow as long as taxpayers know what they are supposed to do, are treated in a procedurally just manner, and are conscious of the fact that there will be follow through by the tax authority if they do not comply.

The tax official's task becomes increasingly harder as taxpayers put more social distance between themselves and the authority. Capitulation describes giving in to authority without necessarily being prepared to take the initiative to get things right in the future; when initiative is demonstrated, commitment is the more apt description. In contrast, the postures of resistance and disengagement reflect a conscious holding back of cooperation. The relationship is adversarial, and the tax official's approach to gaining compliance needs to be more strategic than would be necessary with more cooperative taxpayers. The most difficult stance for a tax official to deal with in the model is disengagement. Here the taxpayer has such contempt for the system that the chances of persuasion working are low: In such circumstances, other strategies may be equally ineffective, leaving incapacitation as the only option (through prosecution, imprisonment, or taking away a license to practice).

The courses of action that a tax official can take in response to compliance problems are many and varied (see Chapters 9, 11, 12), although generally speaking, attention seems to focus on penalties in response to law breaking. As important as these are to an effectively functioning tax system, compliance problems are not always black and white in the field of taxation, and in such circumstances, it is helpful for the tax office to have a range of tools at their disposal to manage the compliance problem well. Possible courses of action that tax officials can take are depicted within the framework of the Compliance Model in Figure 1.1 (middle column). They are arranged to represent different levels of seriousness and intrusiveness on the part of the tax office, the general thesis being that if taxpayers are prepared to meet their obligations with minimum interference by the tax office, they should be left alone to get on with it. Needless to say, the courses of action will change as the nature of the compliance problem changes: What is useful for cash economy problems will not necessarily apply to other problems (see Chapter 9).

While local areas need to develop their own compliance strategies (Sparrow, 2000), the principles that guide enforcement are more stable and are represented on the right hand side of the Compliance Model in Figure 1.1. For those who are willing to cooperate, the principle guiding the choice of strategy is self-regulation. If taxpayers are committed to correcting their own mistakes, they should be encouraged and assisted in doing so. The next level of interference might be called enforced self-regulation. Taxpayers have responsibility for correcting their own mistakes, but a mechanism is in place to ensure they do so, and to provide feedback to indicate whether or not the taxpayers' compliance plan is sound.

Above these levels are the traditional principles of tax office enforcement that have a command and control quality. A soft version of command and control regulation is to wave a big stick, but to exercise discretion around using punishment to improve compliance. The hard version is non-discretionary punishment such that a sanction automatically follows when non-compliance is detected, regardless of the circumstances. The principles of enforcement, from the bottom to the top of the pyramid, involve a transfer of power from the taxpayer to the tax office, and a concomitant loss of freedom on the part of the taxpayer.

At the heart of the Compliance Model are the concepts of responsive regulation and regulatory pyramids to guide an authority's response to non-compliance (Ayres and Braithwaite, 1992). Responsive regulation steps away from a command and control approach to regulation and moves regulators beyond a mentality that if they go strictly by the book in dealing with non-compliance, their problems will be over. A considerable research literature supports the failings of command and control regulation when applied indiscriminately in areas where compliance and non-compliance are multi-faceted and complex phenomena (Bardach and Kagan, 1982; Gunningham and Grabosky, 1998; Sparrow, 2000). It is very easy for a regulatory agency relying on a simplistic conception of enforcement to fall foul of accusations of unreasonableness and unfairness (Bardach and Kagan, 1982). Tax administrations across the world have received their share of criticism of this kind (Report of the National Commission on Restructuring the Internal Revenue Service, 1997; The Report of the Committee of Experts on Tax Compliance, 1999; Senate Economics References Committee, 2001).

Regulatory pyramids are designed to promote self-regulation and they advocate only as much enforcement by the authority as the situation requires to gain compliance. Two basic assumptions underlie their effective use. First, most of the population are assumed to be located at the base of the pyramid. In other words, costly enforcement resources are not wasted on those who are willing to comply, but are reserved for the smaller proportion of the population not willing to cooperate with the authority, clustering around the higher levels of the pyramid. Second, regulatory pyramids demand of an authority the capacity and readiness to follow through on non-compliance, escalating the costs to the taxpayer to the point of incapacitation if necessary.

The essential compliance generating dynamic of the pyramid relies on knowing that it is less costly to resolve a problem at the bottom of the pyramid than to allow it to escalate to the top of the pyramid. This applies to both regulator and regulatee, and incorporates costs of a material, social or psychological kind. The knowledge that drives behaviour comes into play at two levels. First, the cooperative approach at the bottom of the pyramid involves persuasion in both directions: Taxpayers have the opportunity to persuade the tax office at the same time as the tax office is trying to persuade the taxpayer. As the conflict moves up the pyramid, taxpayers lose power to persuade as the tax office moves into command and control mode. Second, the regulatory pyramid communicates consequences of non-compliance, and most importantly, it signals that the delivery of the consequences is contingent upon the next move of the regulatee. If the regulatee chooses a cooperative response, the regulator cooperates. If the regulatee's choice is uncooperative, the regulator moves to a higher level of enforcement that imposes higher costs on the non-complier. This treatment sits comfortably alongside the Taxpayers' Charter with its in-built concept of procedural justice (see Chapter 3).

The implementation of the ATO Compliance Model mainstreamed the Taxpayers' Charter, but at the same time challenged traditional ways of working beyond the human management system. The administrative, technical and legal systems were implicated in the change process as well (see Chapter 8). Foremost in everyone's mind was the fact that the ATO Compliance Model came about through transplanting ideas developed in other regulatory contexts to the field of taxation (see Chapter 6). Adaptation across fields was based on intuitive judgement, and to a considerable extent faith on the part of ATO senior management that it might work (see Chapter 7). In order to progress the use of the Model judiciously, there was a need to monitor and evaluate its effectiveness, making adjustments where required (see Chapter 8). With this purpose in mind, a six-year research partnership was set up between the Australian Taxation Office and the Australian National University in August, 1999 with the establishment of the Centre for Tax System Integrity.

The research program for the Centre for Tax System Integrity revolves around three questions that are relevant to tax administrations around the world: (a) What options do democratic states have for cultivating a voluntary taxpaying culture? (b) How practicable and desirable is the ATO Compliance Model for managing tax compliance and non-compliance? (c) Can evidence-based tax administration be built around a continuing program of experimentation that builds an increasingly rich tool-kit of cost-effective strategies (represented in the middle column of the model) for improving compliance? This volume presents findings from the first phase of our research. Together these chapters present evidence supporting the relevance of the Model to the taxation context, as well as stories of success and frustration as the ATO undertook the systematic process of implementation. Experiences in developing and using the ATO Compliance Model have been shared with a number of other tax authorities including those in Britain, New Zealand, Canada, Bulgaria, Thailand, and East Timor and through training programs for tax administrators in Commonwealth countries in Asia, Africa and the South Pacific. This volume provides an opportunity to share the ideas behind the Model and our current knowledge of its usefulness more broadly with all who are interested in tax administration in the global community of the 21st century.

Part I (The Relationship between the Tax Office and the Community) of this volume examines a set of issues that will be most familiar to readers as arguable causes of non-compliance. In the present context, however, their importance stems from their centrality in establishing a cooperative relationship between a tax authority and the community.

The first question addressed in Chapter 2 is whether or not the concept of motivational postures has relevance in depicting the quality of the relationship of a tax authority with the community. Having established benchmarks for each posture in the community, attention is turned to self-reported compliance. Are individual taxpayers as compliant as their motivational postures suggest? The answer is a resounding no. Non-compliant actions are found among those committed to the system, those who have capitulated to tax authority, those who resist it, and those who have disengaged from it. The readiness of non-compliers to cooperate is varied, as postulated in the ATO Compliance Model.

Chapter 3 addresses one of the most important issues in any relationship between a democratically elected government and its people, perceptions of justice. Michael Wenzel provides a framework for justice research in the taxation context through drawing a distinction between different kinds of justice (distributive, procedural, retributive) and pointing out that justice takes on quite different meanings at different levels of analysis. Justice can be adjudicated at an individual level (am I being treated fairly?) or at a group level (is my group (e.g., taxi drivers) being treated fairly?) or at a societal level (is our tax system fair for all?). Knowing what kind of justice is under consideration is not always clear in tax research that considers justice as a cause of non-compliance. It is particularly important for future research to learn whether or not the kinds of justice that shape non-compliance are different from the kinds of justice that enable tax authorities to manage compliance and claim legitimacy within the democracy.

The question of tax office legitimacy is of central concern in Natalie Taylor's chapter on social identity (Chapter 4). Taylor takes up Michael Wenzel's distinction between whether one thinks of oneself as a member of a group within society or whether one identifies with a more inclusive group such as Australian taxpayer. Using the written responses of 155 Australians to an open-ended question about the tax system, Taylor demonstrates that it is the superordinate inclusive identities that are associated with the granting of legitimacy to the tax office and the readiness to cooperate with the tax system. Taylor concludes by issuing a challenge to tax regimes that continue to adhere to a narrow individualistic conception of self-interest as the fundamental motivation of taxpayers. What such authorities may be giving away, according to Taylor, is the key to their legitimacy.

The cash economy – the compliance problem that gave rise to the ATO Compliance Model – has always been hidden from view, its size being estimated by economists through a variety of indirect methods. In Chapter 5, Friedrich Schneider 'sizes' Australia's cash (shadow) economy in comparison to other countries. Then follows a microanalysis of individual taxpayers who answered survey questions on shadow economy participation in 2000 and 2002. Using these data, Valerie Braithwaite, Friedrich Schneider, Monika Reinhart, and Kristina Murphy examine the importance of deterrence, justice, identity, and motivational postures in determining who moves into the shadow economy, who moves out, who stays involved, and who remains apart from shadow economy activities.

Part II examines the ATO Compliance Model as Change Agent. The section begins with the story of how the Compliance Model was received by operative staff in the Australian Taxation Office (Chapter 6). Jenny Job and David Honaker present a warts and all account of the early stages of implementation of the Model based on interviews conducted by the senior author. While there were enthusiasts, there were also resisters. From both camps there were some who correctly foresaw how far reaching the changes could be for the tax office and for the way it conducted its business in the future. Along with insightfulness, were feelings of threat and loss. Some complained of being pushed into something that was untried and untested, and there were misunderstandings and myths, not uncommon when innovation is in the air.

While the views from below reflected both excitement and cynicism about the prospects of implementing the ATO Compliance Model, those higher up in the organisation showed no reluctance in owning the Model. Kersty Hobson uses transcripts of interviews with champions of the ATO Compliance Model to analyse the ways in which leaders understood the model and presented it to staff (Chapter 7). Hobson draws an interesting distinction in terms of how the ATO Compliance Model was taken on board by senior staff. Some, in the words of one of Hobson's interviewees, worked 'inside the model', while others stood outside, trying to determine where they and their group should be located within the framework. For the first group, the model was a dynamic tool to be played with and pushed to its limits in analysing and managing compliance. For the second, it was a static entity, that was to be used at worst, as another rulebook, at best a cookbook.

In Chapter 8, the action of the ATO Compliance Model moves out of the office and into the field. Neal Shover collected data from ATO field officers in the Cash

Economy Building and Construction Project and from owners of small building and construction firms. These data suggest some progress in the direction of effective implementation and the building of better relationships with taxpayers. Shover warns, however, that it would be premature to claim success for the model at this stage, and recognises some of the real world problems that highlight the need for continuing evaluation. Organisational capacity for reform is fundamental to the introduction of responsive regulation. The ATO provided resources in the early stages, but the organisation was forced to redirect much of its attention to the introduction of a goods and services tax in July 2000. As Shover explains, the ATO lacked 'a calm environment [that] lends itself to the deliberate and self-reflective decision-making that can nurture and sustain [change]'. Consequently, the opportunity to evaluate ATO Compliance Model implementation in a rigorous and systematic way was lost. At the same time, there was a failure in organisational capacity to make the changes in the administrative and technical system to allow responsive regulation to operate fully.

Taking the ATO Compliance Model out of cash economy and recommending its use in other ATO business lines did not occur without considerable scepticism, most notably from the Large Business and International line. In Chapter 9, John Braithwaite provides a review of the relevance of the ATO Compliance Model to large business, arguing that basic ideas translate across contexts, although there may be need to package the model differently. Braithwaite's chapter underlines the point that the principles of responsive regulation travel widely, but that regulatory pyramids cannot and should not be treated as cookbooks. Each compliance group needs to find its own strategies that suit the problem, the context, and the available resources. And they need to consult widely with the community to find these strategies. Braithwaite illustrates this point with the proposal of a compliance-tax-rate-spiral for reducing the incentives for game playing among the very large corporates. The idea is that when the large corporates as a group reach a series of benchmarks in extra dollars collected in tax, they be rewarded through a lowering of company tax rates. The idea of the compliance-tax-rate-spiral is not something that Braithwaite envisages as anything other than a point for debate at this stage: instead it 'signals the kind of world that might one day be possible if only we can learn how to forge a more meaningful business-community-government partnership toward a decent tax system'.

The purpose of responsive regulation and the ATO Compliance Model is to develop, in conjunction with the community, a sophisticated plan that can effectively manage non-compliant taxpayers, while being supportive of those who are compliant. Up to this point, we have assumed that we know what compliance is, and if there is doubt, that the tax office has the authority to clarify things for us. In Part III (Beyond the Compliance Model), the limitations of this worldview are exposed.

In Chapter 10, John Braithwaite, Yvonne Pittelkow and Rob Williams focus on the difficulties of detecting suspected non-compliance in the tax affairs of wealthy individuals in Australia. These authors provide a series of statistical analyses of risk data from 235 high wealth individuals to show how important the expert analyst's hunch is in deciding where the greatest risks to tax revenue lie: When aggressive tax avoidance is obvious, it has long past its use-by date for those with the money to pay for state-of-the-art financial advice.

The game of tax avoidance is addressed by Doreen McBarnet in Chapter 11. McBarnet points out that compliance or non-compliance is a binary classification that falls apart once tax avoidance enters the scene. Tax avoidance creates what McBarnet calls creative compliance whereby taxpayers adhere to the strict letter of the law, but find loopholes and caveats to minimise their tax without regard for the spirit of the law. The ATO Compliance Model, as it stands, offers little help to tax officers dealing with creative compliance because if no law has been broken, there can be no top to the regulatory pyramid to encourage cooperation at lower levels. In such circumstances, management of the human system cannot meaningfully take place in the absence of revision of the legal system. McBarnet describes the practice of introducing principles that span the law in a bid to ensure that the intention of the legislature provides a backstop for legal interpretation of law. McBarnet, however, is pessimistic that the cat and mouse game of creative compliance can be changed by law itself. The change that is required is more fundamental and attitudinal: Law must be seen as something to be 'respected' rather than 'material to be worked on' to one's advantage.

The industry of tax avoidance rests on the talents of financial advisors. In Chapter 12, John Braithwaite reports findings based on interviews with 27 advisors whose clients include the wealthiest people in Australia. Advisors were invited to comment on the performance of the ATO's High Wealth Individuals Taskforce that was set up in 1996, and were also drawn into discussions of better ways of improving compliance among high wealth individuals and identifying deficiencies in the law. The interviews themselves were evidence of the ATO Compliance Model at work, a willingness by all parties to engage in dialogue and share information, allowing persuasion to work in both directions. At the same time, the interviews yielded valuable policy insights about where enforcement capacity should be focused and ways in which the ATO Compliance Model can be misleading if the object of attention is solely the taxpayer. Braithwaite argues that, in the case of high wealth individuals, the dangers of 'enforcement swamping' are so great that the kind of 'simplistic purism' that focuses on the taxpayer as the object of enforcement has to be abandoned. Instead, the High Wealth Individual Taskforce needs to continue along its current path 'of targeting nodes of control over decisions of major import for tax compliance', be they wealthy individuals and the suite of entities they control, tax managers of large corporations, influential advisors, or promoters of aggressive tax avoidance schemes.

In the final chapter, questions of compliance and what it means to comply are embedded within a model that extends across the human, administrative and legal systems that comprise a tax authority. Local compliance solutions do not always sit comfortably alongside other local solutions. The principle introduced to reconcile tensions within the compliance plan of a tax office is integrity defined as unity and soundness of purpose. The argument presented in Chapter 13 is that effective compliance management and institutional integrity are interconnected. Both can be optimised when a tax authority understands and works with the community, bringing interested parties into discussions about the tax system, how it should be designed, and what purpose it should serve. The responsiveness to the outside environment, however, must be matched by responsiveness internally. Tax offices need to have the organisational capacity to change their administrative and legal structures, and to ensure that information flows freely up and down the organisation. Through the quality of responsiveness, internally and externally, tax administrations in the 21st century may lose certainty, but gain an assurance that they greatly need: The acknowledgment of the community that they are indeed taxing in the interests of the democracy as a whole.

Taxing Democracy brings together the contributions of researchers from three continents, all of whom have spent time together in the Centre for Tax System Integrity over its first three years, as full-time research staff, visiting fellows, or research affiliates. Our thanks to the Australian Taxation Office and the Research School of Social Sciences at the Australian National University for funding the Centre and its research. Without their support and their cooperation, this initiative would not have been possible.

Like all enterprises of this kind, there are people, whose names do not appear in the pages that follow, who make it all possible. For her generosity of spirit and infinite wisdom, my thanks to our administrator, Linda Gosnell, who keeps the Centre running smoothly, and seemingly, effortlessly. To Sophie Cartwright who meticulously and patiently prepared this manuscript for publication, thank you from us all. And to the postgraduate students, university colleagues and colleagues from the Australian Taxation Office who have provided critical comments, have participated in conferences and seminars with us, and who have opened doors so that this research could be conducted, our most sincere thanks. Among this very large support team is Andrew Stout who has been our master engineer, building bridges between the academic and bureaucratic worlds and generating a continuing dialogue between the Centre and the Australian Taxation Office. We are indebted to him for contributing in such an important way to the richness of the research that we are able to share in this volume.

The name of one visiting fellow that sadly does not appear in this volume is that of our late colleague, Leslie Whittington. Leslie was a tax economist from Georgetown University, who was to spend study leave at the Centre, with her husband, Charles, and their young daughters, Zoe and Dana. Leslie and her family started their journey on September 11, 2001. All were on board the plane that was hijacked by terrorists and flown into the Pentagon. We dedicate this volume to her memory.

Note

1 The Cash Economy Task Force comprised 13 members spanning non-government (industry, accountancy and commerce, welfare, and university) and government sectors. The Task Force was chaired by Mr. David Butler, now Commissioner of Inland Revenue New Zealand, and Mr. Neil Mann, now Deputy Commissioner, Australian Taxation Office.

References

Australian Taxation Office (1997), *The Taxpayers' Charter*, Australian Taxation Office, Canberra.

_____ (2000), *Cooperative Compliance: Working with Large Business in the New Tax System*, Australian Taxation Office, Canberra.

Ayres, I. and Braithwaite, J. (1992), *Responsive Regulation*, Cambridge University Press, Cambridge.

Bardach, E. and Kagan, R. A. (1982), *Going by the Book: The Problem of Regulatory Unreasonableness*, Temple University Press, Philadelphia.

Braithwaite, V. (1995), 'Games of Engagement: Postures within the Regulatory Community', *Law and Policy*, vol. 17(3), pp. 225-55.

Braithwaite, V., Braithwaite, J. Gibson, D. and Makkai, T. (1994), 'Regulatory Styles, Motivational Postures and Nursing Home Compliance', *Law and Policy,* vol. 16(4), pp. 363-94.

Cash Economy Task Force (1998), *Improving Tax Compliance in the Cash Economy*, Australian Taxation Office, Canberra.

Coleman, C. and Freeman, L. (1997), 'Cultural Foundations of Taxpayer Attitudes to Voluntary Compliance', *Australian Tax Forum*, vol. 13, pp. 311-36.

Grabosky, P. and Braithwaite, J. (1986), *Of Manners Gentle: Strategies of Australian Business Regulatory Agencies*, Oxford University Press, Oxford.

Gunningham, N. and Grabosky, P. (1998), *Smart Regulation: Designing Environmental Policy*, Clarendon Press, Oxford.

Report of the National Commission on Restructuring the Internal Revenue Service (1997), *A Vision for a New IRS*, National Commission on Restructuring the Internal Revenue Service, Washington, D.C.

Senate Economics References Committee (2001), *Inquiry into Mass Marketed Tax Effective Schemes and Investor Protection: Interim Report*, Parliament of the Commonwealth of Australia, Canberra.

Sparrow, M. (2000), *The Regulatory Craft*, Brookings Institution Press, Washington D.C.

The Report of the Committee of Experts on Tax Compliance (1999), *Report for the Treasurer and Minister for Revenue*, http://www.executive.govt.nz/96-99/compliance/index.html.

PART I
THE RELATIONSHIP BETWEEN THE TAX OFFICE AND THE COMMUNITY

Chapter 2

Dancing with Tax Authorities: Motivational Postures and Non-compliant Actions

Valerie Braithwaite

The management of tax systems is a complex business and is likely to become increasingly so in the 21st century as they are forced to adjust to the changes accompanying globalisation. The popular stereotype of the 'taxman' collecting the revenue through the process of detecting non-compliance and imposing penalties provides a simplistic account of the realities of modern tax administration (see Tomkins, Packman, Russell and Colville, 2001). As tax systems are adjusted, the community needs to be educated, persuaded and encouraged to cooperate, long after the vote is cast at the ballot box. Added to this process is the universal problem of tax law, unable to respond adequately to the increasing pressures put on the tax system through the increasingly common practice of tax avoidance. What the law can not fix, tax administration must at least contain until the law catches up to close the offending loopholes, a never ending process since each piece of legislation brings new opportunities for avoidance (see McBarnet, Chapter 11, this volume). Containing problems of tax avoidance, checking problems of tax evasion and convincing the public that tax reforms are for the public good require a conception of taxpayers that is multidimensional and dynamic, but at the same time leaves taxpayers in no doubt about the integrity of the tax administration as a whole. This chapter provides a foundation for this new conception of the taxpayer through drawing a distinction between cooperation (or consent to being regulated) and compliance related actions. This distinction is not only critical to implementing responsive regulation, but also reflects the current state of taxpayer behaviour. This chapter reveals that those who resist most vocally, who challenge tax authority decisions and are openly critical of the institution, are not discernibly more non-compliant as a group than taxpayers who choose other ways of engaging with the system. As resisters exercise their democratic rights, they provide valuable feedback for tax administrations grappling with unprecedented pressures on their systems of revenue collection.

Theoretical Background

As tax authorities approach communities to explain tax obligations and encourage, or indeed, enforce compliance, taxpayers are equally active, practicing their own responsiveness to the authority in ways that meet their own needs and interests (Bardach and Kagan, 1982; McBarnet, Chapter 11, this volume). The regulated are not powerless when faced with authority. They may cooperate or they may withdraw, they may practice defiance, or find ways of sidestepping the issue (Kelman, 1961). And what they do is not unrelated to what the authority does to them (Braithwaite, Braithwaite, Gibson and Makkai, 1994; Tyler, 1990). Community responsiveness to a tax system and tax authority is multidimensional, changeable, and has as much to do with social relationships as with technical and administrative procedures. This observation is not new, but it has only recently begun to resonate through the tax literature (Schmölders, 1970; Smith and Stalans, 1991; Alm, Sanchez and de Juan, 1995; Cullis and Lewis, 1997).

Community responsiveness is defined as the evaluation that individuals or groups make of the tax authority in their community, as well as the actions that taxpayers take in response to the expectations of this authority.[1] In this chapter, two fundamental dimensions of community responsiveness are examined, the first being attitudinal and broad in conception, the second, by contrast, being behavioural and specific. These dimensions translate directly onto the ATO Compliance Model (see Figure 1.1 in Chapter 1). The broad attitudinal kind of responsiveness measured in this chapter is represented by motivational postures. Motivational postures describe the stance of taxpayers that must be managed when a tax authority seeks to change or wants an explanation for taxpaying behaviour.

Compliance related behaviours are different from motivational postures. The behavioural responses of taxpayers that are noticed most keenly by tax authorities are those that are illegal or involve aggressive tax minimisation. Specific actions that signal non-compliance, particularly when undertaken by substantial numbers of taxpayers, provide a trigger for the use of the Compliance Model for management purposes. The taxpaying behaviours that are singled out in this chapter for analysis are those that are traditionally regarded as relevant to compliance: failure to declare income on a tax return, participation in the shadow economy, false declaration of deductions, failure to file a tax return or pay a tax debt, and involvement in tax avoidance (Webley, Robben, Elffers and Hessing, 1991; Kinsey and Grasmick, 1993; Wallschutzky, 1996; Alm, 1999; Schneider and Enste, 2000).

The conceptualisation of attitude and behaviour as separate dimensions of community responsiveness is in keeping with empirical findings in the area of tax compliance, but departs from the expectation of consistency theorists that attitudes and behaviour should be related.[2] The gap between attitude and action extends beyond the taxation context. The criminological literature is rich in accounts of how people do not always obey the law, even when they believe in it. Consistency of thought and action implies a rationality and thoughtfulness that does not always occur in the behaviour of individuals in everyday life (Massey, 2002). Many reasons have been given to explain lack of correspondence between attitudes and behaviour. Circumstances may provide opportunities for non-compliance that tempt us to do things we would not normally do (Carver and Scheier, 1998), or circumstances may present barriers to compliance that make us give up trying to do what is expected (Bandura, 1986). Human actions are not always premeditated. Often they are driven by emotion (Massey, 2002), or by habit (Kuhl and Fuhrmann, 1998). And sometimes, those who act do so with a very inadequate understanding of what the situation demands (Bandura, 1986). In the taxation context, law is complex, changing and ambiguous, and can be broken unintentionally as well as intentionally (James, Lewis and Allison, 1987; Smith and Kinsey, 1987; Long and Swingen, 1988; Coleman and Freeman, 1997).

The second reason for why responsiveness of the broad attitudinal kind needs to be distinguished from responsiveness of the specific behavioural kind is largely methodological (Fishbein and Ajzen, 1974; Epstein, 1983). In order for attitude and action to be consistent, specific attitudes must be paired with specific actions, general attitudes with general actions. The reasoning behind these assertions is that any single act is shaped by multiple factors, and that any small change in context can be a factor that changes specific behaviour. Thus, to predict a specific act, one needs to measure perceptions and attitudes relating to context as well as to the object of interest (see Ajzen, 1991, for an account of how this argument has developed over the years). Attitude measures that are not context sensitive, such as motivational postures, therefore, can only be expected to be a marker of behaviour when we are considering general behaviour, or an amalgam of behaviours.

But the purpose of this chapter, and the regulatory challenge more broadly, is not to find ways to match attitudinal and behavioural measures to extend or modify consistency theories, but rather to move to a different level of analysis and theorise how these different concepts can be used to better manage tax system integrity. Thus, this chapter proceeds from the assumption that responsiveness can be conceptualised in terms of two dimensions, one broad and attitudinal, the other specific and behavioural. These two dimensions bear some relationship to each other as consistency theorists would expect, but in no sense can one be conceived as a proxy for the other. Evaluations of the tax authority of an attitudinal kind and obedience to the tax authority of a behavioural kind are being proposed as distinctly different aspects of the construct of community responsiveness.

Motivational Postures: Evaluating the Tax Authority

Motivational postures have been used in past research to capture the way regulatees position themselves in relation to regulatory authority (Braithwaite et al., 1994; Braithwaite, 1995). Authorities may have legal legitimacy, but this does not guarantee them psychological legitimacy. Individuals and groups evaluate authorities in terms of what they stand for and how they perform. As evaluations are made, revised, shared and accumulated over time, individuals and groups develop positions in relation to the authority. A psychological concept that is central to positioning is social distance (Bogardus, 1928). Bogardus used this term to refer to the degree to which individuals (or groups) had positive feelings for other ethnic groups and ascribed status to other ethnic groups. In the regulatory context, social distance indicates liking and the ascription of status to the regulatory authority. When individuals and groups decide how much they want to associate or be aligned with an authority, and how much they want to be out of reach of and out of contact with the authority, they are indicating the social distance they wish to place between themselves and the authority.[3]

The distance placed between regulatee and regulator may be intuitive at first, but it does not remain that way for long. Individuals and groups articulate their beliefs, develop rationalisations for their feelings, and use values and ideologies to justify the ways they position themselves in relation to legally sanctioned authorities (Sykes and Matza, 1957; Rokeach, 1973; Thurman, St. John and Riggs, 1984; Griffin and Buehler, 1993; Bersoff, 1999). These interconnected sets of beliefs and attitudes are shared, borrowed, challenged, and elaborated upon even further as part of the social life of a community. The interconnected sets of beliefs and attitudes that are consciously held and openly shared with others are called motivational postures. Five motivational postures have been identified as important in the context of taxation compliance: (a) commitment, (b) capitulation, (c) resistance, (d) disengagement, and (e) game playing.

The two postures that reflect an overall positive orientation to authority are commitment and capitulation. The kinds of beliefs and attitudes that comprise these postures are represented in Table 2.1. Commitment reflects beliefs about the desirability of tax systems and feelings of moral obligation to act in the interest of the collective and pay one's tax with good will. Capitulation reflects acceptance of the tax office as the legitimate authority and the feeling that the tax office is a benign power as long as one acts properly and defers to its authority.

In contrast to these postures of deference, are three postures of defiance. The first is the familiar posture of resistance. Resistance reflects doubts about the intentions of the tax office to behave cooperatively and benignly towards those it dominates and provides the rhetoric for calling on taxpayers to be watchful, to fight for their rights, and to curb tax office power. Disengagement is also a motivational posture that communicates resistance, but here the disenchantment is more widespread, and individuals and groups have moved beyond seeing any point in challenging the authorities. The tax office and the tax system are beyond redemption for the disengaged citizen, the main objective being to keep both socially distant and blocked from view.

The fifth posture is game playing. Unlike the previous postures, game playing has not been examined in other regulatory contexts, emerging instead from discussions about posturing with tax officials and taxpayers. The behaviours previously have been described by social scientists working in fields involving economic regulation (McBarnet, 1992; McBarnet and Whelan, 1999). McBarnet (Chapter 11, this volume) sees game playing as a particular kind of attitude to law:

Law is seen as something to be moulded to suit one's purposes rather than as something to be respected as defining the limits of acceptable activity. Game playing was included as a motivational posture for the purposes of testing whether or not players consciously adopted this style of engagement with the tax system and the tax office.

Measuring Motivational Postures

In view of the features of motivational postures, the most convenient measuring procedure is a self-report questionnaire. The statements presented to individuals for their response were modelled on those that had been used successfully in other regulatory contexts. Additional statements were derived from open-ended discussions with people about the tax system and the tax office. In particular, the game playing posture was measured through collecting statements from people about their orientation to the tax system. In all, 29 statements were used to measure the five postures. The statements that were considered to be good indicators of each of the postures are listed in Table 2.1. A brief description of the motivational postures among a sample of Australian taxpayers will be provided shortly. First, the context for the collection of these data requires explanation.

The Community Hopes, Fears and Actions Survey

Between June and December, 2000, a national survey was conducted by the Centre for Tax System Integrity at the Australian National University (for details see Braithwaite, 2001; Braithwaite, Reinhart, Mearns and Graham, 2001). A stratified random sample of 7754 persons was selected from the publicly available electoral rolls. A lengthy questionnaire on tax matters was sent to each person who had been randomly selected, together with a letter explaining the intent of the study and a stamped addressed envelope for the return of the completed questionnaire. Two reminder cards were sent at two to three week intervals. After 5 weeks, a second questionnaire was posted to non-respondents, again followed by two reminder cards. (Details of the methodology of the survey are available in Mearns and Braithwaite, 2001.)

Completed returns of the survey were obtained from 29 per cent of the sample, providing 2040 cases for further analysis. This response rate, while low in absolute terms, compares favourably with rates reported for other tax surveys (Pope, Fayle and Chen, 1993; Wallschutzky, 1996; Kirchler, 1999; Webley, Adams and Elffers, 2002). Interestingly, the sample provided a relatively representative cross-section of the population with regard to sex, ethnicity, education, age, occupation, and marital status (see Mearns and Braithwaite, 2001). The biases that were detected were an over-representation of those in scribing occupations who would have been more comfortable with a detailed response-intense questionnaire, and an under-representation of younger age groups (18 to 25 years) who traditionally are difficult to recruit for self-completion surveys.

Table 2.1 Statements representing motivational postures of commitment, capitulation, resistance, disengagement, and game playing

Commitment
Paying tax is the right thing to do.
Paying tax is a responsibility that should be willingly accepted by all Australians.
I feel a moral obligation to pay my tax.
Paying my tax ultimately advantages everyone.
I think of tax paying as helping the government do worthwhile things.
Overall, I pay my tax with good will.
I resent paying tax. (reversed)
I accept responsibility for paying my fair share of tax.

Capitulation
If you cooperate with the Tax Office, they are likely to be cooperative with you.
Even if the Tax Office finds that I am doing something wrong, they will respect me in the long run as long as I admit my mistakes.
The Tax Office is encouraging to those who have difficulty meeting their obligations through no fault of their own.
The tax system may not be perfect, but it works well enough for most of us.
No matter how cooperative or uncooperative the Tax Office is, the best policy is to always be cooperative with them.

Resistance
If you don't cooperate with the Tax Office, they will get tough with you.
The Tax Office is more interested in catching you for doing the wrong thing, than helping you do the right thing.
It's important not to let the Tax Office push you around.
It's impossible to satisfy the Tax Office completely.
Once the Tax Office has you branded as a non-compliant taxpayer, they will never change their mind.
As a society, we need more people willing to take a stand against the Tax Office.

Disengagement
If I find out that I am not doing what the Tax Office wants, I'm not going to lose any sleep over it.
I personally don't think that there is much the Tax Office can do to me to make me pay tax if I don't want to.
I don't care if I am not doing the right thing by the Tax Office.
If the Tax Office gets tough with me, I will become uncooperative with them.
I don't really know what the Tax Office expects of me and I'm not about to ask.

Game playing
I enjoy spending time working out how changes in the tax system will affect me.
I enjoy talking to friends about loopholes in the tax system.
I like the game of finding the grey area of tax law.
I enjoy the challenge of minimising the tax I have to pay.
The Tax Office respects taxpayers who can give them a run for their money.

Are Motivational Postures Discernible Among Taxpayers and Citizens?

The survey responses, made in relation to each of the 29 motivational posture statements on a 1 (strongly disagree) to 5 (strongly agree) rating scale, provided the data base for answering two questions: First, do individual taxpayers identify with the postures of commitment, capitulation, resistance, disengagement, and game playing; and second, do individuals hold these postures (or a subset of them) simultaneously? Some readers may feel that the statements representing each posture are inconsistent with each other (for instance, compare commitment with game playing). Such would be the case if we subscribed to the idea that each of us has one self. But actually we are not so unitary in our make up. Work by colleagues on aggressive tax planning, for instance, provides evidence of individuals simultaneously holding a conception of self as citizen who should pay taxes with good grace, and a conception of self as a business adviser who makes a living out of game playing on behalf of those who want to avoid their tax obligations (Murphy and Byng, 2002; Braithwaite, J., personal communication). The notion of each individual having multiple selves is now the dominant conception of self in psychology and sociology (Geertz, 1973; Burke, 1980; Baumeister, 1996). The co-existence of different postures boosted or suppressed by various institutional configurations challenges regulation theorists and practitioners to design their systems with an appreciation of the individual. Regulating people through understanding the simultaneous emergence and retreat of various postures means that at the most fundamental level, regulation rests on the art of managing relationships. Before this argument can be convincing, however, there is a need to examine the data on motivational postures to find out about their distinctiveness and co-existence.

In order to confirm the fit of the taxpaying data set to the conceptual schema of five postures of commitment, capitulation, resistance, disengagement, and game playing, a principal components factor analysis with a varimax rotation was performed on responses to the 29 statements. The results showed that each factor was defined predominantly by statements representing one of the postures (see Braithwaite and Reinhart, 2001). This means that the five postures are relatively distinctive, and when we examine the statements that measure each posture as outlined in Table 2.1, we find coherence and consistency in the way that people are responding to statements within each set. In other words, these data provide evidence that the motivational postures are fairly coherent sets of beliefs that are part of the way individuals think about themselves in relation to tax authorities.

The next step was to examine the relationships among the postures: Were they relatively independent of each other, and therefore supportive of the co-existence assumption, or were some postures incompatible with other postures? In order to answer this question, scale scores on each posture were calculated for each person in the sample. Survey respondents had used ratings from 1 (representing strong disagreement) to 5 (representing strong agreement) to indicate the extent to which they agreed or disagreed with each of the statements representing each of the postures in Table 2.1. Ratings for a particular motivational posture were then summed and divided by the number of items used to measure it, producing a scale score ranging from 1 to 5. Having arrived at scores for each person on the scales of commitment, capitulation, resistance, disengagement, and game playing, the scale scores were intercorrelated to find out if there was some consistency in how people were responding to the postures. These Pearson product-moment correlation coefficients appear in Table 2.2, along with an alpha reliability coefficient to reflect the degree of internal consistency within each scale.

These findings show some relationships among the postures. Commitment and capitulation are compatible postures, but where these exist, one is less likely to find disengagement and resistance. Disengagement is a posture that is compatible with resistance, but also with game playing. None of these correlations, however, are sufficiently high (correlations are substantially lower than the alpha reliability coefficients in the diagonal) to justify an assumption that taxpayers can be placed on a simple adversarial-cooperative dimension. On the basis of the findings in Table 2.2, taxpayers' responsive selves are far more multifaceted. Although the correlations demonstrate that the five postures are not likely to be equally strong in any one individual at any one time, having one posture does not rule out the possibility of having another for any individual taxpayer. In other words, the assumption of co-existence remains plausible. Taxpayers can demonstrate more than one posture in any specific encounter.

Table 2.2 Pearson product-moment correlation coefficients among motivational posture scales (alpha reliability coefficients in diagonal)

Posture	1	2	3	4	5
Commitment	.82	-	-	-	-
Capitulation	.38	.63	-	-	-
Resistance	-.30	-.36	.68	-	-
Disengagement	-.36	-.15	.35	.64	-
Game playing	-.13	.16	.17	.33	.69

Note: All Pearson product-moment correlation coefficients are significant at the .01 level.

So what proportion of the population display commitment, capitulation, resistance, disengagement and game playing in response to the tax authority? The mean scores for the survey respondents on commitment, capitulation, resistance, disengagement, and game playing were used to construct the graph in Figure 2.1.

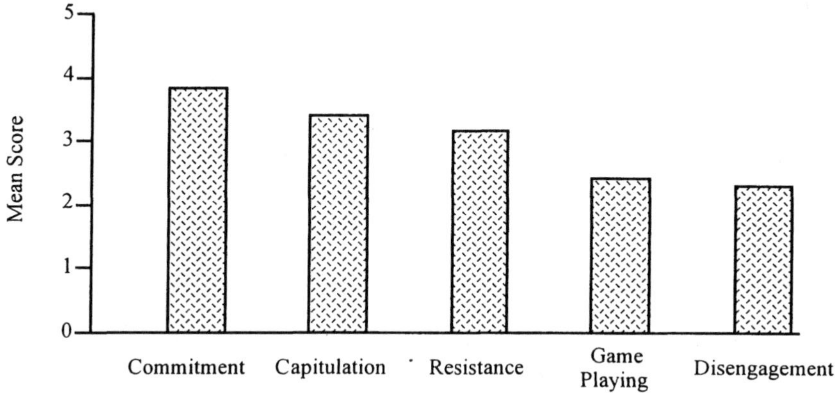

Figure 2.1 Mean scores for motivational postures of commitment, capitulation, resistance, disengagement, and game playing

As expected in a democracy, the dominant postures are those reflecting a positive orientation to authority, that is, commitment (M = 3.85, SD = .54) and capitulation (M = 3.40, SD = .54). Approximately 92 per cent of respondents relate positively to the posture of commitment and 73 per cent recognise themselves in the posture of capitulation. Resistance (M = 3.18, SD = .54) is the next most widely endorsed, again a sign that the democracy is working as it should be in that a sizeable proportion (55%) are willing to question the tax office openly. Least pervasive in the community are disengagement (M = 2.31, SD = .52) and game playing (M = 2.42, SD = .62). Disengagement is the posture that, on the basis of previous research, is the least easy for regulators to manage (Braithwaite et al., 1994). Only 7 per cent of respondents recognised themselves in this posture. Through placing themselves outside the regulatory institution, those who choose to disengage can cut themselves off psychologically from attempts at persuasion and influence. Game playing takes place within the regulatory institution, but players use the letter of the law to circumvent the intention of the law (see McBarnet, Chapter 11, this volume), in time re-creating the regulatory institution itself. The relatively small segment who identify with game playing, 13 per cent, is likely to reflect the fact that such practices have generally been the prerogative of elite groups. As tax avoidance schemes become increasingly available and acceptable to the general public through mass marketing (Commonwealth Ombudsman, 1999; Senate Economics References Committee, 2001), the game playing mindset is expected to increase.

Because motivational postures can be held simultaneously, it is relatively easy for them to wax and wane over time. When instructions arrive in the mail for the yearly tax return we might feel committed, or at least, capitulate to the system. As we look in detail at how much tax we have paid or owe, we might feel resistance, disengagement, or perhaps even a desire to play games. Having completed the transaction, however, we might revert to our committed posture, believing that paying tax is the right thing to do. In other words, as the context in which we find ourselves changes, our motivational postures change, making us cooperative at times, uncooperative at others.

Nevertheless, it is reasonable to assume that individuals have a basic comfort zone in relation to tax, and that survey responses reflect the social distance that individuals generally place between themselves and the tax authority and tax system. Compared with the postures of commitment and capitulation, the defiant postures are more likely to be associated with perceptions of threat from taxation, low satisfaction with the democracy, anti-government and pro-market attitudes, relatively weak identification with being an Australian citizen and an honest taxpayer, higher than average investment in pursuing aggressive tax options, and a desire to abolish the tax system (see Braithwaite, 2002a; Taylor, Chapter 4, this volume). Furthermore, the postures of defiance are more likely to be closed to persuasion of all kinds – education and discussion, as well as the usual deterrence measures of being caught and punished for wrongdoing (Braithwaite, 2002b).

Motivational postures are proving to be useful markers of degree of consent, cooperation and commitment that underlies the human system as it comes into contact with the administrative/technical tax system. When commitment and capitulation are high, the conditions for introducing measures to improve compliance are optimal. These measures may involve setting up social contexts where tax issues can be contested in a constructive and dialogic fashion, and where tax administrators and citizens can co-design tax systems to make them work better for everyone. When the defiant postures of resistance, disengagement and game playing are high, however, a truce will need to be negotiated in all likelihood before any meaningful attempts at the co-design of the tax system can proceed.

Compliance Related Activities: Obeying the Tax Authority

A definition of tax compliance ideally should be one that captures issues of theoretical importance as well as giving practical direction for measuring the concept. James and Alley (1999) offer a definition that does not allow us to back away from the essence of the compliance concept, and at the same time challenges those of us who want to measure tax non-compliance:

> the willingness of individuals and other taxable entities to act…within the spirit as well as the letter of tax law and administration, without the application of enforcement activity (p. 10).

The behavioural dimension of tax compliance measured in this section represents only part of the domain mapped out by this definition. The part that is the focus of attention is compliance related activity by individuals within a self-assessment tax system. Non-compliance is inferred from either: (a) individual taxpayers expressing uncertainty as to whether they have acted within either the letter or the spirit of the law; or (b) individual taxpayers taking actions that are widely recognised in the community as being outside the letter or the spirit of the law. In addition, measures were taken of tax minimisation activities ranging from the cautious to the aggressive. The Australian Taxation Office (ATO) can deny tax benefits where a reasonable person would conclude that the sole or dominant purpose for entering into the tax minimisation arrangement was to obtain a tax benefit (under Part IVA of the *Income Tax Assessment Act 1936*).

The source of data for an analysis of the behavioural dimension of non-compliance and minimisation was the *Community Hopes, Fears and Actions Survey* (Braithwaite, 2001) in which taxpayers were asked to self-report on their activities. In order to ensure that we were measuring the behavioural dimension of tax non-compliance and tax minimisation in ways that were meaningful to the majority of those sampled in the survey, the focus of attention was the personal or individual tax return. Most Australians who have worked are likely to have been required to lodge a tax return at some time in their lives. Five sub-domains of taxpayer activity where tax law and taxpayer obligations are common knowledge were chosen for analysis: (a) lodging a tax return; (b) paying a tax debt; (c) declaring income through an income tax return; (d) engaging in the cash (shadow) economy; and (e) claiming work-related expenses and other deductions. The final sub-domain examined the use of strategies to minimise tax payments comprising cautious (legal) activities, as well as aggressive activities that could fall foul of Part IVA.

In this section of the chapter, the compliance related actions discussed above are reported for this sample from the Australian population. These compliance behaviours are then correlated with each other in order to find out if there is evidence to support the existence of a generalised tendency to not comply with tax requests across a range of contexts. All indications are that whether or not an individual complies or fails to comply depends on context, undoubtedly influenced by a multitude of factors including opportunity, surveillance, social networks, and knowledge (Smith and Kinsey, 1987; Collins, Milliron and Toy, 1992; Andreoni, Erard and Feinstein, 1998; Richardson and Sawyer, 2001). If so, measures of non-compliance, for the most part, should not be highly correlated with each other. Nevertheless, it may be the case that some activities make others possible because of their contextual similarities. In particular, an important question to examine is whether or not cautious minimising strategies of the kind that may be encouraged by government accompany the more aggressive activities that tax authorities are trying to discourage because of the threat they pose to the tax system (Sakurai and Braithwaite, 2001; Murphy and Byng, 2002).

Lodgment

In the *Community Hopes, Fears and Actions Survey*, two questions were asked about lodgment of a 1998-99 tax return. Respondents were asked 'Should you have filed an income tax return in 1998-99' and immediately afterward, 'Did you file an income tax return for 1998-99?' 81.8 per cent of respondents said that they should have lodged a return or that they did not know if they should have lodged a return for the 98-99 financial year.[4] Of this group, 4.7 per cent had not yet lodged their return. When those who did not need to lodge were included with the compliant group, the per cent non-compliant on lodgment in the sample was 3.8 per cent. In other words, 3.8 per cent of the sample acknowledged having the capacity to defy the ATO's request to lodge, and did so.

In addition, respondents were asked: 'Have you any income tax returns not yet completed from previous years?'. Of the total sample, 4.5 per cent said that they were in this situation.

Not having lodged a 98-99 income tax return that respondents said should have been lodged and not having lodged returns for earlier financial years were actions that were significantly and notably correlated ($r = .37$, $p < .001$). Those who had not lodged a 98-99 return were also likely to have not lodged previous returns. Using these data, a non-compliance index called non-lodgment was constructed. The index was calculated by adding together compliance scores for the two time periods. A score of 2, meaning that neither the 98-99 return nor all earlier returns had been filed, was obtained by 1.6 per cent of the sample. A score of 1, meaning that either the 98-99 return or an earlier return had not been lodged, was obtained by 5.1 per cent of the sample. A score of 0, meaning that all tax returns that should have been lodged had been lodged, characterised 93.3 per cent of the sample.

Non-payment of Tax Debt

One question was used to assess having a tax debt: 'Do you have an outstanding debt with the Tax Office?'. Those who said they had an outstanding debt constituted 3.4 per cent of the sample. It should be noted that those with a debt are not necessarily behaving this way without tax office permission: They may have arranged a payment plan with the ATO. It is common knowledge, however, that the law requires taxpayers to pay the money they owe on time, and therefore, carrying an outstanding debt remains an example of not behaving in accordance with the law, even if one is granted an extension of time to pay.

Failure to Declare Income

Respondents were presented with income from a variety of sources and were asked if they 'did not declare it', 'declared some', 'declared most', or 'declared all' in their 98-99 return. They were also given the option of indicating that they received nothing from this income source (scored the same as 'declared all' for the purposes of analysis). The sources of income were: (a) salary, wages; (b) honorariums, allowances, tips, bonuses, director's fees; (c) eligible termination payments; (d) Australian government allowances like Youth Allowance, Austudy, Newstart; (e) Australian government pensions, superannuation pensions, and other pensions or annuities; (f) interest; and (g) dividends. The percentage of the sample failing to declare each type of income is given in Table 2.3. Because of the small percentages in the failure to declare 'some', 'most' and 'all' categories, responses were combined into one non-compliant category (see far right column in Table 2.3).

Table 2.3 Percentage of sample not declaring all income: 'Think about each of the sources of income listed below and select the response that best describes your 1998-99 income tax return'

	Per cent not declaring all			
Income source	did not declare it	declared some	declared most	failure to declare (total)
salary, wages	.4	.7	2.1	3.2
honorariums, tips, allowances, bonuses	1.9	1.3	1.3	4.5
eligible termination payments	.5	.7	.5	1.7
Australian government allowances	.5	.8	.4	1.7
Australian government pensions	1.4	.8	.5	2.7
interest	2.0	1.3	1.8	5.1
dividends	.9	.7	.6	2.2

After answering this set of specific questions about sources of income, respondents were asked: 'As far as you know, did you report all the money you earned in your 1998-99 income tax return?'. 4.3 per cent admitted that they did not declare all their income in their 98-99 return.

Responses to this general question, along with the dichotomised compliant and non-compliant data for the seven sources of income in Table 2.3, were intercorrelated. The correlations ranged from .06 to .60 (median = .36), providing sufficient justification for combining the responses to form an index representing failure to declare income on a tax return (alpha reliability coefficient = .76). The failure to declare income on the 98-99 tax return index revealed that 13 per cent of taxpayers had failed to declare income of some kind. Most episodes of failure to declare income were restricted to one or two categories.

Participation in the Cash Economy

Respondents were asked about whether, in the last 12 months, they had been a provider of services in the cash economy or a purchaser of such services: (a) 'Have you worked for cash-in-hand payments in the last 12 months? By cash-in-hand we mean cash money that tax is not paid on', and (b) 'Have you paid anyone cash-in-hand payments in the last 12 months for work or services they provided to you? By cash-in-hand we mean cash money that tax is not paid on'.

In response to the first question, 6.1 per cent said that they had worked for cash-in-hand payments, and 14.5 per cent said that they had paid for cash-in-hand services. When responses were combined for providers and purchasers, 19.1 per cent of respondents were participating in the cash economy, with 1.5 per cent being both a purchaser and provider.

Over-claiming Deductions

Two questions were asked regarding deductions claimed on the 98-99 income tax return. The first was: 'As far as you know, did you exaggerate the amount of deductions or rebates in your 1998-99 income tax return?'. The majority of respondents (89.8%) answered 'not at all', but 7.1 per cent admitted to exaggerating 'a little', 2.1 per cent 'somewhat', .3 per cent 'quite a lot', and .7 per cent 'a lot'.

The second question on over-claiming was: 'Think of the deductions and rebates you claimed in your 1998-99 income tax return. Would you say you were (a) absolutely confident that they were all legitimate, (b) a bit unsure about some of them, (c) pretty unsure about quite a lot, or (d) haven't a clue, someone else did it'. Most of the sample claimed to be absolutely confident about the legitimacy of the claims (84.8%), 7.9 per cent were a bit unsure about some, .7 per cent were unsure about a lot, and 6.6 per cent did not have a clue because someone else had completed the tax return for them. For this latter group, signing an income tax return appears to be a ritualised activity with a third party being assigned responsibility for its accuracy.

These data show that 10 per cent are willing to admit to some over-claiming and 15 per cent are prepared to express some uncertainty about whether their claims for deductions and rebates are all legitimate. Responses to these two questions were used to form an over-claiming deductions index. Before this could be done, the second question was dichotomised in terms of whether respondents were absolutely confident (84.8%) or not (15.2%). Responses to the two questions were then correlated ($r = .34$, $p < .001$), showing that the more one exaggerates deductions, the less confident one admits to being about the correctness of the claim. Responses to these two items were transformed into standardised scores (mean of 0, standard deviation of 1) and then summed to form an over-claiming deductions index (alpha reliability coefficient = .51). The percentage expressing doubts or admitting to over-claiming deductions was 19.8 per cent of the sample.

Seeking and Using Strategies to Minimise Tax

Respondents were presented with a list of 8 strategies that are known to provide for tax minimisation. Respondents were asked if they were able to minimise their tax through these strategies in the 1998-99 financial year. Respondents were also asked to circle a special category if they did not know what the particular strategy was. The findings are reported in Table 2.4 under two headings. First, the percentage of the sample using the strategy is recorded. The second column represents the percentage of the sample with no knowledge of the strategy as a method of minimising tax. Of particular note is that although tax minimisation is a popular topic for media attention, knowledge about the specific methods of tax minimisation have not penetrated into the community as extensively as had been assumed when the survey was conducted. This apparent lack of understanding of specific methods of tax minimisation among some segments of the population may be comforting to a tax administration that feels in control of its taxpayers and able to shield its constituency from temptation. However, in a world where mass marketed schemes are aggressively promoted and individual taxpayers need to be alert to the dangers, a poor understanding of tax avoidance measures and their consequences leads to vulnerability in the system (Commonwealth Ombudsman, 1999; Murphy, 2002).

The strategies listed in Table 2.4 differ enormously in the degree to which they meet the expectations of the tax office, or to put it another way, the degree to which they risk being defined as avoidance measures by the tax office. Paying into superannuation schemes to minimise tax is explicitly encouraged, for example, whereas using off-shore tax havens is explicitly discouraged. There is no way in which Part IVA of the *Income Tax Assessment Act 1936* can be operationalised in relation to survey responses to divide strategies into those that are legal and those that are illegal. It is possible, however, to divide the strategies in terms of the degree to which they push the limits of legality.[5] With this in mind, the list of 8 was divided into those that are on the more cautious side (negative gearing, employee share arrangements, salary packaging, superannuation planning, and warrants or leveraged investments) and those that are on the more aggressive side (schemes, tax shelters, and off-shore tax havens).

Table 2.4 Percentage of sample using tax minimisation strategies and lacking knowledge of these strategies

	Per cent of sample	
Investment strategies	Used it	No knowledge
Cautious minimisation strategies		
Negative gearing (property & shares)	12.1	8.1
Employee share arrangements	1.7	13.3
Salary packaging	7.2	11.6
Superannuation planning	20.2	6.7
Warrants or leveraged investments	.9	21.2

Risky or aggressive minimisation strategies		
Schemes to convert income into capital gains	1.6	16.4
Tax shelters (e.g. film or agricultural schemes)	1.7	15.2
Off-shore tax havens or other international tax planning	.6	13.9

Evidence to suggest that people who used one strategy were more likely to use others was not strong. The correlations among the 8 strategies were all positive, but they were also relatively low ranging from .02 to .34 (median = .09).[6] It seems most likely that having found one strategy, most individuals really did not need to look for another. As a result, a tax minimisation index was not formed from these measures, but it was still possible to count the number of strategies that were being used by each respondent, of either a cautious or aggressive kind. A count on the use of the five cautious strategies revealed that 69.1 per cent were using none, 22.6 per cent were using one, 7.1 per cent were using two, 1.1 per cent three, .1 per cent four and .1 per cent five. On the three more aggressive strategies, 96.9 per cent were using none, 2.7 per cent one, .3 per cent two, and .1 per cent three.

From a legal perspective, purpose or intent is critically important for ascertaining the acceptability of a tax minimisation scheme to the ATO (Part IVA of the *Income Tax Assessment Act 1936*). In the context of a general population survey in which individuals are asked to self-report on their activities, intent was defined in terms of how much effort the taxpayer dedicated to finding ways to minimise tax. A scale to measure effort to minimise tax was constructed from two items. The first question was: 'Some people put in a lot of effort to plan their financial affairs in order to legally pay as little tax as possible. How much effort did you or your family devote to this objective in preparing for your 1998-99 income tax return?'. In response, 6.7 per cent circled 'a lot', 8 per cent 'quite a bit', 17.2 per cent 'some', 21.2 per cent 'a little', and 46.9 per cent 'none'. The second question asked respondents: 'In preparing for your 1998-99 income tax return, did you look at several ways of arranging your finances to minimise your tax?'. Respondents replied 'yes' (22.2%) or 'no' (77.8%).

These two items correlated positively with each other (r = .49, p < .001), showing that those who put a lot of effort into legal tax minimisation were also likely to have looked at several different ways of arranging their finances to minimise tax. When the responses to these questions were considered conjointly, 45.2 per cent of the sample reported having put no effort into minimising their tax. Scores on the two items were standardised and were summed to produce the tax minimisation effort index (alpha reliability coefficient = .66).

The Overall Picture of Compliance Related Activities

The scores of individuals on 9 indicators of tax non-compliance and minimisation activities were intercorrelated to find out if there was evidence of a broad band practice of tax evasion and avoidance whereby individuals openly acknowledged that they acted in ways to defy the authorities on a number of different compliance dimensions. From Table 2.5, there was not much evidence of broad band defiance of tax office expectations. There were, however, noteworthy correlations in what might be called compatible contexts.

The first area in which there appeared to be some systematic defiance was around the activity of over-claiming deductions. Those over-claiming deductions were more likely to not declare all their income on their tax return. Not declaring all income and over-claiming deductions are associated weakly with working for cash-in-hand as well as being a slow or negligent lodger. And those who were prepared to over-claim deductions acknowledged dedicating special effort to doing their tax return in a way that minimised their tax.

The second area in which there appeared to be links among different activities revolved around tax minimisation. The greater the number of cautious tax minimising strategies adopted by a person, the more likely it was that the person would be engaged in aggressive forms of tax minimisation. Not surprisingly, the greater the number of cautious and aggressive strategies used, the greater the effort devoted to tax minimisation.

Table 2.5 Pearson product-moment correlation coefficients among indicators of tax non-compliance and minimisation

Indicator	1	2	3	4	5	6	7	8
1. Non-lodgment	-	-	-	-	-	-	-	-
2. Non-payment tax debt	.09	-	-	-	-	-	-	-
3. Undeclared income	.18	.05	-	-	-	-	-	-
4. Provider cash-in-hand	.03	.03	.25	-	-	-	-	-
5. Purchaser cash-in-hand	.06	-.01	.02	.08	-	-	-	-
6. Over-claim deductions	.13	.10	.38	.13	.05	-	-	-
7. No. cautious strategies	.03	-.01	.01	.02	.10	.03	-	-
8. No. aggressive strategies	.08	-.02	.09	.04	.07	.09	.23	-
9. Tax minimisation effort	.00	-.02	.10	.02	.06	.15	.30	.19

Note: Coefficients of .08 or over are significant at the .001 level.

While these patterns of behavioural defiance are apparent in the correlation matrix in Table 2.5, the more important story is one of relatively little overlap across these different actions. In each of the 9 instances of defiance listed above, the vast majority of people (over 80%) are doing what the tax office expects of them. If we analyse the problem differently, however, and ask, what proportion of the sample are meeting tax office expectations on all indicators, we get a slightly different picture. In asking this question, the 9 indicators are separated into those that are more commonly linked with evasion (non-lodgment, non-payment of tax debt, failure to declare income, provider of cash-in-hand services, purchaser of cash-in-hand services, and over-claiming deductions) and those more commonly linked with avoidance (number of cautious minimising strategies, number of aggressive minimising strategies, and effort to minimise). The sample segment that claimed to be doing all the right things in terms of lodgment, paying debt, declaring income, correctly claiming deductions, and refraining from participating in the cash economy in any form numbered a rather low 52.2 per cent. The sample segment that was active in tax minimisation was 63.9 per cent, leaving 36.1 per cent claiming complete lack of involvement in tax minimising activities. When cautious minimising was excluded, the percentage engaged in aggressive minimising or effortful minimising dropped to 55.6 per cent, leaving 44.4 per cent in clearly identified 'safe' territory, not committed to tax minimisation activity.

Motivational Postures and Compliance Related Activities

This chapter began with the assertion that how we evaluate the tax authority and the tax system may have little to do with whether we comply with the wishes of that authority: Many factors influence whether or not we obey. The opposite also applies. The level of our obedience does not dictate our readiness to support new tax systems or cooperate with changes to an old one. With a constantly changing taxpaying environment, tax authorities have to worry not only about the community's compliance rates, but also its willingness to accept change and cooperate in the change process. Responsiveness of both the attitudinal and behavioural kind are critical to the effective management of tax systems by tax authorities. In this section, the basic assertion underlying the chapter is tested empirically: Are the motivational postures that people adopt in relation to authorities such as the ATO a reflection of their compliance related actions, or is it best to conceptualise the management of taxpayers in terms of two separate dimensions, one attitudinal and evaluative of the authority, the other behavioural and reactive to tax law?

Correlations were calculated between the motivational postures of commitment, capitulation, resistance, disengagement and game playing and compliance related activities. For the analysis reported in Table 2.6, the compliance related variables were reduced to two kinds of activity. The first variable assigned a score of 1 to any individual who had engaged in at least one of the six evasion-related activities (non-lodgment, carrying a tax debt, failure to declare income, provider of cash-in-hand services, purchaser of cash-in-hand services, over-claiming deductions) and a score of zero to those who did not participate in any of them. The second variable assigned a score of 1 to any individual who had engaged in aggressive strategies or who had put effort into tax minimisation. All others were assigned a score of zero. Through creating variables that reflected compliance actions across contexts, the chances of linking attitudes and behaviour at the general level of measurement should have been optimised. This step was taken to remove the methodological criticism that one cannot expect general attitudes to correlate with specific compliance related actions.[7]

Table 2.6 presents the correlations between motivational postures and evasion or avoidance related actions. As anticipated the relationships are small. Those who try some evasion related activities are more likely to express postures of resistance to and disengagement from the tax system. Interestingly, being committed or captured by the system does not prevent individuals from acting in ways that are likely to get them into trouble with tax authorities.

When we turn our attention to tax avoidance, however, commitment provides a little protection from investing in tax minimising activities. The more committed people are to paying tax, the less likely they are to put effort into the more aggressive forms of tax minimisation. The postures most strongly related to the aggressive minimisation of tax were game playing and resistance. Overall, these data suggest that avoidance is the preferred option of those who dislike tax and can practice their defiance within the letter of the law. Evasion is the option for those who dislike tax and have located themselves outside the reach of the law, at least psychologically.

Table 2.6 Point-biserial correlation coefficients between motivational postures and compliance related actions

Motivational postures	Evasion related actions	Avoidance related actions
Commitment	-.05	-.11
Capitulation	-.04	-.06
Resistance	.12	.12
Disengagement	.14	.07
Game playing	.07	.17

Note: Coefficients of .08 or over are significant at the .001 level.

It is worth noting that all relationships between motivational postures and compliance related activities are in the expected direction from a consistency theory perspective. It must be emphasised, however, that the correlations are uniformly low. Figures 2.2 and 2.3 show that evaders, avoiders, and model citizens do not differ much from each other when they are sitting by themselves completing a questionnaire. If their postures change in the course of acting out their non-compliance, they are responding to triggers from reference groups, the environment, or perhaps even tax authorities. Thus, we can conclude that the motivational postures that people generally espouse in relation to taxation, and the compliance related actions these same people take in response to tax authority demands, while weakly related to each other, provide different information about community responsiveness.

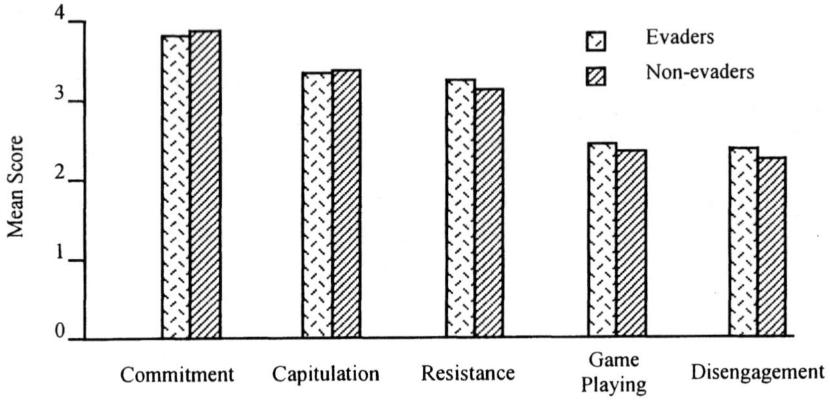

Figure 2.2 Motivational posture mean scores for evaders and non-evaders

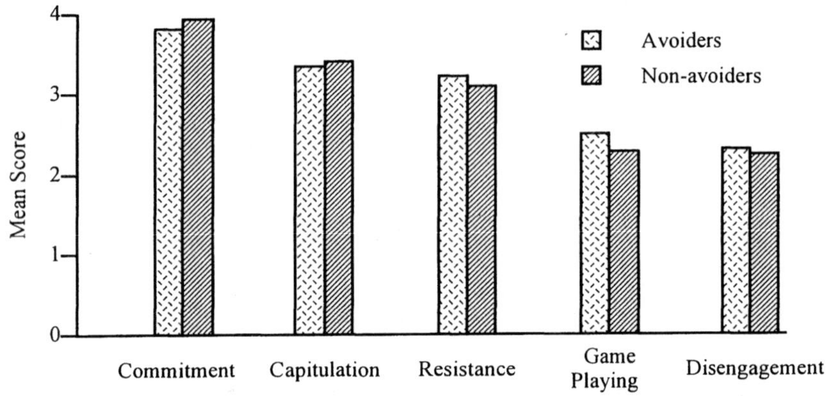

Figure 2.3 Motivational posture mean scores for avoiders and non-avoiders

Conclusion

This chapter theoretically and empirically differentiates the compliance related actions of taxpayers from their evaluation of the tax system and the tax office, expressed in terms of motivational postures. Motivational postures reflect the social distance that individuals wish to place between themselves and the tax authority. Increasing social distance indicates increasing dislike for the authority and a lowering of the status ascribed to that authority. It does not, necessarily, signal disobedience. In some ways, motivational postures can be thought of as an indicator of the degree to which an individual is giving consent to the authority: Consent to consider that individual as a participant in the tax system and consent to being regulated by the authority. Giving consent is a different phenomenon from obeying a request from a legally designated authority.

When framed in terms of consent and compliance related action, the two-dimensional conception of responsiveness offered in this chapter is less puzzling. Non-compliant actions may be initiated for any number of reasons, only some of which are attitudinal. Once non-compliance has occurred, it requires a response by the authority. All too often, authorities make the assumption of consistency between attitude and behaviour: People who do the wrong thing are bound to be nasty pieces of work, and need to be treated like the villains they are (Braithwaite et al., 1994). This is not always the case, as this chapter demonstrates. The important question then is does this simplistic formulation of 'bad guys do bad things' cause harm? From the perspective of an authority, part of dealing with an individual's non-compliance is to ensure that it will not happen again, and part is to show the community that compliance standards are high and will be maintained. Neither of these goals is served well through management strategies that provoke non-compliant individuals into revoking their consent to be a participant in the system. No-one is going to like being sanctioned for non-compliance, but few benefit when discontent of this kind is fuelled by disrespectful treatment from the authorities, leaving individuals with a life long passion for resistance and defiance. Furthermore, community confidence in standards is unlikely to be boosted when the story of detected non-compliance is trumped by a horror story of unfair treatment at the hands of the authority. When individuals withdraw their consent to being part of the tax system, the legitimacy of the system itself is vulnerable.

Thus, non-compliant actions on the part of taxpayers must be met by a responsiveness from authority that recognises and deals with the wrongful act, but at the same time works to bring the more cooperative motivational postures to the fore (Braithwaite, 2002). Resentment and anger may be present, but the findings presented in this chapter suggest that there is also likely to be goodwill and acceptance of the rules of the game, if they can be brought into the discussion and the resolution of the problem. The challenge for tax administrators is to play a two-handed game: To deal with the wrongdoing today, while nurturing consent for tomorrow.

Notes

1 These two aspects of community responsiveness were recognised by Schmölders (1970) in his early work on tax systems in different cultures.

2 The poor relationship between attitude and behaviour has been widely recognised and has given rise to research that has tried to build theory that provides a better fit between attitudes and behaviour in line with consistency theorists' general expectations (see, for example, Lewis, 1982; Hessing, Elffers and Weigel, 1988; McGraw and Scholz, 1991; Scholz, McGraw and Steenbergen, 1992; Taylor, Chapter 4, this volume). This chapter, however, pursues a different direction.

3 Black (1976) has used the term, relational distance, to describe social distance from the regulator's perspective. In the present context, social distance is used to represent the regulatee's perspective.
4 Of the respondents, 32 (1.6%) said that they did not know if they should have filed a return. Given that citizens have a responsibility to find out if they are exempt, this group was included with those who agreed that they should have filed a return.
5 Tax researchers use the term, avoision, to capture the problem associated with differentiating legal and illegal tax effective schemes (Seldon, 1979; Sawyer, 1996; see also James and Alley, 1999).
6 For the correlational analyses, respondents who had never heard of the strategy were included with those who had not used the strategy.
7 In order to exhaust all possibilities, the motivational postures were correlated with the 9 specific compliance related measures. The results did not change substantively: Significant correlations with specific compliance-related actions were reflected in the amalgamated action measures presented in Table 2.6.

References

Ajzen, I. (1991), 'The Theory of Planned Behavior', *Organizational Behavior and Human Decision Processes*, vol. 50, pp. 179-211.

Alm, J. (1999), 'Tax Evasion', in J.J. Cordes, R.D. Ebel and J.G. Gravelle (eds), *The Encyclopedia of Taxation and Tax Policy*, The Urban Institute Press, Washington D.C., pp. 374-76.

Alm, J., Sanchez, I. and de Juan, A. (1995), 'Economic and Non-economic Factors in Tax Compliance', *Kyklos*, vol. 48(1), pp. 3-18.

Andreoni, J., Erard, B. and Feinstein J. (1998), 'Tax Compliance', *Journal of Economic Literature*, vol. 36, pp. 818-60.

Bandura, A. (1986), *Social Foundations of Thought and Action: A Social Cognition Theory*, Prentice Hall, New Jersey.

Bardach, E. and Kagan, R.A. (1982), *Going by the Book: The Problem of Regulatory Unreasonableness*, Temple University Press, Philadelphia.

Baumeister, R.F. (1996), 'Self', in A.S.R. Manstead and M. Hewstone (eds), *The Blackwell Encyclopedia of Social Psychology*, Blackwell Publishers, Oxford, pp. 496-501.

Bersoff, D.M. (1999), 'Why Good People Sometimes Do Bad Things: Motivated Reasoning and Unethical Behavior', *Personality and Social Psychology Bulletin*, vol. 25(1), pp. 28-39.

Black, D. (1976), *The Behavior of Law*, Academic Press, New York.

Bogardus, E.S. (1928), *Immigration and Race Attitudes*, D.C Heath and Company, Boston.

Braithwaite, J. (2002), *Restorative Justice and Responsive Regulation*, Oxford University Press, Oxford.

Braithwaite, V. (1995), 'Games of Engagement: Postures within the Regulatory Community', *Law and Policy*, vol. 17, pp. 225-55.

_____ (2001), 'The Community Hopes, Fears and Actions Survey: Goals and Measures', *Centre for Tax System Integrity Working Paper No. 2*, The Australian National University, Canberra.

_____ (2002a), 'Motivational Postures and the Social Distancing of Taxpayers', (unpublished manuscript).

_____ (2002b), 'Shame Acknowledgment and Social Regulation', Paper presented at the Joint Meetings of the Law and Society Association and the Canadian Law and Society Association, May 30-June 1, Vancouver.

Braithwaite, V., Braithwaite, J., Gibson, D. and Makkai, T. (1994), 'Regulatory Styles, Motivational Postures and Nursing Home Compliance', *Law and Policy*, vol. 16, pp. 363–94.

Braithwaite, V. and Reinhart, M. (2001), 'Tensions between the Citizen Taxpaying Role and Compliance Practices', *Centre for Tax System Integrity Working Paper No. 13*, The Australian National University, Canberra.

Braithwaite, V., Reinhart, M., Mearns, M. and Graham, R. (2001), 'Preliminary Findings from the Community Hopes, Fears and Actions Survey', *Centre for Tax System Integrity Working Paper No. 3*, The Australian National University, Canberra.

Burke, P.J. (1980), 'The Self: Measurement Requirements from an Interactionist Perspective', *Social Psychology Quarterly*, vol. 43(1), pp. 18-29.

Carver, C.S. and Scheier, M.F. (1998), *On the Self-regulation of Behaviour*, Cambridge University Press, Cambridge.

Coleman, C. and Freeman, L. (1997), 'Cultural Foundations of Taxpayer Attitudes to Voluntary Compliance', *Australian Tax Forum*, vol. 13, pp. 311-36.

Collins, J.H., Milliron V.C. and Toy, D.R. (1992), 'Determinants of Tax Compliance: A Contingency Approach', *Journal of the American Taxation Association*, vol. 14, pp. 1-29.

Commonwealth Ombudsman (1999), *The ATO and Budplan: Report of the Investigation into the Australian Taxation Office's Handling of Claims for Tax Deductions by Investors in a Tax-effective Financing Scheme Known as Budplan*, June, Commonwealth Ombusdsman Office, Canberra.

Cullis, J.G. and Lewis, A. (1997), 'Why People Pay Taxes: From a Conventional Economic Model to a Model of Social Convention', *Journal of Economic Psychology*, vol. 18, pp. 305-21.

Epstein, S. (1983), 'Aggregation and Beyond: Some Basic Issues on the Prediction of Behavior', *Journal of Personality*, vol. 51, pp. 360-92.

Fishbein, M. and Ajzen, I. (1974), 'Attitudes Toward Objects as Predictors of Single and Multiple Behavioural Criteria', *Psychological Review*, vol. 81, pp. 59-74.

Geertz, C. (1973), *The Interpretation of Cultures*, Basic Books, New York.

Griffin, D. and Buehler, R. (1993), 'Role of Construal Processes in Conformity and Dissent', *Journal of Personality and Social Psychology*, vol. 65(4), pp. 657-69.

Hessing, D.J., Elffers, H. and Weigel, R.H. (1988), 'Exploring the Limits of Self-reports and Reasoned Action: An Investigation of the Psychology of Tax Evasion Behavior', *Journal of Personality and Social Psychology*, vol. 54(3), pp. 405-13.

James, S. and Alley, C. (1999), 'Tax Compliance, Self-assessment and Administration in New Zealand – Is the Carrot or the Stick More Appropriate to Encourage Compliance?', *New Zealand Journal of Taxation Law and Policy*, vol. 5(1), pp. 3-14.

James, S., Lewis, A. and Allison, F. (1987), *The Comprehensibility of Taxation*, Avebury, Aldershot.

Kelman, H.C. (1961), 'Processes of Opinion Change', *Public Opinion Quarterly*, vol. 25, pp. 57-78.

Kinsey, K.A. and Grasmick, H.G. (1993), 'Did the Tax Reform Act of 1986 Improve Compliance? Three Studies of Pre- and Post-TRA Compliance Attitudes', *Law and Policy*, vol. 15(4), pp. 295-325.

Kirchler E. (1999), 'Reactance to Taxation: Employers' Attitudes towards Taxes', *Journal of Socio-Economics*, vol. 28, pp. 131-38.

Kuhl, J. and Fuhrmann, A. (1998), 'Decomposing Self-regulation and Self-control: The Volitional Components Inventory', in J. Heckhausen and C.S. Dweck (eds), *Motivation and Self-regulation Across the Life Span*, Cambridge University Press, Cambridge, pp. 15-49.

Lewis, A. (1982), *The Psychology of Taxation*, Martin Robertson, Oxford.
Long S.B. and Swingen, J.A. (1988), 'The Role of Legal Complexity in Shaping Taxpayer Compliance', in P.J. van Koppen, D.J. Hessing and G. van den Heuvel (eds), *Lawyers on Psychologists and Psychologists on Law*, Swets North America, Berwyn, pp. 128-46.
Massey, D.S. (2002), 'A Brief History of Human Society: The Origin and Role of Emotion in Social Life', *American Sociological Review*, vol. 67, pp. 1-67.
McBarnet, D. (Chapter 11, this volume), 'When Compliance is not the Solution but the Problem: From Changes in Law to Changes in Attitude'.
_____ (1992), 'Legitimate Rackets: Tax Evasion, Tax Avoidance, and the Boundaries of Legality', *The Journal of Human Justice*, vol. 3(2), pp. 56-74.
McBarnet, D. and Whelan, C. (1999), *Creative Accounting and the Cross-eyed Javelin Thrower*, John Wiley, Chichester.
McGraw, K.M. and Scholz, J.T. (1991), 'Appeals to Civic Virtue Versus Attention to Self-interest: Effects on Tax Compliance', *Law and Society Review*, vol. 25, pp. 471-98.
Mearns, M. and Braithwaite, V. (2001), 'The Community Hopes, Fears and Actions Survey: Survey Method, Sample Representativeness and Data Quality', *Centre for Tax System Integrity Working Paper No. 4*, The Australian National University, Canberra.
Murphy, K. (2002), 'Procedural Justice and the Australian Taxation Office: A Study of Tax Scheme Investors', *Centre for Tax System Integrity Working Paper No. 35*, The Australian National University, Canberra.
Murphy, K. and Byng, K. (2002). 'Preliminary Findings from the Australian Tax System Survey of Tax Scheme Investors', *Centre for Tax System Integrity Working Paper No. 40*, The Australian National University, Canberra.
Pope, J., Fayle, R. and Chen, D.L. (1993), *The Compliance Costs of Employment-Related Taxation in Australia*, Australian Tax Research Foundation, Sydney.
Richardson, M. and Sawyer, A.J. (2001), 'A Taxonomy of the Tax Compliance Literature: Further Findings, Problems and Prospects', *Australian Taxation Forum*, vol. 16(2), pp. 137-320.
Rokeach, M. (1973) *The Nature of Human Values*, Free Press, New York.
Sakurai, Y. and Braithwaite, V. (2001), Taxpayers' Perceptions of the Ideal Tax Advisor: Playing Safe or Saving Dollars?', *Centre for Tax System Integrity Working Paper No. 5*, The Australian National University, Canberra.
Sawyer, A. (1996), 'Blurring the Distinction between Avoidance and Evasion: The Abusive Tax Position', *British Tax Review*, vol. 5, pp. 483-504.
Schmölders, G. (1970), 'Survey Research in Public Finance – A Behavioural Approach to Fiscal Theory', *Public Finance*, vol. 25, pp. 300-6.
Schneider, F. and Enste, D. (2000), 'Shadow Economies: Size, Causes, and Consequences', *The Journal of Economic Literature*, vol. 38(1), pp. 77-114.
Scholz, J.T., McGraw, K.M. and Steenbergen, M.R. (1992), 'Will Taxpayers Ever Like Taxes? Responses to the U.S. Tax Reform Act of 1986', *Journal of Economic Psychology*, vol. 13(4), pp. 625-56.
Seldon, A. (1979), *Tax Avoision: The Economic, Legal and Moral Inter-relationships between Avoidance and Evasion*, Institute of Economic Affairs, London.
Senate Economics References Committee (2001), *Inquiry into Mass Marketed Tax Effective Schemes and Investor Protection: Interim Report*, Parliament of the Commonwealth of Australia, Canberra.
Smith, K.W. and Kinsey, K.A. (1987), 'Understanding Taxpaying Behavior: A Conceptual Framework with Implications for Research', *Law and Society Review*, vol. 21(4), pp. 639-63.

Smith, K.W. and Stalans, L.J. (1991), 'Encouraging Tax Compliance with Positive Incentives: A Conceptual Framework and Research Directions', *Law and Policy*, vol. 13(1), pp. 35-53.

Sykes, G. and Matza, D. (1957), 'Techniques of Neutralization: A Theory of Delinquency', *American Sociological Review*, vol. 22, pp. 488-98.

Taylor, N. (Chapter 4, this volume), 'Understanding Taxpayer Attitudes Through Understanding Taxpayer Identities'.

Thurman, Q.C., St John, C. and Riggs, L. (1984), 'Neutralization and Tax Evasion: How Effective would a Moral Appeal be in Improving Compliance to Tax Laws?', *Law and Policy*, vol. 6, pp. 309-27.

Tomkins, C., Packman, C., Russell, S. and Colville, I. (2001), 'Managing Tax Regimes: A Call for Research', *Public Administration*, vol. 79(3), pp. 751-58.

Tyler, T.R. (1990), *Why People Obey the Law: Procedural Justice, Legitimacy, and Compliance,* Yale University Press, New Haven.

Wallschutzky, I.G. (1996), 'Issues in Research Methods: With Reference to Income Tax Research', Department of Commerce, University of Newcastle, Newcastle.

Webley, P., Adams, C. and Elffers, H. (2002), 'VAT Compliance in the United Kingdom', *Centre for Tax System Integrity Working Paper No. 41*, The Australian National University, Canberra.

Webley, P., Robben, H., Elffers, H. and Hessing, D. (1991), *Tax Evasion: An Experimental Approach*, Cambridge University Press, Cambridge.

Chapter 3

Tax Compliance and the Psychology of Justice: Mapping the Field

Michael Wenzel

'In this world nothing can be said to be certain, except death and taxes.'

Benjamin Franklin writing to Jean Baptiste Le Roy, 13 November 1789

According to this popularised aphorism, taxes are ubiquitous, as they affect practically everybody, and surely they are as little in our personal interest as death. Yet, while the everyday use of the expression does not occur without a wink, science seems to have missed the humour in it. It is certainly true that taxation deserves the closest scientific attention, as hardly any other legislation has such a widespread impact on our lives, from 'impacting personal decisions to shaping economic phenomena, political forces and the institutional fabric of our society' (Long and Swingen, 1991, p. 638). Furthermore, the failure to comply with tax laws costs states billions of dollars each year, thus impacting severely on their provision of government services and their socio-economic functioning (see Andreoni, Erard and Feinstein, 1998). However, the dominant theoretical paradigm that understands tax compliance in terms of individual self-interest, that is, as an individual's rational choice aimed at maximising individual outcomes under conditions of uncertainty (in the tradition of Allingham and Sandmo, 1972), misses important dimensions of the phenomenon. In recent years, a number of researchers have pointed to the limited understanding this paradigm provides and delivered empirical evidence for the role of 'non-economic' factors in tax compliance (see Grasmick and Bursik, 1990; De Juan, Lasheras and Mayo 1994; Reckers, Sanders and Roark, 1994; Alm, Sanchez and De Juan, 1995). At the same time, there have been attempts to incorporate factors such as equity considerations and moral constraints into traditional expected utility theory, as another category of individual outcomes to be maximised (see Gordon, 1989; Cowell, 1992; Bordignon, 1993; Falkinger, 1995).

Research so far has referred to non-economic factors in a rather selective fashion. A more systematic analysis of these factors seems necessary for further progress in the explanation of tax non-compliance. The present chapter focuses on *justice* and *fairness* considerations that could play a role in taxpayers' evaluations of the tax system and therefore in their decision to comply or not comply with tax laws. I will offer a conceptual framework for such justice considerations based on conceptual distinctions made in social psychological justice research. I will review research on fairness perceptions in the area of taxation as it relates to the suggested taxonomy and finally discuss implications of the conceptual framework. Specifically, the review will demonstrate the wealth of justice issues potentially relevant to tax compliance and the neglect of certain justice perceptions in existing research. The taxonomy raises the question of the relative importance of the various justice issues for tax compliance as well as the conditions of their importance.

Firstly, however, I will present arguments for the limitations of a purely economic self-interest approach to tax compliance. While similar critiques have been put forward elsewhere (see Cowell, 1992; Scholz, 1998), my arguments will specifically make a case for a consideration of justice issues at different levels of analysis.

Beyond Individual Self-interest: A Multi-level Approach to Tax Evasion

Traditional economic models of tax evasion (see Allingham and Sandmo, 1972) regard tax compliance as an outcome-maximising decision between the alternatives of: (a) truthfully paying tax which results in a certain loss, and (b) evading tax which results, with some uncertainty, in either a reduced loss (in terms of taxes not paid) or an even greater loss (due to the fines imposed if the evasion is detected and penalised). These early models, however, neglect the fact that taxpayers also have their share in government services and public goods that are funded by the tax revenue. Taxpayers receive some gains in exchange for the taxes they pay, and not only may they consider these outcomes in their rational equation, but they may also evaluate whether the exchange is an *equitable* one or not (Cowell, 1992; Falkinger, 1995).

Further, the issue of public goods in return for taxes adds a social dimension to the problem, because the amount of revenue available, and the quantity and quality of public goods provided, is not solely dependent on the single taxpayer's choice to pay or evade taxes. Rather, taxpayers are interdependent, as their outcomes in terms of the public goods they share are a function of their combined behavioural choices. The issue of tax compliance can therefore be considered a social dilemma (see Dawes, 1980). Individual taxpayers may choose to evade tax in order to maximise their personal outcomes and still enjoy their share of the public good, which is not affected by single defective choices. However, if many taxpayers chose to do so, revenue would fall to a level where certain public goods would be no longer affordable and everyone's outcomes would be reduced (Weigel, Hessing and Elffers, 1987; Elffers, 2000). Models of tax compliance would have to incorporate taxpayers' awareness of their mutual interdependence in their rational decision of how to maximise individual outcomes. Furthermore, as research on social dilemmas informs us (see Pepitone, 1971; Wit, Wilke and Oppewal, 1992; van Dijk and Wilke, 1993), taxpayers may also evaluate what would be *fair* for them to contribute to the public good, considering their relative resources and relative share of the public good as well as others' level of evasion (Bordignon, 1993).

Social psychological research also informs us that social dilemmas assume a quality of greater competitiveness and less cooperativeness when the involved parties define themselves as members of *different groups* rather than as individuals (see Brewer and Schneider, 1990; Schopler and Insko, 1992). A crucial factor contributing to this effect may be the perceived sharedness of and consensus on distinctive group interests that give social-normative support for one's tendency to act in the interests of one's group (Zander, 1971; Haslam, 2001). Importantly, once one identifies with a group, norms and perceived consensus within the group should make members act in the interests of their own group, even if they personally would not profit from their own behaviour. Most models of tax evasion assume that taxpayers are motivated to maximise their individual outcomes; they do not consider the possibility that taxpayers define themselves as members of social groups and act in terms of the interests and norms of their group and fellow group members (Sigala, Burgoyne and Webley, 1999). Again, it also holds for this level of analysis that group members are not only concerned about maximising their group's outcomes but also about their group receiving the outcomes it is perceived to be entitled to, according to ingroup norms of *justice* and *fairness*. Research on relative deprivation has repeatedly shown that group deprivation is a stronger predictor for social protest and resistance than feelings of personal deprivation (see Dubé and Guimond, 1986; Walker and Mann, 1987; Hafer and Olson, 1993). The possibility that tax evasion is an act of social protest against a tax system perceived to be unfair to their ingroup needs to be considered.

Finally, research shows that persons or groups involved in a social dilemma are more cooperative and show more concern for collective outcomes when they identify themselves in terms of the same inclusive group (Brewer and Schneider, 1990); for instance, the society including all individuals and all different groups of taxpayers. Defining themselves more inclusively, their selves and correspondingly their self-interests become so transformed that they include the interests of others and of the collective as a whole (Brewer, 1991; Morrison, 1997). A concern for the interests, goals and values of the inclusive category has rarely been taken into account in research and models on tax evasion (see Taylor, Chapter 4, this volume for a departure from general practice). Again, based on a collective self-identification, taxpayers might feel committed to maximising their collective outcomes as well as committed to socially shared and normative representations of their collective identity that prescribe certain distributions of burdens and goods as appropriate and just. A concern for a fair society rather than for one's personal or group interests would then motivate taxpayers. Tax evasion would depend on taxpayers' (socially mediated) perceptions of whether the current tax practice is either conducive to maximising the collective's welfare or consistent with a representation of how society should look.

To sum up, research on tax evasion has been dominated so far by individualistic approaches that focus exclusively on the motivation to maximise personal material outcomes. The analysis needs to be extended to also include the possibility of taxpayers defining themselves in more inclusive ways, either as members of different social groups or, most inclusively, as members of the society as a whole, implying a concern for outcomes of their ingroup or the welfare of their whole nation, respectively. Furthermore, models of tax evasion need to take into account that taxpayers may not only want to maximise their interests, however defined, but also desire to see justice and fairness realised (see Kinsey, Grasmick and Smith, 1991). In the remainder of this chapter, I will look more closely at different *justice* considerations that may play a role in tax compliance and differentiate between an individual, group and inclusive (societal) level of analysis.

Justice, Fairness and Tax Compliance: A Taxonomy

Empirical research on tax compliance often refers to issues of justice and fairness in a rather undifferentiated and/or selective manner. Given the dominance of the rational actor approach, authors interested in issues of justice and fairness seem to have found it their main challenge to demonstrate the general importance of these perceptions for tax compliance. Justice perceptions have often been either operationalised through global measures, or selected aspects (e.g., one's relative tax burden) have been treated as representative indicators of generic concepts such as 'fiscal fairness' (see De Juan et al., 1994). Other research has looked at single justice issues in more depth, but in isolation. Although some authors have demanded that attention be 'directed toward what forms of inequity are likely to affect tax evasion behavior' (Spicer and Becker, 1980, p. 174) and 'that one has to specify fairly carefully what one means by the inequity or injustice that is often cited as a motive for evading taxes' (Cowell, 1992, p. 540), so far these questions have not been systematically addressed.

The most common differentiation in research on tax compliance refers to the concepts of exchange equity, vertical equity and horizontal equity (e.g., Kinsey and Grasmick, 1993). Exchange equity concerns the perceived value of tax-funded government benefits and services received relative to one's tax contribution. Vertical equity concerns the burden of taxes for certain social strata relative to other strata. Horizontal equity concerns the burden of taxes for members relative to others within a given social stratum. Other studies have focussed on the structure of tax rates (e.g., Roberts, Hite and Bradley, 1994) or on procedural fairness in audits (e.g., Stalans and Lind, 1997). A few studies have tried to specify empirically the dimensionality of the fairness concept. Based on factor analysis, Gerbing (1988, cited in Roberts and Hite, 1994) found four dimensions of tax fairness, namely general fairness and distribution of tax burden, exchange with government, taxes of the wealthy and progressivity of tax rates. Christensen,

Weihrich and Newman (1994) also used factor analysis and found five factors: personal payment level, exchange with government, tax rate structure, special provisions and overall fairness.

However, outcomes of factor analyses depend on the measures fed into the analyses; the dimensionality of a concept cannot be decided on purely empirical grounds. We require a theoretical framework that guides the formulation of measures and that aids us in systematically investigating the role of fairness for taxpaying attitudes and behaviour. Such a framework should also help us integrate diverse research findings, point to areas that have been neglected so far and identify areas where the evidence is either inconsistent or conclusive. In the following, I will suggest a taxonomy for this purpose and review the literature on this basis.

Three Areas of Justice

In social psychology it has become common practice to differentiate between three areas of justice (Tyler and Smith, 1998). *Distributive justice* refers to the fairness of the outcomes of a resource allocation or distribution and has the longest research tradition in social psychology (Homans, 1961; Adams, 1965; Walster, Berscheid and Walster, 1973). At its core lies the concept of entitlement or deservingness; that is, a situation is considered just when a given social unit receives the amount or share of resources it is perceived to deserve (Lerner, 1991; Major, 1994; Feather, 1999; Wenzel, 2000).[1] Resources may be understood here in a wide sense and include material and non-material, positive and negative resources (e.g., tax burden). Distributive justice thus refers to a perceiver's view of how to distribute a given pool of resources so that a certain target, or all social units involved, receive what they are entitled to (proactive); and it refers to the post-decisional perception of whether a target, or all social units, have received what they are entitled to (reactive) (Greenberg, 1982). The reactive version, furthermore, includes attributions of responsibility and blame when entitlements are perceived not to be met (Mikula, 1993).

Procedural justice refers to the fairness of the processes of a resource allocation or distribution. While distributive justice concerns decision outcomes, procedural justice pertains to the ways, modes and procedures of reaching the decision (Thibaut and Walker, 1978; Leventhal, 1980; Lind and Tyler, 1988). Although not yet established practice, the entitlement concept may also be applied to the procedural arena (Heuer, Blumenthal, Douglas and Weinblatt, 1999; Wenzel, 2000). An allocation decision will be regarded as procedurally fair when a certain target, or all social units involved, are perceived to be granted the treatment, role and quality of decision-making they are entitled to. It is inherent to the concept that entitlements are not constant but relative and variable in that they involve social comparisons and context effects. Perceptions of procedural justice would therefore be understood as equally variable and context-dependent. Indeed, Barrett-Howard and Tyler (1986) found that the importance of Leventhal's (1980) six rules of procedural justice – consistency, bias suppression, accuracy, correctability, representativeness and ethicality – varied between different situations. However, compared to the distributive arena, researchers often regard variability and context-dependence of criteria to be less intrinsic to the procedural justice concept. Given the empirical invariance of criteria between different ethnic groups, Tyler, Boeckmann, Smith and Huo (1997) argue that procedural justice has the potential to bridge across norm and value conflicts (e.g., conflicts due to differing notions of distributive justice).

Retributive justice refers to the fairness of sanctions and reactions to the breaking of social rules and norms (Hogan and Emler, 1981; Miller and Vidmar, 1981; Tyler et al., 1997). Retributive justice is distinct from distributive and procedural justice because, as Tyler and Smith (1998) argue, if a norm of distributive justice has been violated, that norm would only demand the restitution of the just situation (as the norm defines it). In fact, however, people may not only demand restitution but also punishment of the actor, going beyond the distributive norm and requiring a further category of justice principles for its justification. Again, a concept of entitlement or deservingness can be considered to be at the core of retributive justice (the term 'entitlement' is of course awkward for negative outcomes). The central question of retributive justice is what treatment and degree of sanction the rule-breaker deserves. Deservingness of punishment should depend on the perceived importance of the violated rule, the severity of rule violation and the degree of responsibility and blame attributed to the actor (Miller and Vidmar, 1981; Weiner, 1995).

It is beyond the focus of the present chapter to further discuss and review the research on these three areas in the abstract. As I will argue below, all three aspects of justice play a role in the realm of taxation and it will be shown that taxpayers' perceptions of each justice aspect could impact on their level of tax compliance.

Three Analytic Levels of Justice

As argued earlier, the expected utility approach to tax compliance is limited in its assumption that taxpayers try to maximise the absolute utility or favourability of outcomes rather than also being concerned about their fairness and appropriateness. Moreover, the approach focuses on the *individual's* outcomes alone and does not acknowledge potential concerns for outcomes of certain societal groups with which taxpayers may identify, or outcomes of the society at large. Justice and fairness perceptions at an *individual, group* and *societal* level might impact on tax compliance. To clarify this differentiation, I will distinguish it from the related concepts of micro and macro-justice as suggested by Brickman, Folger, Goode and Schul (1981) (see Tyler et al., 1997; Tyler and Smith, 1998).

At an *individual* level, people can be concerned about the justice and fairness of their individual outcomes and treatment. The perceived recipient unit (Eckhoff, 1974) of the outcome allocation is the individual; and people want a certain target individual (normally themselves) to be treated in a way they feel they are entitled to. This seems close to what Brickman et al. (1981) define as microjustice; that is, individuating principles prescribing that individuals be treated according to an assessment of their individual attributes (e.g., merits, efforts, needs). However, individuals' entitlements can also be based on what Brickman et al. (1981) define as principles of macrojustice; that is, deindividuating principles that do not consider individual attributes as a basis for resource distributions and rather prescribe properties of the distributions themselves. For instance, a macro-principle could prescribe a flat distribution (e.g., a flat tax rate), implying that each social unit should receive an equal share (or burden) regardless of their individual differences (i.e., the equality principle). So, independent of the nature of the principles applied, it is essential for individual level justice that the perceiver regards the individual as the recipient unit and evaluates the degree to which the entitlements of a certain target individual are met (e.g., one's own entitlements).

At a *group* level of analysis, people can be concerned about the justice and fairness of a group's outcomes and treatment. The group is regarded as the recipient unit and people want a certain target group (in most cases the group they identify with, i.e., their ingroup) to be treated in a way they feel the group is entitled to. Again, these entitlements can be based on micro-principles that prescribe a treatment based on an assessment of relevant attributes of the target group relative to other groups. Alternatively, the group's entitlement can be based on macro-principles that prescribe certain features of the distribution as a whole. For instance, a macro-principle could specify the maximum burden (e.g., tax rate) any group should have to bear, implying that a certain target group (e.g., high-income earners) is entitled to carry a burden no higher than the specified maximum.

Thus, it is essential to the group-level analysis that groups, rather than individuals, are the recipient units whose entitlements are to be judged, on the basis of intergroup rather than interpersonal comparisons (Markovsky, 1985; Major, 1994). In research on relative deprivation, we find a related distinction between personal and group relative deprivation (Runciman, 1966; see Kessler, Mummendey and Leisse, 2000). Note that even in cases where single persons receive certain resources (e.g., a job), they might be considered as members of social groups rather than individuals; and they might receive these resources based on perceived entitlements of their group rather than individual entitlements (e.g., in affirmative action programs). Hence, the level of abstraction of the recipient unit is a function of social categorisation (Smith, Spears and Oyen, 1994), which in turn is an act of social construction and sense-making rather than objective criteria (Oakes, 1996). Also, the level of abstraction of the recipient unit can vary beyond a simple dichotomy of individuals versus groups; it can vary on a continuum of inclusiveness (e.g., individual, carpenter, trades people, employees, taxpayers) (see Turner, Oakes, Haslam and McGarty, 1994).

At a *societal level*, people can be concerned about outcomes, their general level or the form of their distribution, of the society at large (see Wenzel, 2000, 2001a, 2002). Either individuals or groups can be the recipient unit of the distribution; however, people would want the collective of all individuals or groups to be treated in a way they consider fair or appropriate. That means, the *societal* level of analysis deals most directly with Brickman et al.'s (1981) concept of macrojustice. Different from the previous two levels of analysis, macrojustice principles are not merely applied to evaluate the outcomes of a target person or group; rather, the overall realisation of these principles is evaluated across all individuals or groups, across all potential recipients.

Following this discussion, the present taxonomy distinguishes between an *individual, group* and *societal level* of analysis and applies these to the three areas of justice, namely *distributive, procedural* and *retributive justice*. Instead of doing this in the abstract, however, I will refer to research on the relation between justice and tax compliance to illustrate the taxonomy and, conversely, use the taxonomy to systematically review relevant research.

Justice and Tax Compliance

Justice aspect (distributive, procedural, retributive) and level of analysis (individual, group, societal) are considered here as two dimensions of a taxonomy used to differentiate research and findings on the role of justice in tax compliance. Note that I do not suggest that this (or any other) taxonomy in itself provides us with a theoretical understanding of the relationship between justice and compliance. We might have better glasses to see the world, but that does not replace efforts to comprehend what we see, namely by applying, testing and developing substantial theoretical propositions about underlying processes (e.g., Tyler, 2000; Wenzel, 2001b).

Distributive Justice and Tax Compliance

Similar to the priority that social psychology has historically given to distributive justice (Adams, 1965; Walster et al., 1973; Leventhal, 1976; Lerner, 1977), tax compliance research has so far mainly focussed on distributive aspects of taxation. It has done so on all three levels of analysis, as defined above, however without differentiating them explicitly in most cases. Some research has used measures that did not specify the level of analysis and so these cases cannot be categorised unambiguously into the present schema (see Table 3.1).

Table 3.1 Distributive justice in taxation: examples for three levels of analysis

	Individual level	Group level	Societal level
Tax burdens	personal tax burden; compared to others; other times; one's relative income	ingroup's tax burden; compared to other groups; other times; its relative income	tax level; distribution; progressivity
Tax-based benefits	personal benefits compared to others; other times; one's relative taxes	ingroup's benefits; compared to other groups, other times; its relative taxes	level of spending; efficiency; distribution over different policies
Avoidance/ evasion opportunities	personal options compared to others; other times	ingroup's options relative to other groups	level; distribution of opportunities

Two issues of taxation have commonly been considered in terms of distributive fairness, namely (a) tax burdens and (b) tax-funded benefits or government services. Another 'resource' distributed among taxpayers are (c) opportunities to avoid (or evade) tax. The latter issue also involves elements of procedural justice (and retributive justice) but is considered here primarily as a distributive justice issue, because such opportunities can affect one's actual tax burden. In fact, one might argue that this issue could be subsumed under (a). However, having opportunities to avoid or evade taxes does not mean that one actually uses them to reduce the tax burden; and yet, the distribution of opportunities itself could be evaluated in terms of fairness. Hence, the issues will be dealt with separately.

At an *individual level*, taxpayers might evaluate the distributive fairness of their personal tax burden, share in tax-funded benefits or avoidance opportunities. They may evaluate their tax burden compared to other taxpayers; in particular those taxpayers they would consider equivalent and comparable in terms of their economic circumstances. This would be a case of horizontal justice. Dean, Keenan and Kenney (1980) found in a survey with taxpayers in Scotland that perception of horizontal injustice were very prevalent, with 26 per cent of taxpayers believing they paid 'far too much' relative to other taxpayers of the same income level. Other studies investigated the impact of such perceptions on tax evasion. In an experimental simulation study, Spicer and Becker (1980) manipulated people's relative tax burden. Participants' tax burden was portrayed as either lower, equal or higher than others. They found that disadvantageous inequity increased tax evasion and advantageous inequity decreased tax evasion. However, Webley, Robben and Morris (1988) used a similar manipulation for relative tax-free allowances and did not find an effect on tax evasion. Again using a similar manipulation (but with only two levels, i.e., horizontal equity and unfavourable inequity), Moser, Evans and Kim (1995) also failed to find a main effect of horizontal justice on the amount of income correctly reported (however, they found an interaction effect with exchange equity; see below).

Taxpayers may also refer to other comparison referents when evaluating the fairness of their tax burden. For instance, they could compare their current tax level with their earlier tax burdens (Calderwood and Webley, 1992). Wartick (1994) investigated effects of tax law changes and found that the changes were considered more unfair when participants felt they made them worse off (however, the effect was moderated by whether or not justifications for the changes were provided; see below). Furthermore, individuals could also compare their tax burden with others who are in a different economic situation than they are and evaluate their own and others' tax rates relative to their income levels (i.e., considering income levels as inputs, according to the equity calculus) (Walster, Walster and Berscheid, 1978).

Similarly, taxpayers could be concerned about the fairness of their share in tax-based benefits. They could evaluate their benefits relative to their tax burden, the benefits of others (either in absolute terms or relative to their different tax burdens) or the benefits they enjoyed at an earlier time.[2] These issues have been studied under the label 'exchange equity', although only a comparison of benefits relative to taxes paid would be a strict case of exchange equity (Vogel, 1974; Spicer and Lundstedt, 1976). Wallschutzky (1984) surveyed a group of convicted tax evaders and a control group in Australia and found no difference in their evaluations of income tax relative to government services. In an interview study in Oregon, Mason and Calvin (1978) asked taxpayers to evaluate their tax levels compared to the benefits they received, and the amount of their benefits compared to the benefits of the average person in the state. Neither rating was related to self-reported evasion. However, Porcano (1988) applied very similar measures in a survey with American taxpayers. He combined the two questions into one score and found that self-reported evaders perceived the exchange as more unfair than non-evaders did. In an experimental study, Alm, McClelland and Schulze (1992) manipulated the magnitude of returns relative to the taxes paid and found that compliance increased with the favourability of that ratio (note that the manipulation applied to the whole group and can also be interpreted as affecting the exchange relationship at a 'societal' level; see below). Finally, Moser et al. (1995) found that exchange equity (manipulated via different tax rates while the amount of tax-funded benefits was constant, namely nil) interacted with horizontal inequity and affected the correct reporting of income only when one's tax rate was higher than others' tax rate.

Taxpayers may also evaluate the fairness of their opportunities to avoid or evade tax, again compared to others' minimisation or evasion options or one's own options at different times. However, most studies that investigated perceived opportunities to avoid or evade tax dealt with their absolute level but not their perceived fairness (Vogel, 1974; Wallschutzky, 1984; Porcano, 1988). In fact, when fairness of avoidance opportunities was addressed, it was usually done at a *group* level of analysis (see below). This is not surprising, because, minimisation opportunities are given in the structure of the law, specifying circumstances that apply to groups of taxpayers (rather than individuals). Moreover, differences between taxpayers in terms of their resources to employ tax minimisation strategies, and strategists, define salient groups in the context of taxation (e.g., the rich versus the poor).

At a *group* level, taxpayers may evaluate the fairness of the same three issues – tax burden, tax-funded benefits and avoidance/evasion opportunities – for their group (or any group). They could evaluate these outcomes again relative to other social referents (i.e., groups), temporal (i.e., former times) or counterfactual referents (i.e., an imagined world). However, only a small amount of published research applied such a *group* level analysis, despite Schmölders' (1970) early contention that 'success of an income tax depends on cooperation; this means not so much on individual but group cooperation' (p. 305). Kinsey and Grasmick (1993) found that American taxpayers' belief that the tax system (after the *Tax Reform Act* of 1986) benefited the rich had a significant effect on respondents' expressed acceptability of tax cheating. Recall also that Gerbing (1988) found attitudes towards taxes of the wealthy as a factor of fairness in taxation. This was also one of the aspects Roberts (1994) addressed in his televised appeal messages that successfully affected perceptions of fairness and attitudes to non-compliance. Admittedly, such *group* level issues are at times difficult to distinguish from research applying a *societal* level of analysis (see the concept of vertical justice below).

Further evidence for the role of *group* level injustice for tax evasion comes from some qualitative data concerning avoidance/evasion opportunities. Spicer and Lundstedt (1976) report that 75 per cent of those who found the distribution of tax burdens unfair stated as the major reason the 'extensive tax avoidance by affluent taxpayers and corporations' (p. 301). Likewise, in Wallschutzky's (1984) survey, respondents in both the group of convicted evaders and the control group 'expressed grave concern [about] the lack of opportunity for wage and salary earners to evade tax [with] the consequent shift of the weight of tax burdens' (p. 381). Conversely, it could be that more affluent people, who pay a higher tax rate but are less likely to be recipients of tax-funded welfare benefits, feel that their exchange relationship with the government is unfair when compared to lower income groups (Vogel, 1974).

At a *societal* level, taxpayers could evaluate whether the tax system yields good and fair distributions of tax burdens, tax-funded benefits or minimisation/evasion opportunities. They could do so in comparison with other societies, different times and counterfactual systems – generally on the basis of an idea of how their society should look. Concerning *tax burdens*, people could evaluate various parameters of their distribution; for instance, the level of taxes for different societal groups, the degree of progressivity of tax rates, the taxable income threshold or the maximum tax rate. Or, they could evaluate the degree to which the tax system overall realises, or deviates from, a good distribution of tax burdens. Porcano (1988) used a rather global measure of such an evaluation, asking whether the current tax system treats everyone fairly and whether certain types of taxpayers (based on income) received favourable treatment. Aggregated into one scale, the measure did not account for differences in hypothetical or self-reported evasion.

A more sophisticated method was used by Kinsey and Grasmick (1993), who asked respondents to rate the fairness of tax burdens (on a scale from less to more than their fair share) for four categories of taxpayers representing lower versus upper income strata. For each respondent they calculated the standard deviation across the four ratings, as a measure of how strongly his/her fairness ratings varied between the different groups. Note that this measure would yield a low score even if all tax burdens were considered as unfair but deviating in the same direction from fairness. This would be the case, for instance, if tax burdens were generally considered too high. Hence, the mean level of ratings across groups could be used as an additional *societal* level fairness measure of the level of tax burden or the government-taxpayer exchange relationship (Kinsey et al., 1991). The standard deviation measure, in contrast, is a measure of discrepancies between different groups or, as used by Kinsey and Grasmick (1993), between different economic strata, and is thus a measure of vertical injustice. In Kinsey and Grasmick's (1993) third study, the measure significantly contributed to the prediction of future intentions to cheat on taxes.

Fairness of the tax rate structure and its degree of progressivity is another aspect of vertical justice. With a regressive tax rate, taxes are less than proportional to income (even though people with higher income may pay higher taxes); with a flat tax rate, taxes paid are strictly proportional to income; and with a progressive tax rate, taxes are more than proportional to income. Preferences for a more or less progressive tax structure may be based on views about the relative benefits from tax-funded services for low and high-income earners, the belief that those able to pay more should pay more tax or some notion that the disutility of tax sacrifices varies with income (see Musgrave, 1994). The concept of progressivity is, however, a complex one and respondents often misunderstand it (Sheffrin, 1994), which is why results are often inconsistent (e.g. results depend on how abstractly or concretely the questions are put) (Roberts et al., 1994). While various studies have investigated taxpayers' preferences concerning a more or less progressive tax structure (e.g., Lewis, 1978; Porcano, 1984; Hite and Roberts, 1991; Copeland and Harmelink, 1995), few studies have shown how these preferences, or their perceived frustrations, are related to taxpaying attitudes and tax compliance. Roberts and Hite (1994) distinguished between three groups of participants who found a flat rate, a mildly progressive rate and a steeply progressive rate most fair, respectively. Respondents tending towards a flat rate evaluated the overall tax system as more unfair, while the level of compliance in terms of underreporting of cash income did not differentiate between the groups. For all groups, attitudes about current tax rates were related to the perceived overall fairness of the tax system. Interestingly, however, overall fairness ratings of respondents who preferred progressive rates were also influenced by their concerns about the existence of loopholes for the wealthy.

Thus, preference for progressive tax rates can partly be a response to a perceived *societal* level unfairness of a different kind, namely the unfair distribution of *avoidance* and *evasion opportunities*. As reported earlier, Spicer and Lundstedt (1976) and Wallschutzky (1984) also found evidence for the view that taxpayers are very concerned about inequities with regard to minimisation and evasion options (see Song and Yarbrough, 1978). In his televised appeal campaigns, Roberts (1994) addressed both the reduction in tax shelter activity and the decrease of opportunities for tax evasion (next to other issues). The campaigns proved effective in increasing fairness ratings and compliance attitudes. However, more controlled research would be needed on the impact of this *societal* level justice perception before any firm conclusions could be drawn.

Finally, taxpayers can also evaluate the fairness of the *taxpayer-government exchange* relationship at a *societal* level. As noted earlier, the fairness of the general level of taxes can be seen as part of the *societal* level exchange equity. Kinsey et al.'s (1991) measure of mean fairness across groups offers one possible operationalisation of this construct. More specifically, however, this fairness aspect would concern the satisfaction with the government's use of revenue. Revenue use could be evaluated in terms of the perceived general level and efficiency of spending as well as the distribution of revenue across different policies, portfolios and taxpayer groups. Wallschutzky (1984) did not find a significant difference between convicted evaders and a control group with regard to their overall satisfaction with government spending (satisfaction was generally low). In a study referred to earlier at the individual level, Alm et al. (1992) manipulated the efficiency of revenue use and, correspondingly, the relative level of benefits in return for taxes paid. They varied the level of benefits as a multiple of taxes paid by the collective (multiplying tax revenue by 0, 2 and 6, respectively); hence, a societal-level interpretation may be appropriate. Indeed, compliance increased with efficiency of provision of social goods. In another simulation study, Alm, Jackson and McKee (1993) manipulated the favourability of the 'policy' on which revenue would be spent (when the choice for one out of two options was imposed on them). Compliance was significantly lower when the revenue was supposed to be spent on the less favoured public good. Interestingly, the study indicated a clear social dimension of the effect of public good preference. Namely, in two other conditions participants decided per majority rule on the use of the tax revenue and were given feedback about the vote outcome. When the vote was clearly in favour of one option (rather than an unattractive alternative), compliance was significantly higher than when the vote showed a narrow preference for the same option with an attractive alternative. This finding suggests that when the preference for a public good to be funded by tax was socially shared, tax compliance was increased. Moreover, the research showed that compliance was higher when revenue use was decided on by majority vote rather than imposed; this, however, leads us to a different area of justice.

Procedural Justice and Tax Compliance

Compared to distributive justice, procedural justice has received considerably less research attention in the area of taxation, but undeservedly so. Four issues of procedural justice are distinguished here: (a) the quality of treatment in interactions between taxpayers and tax authorities, (b) the degree to which taxpayers have a say (voice and control), (c) the extent and quality of information provided by tax authorities, and (d) compliance and administration costs. The last issue also has a distributive justice dimension, as compliance costs can mean a material burden on taxpayers and administration costs can imply a waste of revenue. However, because inappropriate procedures are the cause of the problem, and there are other possible effects apart from material losses, the issue is dealt with here as a procedural one. Again, all these issues can be analysed at an *individual, group* and *societal* level (see Table 3.2).

At an *individual* level, taxpayers could evaluate how fairly the Australian Taxation Office (ATO) treats them personally (or any other target individual, such as a family member or friend) in terms of respectfulness, neutrality and trustworthiness (see Tyler, 1989, 1997). Following Tyler's (1990) work, Smith and Stalans (1991) regard respectful and responsive treatment as a 'positive incentive' that could increase taxpaying attitudes and behaviour through strengthening the allegiance to tax authorities. Smith (1992) indeed found a measure of taxpayers' perceived fairness of the tax authority (consisting of items tapping respect and trustworthiness) to be negatively related to perceived acceptability of non-compliance (i.e., cash under reporting). Stalans and Lind (1997) interviewed taxpayers, or their representatives, after being audited by the ATO. Respondents who mentioned in their open-format evaluations that they had been treated respectfully rated the auditor as procedurally fairer than those who did not mention respectful treatment. Likewise, perceived neutrality of the auditors' decision-making was related to perceived fairness. However, the study did not include any findings on whether or not perceived fairness had any implications for compliance attitudes or behaviour.

Table 3.2 Procedural justice in taxation: examples for three levels of analysis

	Individual level	Group level	Societal level
Interactional treatment	respect for the individual; consistency relative to other individuals	respect for the ingroup; consistency relative to other groups	rights for taxpayers and service standards
Process and decision control	voice; control; consultation of individual	voice; control; consultation and representation of ingroup	consultation of taxpayers in general; democratic structures
Information and explanation	explanations and justifications for decisions affecting the individual	explanations and justifications for decisions affecting the ingroup	transparency; presentation in media
Compliance costs	efficiency; service vs. costs for the individual	efficiency; service vs. costs for the ingroup	administration and compliance costs; complexity of the tax system

Taxpayers can also evaluate the amount of voice or control they have in decision processes; that is, the degree of consultation and representation in tax matters. In their study on audits, Stalans and Lind (1997) found that taxpayers who mentioned that auditors were unresponsive to their views and comments thought auditors tried less hard to be fair. Alm et al.'s (1993) finding falls in the same category of fairness effects. As mentioned earlier, participants who could decide over the use of tax revenue by vote and majority rule, rather than the spending purpose being imposed on them, were more compliant (see Tyler, Rasinski and Spodick, 1985).

Another potential subject of fairness evaluations is the extent and quality of information provided by the ATO. While access to and provision of information may also impact on compliance costs (see below), they are first of all understood here in their intrinsic value of providing transparency, justifications and explanations for decisions (informational justice) (Greenberg, 1993). Magner, Johnson, Sobery and Welker (2000) found that perceived attempts to justify a revenue spending decision did not contribute uniquely, that is, beyond the effects of other fairness criteria, to perceived procedural justice. However, Wartick's (1994) research, referred to earlier, showed that the provision of explanations for a tax law change can increase perceptions of fairness. However, the outcomes of her two studies were inconsistent in that the justification effect occurred either only for those less well off due to the change (study 1) or only for those unaffected by the change (study 2). As Wartick argues, the results might reflect the fact that the justification needs to be found adequate in order to be effective (Greenberg, 1993).

Moreover, procedural justice was defined earlier as implying a concept of entitlement. Hence, it could be argued that taxpayers would regard a certain treatment as particularly fair when it satisfies their perceived entitlements. In a study with a student sample in Australia, I asked respondents to rate their perceptions of and response to a reminder letter that they hypothetically received from the ATO (Wenzel, 2001c). The letter either contained respectful treatment (interpersonal justice), provided explanations and justifications (informational justice), or was a usual, rather concise, letter from the ATO (control). Furthermore, each letter highlighted one of three rights from the Taxpayers' Charter (Australian Taxation Office, 1997), namely, rights to respectful treatment, explanation of decisions, or minimisation of costs (control). In line with the prediction, the interpersonal justice letter was considered fairer than the other two letters, when the interpersonal right (respect) was salient. The informational justice letter was considered fairer than the other two letters when the information right (explanation) was salient. Feelings of entitlement seem to play a role for perceptions of procedural fairness. The results suggest that tax authorities could indeed profit from alerting attention to and granting taxpayer rights, but they would need to assure that the rights are indeed fulfilled.

Finally, individuals may also be concerned about the efficiency of their interactions with the ATO or, conversely, the costs of their attempts to be compliant. Possible issues could be the promptness of correspondence, provision of assistance and clear instructions, waiting time on the phone and length of queues at information desks (see Smith and Stalans, 1991). For instance, in Stalans and Lind's (1997) study, respondents' satisfaction with their audit treatment was affected by the perceived time the auditor used to gather information and make a decision. Likewise, respondents were more dissatisfied, the longer it objectively took to reach a decision. Wallschutzky (1984) found that convicted evaders were less satisfied than the control group with the efficiency and speed of the ATO's handling of their tax returns.

The same issues of procedural justice could be analysed at a *group level*, which research has so far neglected. For instance, taxpayers could feel they are treated disrespectfully as members of a certain group (rather than as individuals) (see Hobson, 2002; Murphy, 2002a). They could believe that the ATO is not neutral and treats their group differently from another group (see Hobson, 2002; Murphy, 2002b). Likewise, they could feel that the ATO allows voice, and listens, to certain *societal* groups rather than others. They could think that the ATO goes to great lengths to explain decisions to, and try to receive consent from, some groups but not when it comes to their group. Or, they could believe that their dealings with the ATO are less efficient and the costs of complying with the laws are higher for their group than for others. A good example of this latter issue is the strong dissatisfaction small business owners expressed after the introduction of Tax Reform in Australia in 2000. With the introduction of the Goods and Services Tax (GST), and the (initial) requirement to lodge quarterly tax statements, they felt small business was carrying the greatest burden of the tax changes. They also felt disadvantaged compared to larger business who were in a better position to make one-off investments in structural changes to cope with the new system.

At a *societal* level, the same four issues and how they apply to the ATO's treatment of *all* taxpayers could be of concern. For instance, the ATO's formal granting of respective rights and service standards could be seen as a measure of procedural fairness at a *societal* level. Based on a survey with Australian citizens, Braithwaite and Reinhart (2000) found that respondents had greater trust in, and more favourable attitudes towards, the ATO when they believed that the ATO met their obligations set out in the Taxpayers' Charter. The Australian Taxpayers' Charter not only grants fair and respectful treatment and confidentiality, but also makes explicit taxpayers' options for making complaints and appealing decisions. The latter would be an instance of voice and process control at a *societal* level. Perceptions of large-scale voice and control about taxation issues, however, are also based on views about the presence of participatory and democratic political structures (as simulated in the study by Alm et al., 1993 or referred to in the vignette study by Tyler et al., 1985). The third issue of informational justice is played out at the *societal* level in terms of the ATO's transparency towards the public, its presentation in the media and the extent of communication with taxpayers.

Overall, these societal-level issues have rarely been investigated in their potential impact on tax compliance. In contrast, the fourth issue, namely the efficiency or costliness of the tax system, has attracted quite a lot of research attention. This issue has been dealt with in particular under the labels of administration and compliance costs (e.g., Sandford, Godwin and Hardwick, 1989) and the complexity of the tax system (e.g., Milliron, 1985). Both topics are related (e.g., Blumenthal, 2000), but only the latter has been discussed explicitly in relation to perceptions of fairness, with authors disagreeing about how, or whether at all, complexity is related to fairness) (see Carnes and Cuccia, 1996). According to Carnes and Cuccia (1996), complexity overall is negatively related to perceived equity; however, taxpayers can regard specific complexities as justified and thus these would contribute less to perceptions of unfairness. Yet, Smith asked respondents to rate the probable effectiveness of eight possible 'ways that might help the IRS [Internal Revenue Service] do a better job' (1992, p. 237). Respondents most strongly recommended a simplification of the tax system; and the more unfair they thought the current tax system was, the more they recommended simplification. It may be added here that respondents' second strongest recommendation was to increase the likelihood of tax offenders being caught. This leads us to the third area of justice.

Retributive Justice and Tax Compliance

Issues of retributive justice have rarely been explicitly studied in the context of tax compliance. Findings like Smith's (1992), however, suggest that they deserve our attention, as the results seem to indicate that honest taxpayers (i.e., presumably the majority of taxpayers) are concerned about others betraying the system and getting away with it. In fact, however, questions of retributive justice have two perspectives. First, as just stated, honest taxpayers could perceive it as unfair, and consider their sense of responsibility to be disrespected or ridiculed, when they see others violate the law, disregard civic duties, make their profit and go unpunished. Second, taxpayers who violate tax laws could find the penalty they receive unfair, disproportional to the offence, or for other reasons unjustified. In its narrow sense, retributive justice deals here with the question of fair and appropriate punishment for tax evaders. In a wider sense, this could also include the appropriateness of procedures involved in investigating tax evasion. Thus, there is some overlap with the category of procedural justice, where we already discussed research on fairness in the context of audits.

As with distributive and procedural justice, issues of retributive justice could be relevant at three different levels of analysis (see Table 3.3).

Table 3.3 Retributive justice in taxation: examples for three levels of analysis

	Individual level	Group level	Societal level
Penalties	appropriateness of penalty for individual (relative to the offence, others)	appropriateness of penalty for ingroup (relative to the offence, others)	severity of penalties; distribution penalties for different offences; quality of penalties
Audits	rigidity or inconsiderateness of audit for individual case	rigidity or inconsiderateness of audit for ingroup cases	rigidity or inconsiderateness of audits in general

Taxpayers could question the fairness of the treatment that they (or another target *individual*) receive as a response to a suspected or established act of tax evasion. They could find a penalty too severe (or not severe enough) relative to the offence, given the degree of blame attributed to oneself (or the other person) or compared to other cases. They could find the audit process too rigid, ignorant of possible harm to the person or their business, or a mere harassment. At a *group* level, the same issues could be considered for the treatment of one's own group relative to other groups. At a *societal* level, some possible issues could be the perceived fairness of the general severity of penalties for tax offences, the relative severity of penalties for small versus serious offences (i.e., a version of vertical justice), or the perceived quality of the punishments such as their punitive versus reintegrative character (see Braithwaite, 1989).

As stated above, there is not much research available on these issues. Vogel (1974) asked participants to select appropriate penalties (no penalty, fine, imprisonment) for acts of tax evasion differing in seriousness. However, he compared the responses with the penalties suggested for other offences, but not with the perceived actual penalties for tax evasion. Thus, the questions were used as an indirect measure of people's attitudes towards tax evasion as an offence compared to other offences (see Song and Yarbrough, 1978), but not people's perceived fairness of the current system of penalties for tax evasion. There is, however, much anecdotal evidence for taxpayers' resentment over incidences where individuals defied the ATO, evaded or avoided tax, and yet escaped prosecution. In fact, the resentment is often better understood as an intergroup phenomenon in that certain groups of people (e.g., the rich, big business) are considered to be able to dodge their taxpaying responsibilities and the ATO is perceived as being soft on 'them' (see Shover, Job and Carroll, Chapter 8, this volume; Braithwaite, Chapter 12, this volume).

Likewise, researchers have argued that taxpayers subject to investigation or punishment could resent their treatment, find penalties unfair or audits unreasonably intrusive, and as a consequence develop more negative attitudes towards the ATO (Strümpel, 1969; Spicer and Lundstedt, 1976; Sheffrin and Triest, 1992; Murphy, 2002a, 2002b). At a group level, taxpayers could also question the consistency of the ATO's enforcement procedures and penalty regimes across different *societal* groups. For instance, in the 1990s, tax miminisation schemes gained popularity, and were strongly promoted, among groups of middle and working-class Australians (see Murphy and Byng, 2002). While the ATO tolerated the practices for several years, in early 1998 it decided to crack down on the schemes, declared them illegal and amended previous tax assessments. Taxpayers involved in the schemes faced large tax bills, penalties and interest charges (Murphy, 2002a, 2002b). There was not merely a perceived inconsistency over time; more crucially people resented the decision because they thought it reflected discriminatory treatment of them, the normal middle or working-class people, versus the rich who always go unpunished. As one tax scheme promoter put it: 'You see, it was OK while it was the top end of town, but when it was the mums and dads of Australia starting to take advantage of the same tax breaks, then, of course, it was time to call a halt' (Australian Broadcasting Commission, *Four Corners*, 2001) (see also Senate Economics References Committee, 2001; Hobson, 2002; Murphy, 2002a, 2002b, for work on perceptions of ATO fairness by scheme investors).

Issues of retributive justice may also play a role in the success or failure of tax amnesties (Hasseldine, 1998); however, tax amnesties have been analysed so far mainly from an economic expected utility perspective (e.g., Alm and Beck, 1990; Stella, 1991). Under these programs, previously non-compliant taxpayers are asked to come forward and disclose their tax deficiencies, normally with the incentive of penalties being waived before a certain deadline. The aims of such measures are twofold: to get hold of revenue that would otherwise be lost because detection of the evasion would be either unlikely or costly, and to bring taxpayers who dropped out of the system back into the system. Taxpayers who previously evaded tax but have changed their attitude would no longer feel forced to repeat their previous behaviour out of fear of receiving high penalties. They might therefore view the amnesty as a way of giving them a fair chance. In contrast, taxpayers who are already honest may consider a tax amnesty unfair, because it does not acknowledge their integrity, disadvantages them materially and rewards tax evasion (Hasseldine, 1998). The perceived unfairness of tax amnesties, in addition to their potential impact on expected utilities from evasion behaviour, may undermine tax morality in the long run.

Conclusion

The evidence for the role of justice perceptions for tax compliance, as reviewed in the previous sections, supports my introductory argument that a pure self-interest account is insufficient for a proper understanding of taxpaying behaviour. Furthermore, the review demonstrates the complexity of questions of fairness in the area of taxation and supports my view that we need to differentiate more precisely the aspects of justice we are talking about. The distinction between distributive, procedural and retributive justice is an established one in psychological research on justice (Tyler and Smith, 1998). As shown, all three areas seem to be potentially relevant to the phenomenon of tax compliance. Likewise, the distinction between different levels of analysis, even though often overlooked, is considered valuable in psychological research on justice (Tyler and Smith, 1998). To some extent, this distinction was already implicit in the fairness concepts applied to tax compliance (e.g., horizontal versus vertical justice), but an explicit and systematic application of different levels of analysis proved possible and instructive. In particular, an intermediate *group* level analysis has been largely neglected in tax compliance research, whereas studies on justice and relative deprivation have demonstrated the distinctive dynamics when people do not consider themselves as individuals but rather as members of social groups (e.g., Smith et al., 1994; Platow, O'Connell, Shave and Hanning, 1995; Wenzel, 2002). An analysis of tax non-compliance as a *group* level response that is based on an interpretation of the situation shared within one's relevant ingroup, and that is justified as a response against the perceived unfair treatment of one's ingroup (relative to other groups), is more than plausible. Unfortunately, however, there is limited research that speaks directly to such an account.

Indeed, the main value of the present review is less likely to consist in its statement about what we know about the role of justice perceptions for tax compliance, but rather what we do not know. For several issues, the review revealed inconsistent findings that could not be resolved here, because a more thorough analysis of the different methodologies and operationalisations would be required. More importantly, however, the argument is that we cannot expect all findings to be consistent as they refer to various forms of fairness perceptions. The taxonomy suggests which results should be comparable and therefore which inconsistencies need to be resolved. Moreover, the review showed that a number of issues identified on the basis of the present taxonomy have rarely been investigated at all. Specifically, questions of retributive justice at all three levels of analysis have been largely ignored. Likewise, only a few studies have looked at the role of procedural justice for tax compliance. Further, even in the area of distributive justice, which has been the main focus of research, a *group* level analysis has been clearly neglected so far. Future research needs to address these issues.

Future research would also need to test for independent and unique effects of the various justice considerations, as they are likely to be empirically correlated with each other. Research could try to establish which of the more finely differentiated justice considerations are most strongly related to, and most predictive of, tax compliance (Wenzel, 2001d). The results could be valuable for tax legislators and tax authorities, not only by providing a more differentiated diagnosis of the underlying problem, but also by suggesting priorities for addressing the issues.

However, contextual conditions should furthermore moderate the impact of the various justice concerns on taxpaying behaviour. We need to apply and develop more refined theoretical accounts for the relevance of justice concerns. Empirical inconsistencies revealed in the present chapter, where consistency was expected, may be partly due to methodological differences between the studies; however, they also encourage us to look for moderating factors and gain a better understanding of when and why people are concerned about fairness at all.

In a recent study on tax compliance (Wenzel, 2001b), I tested the prediction that concerns for procedural and distributive justice would depend on the level of identification with the inclusive category (i.e., one's nation) within which procedures were applied and resources distributed (Tyler, 1997; Tyler and Smith, 1999; Wenzel, 2000, 2001a, 2002). Based on a survey with Australian citizens (Braithwaite, 2001), the results confirmed the predictions for two forms of tax compliance (i.e., under reporting of non-pay income, exaggerations of deductions). Self-interest variables were more influential when respondents were less identified as Australians, while perceptions of procedural and distributive justice were more positively related to compliance when respondents identified strongly as Australians. Two other forms of compliance were not related to fairness concerns but to self-interest considerations. These two forms, namely cash under reporting and tax minimisation, could be considered more legitimate behaviours, at least for certain reference groups, and might therefore constitute rational choices rather than a protest against perceived injustices. Thus, not only could social identity influence whether or not people are concerned about justice, but qualities of the specific behaviours could moderate whether or not these would be used as a response to perceived unfairness.

Certainly, further research in this direction is necessary. The present chapter was not meant to offer substantial theoretical propositions about underlying psychological processes. Rather, it provides a map to the field, using a larger scale and covering familiar and unfamiliar territory that will hopefully act as a tool for future expeditions.

Notes

1 I will not distinguish here between entitlement and deservingness, but see Feather (1999) and Steil (1994).

2 In fact, they could also compare their share in tax-funded benefits with their share at future times or under counterfactual conditions; for instance, when the opposition party suggests a different use of tax revenue (see Folger, 1986).

References

Adams, J.S. (1965), 'Inequity in Social Exchange', in L. Berkowitz (ed), *Advances in Experimental Social Psychology* (Vol. 2), Academic Press, New York, pp. 267-99.

Allingham, M. and Sandmo, A. (1972), 'Income Tax Evasion: A Theoretical Analysis', *Journal of Public Economics*, vol. 1, pp. 323-38.

Alm, J. and Beck, W. (1990), 'Tax Amnesties and Tax Revenues', *Public Finance Quarterly*, vol. 18, pp. 433-53.

Alm, J., Jackson, B.R., and McKee, M. (1993), 'Fiscal Exchange, Collective Decision Institutions, and Tax Compliance', *Journal of Economic Behavior and Organization*, vol. 22, pp. 285-303.

Alm, J., McClelland, G. and Schulze, W. (1992), 'Why do People Pay Taxes?', *Journal of Public Economics*, vol. 48, pp. 21-38.

Alm, J., Sanchez, I. and De Juan, A. (1995), 'Economic and Noneconomic Factors in Tax Compliance', *Kyklos*, vol. 48, pp. 3-18.

Andreoni, J., Erard, B. and Feinstein, J. (1998), 'Tax Compliance', *Journal of Economic Literature*, vol. 36(2), pp. 818-60.

Australian Broadcasting Corporation (2001), *Four Corners: The Crackdown*, Broadcast on 18 June 2001, http://www.abc.net.au/4corners/

Australian Taxation Office (1997), *The Taxpayers' Charter*, Australian Taxation Office, Canberra.

Barrett-Howard, E. and Tyler, T.R. (1986), 'Procedural Justice as a Criterion in Allocation Decisions', *Journal of Personality and Social Psychology*, vol. 50, pp. 296-304.

Blumenthal, M. (2000), 'Leaping Tall Buildings: Pursuing Greater Compliance and Less Burden in the United States', *Bulletin for International Fiscal Documentation*, vol. 54, pp. 351-56.

Bordignon, M. (1993), 'A Fairness Approach to Income Tax Evasion', *Journal of Public Economics*, vol. 52, pp. 345-62.

Braithwaite, J. (1989), *Crime, Shame, and Reintegration*, Cambridge University Press, Cambridge.

_____ (chapter 12, this volume), 'Through the Eyes of the Advisers: A Fresh Look at High Wealth Individuals'.

Braithwaite, V. (2001), 'The Community Hopes, Fears and Actions Survey: Goals and Measures', *Centre for Tax System Integrity Working Paper No. 2*, The Australian National University, Canberra.

Braithwaite, V. and Reinhart, M. (2000), 'The Taxpayers' Charter: Does the Australian Tax Office Comply and Who Benefits?', *Centre for Tax System Integrity Working Paper No. 1*, The Australian National University, Canberra.

Brewer, M.B. (1991), 'The Social Self: On Being the Same and Different at the Same Time', *Personality and Social Psychology Bulletin*, vol. 17, pp. 475-82.

Brewer, M.B. and Schneider, S.K. (1990), 'Social Identity and Social Dilemmas', in D. Abrams and M.A. Hogg (eds), *Social Identity Theory: Constructive and Critical Advances*, Harvester-Wheatsheaf, London, pp. 169-84.

Brickman, P., Folger, R., Goode, E. and Schul, Y. (1981), 'Microjustice and Macrojustice', in M.J. Lerner and S.C. Lerner (eds), *The Justice Motive in Social Behaviour*, Plenum Press, New York, pp. 173-202.

Calderwood, G. and Webley, P. (1992), 'Who Responds to Changes in Taxation? The Relationship Between Taxation and Incentive to Work', *Journal of Economic Psychology*, vol. 13(4), pp. 735-48.

Carnes, G.A. and Cuccia, A.D. (1996), 'An analysis of the Effect of Tax Complexity and its Perceived Justification on Equity Judgments', *The Journal of the American Taxation Association*, vol. 18, pp. 40-56.

Christensen, A.L., Weihrich, S.G. and Newman, M.D.G. (1994), 'The Impact of Education on Perceptions of Tax Fairness', in T.M. Porcano (ed), *Advances in Taxation* (Vol. 6), JAI Press, Greenwich, pp. 63-94.

Copeland, P.V. and Harmelink, P.J. (1995), 'Using Taxpayer Perception of Fairness to Redesign the Federal Income Tax Structure', in T.M. Porcano (ed), *Advances in Taxation* (Vol. 7), JAI Press, Greenwich, pp. 43-72.

Cowell, F.A. (1992), 'Tax Evasion and Inequity', *Journal of Economic Psychology*, vol. 13(4), pp. 521-43.

Dawes, R.M. (1980), 'Social Dilemmas', *Annual Review of Psychology*, vol. 31, pp. 169-93.

De Juan, A., Lasheras, M.A. and Mayo, R. (1994), 'Voluntary Tax Compliant Behavior of Spanish Income Tax Payers', *Public Finance*, vol. 49, pp. 90-105.

Dean, P., Keenan, T. and Kenney, F. (1980), 'Taxpayers' Attitudes to Income Tax Evasion: An Empirical Study', *British Tax Review*, vol. 25, pp. 28-44.

Dubé, L. and Guimond, S. (1986), 'Relative Deprivation and Social Protest: The Personal Group Issue', in J. Olson, C.P. Herman and M. Zanna (eds), *Relative Deprivation and Social Comparison*, Erlbaum, Hillsdale, pp. 201-16.

Eckhoff, T. (1974), *Justice: Its Determinants in Social Interaction*, Rotterdam University Press, Rotterdam.

Elffers, H. (2000), 'But Taxpayers do Cooperate!', in M. van Vugt, M. Snyder, T.R. Tyler and A. Biel (eds), *Cooperation in Modern Society*, Routledge, London, pp. 184-94.

Falkinger, J. (1995), 'Tax Evasion, Consumption of Public Goods and Fairness', *Journal of Economic Psychology*, vol. 16(1), pp. 63-72.

Feather, N.T. (1999), *Values, Achievement, and Justice: Studies in the Psychology of Deservingness*, Kluwer/Plenum, New York.

Folger, R. (1986), 'Rethinking Equity Theory: A Referent Cognitions Model', in H.W. Bierhoff, R.L. Cohen and J. Greenberg (eds), *Justice in Social Relations*, Plenum, New York, pp. 145-62.

Gerbing, M.D. (1988), 'An Empirical Study of Taxpayer Perceptions of Fairness', Paper presented at the Annual Meeting of the American Accounting Association, August, Orlando.

Gordon, J.P.F. (1989), 'Individual Morality and Reputation Costs as Deterrents to Tax Evasion', *European Economic Review*, vol. 33, pp. 797-805.

Grasmick, H.G. and Bursik Jr, R.J. (1990), 'Conscience, Significant Others, and Rational Choice: Extending the Deterrence Model', *Law and Society Review*, vol. 24, pp. 837-61.

Greenberg, J. (1982), 'Approaching Equity and Avoiding Inequity in Groups and Organizations', in J. Greenberg and R.L. Cohen (eds), *Equity and Justice in Social Behavior*, Academic Press, New York, pp. 389-435.

_____ (1993), 'The Social Side of Fairness: Interpersonal and Informational Classes of Organizational Justice', in E. Cropanzano (ed), *Justice in the Workplace: Approaching Fairness in Human Resource Management*, Erlbaum, Hillsdale, pp. 79-103.

Hafer, C. and Olson, J.M. (1993), 'Beliefs in a Just World, Discontent and Assertive Actions by Working Women', *Personality and Social Psychology Bulletin*, vol. 19, pp. 30-8.

Haslam, S.A. (2001), *Psychology in Organizations: The Social Identity Approach*, Sage, London.

Hasseldine, J. (1998), 'Tax Amnesties: An International Review', *Bulletin for International Fiscal Documentation*, vol. 52, pp. 303-10.

Heuer, L., Bumenthal, E., Douglas, A. and Weinblatt, T. (1999), 'A Deservingness Approach to Respect as a Relationally Based Fairness Judgment', *Personality and Social Psychology Bulletin*, vol. 25, pp. 1279-92.

Hite, P.A. and Roberts, M.L. (1991), 'An Experimental Investigation of Taxpayer Judgments on Rate Structure in the Individual Income Tax System', *Journal of the American Taxation Association*, vol. 13, pp. 47-63.

Hobson, K. (2002), 'Say No to the ATO: The Cultural Politics of Protest Against the Australian Taxation Office', *Centre for Tax System Integrity Working Paper No. 37*, The Australian National University, Canberra.

Hogan, R. and Emler, N.P. (1981), 'Retributive Justice', in M.J. Lerner and S.C. Lerner (eds), *The Justice Motive in Social Behavior*, Academic Press, New York, pp. 125-44.

Homans, G.C. (1961), *Social Behavior: Its Elementary Forms*, Routledge and Kegan Paul, London.

Kessler, T., Mummendey, A. and Leisse, U.K. (2000), 'The Personal-group Discrepancy: Is there a Common Information Basis for Personal and Group Judgment?', *Journal of Personality and Social Psychology*, vol. 79, pp. 95-109.

Kinsey, K.A. and Grasmick, H.G. (1993), 'Did the Tax Reform Act of 1986 Improve Compliance? Three studies of Pre-and Post-TRA Compliance Attitudes', *Law and Policy*, vol. 15, pp. 239-325.

Kinsey, K.A., Grasmick, H.G. and Smith, K.W. (1991), 'Framing Justice: Taxpayer Evaluations of Personal Tax Burdens', *Law and Society Review*, vol. 25, pp. 845-73.

Lerner, M.J. (1977), 'The Justice Motive: Some Hypotheses as to its Origins and Forms', *Journal of Personality*, vol. 45, pp. 1-52.

_____ (1991), 'Integrating Societal and Psychological Rules of Entitlement', in R. Vermunt and H. Steensma (eds), *Social Justice in Human Relations* (Vol. 1), Plenum Press, New York, pp. 13-32.

Leventhal, G.S. (1976), 'Fairness in Social Relationships', in J.W. Thibaut, J.T. Spence and R.C. Carson (eds), *Contemporary Topics in Social Psychology*, General Learning Press, Morristown, pp. 211-39.

_____ (1980), 'What Should be Done with Equity Theory? New Approaches to the Study of Fairness in Social Relationships', in K.J. Gergen, M.S. Greenberg and R.H. Willis (eds), *Social Exchange*, Plenum, New York, pp. 27-55.

Lewis, A. (1978), 'Perceptions of Tax Rates', *British Tax Review*, vol. 6, pp. 358-66.

Lind, E.A. and Tyler, T.R. (1988), *The Social Psychology of Procedural Justice*, Plenum Press, New York.

Long, S.B. and Swingen, J.A. (1991), 'Taxpayer Compliance: Setting New Agendas for Research', *Law and Society Review*, vol. 25, pp. 637-83.

Magner, N.R., Johnson, G.G., Sobery, J.S. and Welker, R.B. (2000), 'Enhancing Procedural Justice in Local Government Budget and Tax Decision Making', *Journal of Applied Social Psychology*, vol. 30, pp. 798-815.

Major, B. (1994), 'From Social Inequality to Personal Entitlement: The Role of Social Comparisons, Legitimacy Appraisals, and Group Membership', in M.P. Zanna (ed), *Advances in Experimental Social Psychology* (Vol. 26), Academic Press, New York, pp. 293-355.

Markovsky, B. (1985), 'Multilevel Justice Theory', *American Sociological Review*, vol. 50, pp. 822-39.

Mason, R. and Calvin, L.D. (1978), 'A Study of Admitted Income Tax Evasion', *Law and Society Review*, vol. 13, pp. 73-89.

Mikula, G. (1993), 'On the Experience of Injustice', in W. Stroebe and M. Hewstone (eds), *European Review of Social Psychology* (Vol. 4), Wiley, Chichester, pp. 223-44.

Miller, D.T. and Vidmar, N. (1981), 'The Social Psychology of Punishment Reactions', in M.J. Lerner and S.C. Lerner (eds), *The Justice Motive in Social Behavior*, Academic Press, New York, pp. 145-72.

Milliron, V. (1985), 'A Behavioral Study of the Meaning and Influence of Tax Complexity', *Journal of Accounting Research*, vol. 23, pp. 794-816.

Morrison, B.E. (1997), 'Social Cooperation: Re-defining the Self in Self-interest', Unpublished PhD thesis, The Australian National University, Canberra.

Moser, D.V., Evans III, J.H., and Kim, C.K. (1995), 'The Effects of Horizontal and Exchange Inequity on Tax Reporting Decisions', *The Accounting Review*, vol. 70, pp. 619-34.

Murphy, K. (2002a), 'Procedural Justice and the Australian Taxation Office: A Study of Tax Scheme Investors', *Centre for Tax System Integrity Working Paper No. 35*, The Australian National University, Canberra.

Murphy, K. (2002b), 'Trust Me, I'm the Taxman: The Role of Trust in Nurturing Compliance', *Centre for Tax System Integrity Working Paper No. 43*, The Australian National University, Canberra.Murphy, K. and Byng, K. (2002), 'Preliminary Findings from the Australian Tax System Survey of Tax Scheme Investors', *Centre for Tax System Integrity Working Paper No. 40*, The Australian National University, Canberra.

Musgrave, R.A. (1994), 'Progressive Taxation, Equity, and Tax Design', in J. Slemrod (ed), *Tax Progressivity and Income Inequality*, Cambridge University Press, Cambridge, pp. 341-56.

Oakes, P.J. (1996), 'The Categorisation Process: Cognition and the Group in the Social Psychology of Stereotyping', in W.P. Robinson (ed.), *Social Groups and Identities: Developing the Legacy of Henri Tajfel*, Butterworth-Heinemann, Oxford, pp. 95-119.

Pepitone, A. (1971), 'The Role of Justice in Interdependent Decision Making', *Journal of Experimental Social Psychology*, vol. 7, pp. 144-56.

Platow, M., O'Connell, A., Shave, R. and Hanning, P. (1995), 'Social Evaluations of Fair and Unfair Allocators in Interpersonal and Intergroup Situations', *British Journal of Social Psychology*, vol. 34, pp. 363-81.

Porcano, T.M. (1984), 'Distributive Justice and Tax Policy', *The Accounting Review*, vol. 59, pp. 619-36.

_____ (1988), 'Correlates of Tax Evasion', *Journal of Economic Psychology*, vol. 9(1), pp. 47-67.

Reckers, P.M.J., Sanders, D.L. and Roark, S.J. (1994), 'The Influence of Ethical Attitudes on Taxpayer Compliance', *National Tax Journal*, vol. 47, pp. 825-36.

Roberts, M.L. (1994), 'An Experimental Approach to Changing Taxpayers' Attitudes Towards Fairness and Compliance Via Television', *The Journal of the American Taxation Association*, vol. 16, pp. 67-86.

Roberts, M.L. and Hite, P.A. (1994), 'Progressive Taxation, Fairness and Compliance', *Law and Policy*, vol. 16, pp. 27-47.

Roberts, M.L., Hite, P.A. and Bradley, C.F. (1994), 'Understanding Attitudes Toward Progressive Taxation', *Public Opinion Quarterly*, vol. 58(2), pp. 165-90.

Runciman, W.G. (1966), *Relative Deprivation and Social Justice: A Study of Attitudes to Social Inequality in Twentieth-century England*, University of California Press, Berkeley.

Sandford, C., Godwin, M. and Hardwick, P. (1989), *Administrative and Compliance Costs of Taxation*, Fiscal Publications, Bath.

Schmölders, G. (1970), 'Survey Research in Public Finance – A Behavioural Approach to Fiscal Theory', *Public Finance*, vol. 25, pp. 300-6.

Scholz, J.T. (1998), 'Trust, Taxes and Compliance', in V. Braithwaite and M. Levi (eds), *Trust and Governance*, Russell Sage Foundation, New York, pp. 135-66.

Schopler, J. and Insko, C.A. (1992), 'The Discontinuity Effect in Interpersonal and Intergroup Relations: Generality and Mediation', in W. Stroebe and M. Hewstone (eds), *European Review of Social Psychology* (Vol. 3), Wiley, Chichester, pp. 121-51.

Senate Economics References Committee (2001), *Inquiry into Mass Marketed Tax Effective Schemes and Investor Protection: Interim Report*, Parliament of the Commonwealth of Australia, Canberra.

Sheffrin, S.M. (1994), 'Perceptions of Fairness in the Crucible of Tax Policy', in J. Slemrod (ed), *Tax Progressivity and Income Inequality*, Cambridge University Press, Cambridge, pp. 309-40.

Sheffrin, S. and Triest, R. (1992), 'Can Brute Deterrence Backfire? Perceptions and Attitudes in Taxpayer Compliance', in J. Slemrod (ed), *Who Pays Taxes and Why? Tax Compliance and Enforcement*, University of Michigan Press, Ann Arbor, pp. 193-218.

Shover, N., Job, J. and Carroll, A. (Chapter 8, this volume), 'The Compliance Model in Action: A Case Study of Building and Construction'.

Sigala, M., Burgoyne, C. and Webley, P. (1999), 'Tax Communication and Social Influence: Evidence from a British Sample', *Journal of Community and Applied Social Psychology*, vol. 9, pp. 237-41.

Smith, H.J., Spears, R. and Oyen, M. (1994), '"People like us": The Influence of Personal Deprivation and Group Membership Salience on Justice Evaluations', *Journal of Experimental Social Psychology*, vol. 30, pp. 277-99.

Smith, K.W. (1992), 'Reciprocity and Fairness: Positive Incentives for Tax Compliance', in J. Slemrod (ed), *Why People Pay Taxes: Tax Compliance and Enforcement*, University of Michigan Press, Ann Arbor, pp. 223-50.

Smith, K.W. and Stalans, L.J. (1991), 'Encouraging Tax Compliance with Positive Incentives: A Conceptual Framework and Research Directions', *Law and Policy*, vol. 13(1), pp. 35-53.

Song, Y.D. and Yarbrough, T.E. (1978), 'Tax Ethics and Taxpayer Attitudes: A Survey', *Public Administration Review*, vol. 38, pp. 442-52.

Spicer, M.W. and Becker, L.A. (1980), 'Fiscal Inequity and Tax Evasion: An Experimental Approach', *National Tax Journal*, vol. 33, pp. 171-75.

Spicer, M.W. and Lundstedt, S.B. (1976), 'Understanding Tax Evasion', *Public Finance*, vol. 31, pp. 295-305.

Stalans, L. and Lind, E.A. (1997), 'The Meaning of Procedural Fairness: A Comparison of Taxpayers' and Representatives' Views of Their Tax Audits', *Social Justice Research*, vol. 10, pp. 311-31.

Steil, J. (1994), 'Equality and Entitlement in Marriage: Benefits and Barriers', in M.J. Lerner and G. Mikula (eds), *Entitlement and the Affectional Bond: Justice in Close Relationships*, Plenum, New York, pp. 229-58.

Stella, P. (1991), 'An Economic Analysis of Tax Amnesties', *Journal of Public Economics*, vol. 46, pp. 383-400.

Strümpel, B. (1969), 'The Contribution of Survey Research to Public Finance', in A.T. Peacock (ed), *Quantitative Analysis in Public Finance*, Praeger, New York, pp. 13-22.

Taylor, N. (Chapter 4, this volume), 'Understanding Taxpayer Attitudes Through Understanding Taxpayer Identities'.

Thibaut, J. and Walker, L. (1978), 'A Theory of Procedure', *California Law Review*, vol. 66, pp. 541-66.

Turner, J.C., Oakes, P.J., Haslam, S.A. and McGarty, C. (1994), 'Self and Collective: Cognition and Social Context', *Personality and Social Psychology Bulletin*, vol. 20, pp. 454-63.

Tyler, T.R. (1989), 'The Psychology of Procedural Justice: A Test of the Group Value Model', *Journal of Personality and Social Psychology*, vol. 57, pp. 830-38.

_____ (1990), *Why People Obey the Law: Procedural Justice, Legitimacy, and Compliance*, Yale University Press, New Haven.

_____ (1997), 'The Psychology of Legitimacy: A Relational Perspective on Voluntary Deference to Authorities', *Personality and Social Psychology Review*, vol. 1, pp. 323-45.

_____ (2000), 'Why Do People Obey the Law?', Paper presented at the 1st International Conference of the Centre for Tax System Integrity, December 4-5, The Australian National University, Canberra.

Tyler, T.R. and Smith, H.J. (1998), Social Justice and Social Movements', in D.G. Gilbert, S.T. Fiske and G. Lindzey (eds), *The Handbook of Social Psychology* (4th ed, Vol. 2), McGraw-Hill, Boston, pp. 595-629.

_____ (1999), 'Justice, Social Identity, and Group Processes', in T.R. Tyler, R.M. Kramer and O.P. John (eds), *The Psychology of the Social Self*, Erlbaum, Mahwah, pp. 223-64.

Tyler, T.R., Boeckmann, R.J., Smith, H.J. and Huo, Y.J. (1997), *Social Justice in a Diverse Society*, Westview, Boulder.

Tyler, T.R., Rasinski, K. and Spodick, N. (1985), 'The Influence of Voice on Satisfaction with Leaders: Exploring the Meaning of Process Control', *Journal of Personality and Social Psychology*, vol. 48, pp. 72-81.

van Dijk, E. and Wilke, H.A.M. (1993), 'Differential Interests, Equity, and Public Good Provision', *Journal of Experimental Social Psychology*, vol. 29, pp. 1-16.

Vogel, J. (1974), 'Taxation and Public Opinion in Sweden: An Interpretation of Recent Survey Data', *National Tax Journal*, vol. 27, pp. 499-513.

Walker, I. and Mann, L. (1987), 'Unemployment, Relative Deprivation and Social Protest', *Personality and Social Psychology Bulletin*, vol. 13, pp. 275-83.

Wallschutzky, I.G. (1984), 'Possible Causes of Tax Evasion', *Journal of Economic Psychology*, 5(4), pp. 371-84.

Walster, E., Berscheid, E. and Walster, G.W. (1973), 'New Directions in Equity Research', *Journal of Personality and Social Psychology*, vol. 25, pp. 151-76.

Walster, E., Walster, G.W. and Berscheid, E. (1978), 'Equity: Theory and Research', Allyn and Bacon, Boston.

Wartick, M. (1994), 'Legislative Justification and the Perceived Fairness of Tax Law Changes: A Reference Cognitions Theory Approach', *The Journal of the American Tax Association*, vol. 16, pp. 106-23.

Webley, P., Robben, H. and Morris, I. (1988), 'Social Comparison, Attitudes and Tax Evasion in a Shop Simulation', *Social Behaviour*, vol. 3, pp. 219-28.

Weigel, R.H., Hessing, D.J. and Elffers, H. (1987), 'Tax Evasion Research: A Critical Appraisal and Theoretical Model', *Journal of Economic Psychology*, vol. 8, pp. 215-35.

Weiner, B. (1995), *Judgments of Responsibility: A Foundation for a Theory of Social Conduct*, Guilford, New York.

Wenzel, M. (2000), 'Justice and Identity: The Significance of Inclusion for Perceptions of Entitlement and the Justice Motive', *Personality and Social Psychology Bulletin*, vol. 26, pp. 157-76.

_____ (2001a), 'A Social Categorisation Approach to Distributive Justice: Social Identity as the Link Between Relevance of Inputs and Need for Justice', *British Journal of Social Psychology*, vol. 40, pp. 315-35.

_____ (2001b), 'The Impact of Outcome Orientation and Justice Concerns on Tax Compliance: The Role of Taxpayers' Identity', *Centre for Tax System Integrity Working Paper No. 6*, The Australian National University, Canberra.

_____ (2001c), 'Principles of Procedural Fairness in Reminder Letters and Awareness of Entitlements: A Prestudy', *Centre for Tax System Integrity Working Paper No. 10*, The Australian National University, Canberra.

_____ (2001d), *Which Fairness Perceptions are Related to Tax Compliance?: An Empirical Analysis*, Manuscript in preparation, The Australian National University, Canberra.

Wenzel, M. (2002), 'What is Social About Justice? Inclusive Identity and Group Values as the Basis of the Justice Motive', *Journal of Experimental Social Psychology*, vol. 38, pp. 205-18.

Wit, A., Wilke, H.A.M. and Oppewal, H. (1992), 'Fairness in Asymmetric Social Dilemmas', in W.B.G. Liebrand, D.M. Messick and H.A.M. Wilke (eds), *Social Dilemmas: Theoretical Issues and Research Findings*, Pergamon Press, Elmsford, pp. 183-97.

Zander, A. (1971), *Motives and Goals in Groups*, Academic Press, New York.

Chapter 4

Understanding Taxpayer Attitudes Through Understanding Taxpayer Identities

Natalie Taylor

Understanding why taxpayers do or do not comply with tax regulation has been the focus of much research over the past three decades. Quite naturally, it is assumed that if we were able to acquire a good understanding of why taxpayers do or do not comply, we would be in a much better position to obtain greater levels of compliance with tax reporting, and bridge the tax-gap (Internal Revenue Service, 1997) more effectively. However, despite the wealth of research conducted on this question, a satisfactory explanation remains elusive. The task is not helped by the fact that defining what constitutes compliance is in itself difficult, with the subtleties surrounding evasion, avoidance, mere error, and intention often making them indistinguishable (see Long and Swingen, 1991; Roth, Scholz and Witte, 1989). Even so, our ability to pinpoint underlying motivations for compliant or non-compliant behaviour, however defined, remains weak.

Researchers from various disciplines have investigated the effects of variables such as legal sanctions (Grasmick and Scott, 1982), stigmatisation (e.g., Porcano and Price, 1993), probability of audit (Webley, 1987), conscience appeals (Schwartz and Orleans, 1967), self-interest (McGraw and Scholz, 1991), opportunity (Klepper and Nagin, 1989), omission and commission (e.g., Christensen and Hite, 1997), message framing (Schisler, 1994), perceptions of fairness (e.g., Roberts and Hite, 1994) and, of course, demographic features (e.g., Baldry, 1987). Investigation of these variables has made use of (a) self-reports of actual behaviour, attitudes, or intentions (see Kinsey, 1984), (b) analytical models of tax evasion which rely heavily on economic deterrence theory (e.g., Allingham and Sandmo, 1972), (c) actual data obtained from tax agencies (e.g., McGraw and Scholz, 1991), and (d) experimental studies which explicitly manipulate variables of interest (e.g., Beck, Davis and Jung, 1991).

While each of these variables appears to have some causal or correlational connection with compliance, there is often difficulty in replicating findings, and links between variables have not been established (see Andreoni, Erard and Feinstein, 1998). Further, it has become clear that techniques to improve compliance based solely on surveillance and sanctions are inadequate (Kirchler, 1998; James and Nobes, 1998; Tyler, 1998) or counterproductive (Schwartz and Orleans, 1967; Blumenthal, Christian and Slemrod, 1998), and do not explain the voluntary compliance that occurs in the absence of surveillance (Alm, 1991), or changes in attitude as a result of an appeal to conscience (e.g., McGraw and Scholz, 1991; Mason and Mason, 1992). For tax systems that rely on voluntary self-reporting of tax obligations, the need to understand the processes underlying compliance is increasingly urgent.

The purpose of this chapter is to argue for a different approach to understanding the motivations underlying taxpaying behaviour. This approach is social-psychological in nature and aims to show that attitudes towards paying tax are not stable, but are fluid and are an outcome of how one defines oneself in relation to the tax system, the tax authorities and other groups of taxpayers. It will be argued that the variables that are important in motivating behaviour will be an outcome of this self-definition.

The chapter begins with a brief explanation of why current approaches are inadequate for explaining taxpayer motivations and why a self-definitional approach is useful. It will be shown, by analysing spontaneous taxpayer comments written at the end of a tax questionnaire, that how one defines oneself in relation to tax authorities and other groups of taxpayers affects attitudes to paying tax, the strength of objection to or acceptance of paying tax, the perceived fairness of tax, and the degree to which self-interest versus civic duty is likely to be a motivating factor. It is concluded that understanding how taxpayers perceive themselves in the tax system is fundamental to understanding the motivations that underlie taxpaying behaviour.

Self-interest Models of Non-compliance

A dominant approach to research on taxpayer compliance is a financial self-interest model (Fischer, Wartick and Mark, 1992). This approach assumes that individuals are intrinsically motivated to maximise their own outcomes by weighing up the risks of detection and punishment for non-compliance against the probabilities of successfully evading tax. Individuals essentially engage in a cost-benefit analysis. They are rational actors who are interested only in their own financial well-being and their taxpaying behaviour depends upon their beliefs about the probability of detection and legal sanctions. If the probability of being caught and/or punished is deemed too high, compliance will result. While there is support for this general approach (e.g., Allingham and Sandmo, 1972; Beck and Jung, 1989), self-interest models would suggest that when income is not subject to third party reporting, individuals should evade their tax obligations (Alm, 1991). This, however, does not always appear to be the case.

Grasmick and Scott (1982) found that while the relationship between the threat of legal punishment (detection probability) and intention to evade taxes in the future was statistically significant, anticipated feelings of guilt and possible social stigma attached to tax evasion were more strongly associated with deterrence. They concluded from their data that policies increasing the public's sense of moral duty to comply should be the most effective strategy for improving compliance. In a similar vein, Mason and Mason (1992) have drawn on the moral development literature to argue that an appeal to conscience or civic virtue, if correctly targeted, should improve tax compliance over and above a fear of sanction or threat. Schwartz and Orleans (1967) found that when questions were asked in a way that emphasised conscience rather than sanctions, a stronger effect was found for increasing reported income. This emphasis on conscience is consistent also with the co-operative citizen approach being adopted by James and Nobes (2000) in their research on compliance. Clearly, it would seem that factors other than pure self-interest must be involved in compliance (Alm, 1991).

A quasi-replication of the Schwartz and Orleans study (McGraw and Scholz, 1991) examined the effects of a normative appeal in contrast to a personal consequences appeal on compliance. The former appeal invokes the question 'What am I obligated to do?' while the latter appeal invokes the question 'What will make me better off?'. McGraw and Scholz (1991) found that a normative appeal resulted in an increased perception that the tax system and their own personal tax situation were fair; and that respondents were more likely to adopt an impersonal, rather than self-interested, standard to evaluate the fairness of the tax system. In contrast, those who were exposed to a personal consequences appeal showed the strongest self-interest bias in evaluating the fairness of the tax system. Although these attitudinal differences did not translate into actual differences in tax filing behaviour, a likely explanation is that the appeal manipulation had occurred over three months before tax filing was due. In other words, the induced attitude change may have decayed over time. The observed differences in attitude immediately following the manipulation, however, suggest that tax-related attitudes can be affected by how an appeal is directed and, moreover, that such attitudes are not simply determined by reference to personal self-interest, but by civic virtue or obligation.

But what does appealing to civic virtue actually mean? An appeal to self-interest is clearly in line with the cost-benefit approach outlined earlier. Unsurprisingly, emphasising how one can maximise one's income through evading tax leads to a desire to do precisely that. Why? Because the issue of tax is reframed so as to emphasise that everyone is in it for themselves, which motivates a desire to maximise what one can get out of the system. As Spicer (1975) has noted, the perception that cheating is widespread tends to undermine the resolve of honest taxpayers. It is likely that it is against this backdrop that self-interest motivates behaviour. However, an appeal to civic virtue is less easy to interpret. While McGraw and Scholz (1991, p. 472) themselves note that this perspective 'emphasises moral reasoning and the processes of socialisation and internalisation of norms' and that both approaches 'are important for understanding citizen responses to legal obligations', the implication is that these two approaches are essentially pitted against each other. That is, self-interest ('what will make me better off?') is pitted against obligation ('what am I obligated to do?'). There is an implicit underlying assumption that self-interest is the dominant motivation and that obligation is a means to try and deflect that motivation.

While it is agreed that these two approaches are important for a fuller understanding of the processes underlying compliance, it is argued that investigating them as if they involve an individual cost-benefit analysis reduces the focus, once again, to an expected utility approach. This is inadequate, and ignores the fundamental point that the socialisation and internalisation of norms associated with appeals to civic virtue may lead to qualitative differences in self-perception and not just quantitative differences in attitudes.

A Social Identity Approach to Understanding Compliance

This chapter presents a different approach to understanding the motivations underlying taxpaying behaviour, a social psychological approach that is based on an understanding of processes of social identity (Turner, 1985; Tajfel and Turner, 1986; Turner, Hogg, Oakes, Reicher and Wetherell, 1987). Turner (1985) developed a theory of self-categorisation, in which he argued that self can be perceived as unique and individual, and different in comparison with others ('me' in contrast to 'you/him/her'). At other times, however, self can be perceived as belonging to some social category (ingroup), and relatively interchangeable with members of it, in contrast to another category to which self does not belong (outgroup). This involves a psychological transformation from 'me' to 'we', and 'him/her' to 'them', and occurs as a result of changes in perceiver factors (knowledge, goals and motivations) and situational context. As the context changes (i.e., the issue, those involved, the frame of reference), so does self-perception. It is when self-perception is at the level of social identity, where greater similarity to ingroup others and greater dissimilarity to outgroup others is perceived, that attitudes and behaviour become more aligned with ingroup norms. Influence is argued to be an outcome of self-categorisation and is specific to ingroups. Outgroups possess no ability to influence. As a result, attitudes, behaviour, perceptions of fairness, what is right and what is wrong are outcomes of, and vary with, self-categorisation.

It is important to note that, from this perspective, both personal and social identities are psychologically valid and meaningful expressions of self. One is not regarded as more real or important than the other; rather, they are contextually-dependent and hence valid self-definitions, driving attitudes and behaviour, given a particular context. Perception 'varies not only with the perceiver but also with the salient self-category for a given perceiver – different people see the same thing differently, and the same perceiver sees the same thing differently as the varying self changes' (Turner and Oakes, 1997, p. 367).

This analysis implies that self-interest and civic virtue are not in direct competition with each other; rather, self-interest (i.e. personal self-interest) is likely to motivate behaviour when people see themselves as individuals (in contrast with other individuals), while civic virtue (what is good for the group collectively) is likely to motivate behaviour when people see themselves as being members of (positively valued) social categories, in contrast to other (negatively valued) social categories. An appeal to civic virtue changes the psychological situation by situating the recipient in a wider, more inclusive category in a different social context.

In the McGraw and Scholz (1991) study, the normative appeal referred to the importance Americans placed on the norms of social responsibility and patriotism, emphasising how these norms related to tax compliance. That is, the context was manipulated to include 'all good Americans who believe in social responsibility and patriotism' (ingroup), which implied that not taking social responsibility seriously (i.e., not complying with tax rules) was essentially bad and un-American (outgroup). On the assumption that most of the recipients would have regarded themselves as good Americans (or at least would not have liked to think of themselves as bad Americans), this would have led to a self-categorisation of 'good American', which meant adopting more closely the attitudinal and behavioural norms associated with that category. At this superordinate level of identity, all Americans would then have the potential to be influential. This stems from the fact that those who are seen as similar to self are also perceived as more legitimate, fair, accurate, and trustworthy (Tyler and Lind, 1992; Haslam, 2001).

Hence, the appeal to civic virtue is associated with a qualitative shift in self-perception from 'me' to 'us', a corresponding shift in who is included in the frame of reference, and a corresponding decrease in personal self-interest and more concern about outcomes for all good Americans. It is due to the fact that attitudes, behaviours, and motivations are outcomes of the self-categorisation process that self-interest and civic virtue are not competing in a cost-benefit analysis. Whether self-interest or civic virtue will motivate behaviour will depend on whether personal or social identity is salient, and whether the salient social identity is one which includes a majority of people and groups within the self-concept (a superordinate identity, such as 'American'), or one which includes only a subset of people within the self-concept (a subgroup identity, such as 'the rich' or 'the poor').

Most compliance with tax laws is to be expected at a more superordinate level of identity, because that is the level at which most people are included in one's self-definition and few people are excluded. Hence, if I perceive myself as American, then I care about America and all Americans, and want what is best for Americans. Least compliance with tax laws is to be expected at a subgroup level of identity, because this level includes fewer people and is more likely to be situated in conflict with other subgroup groups (e.g., 'us poor versus them rich'), focusing the concern on distributive outcomes and maximising the ingroup's interests.

Perceived Representativeness of Authorities

Approaching compliance from a social identity perspective, we can see that attitudes and behaviour in relation to compliance are outcomes of the self-categorisation process. It has been argued that compliance with tax laws is much more likely to occur when a superordinate identity is salient than when a subgroup identity is salient. Further, it has been argued (Smith and Tyler, 1996) that compliance should be most likely when the authority in question is included in that superordinate identity. The degree to which authorities are perceived to be representative of those over whom they have power has important implications for attitudes and behaviour. Research into procedural justice has shown that when authorities are perceived to behave fairly and respectfully, greater compliance results (Worsham, 1996; Tyler, 2001). When authorities are perceived as representative, their decisions are seen as legitimate because they are acting in the collective interests of 'us' (Ellemers, van Rijswijk, Bruins and de Gilder, 1998; Haslam, 2001). Legitimacy, in turn, leads to acceptance of decisions that authorities make and obedience to rules, regardless of whether people agree with them or dislike the outcomes (Tyler, 1998). Further, representative authorities confer a sense of pride in being a member of groups over which those authorities reign (Tyler and Degoey, 1996).

The implications in relation to tax authorities, then, are clear. Tax revenue authorities are designated by governments to collect revenue on behalf of governments. If governments are perceived as representative, then the role of tax authorities should be perceived as legitimate. If authorities are included within one's self-categorisation, they will be perceived to be legitimate, fair, accurate and trustworthy because they are perceived as representative of self, leading to greater compliance with rules and regulations (Smith and Tyler, 1996). Unrepresentative authorities, then, face greater difficulty obtaining compliance because they are more likely to be perceived as illegitimate, unjust, wrong and untrustworthy. What is important about this latter point is that if self-perception is located at a subgroup level (e.g., rich versus poor), the tax authority may be perceived as being part of, or representing the interests of the outgroup, in which case the authority's ability to influence is dramatically reduced and even rejected outright.

While we can attempt to manipulate experimentally superordinate identities so that the tax authority is included in them (along similar lines to civic virtue), it is important to know how and why particular identities spontaneously become salient in the context of tax, and what those spontaneous identities are. After all, it is these spontaneously generated identities that, it is argued, drive actual taxpayer attitudes and behaviour. Their existence needs to be established and their implications explored, both in terms of demonstrating the nature and importance of social identity, and in terms of obtaining a deeper understanding of the processes involved in taxpayer behaviour. For this reason, the study outlined in this chapter analysed unsolicited, spontaneously written comments made by taxpayers at the end of a tax survey (i.e., when they were thinking about paying tax). It was predicted that identities (both personal and social) would be discernible from what taxpayers wrote (Hypothesis 1), and that there would be a positive correlation between the extent to which respondents perceived the government to be representative of them and the extent to which they perceived the tax revenue authority to be representative of them (Hypothesis 2).

Social Identity, Justice and Compliance

Perhaps one of the distinguishing features of the Australian tax system is that it is purportedly about achieving justice and fairness, and turning inequality into equality. Everyone who earns above a certain amount of income is required to pay a certain amount of tax. Further, those who earn more are required to pay a higher level of tax than those who earn less. This is deemed to be a fair process as it essentially relies on the ability to pay. Apart from providing essential services from which everyone benefits, tax revenue is also used to provide a safety net for those in need.

Justice, fairness and equality, however, are not objective standards (Tyler, Boeckmann, Smith and Huo, 1997). Perceptions of these standards vary with self-categorisations (Wenzel, 2000). What might be perceived as being fair at the superordinate level (e.g., paying more tax than others) could be perceived as being highly unfair at the subgroup level. As Smith and Tyler note:

> Distinguishing between levels of inclusiveness suggests that when a superordinate category is more important to people, inequities between different groups represent an *intra*group situation with implications for collective cooperation and harmony. In contrast, if a particular group is more important to people, inequities between different groups represent an *inter*group situation with different groups competing for resources and power (1996, p. 175).

This suggests that when a subgroup identity is salient, what is perceived as fair or just is determined with reference to what *other* groups on similar dimensions have. This is similar to the notion of horizontal inequity (Moser, Evans and Kim, 1995), except that the perceived inequity relates to comparison with other groups rather than individuals. If other groups of taxpayers are perceived to be doing better than one's own, and this is deemed to be illegitimate and unfair (no obvious reason why 'they' should be getting a better deal than 'us'), collective relative deprivation can result (see Walker and Mann, 1987); that is, a subjective sense of collective, group-based injustice ('we have been treated unfairly'), generating anger and resentment and a strong desire to remedy the situation.

However, perceptions of injustice are not simply related to inequality in outcomes (distributive justice), but can also be related to the perceived unfairness of the methods and procedures used to determine the outcomes (procedural justice). If the methods by which outcomes are distributed are perceived to be fair, then discrepancies in outcomes may also be judged to be fair (Tyler, 2001). Song and Yarbrough (1978) noted that the taxpayers' complaint is not that too many citizens cheat the government and get away with it, but that the government provides unequal opportunities to different income groups.

Evaluations of procedural justice have been linked to voluntary acceptance of decisions made by authorities, obedience to laws and legitimacy of authorities (Tyler, 1990; Tyler and Lind, 1992). This implies that if inequities in outcome (paying more tax than others) are perceived to result from unfair procedures in the tax system, perceptions of group deprivation should increase, subgroup identities should become stronger, intergroup hostility should increase, and attitudes towards paying tax should become negative. In particular, Smith and Tyler (1996) have argued that procedural justice concerns should be dominant at the superordinate level for two reasons. First, distributive injustice concerns are associated with subgroup differentiation that is not found at a superordinate level. Second, being treated in a procedurally fair manner conveys that one is valued and respected by other group members; a message that promotes self-esteem and shapes behaviour toward other group members. At the subgroup level, however, the distinctions between subgroups, which are not so apparent at the superordinate level, are highly apparent, focusing concerns on distributive outcomes ('what they are getting in relation to what we are getting'). Hence, in the study being presented, it was predicted that taxpayer comments would relate both to distributive and procedural justice concerns (Hypothesis 3). Further, in line with Smith and Tyler (1996), it was predicted that concerns about distributive justice would be greater at a subgroup than at a superordinate level of identity (Hypothesis 4).

Attitudes and Motivational Postures Towards Tax

Taxpayers have been described in terms of a set of motivational postures (see Braithwaite, Chapter 2, this volume; Braithwaite and Braithwaite, 2001). These postures reflect underlying values, attitudes and beliefs and are the result of the dynamic interplay between taxpayers and tax authorities. The motivational postures of commitment, capitulation, resistance and disengagement embody psychological and behavioural orientations that are of particular interest in this chapter.

Commitment reflects a high level of internalised acceptance of the rules and regulations associated with the tax system (meaning that surveillance is unnecessary), while capitulation reflects an explicit and conscious decision to comply, in the knowledge that the tax authority has power and will use it if necessary. These motivational postures are orientated towards compliance. Resistance and disengagement reflect a psychological increase in social distance between taxpayers and the regulatory system. Those who adopt these postures do not wish to be part of the tax system, are motivated to avoid it and are more likely to engage in conflictual behaviour in relation to it. These postures describe an escalating process of non-compliance, accompanied by escalations in the degree to which surveillance and punishment are necessary to produce compliance with tax regulation.

Importantly, it is explicitly acknowledged that these motivational postures are not stable individual traits, but reflect the dynamic context in which the taxpayer is situated. This means that the motivational postures are fluid and taxpayers can shift between them. However, the specific processes that might lead to taxpayers adopting one motivational posture over another are not specified. It is proposed in this chapter that levels of inclusiveness of self-categorisation and the perceived representativeness of authorities may be two factors affecting the shift from one posture to another. Specifically, it was predicted that the less representative the government and the Australian Taxation Office (ATO) were perceived to be, the less cooperative and more resistant taxpayers would be in their motivational postures (Hypothesis 5).

Research Design

The primary purpose of this chapter is to demonstrate that how people spontaneously perceive themselves in relation to the tax system and other taxpayers is fundamentally important in understanding taxpayer attitudes and behaviour. It has been argued that social identity is central in this process, and that how people categorise themselves and others affects their perceptions of the fairness of the tax system and their attitudes towards tax in general. Studies which manipulate variables and then attempt to measure their effect on actual taxpaying behaviour, while rare, tend to find small effects, if any, on actual taxpaying behaviour (e.g., McGraw and Scholz, 1991; Blumenthal, Christian and Slemrod, 2001). From the perspective being advocated in this chapter, this is because the context in which taxpayers are situated at tax filing time may bear no relation to the context at the time when the variables were being manipulated (often some time earlier). If so, it becomes important to investigate how taxpayers might spontaneously perceive themselves and others when they are thinking about tax.

This was done in the present study by analysing unsolicited comments written by taxpayers at the end of a questionnaire investigating tax-related attitudes. The questionnaire immersed these taxpayers in a situation in which they had been thinking about tax for a substantial period of time. Analysis of what taxpayers express in words is important because 'the various aspects of context and self-categorisation are actively constructed and contested through language. This means that we need to treat text seriously, examining the precise words that are used, analysing what categorical definitions are offered, how they are warranted or else challenged' (Reicher and Hopkins, 1996, p. 301).

As part of a larger research project in May 2000, the Community Hopes, Fears and Actions Survey (Braithwaite, 2001) was mailed to 7754 Australian taxpayers, selected randomly from the publicly available Australian electoral roll. After allowing for out-of-scope responses (e.g., return to sender, recipient deceased), the response rate was 29 per cent (see Mearns and Braithwaite, 2001, for more details of the design and methodology). Approximately 500 questions covered a wide range of tax-related issues and took about one and a half hours to complete. As a Goods and Services Tax (GST) was being introduced in Australia from 1 July 2000, this date was used as a cut-off for inclusion of returned responses in the present study in order to eliminate extra variability in responses due to the introduction of the GST. This yielded 1044 usable questionnaires. Although the survey contained a large number of questions about various matters, the focus here will be on those directly related to testing the hypotheses developed in this chapter.

Measuring Self-categorisation

Self-categorisation was investigated by analysing comments written spontaneously at the end of the questionnaire. At the top of a blank page were the words 'If you have any comments which you would like to add, please write them below'. Comments written on this page were therefore unsolicited, allowing spontaneously generated self-categorisations to emerge. As the questions of interest in this chapter revolve around self-definition, only those who wrote comments at the end of the questionnaire in relation to tax were included in the analyses. The number of respondents who wrote comments relating to tax was 155 (15% of the pre-July sample). Ages ranged from 19 to 80, with a median age of 46. Fifty-two per cent of these respondents were male, while 48 per cent were female. Thirty-seven per cent of respondents wrote half a page, 21 per cent wrote a whole page, and 8 per cent wrote two pages.

To investigate whether social identities could be detected in the comments respondents wrote, three different coders (two of whom were familiar with the concept of self-categorisation) classified each respondent as reflecting personal, social or unclear identities. A social identity was coded as existing if the respondent referred to him/herself in a way that clearly indicated social group membership. When a social identity was detected, the coders were required to identify which social ingroup the respondent belonged to. The groups identified were: average Australian; pay-as-you-earn; homemaker; single parents; single income families; families with children; welfare recipients; retired; working singles or couples; rural Australians; Australian; low income; hardworking Australian; or small business owners. A consensus code (cf. Lupfer, Weeks, Doan and Houston, 2000) was established if two or three of the coders agreed in their codings. Consensus codes were established for 96 per cent of the coding decisions. Of the 155 respondents, 40 were unable to be classified.

To establish level of inclusiveness, these social groups were collapsed into two categories: superordinate (i.e., Australian; average Australian; hardworking Australian) and subgroup (i.e., the remainder of the groups). These categories reflected the degree to which others were included in one's self-concept, and hence provided the means for investigating how self-categorisation affects attitudes.

Measuring Motivational Postures

Based on previous research (Braithwaite, Braithwaite, Gibson and Makkai, 1994; Braithwaite, Chapter 2, this volume), a priori scales were constructed from the questionnaire for each of the four postures: (a) disengagement (e.g., 'I personally don't think that there is much the ATO can do to me to make me pay tax if I don't want to'); (b) resistance (e.g., 'The ATO is more interested in catching you for doing the wrong thing, than helping you do the right thing'); (c) capitulation (e.g., 'The ATO is encouraging to those who have difficulty meeting their obligations through no fault of their own'); and (d) commitment (e.g., 'Paying tax is a responsibility that should be willingly accepted by all Australians'). Each item was rated on a 5-point scale from 1 (strongly disagree) to 5 (strongly agree), and each scale was computed by averaging responses across items (see Braithwaite, Chapter 2, this volume for more details).

Measuring Perceived Representativeness of Authorities

Scales were constructed from the questionnaire to reflect the degree to which government was perceived as representative of self (Government-self) and the degree to which the ATO was perceived as representative of self (ATO-self). Government-self (α = .75) comprised six items and was computed by averaging responses across items. The first item was 'how dissatisfied or satisfied are you with the way the government spends taxpayers' money?'. Responses were made on a scale ranging from 1 (dissatisfied) to 5 (satisfied). The other five items were rated on a 5-point scale from 1 (strongly disagree) to 5 (strongly agree) and were reverse scored: (a) 'Our government is attempting to mould our society to the needs of a profit-oriented market'; (b) 'There's a dollar democracy that runs through our supposed democracy'; (c) 'I don't think we have enough input into legislation and the decisions that are important'; (d) 'I'm always cynical about government processes'; and (e) 'All political parties seem to be appalling'.

Tax-self (α = .84) comprised eight items, with responses measured on the same 1 to 5 rating scale: (a) 'The ATO listens to powerful interest groups, not to ordinary Australians' (reverse scored); (b) 'The ATO can be trusted to administer the tax system so that it is right for the country as a whole'; (c) 'The ATO's decisions are too influenced by political pressures' (reverse scored); (d) 'The ATO has acted in the interests of all Australians'; (e) 'The ATO has turned its back on its responsibility to Australians' (reverse scored); (f) 'The ATO has caved in to pressure from special interest groups' (reverse scored); (g) 'The ATO is trusted by you to administer the tax system fairly'; and (h) 'The ATO takes advantage of people who are vulnerable' (reverse scored).

Measuring Perceptions of Injustice

Taxpayer comments were coded in terms of perceptions of distributive and procedural injustice. The coding procedure was similar to that developed and used by Lupfer et al. (2000). Distributive (in)justice comprised three criteria: (a) received inequitable outcome, (b) received unequal outcome, or (c) need was not considered in outcome. Four procedural justice categories were created for the purpose of this coding task. This reflected the fact that the procedural justice criteria as identified by Lupfer et al. did not adequately capture other criteria specifically relating to the nature of the issues raised in the taxpayer comments. Procedural (in)justice comprised four categories. Procedural waste referred to any reference that politicians waste money, taxes are generally wasted, taxes are wasted while health, superannuation, education, or public transport suffer. Procedural inequity referred to suggestions that the tax system was wrong, the tax system was inequitable, the system did not consider need, the system benefits the wealthy, welfare recipients, or big business. Procedural violation referred to explicit promises and agreements broken, rules applied inconsistently, too many loopholes in the system, or no disclosure of where taxes go. Procedural illegitimacy referred to the ATO or politicians being disrespectful, incompetent, untrustworthy, or lack of confidence in the system. This resulted in 24 different criteria against which each taxpayer's comments were to be coded.

Following Lupfer et al. (2000), the coder's task was to decide whether or not each criterion was reflected in the comments, and to assign a code of 0 (not reflected) or 1 (reflected) to each criterion. In the event that coders felt the coding categories were incomplete or unclearly defined, they were asked to note down extra categories they felt were applicable. Three coders coded each of the taxpayer comments in terms of the justice criteria. A consensus code was established if two or three of the coders agreed in their codings. Consensus codes were established for 93 per cent of the justice coding decisions.

Findings on Self-categorisation

Taxpayers' comments relating to tax at the end of the questionnaire (n = 155) were coded by two independent raters into categories of issues raised (Cohen's kappa coefficient = .67, which Fleiss (1981) regards as an acceptable level of intercoder reliability). The issues raised in the comments, and the proportion of respondents who referred to each issue, are shown in Table 4.1. Almost all the comments referred to perceptions of injustice. The most common complaint was that the tax system was inequitable (51%).

It was hypothesised that the social identities of taxpayers would be discernible from their comments (Hypothesis 1). This was so for the majority of those who wrote comments (74%). Further, it was possible to determine the level of inclusiveness of social identities. Sixty-seven per cent comprised a superordinate level of identity, 48 per cent a subgroup level.

Findings on Perceived Representativeness of Authorities and Motivational Postures

It was hypothesised that if the government was perceived to be representative of self, the more likely it was that the ATO would be perceived as representative of self (Hypothesis 2). This correlation was moderately strong, $r(153) = .59$, $p < .001$, implying that perceived legitimacy of government is related to perceived legitimacy of the ATO. It was further hypothesised that the more unrepresentative authorities were perceived to be, the more resistant and less compliant taxpayers' motivational postures. The data supported this hypothesis. The more representative the government and ATO were perceived to be of individual respondents, the less disengaged (r = -.34 and r = -.27 respectively) and resistant (r = -.41 and r =-.57 respectively) taxpayers were, and the more capitulating (r = .32 and .60 respectively) and committed (r = .30 and .39 respectively) they were.

Findings on Perceptions of Injustice

The data in Table 4.1 were averaged across the specific coding criteria to produce a mean probability for respondents mentioning (a) distributive injustice, (b) procedural waste, (c) procedural inequity, (d) procedural violation, and (e) procedural illegitimacy. These probabilities were calculated separately for those displaying a superordinate identity and those displaying a subgroup identity. The results are depicted graphically in Figure 4.1. Consistent with Smith and Tyler's (1996) argument, the probability of concerns being mentioned about distributive injustice were significantly higher at the subgroup level ($M = .18$, $SD = .27$) than at the superordinate level ($M = .02$, $SD = .27$), $t(107) = 4.67$, $p = .000$.

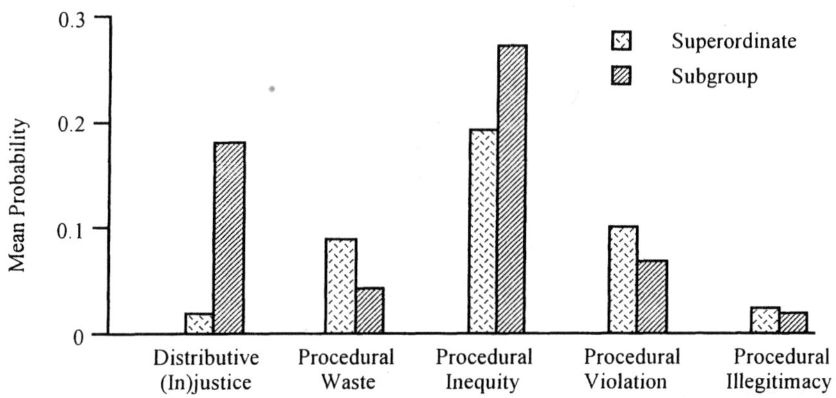

Figure 4.1 Mean probability of each justice category being mentioned by respondents with superordinate or subgroup identity

While procedural waste, procedural violation and procedural illegitimacy did not differ between levels of inclusiveness, procedural inequity was also mentioned significantly more often at the subgroup level ($M = .27$, $SD = .15$) than at the superordinate level ($M = .19$, $SD = .18$), $t(107) = 2.43$, $p = .017$.

These findings demonstrate that those at the subgroup level were more concerned about unfair outcomes *and* more concerned about the unfair procedures that produced those unfair outcomes than those at the superordinate level.

Table 4.1 Percentage of respondents referring to each issue (n = 155)

Issue referred to	%
Tax system is inequitable	51.0
Introduction of GST is unfair	23.9
System benefits wealthy	22.6
Taxes generally wasted	18.1
System does not consider need	14.8
Politicians waste money	14.2
Tax system is wrong	14.2
Too many loopholes in the system	11.6
Little people pay while rich do not	11.0
Rules applied inconsistently	9.0
Government is untrustworthy	8.4
System benefits welfare recipients	7.7
Problems with health insurance	7.7
Explicit promises and agreements broken	7.1
Tax system removes incentive to work	7.1
Taxes are unequal	5.8
Taxes are too high	5.8
Tax is unfair because not everyone pays	5.8
Reference to Kerry Packer[1]	5.8
Government, not ATO, responsible	5.8
Problems with superannuation	5.2
Tax forms difficult/costly to complete	5.2
No confidence in system	5.2
System benefits big business	3.9
Problems with education	3.9
ATO is incompetent	3.9
Government is incompetent	3.9

Were Authorities Perceived as More Representative at the Superordinate Level?

To investigate whether authorities were more likely to be included in the self-concept at the superordinate level of identity, taxpayers at both superordinate and subgroup levels were analysed with respect to the degree to which authorities were perceived as representative of them. Based on a median split of both Government-self and ATO-self, taxpayers were categorised as perceiving high or low representativeness of both authorities. Interestingly, the frequencies were similar in terms of high and low representativeness of government at both the superordinate (45% versus 55%) and subgroup (50% versus 50%) levels. The same pattern emerged for judgments of the ATO at the superordinate (43% versus 57%) and subgroup (49% versus 51%) levels. Clearly, authorities were not perceived as more representative at the superordinate level than at the subgroup level, which may help to explain why procedural justice concerns were not stronger at the superordinate level, as would be predicted by Smith and Tyler (1996).

Attitudes to Tax

In order to understand better the role of authorities in attitudes to tax, a more detailed analysis was undertaken of taxpayers who had been categorised as perceiving the ATO as exhibiting high or low representativeness. Those who perceived the ATO as exhibiting low representativeness regarded being an honest taxpayer as less important, felt more resentment about paying tax, and felt less obligated to obey the rules, than those who perceived the ATO as exhibiting high representativeness. Further, those who perceived low representativeness of the ATO were also more disengaged, resistant, and less likely to display capitulation and commitment in their motivational postures than those who perceived high representativeness.

Implications of Findings

It seems clear that attitudes towards tax are not simply driven by personal self-interest variables but are also affected by how taxpayers perceive themselves, other taxpayers and tax authorities. Clearly, taxpayers can see themselves as relatively interchangeable with other taxpayers, and interchangeable with a subgroup of taxpayers in contrast to another group, or interchangeable with the group of taxpayers as a whole. Self-interest, then, which might drive attitudes and behaviour at a personal level of identity, is transcended by group values and interests. The question of 'what is good/right for me' becomes 'what is good/right for us'. Judgments about fairness reflect the degree to which other taxpayers are perceived as similar to self or not. At a subgroup level, the focus is on distributive injustice because the distinction between subgroups and unfair outcomes is more clearly defined than at the superordinate level ('what are they getting that we aren't?').[2]

The role of authorities, however, is also very important in affecting tax-related attitudes. The less representative of taxpayers authorities are perceived to be, the more resistant taxpayers are in their motivational postures and the more negative their attitudes are towards paying tax. This, it is argued, stems from the fact that unrepresentative authorities are perceived as illegitimate because they do not represent 'us' appropriately (Haslam, 2001). Decisions made by an illegitimate authority, then, are seen as invalid, removing the obligation to accept or obey them (Tyler, 1998). The importance of this point in relation to social identity should perhaps be spelt out a little more clearly.

In their argument, Smith and Tyler (1996) noted that procedural justice concerns should be greater at a superordinate level because fair treatment by those included within one's self-concept confers a sense of respect and pride in oneself, which is important for self-worth. This sense of self-respect and pride then leads to acceptance of rules and decisions made by ingroup others, even if the outcomes do not personally benefit oneself. However, these authors also point out that in order for authorities to gain obedience to rules and decisions, those authorities must be included within the superordinate category. If they are excluded, their influence is reduced because their treatment of group members does not affect perceptions of self-worth (Tyler and Smith, 1999). While it might be expected that at a superordinate level of identity (e.g., Australian) authorities might normally be included within the self-concept, it seems clear that this was not so in the present study. The degree to which authorities (both the government and ATO) were perceived as representative was not greater at the superordinate level than at the subgroup level. Given that the comments expressed by taxpayers were in the form of complaints (i.e., negative), it seems likely that those who perceived themselves as similar to other Australians were defining themselves in contrast to authorities, while those at the subgroup level were defining themselves in contrast to other subgroups as well as in contrast to authorities. After all, if one's subgroup is perceived to be unfairly disadvantaged in comparison to another subgroup, it is presumably natural to also focus on those who have allowed the injustice to occur.

Two issues, however, render perceptions of authorities more problematic when social rather than personal identity is salient. Firstly, perceptions of group-based injustice become stronger when social rather than personal identity is salient (Walker and Mann, 1987). Second, authorities not included within one's own category membership run the risk of being perceived as condoning or representing outgroup interests, making the potential for intergroup hostility even stronger.

It is also interesting to note that while procedural waste, procedural violation and procedural illegitimacy were referred to equally often at the superordinate and subgroup levels, procedural inequity was referred to significantly more often at the subgroup level. When distributive outcomes were perceived as unfair, taxpayers focused on the unfair procedures that were directly relevant to producing those outcomes. This, of course, makes sense because judgments about unfair outcomes are not made in a vacuum. To judge an outcome as unfair must mean that the procedures that produced the outcome are also judged as unfair. It is difficult to see that an outcome could be judged as unfair if the procedures that produced the outcome are judged as fair. This result also shows the interdependence between distributive and procedural justice, a link that is sometimes lacking in justice research (see Tyler, 2001).

The Social Identity Perspective for Understanding Tax Attitudes and Tax Compliance

It has been argued in this chapter that attitudes towards tax are not simply driven by individual self-interest. The way in which taxpayers categorise themselves, other taxpayers and relevant tax authorities (that is, the degree to which others are included within one's self-category) affects the degree to which personal self-interest dictates attitudes and behaviour. When social category membership is salient, self-interest is transformed into a 'collective we-group interest' (Turner and Haslam, 2001, p. 39). This means that concerns about what is right/good/fair for all group members becomes the dominant focus. As previously mentioned, the concept of civic virtue is precisely a collective group interest, resulting from social category membership. It is not a soft or irrational deviation from the true self, something to be appealed to as a means of trying to deflect the true self-interested nature of the individual. Rather, it reflects the perception of self as a member of a valued broader community, the knowledge of which makes salient shared norms, values and expectations associated with such membership. Perceiving self as a member of the community leads to adopting attitudes and behaviour that benefit the community rather than self because the community is reflected in self. Thoughts and actions, then, do not revolve around a conflict between doing what is right for self versus doing what is morally or legally right. Personal self-interest will dominate thinking when personal identity is salient. Group-based concerns (collective self-interest) will dominate thinking when social identity is salient.

The facts that taxpayers can and do think of themselves as members of social categories (shown empirically in this chapter), and that social identity leads to group-based rather than personal concerns, have important implications for the use of surveillance and deterrence as instruments for ensuring compliance with tax laws. First, if factors other than self-interest are motivating behaviour, then surveillance and deterrence are unlikely to be effective for the simple reason that the assumptions underlying their usage are questionable (cf. Alm, 1991; James and Nobes, 1998; Tyler, 1998).

Second, power relations between groups become more distinctive when social identity is salient. Psychological ingroup members are perceived as more likeable, honest, trustworthy, accurate, legitimate, and fair than psychological outgroup members (e.g., Turner, 1991; Hogg, 1993; Ellemers et al., 1998; Haslam, McGarty and Reynolds, 1999; Haslam, 2001). For these reasons, ingroup members are persuasive and produce internalised attitudinal and behavioural change. Outgroup members, however, are not attributed with these characteristics, and hence persuasion is not an option. In order to effect change, outgroups must resort to coercion and threat (Turner, 1991). Further, however, the more those trying to change behaviour are perceived to belong to a different social category (outgroup), the more the relationship between self and outgroup others is likely to be characterised by perceptions of coercion (Haslam, 2001; Taylor and McGarty, 2001). This has clear and counterproductive implications for tax authorities who are excluded from self-categories and who use threat and deterrence to obtain compliance.

Third, and quite apart from social identity effects, research into reactance (Brehm and Brehm, 1981) has shown that the use of threat and coercion can lead to the opposite behaviour from that sought. Essentially, people react against the use of power, particularly when such power use is perceived as unwarranted and illegitimate (Biner, 1988). It is not difficult to see that if social identity increases perceptions of outgroup power, reactance may become more likely the more that an outgroup uses threat and coercion. It is also not difficult to see that the use of threat and coercion can undermine perceptions of the legitimacy of the tax system and tax authorities. In terms of the motivational postures, this is likely to lead to the adoption of non-compliant rather than compliant postures, reflecting increasing distance between self and tax authorities.

In order to improve voluntary compliance with tax laws, it is absolutely essential that tax authorities are included within the self-category (see Smith and Tyler, 1996). This means tax authorities must be perceived as representative of taxpayers through embodying the values and ideals of being fair, neutral and trustworthy (Tyler, 1998). As has been shown in this chapter, unrepresentative authorities affect attitudes on a range of tax-related dimensions, and are associated with non-compliant motivational postures. The importance of being representative of taxpayers is grounded in the fact that those who are seen as representative of self are also seen as legitimate. Acceptance of, and voluntary compliance with, the rules and regulations laid down by tax authorities are underscored by a belief in the legitimacy of the broader tax system and its objectives. This, of course, is the level reflected by the motivational posture of commitment and is the level of most benefit to tax authorities, as compliance is driven less by surveillance or personally favourable outcomes.

Indeed, it could be argued that most taxpayers take for granted the legitimacy of the tax system and its overarching objectives. For example, it has been shown that the majority of people believe themselves to be honest in their tax dealings (see Wenzel, 2001) and clearly they are if the gross individual income tax gap (estimated non-compliance rate of 17%) is a good indicator of individual non-compliance (Internal Revenue Service, 1997). This point is further exemplified by the structuring of the compliance model pyramid (see Braithwaite, Chapter 1, this volume; Braithwaite and Braithwaite, 2001) in which the majority of taxpayers are located at the bottom and middle of the pyramid rather than the top. This point again reinforces the argument that personal self-interest cannot be the major motivation for taxpaying behaviour since a system based totally on personal self-interest would clearly be unworkable. It is argued that the non-compliance from the small minority of resistant or disengaged taxpayers at the top of the pyramid reflects a lack of belief in the legitimacy of the system and a corresponding increase in social distance from those trying to regulate their behaviour.

Conclusion

The purpose of this chapter has been (a) to argue that an understanding of social identity processes is fundamental to understanding why particular factors might motivate behaviour in some situations and not others, (b) that to treat taxpayers as rational, self-interested, utility-maximising actors in all situations is to limit our ability to understand the processes involved in taxpaying behaviour, and (c) to show that taxpayer social identities exist and vary according to the situational and psychological contexts in which taxpayers find themselves. Resulting differences in attitudes and perceptions of fairness are natural outcomes of this self-categorisation process.

The attention given to the role of unrepresentative authorities in this chapter is not to downplay the importance of a superordinate identity which incorporates the ATO, the government and other taxpayers. As hypothesised earlier in this chapter, self-categorisation at this level is where most compliance is to be expected, since all subgroups become incorporated into the self-concept, making better outcomes for everyone an important goal. The focus on self-interest is replaced by a desire to ensure that all category members get a better deal, even if this is not to one's personal advantage. This, as mentioned earlier, is what researchers who focus on trying to induce 'civic virtue' essentially do. However, the requirement is that the organisations in question (here the tax authorities and government) are included within that superordinate category (Smith and Tyler, 1996; Haslam, 2001). Clearly, this is not an easy task. Perceptions of the ATO are affected by perceptions of the government. Illegitimacy of one implies some illegitimacy of the other. Further, it is possible that the context in which taxpayers find themselves may be too well-defined to allow an easy transition to a context in which category membership is more inclusive. While these issues are obviously problematic, acknowledgement of them is a step towards understanding taxpayer attitudes. A next step is to identify ways in which it is possible and feasible for tax authorities to be seen as representing, as far as possible, the interests of all taxpayers, rather than just a few.

Notes

1 Kerry Packer is Australia's wealthiest individual whose taxpaying activities were subject to public scrutiny in 1991 (House of Representatives Select Committee on the Print Media, 1992) and in 2000 (The Australian, 'Packer Sues over Internet Tax Ads', 5 September, A. McGilvray and A. McKenzie, p. 1).

2 See also Wenzel, Chapter 3, this volume for a further discussion of level of identity and justice.

References

Allingham, M. and Sandmo, A. (1972), 'Income Tax Evasion: A Theoretical Analysis', *Journal of Public Economics*, vol. 1, pp. 323-38.

Alm, J. (1991), 'A Perspective on the Experimental Analysis of Taxpayer Reporting', *The Accounting Review*, vol. 66, pp. 577-93.

Andreoni, J., Erard, B. and Feinstein, J. (1998), 'Tax Compliance', *Journal of Economic Literature*, vol. 36, pp. 818-60.

Baldry, J.C. (1987), 'Income Tax Evasion and the Tax Schedule: Some Experimental Results', *Public Finance*, vol. 42, pp. 357-83.

Beck, P.J., Davis, J.S. and Jung, W. (1991), Experimental Evidence on Taxpayer Reporting Under Uncertainty', *Accounting Review*, vol. 66(3), pp. 535-58.

Beck, P.J. and Jung, W. (1989), 'Taxpayers' Reporting Decisions and Auditing Under Information Asymmetry', *Accounting Review*, vol. 64(3), pp. 468-87.

Biner, P.M. (1988), 'Effects of Cover Letter Appeal and Monetary Incentives on Survey Response: A Reactance Theory Application', *Basic and Applied Social Psychology*, vol. 9, pp. 99-106.

Blumenthal, M., Christian, C. and Slemrod, J. (1998), 'The Determinants of Income Tax Compliance: Evidence from a Controlled Experiment in Minnesota', *National Bureau of Economic Research Working Paper No. 6575*, Cambridge.

_____ (2001), 'Do Normative Appeals Affect Tax Compliance? Evidence from a Controlled Experiment in Minnesota', *National Tax Journal*, vol. 54(1), pp.125-38.

Braithwaite, V. (Chapter 1, this volume), 'A New Approach to Tax Compliance'.

Braithwaite, V. (Chapter 2, this volume), 'Dancing with Tax Authorities: Motivational Postures and Non-compliant Actions'.

Braithwaite, V. (2001), 'The Community Hopes, Fears and Actions Survey: Goals and Measures', *Centre for Tax System Integrity Working Paper No. 2*, The Australian National University, Canberra.

Braithwaite, V. and Braithwaite, J. (2001), 'An Evolving Compliance Model for Tax Enforcement', in N. Shover and J.P. Wright (eds), *Crimes of Privilege*, Oxford University Press, New York, pp. 405-19.

Braithwaite, V., Braithwaite, J., Gibson, D. and Makkai, T. (1994), 'Regulatory Styles, Motivational Postures and Nursing Home Compliance', *Law and Policy*, vol. 16, pp. 363-94.

Brehm, S.S. and Brehm, J.W. (1981), *Psychological Reactance: A Theory of Freedom and Control*, Academic Press, New York.

Christensen, A. and Hite, P. (1997), 'A Study of the Effect of Taxpayer Risk Perceptions on Ambiguous Compliance Decisions', *The Journal of the American Taxation Association*, vol. 19, pp. 1-18.

Ellemers, N., van Rijswijk, W., Bruins, J. and de Gilder, D. (1998), 'Group Commitment as a Moderator of Attributional and Behavioural Responses to Power Use', *European Journal of Social Psychology*, vol. 28, pp. 555-73.

Fischer, C.M., Wartick, M. and Mark, M.M. (1992), 'Detection Probability and Taxpayer Compliance: A Literature Review', *Journal of Accounting Literature*, vol. 11, pp.1-46.

Fleiss, J.L. (1981), *Statistical Methods for Rates and Proportions* (2nd ed), John Wiley and Sons, New York.

Grasmick, H. and Scott, W. (1982), 'Tax Evasion and Mechanisms of Social Control: A Comparison with Grand and Petty Theft', *Journal of Economic Psychology*, vol. 2, pp. 213-30.

Haslam, S.A. (2001), *Psychology in Organizations: The Social Identity Approach*, Sage, London.

Haslam, S.A., McGarty, C. and Reynolds, K.J. (1999), The Role of Self-categorization in the Interpretation of Power Use, unpublished manuscript, The Australian National University, Canberra.

Hogg, M.A. (1993), 'Group Cohesiveness: A Critical Review and Some New Directions', in W. Stroebe and M. Hewstone (eds), *European Review of Social Psychology* (Vol. 4), John Wiley and Sons, Chichester, pp. 85-111.

House of Representatives Select Committee on the Print Media (1992), *Report from the House of Representatives Select Committee on the Print Media News & Fair Facts: The Australian Print Media Industry*, Australian Government Publishing Service, Canberra.

Internal Revenue Service (1997), 'The Individual Income Tax Gap and Accounts Receivable', *IRS Fact Sheet, #FS-97-14*, http://www.unclefed.com/Tax-News/1997/Nrfs97-14.html.

James, S. and Nobes, C. (1998), *The Economics of Taxation: Principles, Policy and Practice*, Prentice Hall, New York.

Kinsey, K. (1984), 'Survey Data on Tax Compliance: A Compendium and Review', *American Bar Foundation Working Paper #8716*, American Bar Foundation, Chicago.

Kirchler, E. (1998), 'Differential Representations of Taxes: Analysis of Free Associations and Judgments of Five Employment Groups', *Journal of Socio-Economics*, vol. 27, pp. 117-31.

Klepper, S. and Nagin, D. (1989), 'The Anatomy of Tax Evasion', *Journal of Law, Economics, and Organisation*, vol. 5(1), pp. 1-24.

Long, S. and Swingen, J. (1991), 'Taxpayer Compliance: Setting New Agendas for Research', *Law and Society Review*, vol. 25, pp. 637-83.

Lupfer, M.B., Weeks, K.P., Doan, K.A. and Houston, D.A. (2000), 'Folk Conceptions of Fairness and Unfairness', *European Journal of Social Psychology*, vol. 30, pp. 405-28.

Mason, L. and Mason, R. (1992), 'A Moral Appeal for Taxpayer Compliance: The Case for a Mass Media Campaign', *Law and Policy*, vol. 14, pp. 381-99.

McGraw, K.M. and Scholz, J.T. (1991), Appeals to Civic Virtue Versus Attention to Self-interest: Effects on Tax Compliance', *Law and Society Review*, vol. 25, pp. 471-98.

Mearns, M. and Braithwaite, V. (2001), 'The Community Hopes, Fears and Actions Survey: Survey Method, Sample Representativeness and Data Quality', *Centre for Tax System Integrity Working Paper No. 4*, The Australian National University, Canberra

Moser, D.V., Evans, J.H. and Kim, C.K. (1995), 'The Effects of Horizontal and Exchange Inequity on Tax Reporting Decisions', *The Accounting Review*, vol. 70, pp. 619-34.

Porcano, T. and Price, C. (1993), 'The Effects of Social Stigmatization on Tax Evasion', *Advances in Taxation*, vol. 5, pp. 197-217.

Reicher, S. and Hopkins, N. (1996), 'Seeking Influence through Characterizing Self-categories: An Analysis of Anti-abortionist Rhetoric', *British Journal of Social Psychology*, vol. 35, pp. 297-311.

Roberts, M.L. and Hite, P.A. (1994), 'Progressive Taxation, Fairness, and Compliance', *Law and Policy*, vol. 16, pp. 27-47.

Roth, J., Scholz, J. and Witte, A. (1989), *Taxpayer Compliance* (Vol. 1), University of Pennsylvania Press, Philadelphia.

Schisler, D. (1994), 'An Experimental Examination of Factors Affecting Tax Preparers' Aggressiveness: A Prospect Theory Approach', *The Journal of the American Tax Association*, vol. 16, pp. 124-42.

Schwartz, R. and Orleans, S. (1967), 'On Legal Sanctions', *University of Chicago Law Review*, vol. 25, pp. 274-300.

Smith, H.J. and Tyler, T.R. (1996), 'Justice and Power: When will Justice Concerns Encourage the Advantaged to Support Policies which Redistribute Economic Resources and the Disadvantaged to Willingly Obey the Law?' *European Journal of Social Psychology*, vol. 26, pp. 171-200.

Song, Y. and Yarbrough, T.E. (1978), 'Tax Ethics and Taxpayers' Attitudes: A Survey', *Public Administration Review*, vol. 38, pp. 442-52.

Spicer, M.N. (1975), 'New Approaches to the Problem of Tax Evasion', *British Tax Review*, vol. 3, pp. 152-54.

Tajfel, H. and Turner, J.C. (1986), 'The Social Identity Theory of Intergroup Behavior', in S. Worchel and W.G. Austin (eds), *Psychology of Intergroup Relations*, Nelson-Hall, United States of America, pp. 7-24.

Taylor, N. and McGarty, C. (2001), 'The Role of Subjective Group Memberships and Perceptions of Power in Industrial Conflict', *Journal of Community and Applied Social Psychology*, vol. 11, pp. 389-93.

Turner, J.C. (1985), 'Social Categorization and the Self-concept: A Social Cognitive Theory of Group Behavior', in E.J. Lawler (ed), *Advances in Group Processes* (Vol. 2), JAI Press, Greenwich, pp. 77-122.

_____ (1991), *Social Influence*, Open University Press, United Kingdom.

Turner, J.C. and Haslam, S.A. (2001), 'Social Identity, Organizations and Leadership', in M.E. Turner (ed), *Groups at Work: Advances in Theory and Research*, Erlbaum, Hillsdale, pp. 25-65.

Turner, J.C. and Oakes, P.J. (1997), 'The Socially Structured Mind', in C. McGarty and S.A. Haslam (eds), *The Message of Social Psychology*, Blackwell Publishers, Oxford, pp. 355-73.

Turner, J.C., Hogg, M.A., Oakes, P.J., Reicher, S.D. and Wetherell, M.S. (1987), *Rediscovering the Social Group: A Self-categorization Theory*, Basil Blackwell, Oxford.

Tyler, T.R. (1990), *Why People Obey the Law*, Yale University Press, New Haven.

_____ (1998), 'Trust and Democratic Governance', in V. Braithwaite and M. Levi (eds), *Trust and Governance*, Russell Sage Foundation, New York, pp. 269-94.

_____ (2001), 'Social Justice', in R. Brown and S. Gaertner (eds), *Blackwell Handbook of Social Psychology: Intergroup Processes*, Blackwell, Oxford, pp. 344-64.

Tyler, T.R. and Degoey, P. (1996), 'Trust in Organizational Authorities: The Influence of Motive Attributions on Willingness to Accept Decisions', in R. Kramer and T.R. Tyler (eds), *Trust in Organizations*, Sage, Thousand Oaks, pp. 331-56.

Tyler, T.R. and Lind, E.A. (1992), 'A Relational Model of Authority in Groups', in M.P. Zanna (ed), *Advances in Experimental Social Psychology* (Vol. 25), Academic Press, New York, pp. 115-91.

Tyler, T.R. and Smith, H.J. (1999), 'Justice, Social Identity, and Group Processes', in T.R. Tyler, R.M. Kramer and O.P. John (eds), *The Psychology of the Social Self*, Lawrence Erlbaum Associates, New Jersey, pp. 223-64.

Tyler, T.R., Boeckmann, R.J., Smith, H.J. and Huo, Y.J. (1997), *Social Justice in a Diverse Society*, Westview, Boulder.

Walker, I. and Mann, L. (1987), 'Unemployment, Relative Deprivation and Social Protest', *Personality and Social Psychology Bulletin*, vol. 13, pp. 275-83.

Webley, P. (1987), 'Audit Probabilities and Tax Evasion in a Business Simulation', *Economic Letters*, vol. 25(3), pp. 267-70.

Wenzel, M. (Chapter 3, this volume), 'Tax Compliance and the Psychology of Justice: Mapping the Field'.

Wenzel, M. (2000), 'Justice and Identity: The Significance of Inclusion for Perceptions of Entitlement and the Justice Motive', *Personality and Social Psychology Bulletin*, vol. 26, pp. 157-76.

Wenzel, M. (2001), 'Misperceptions of Social Norms about Tax Compliance (1): A Prestudy', *Centre for Tax System Integrity Working Paper No. 7*, The Australian National University, Canberra.

Worsham, R.G. (1996), 'The Effect of Tax Authority Behavior on Taxpayer Compliance: A Procedural Justice Approach', *The Journal of the American Taxation Association*, vol. 18(2), pp. 19-39.

Chapter 5

Charting the Shoals of the Cash Economy

Valerie Braithwaite, Friedrich Schneider, Monika Reinhart and Kristina Murphy

In this chapter, we examine the issue of movement into and out of the cash economy. All indications are that the cash economy is on the increase worldwide and is posing a challenge for sovereign states aiming to control its growth. An increasing economic literature is addressing the factors that drive its development and map its effects on the official economy, and society at large. Less widely researched is the behaviour of those moving into and out of the cash economy, what motivates them to take part, and what keeps them at a distance from this kind of activity (see Wiegand (1994) as a notable exception). The literature on individual tax evasion points to a number of possible explanatory variables, among them perceptions of justice, civic virtue, moral obligation, social identity, and social norms, to say nothing of the classic self-interest variables of human greed as an instigator, and fear of punishment as an inhibitor (see Webley, Robben, Elffers and Hessing, 1991; Andreoni, Erard and Feinstein, 1998; Richardson and Sawyer, 2001). In this chapter, some of these ideas are drawn together through the concept of motivational postures. Motivational postures are central to the operation of the social rift model of regulatee responsiveness, which comprises a set of explanatory propositions for how and why people distance themselves from authority and find the psychological freedom to act outside the constraints imposed by that authority. While social distancing is not a sufficient condition for taking part in the cash economy (people must find the prospect attractive or advantageous to them), it is a necessary condition for throwing off the constraints imposed by an authority through laws and regulatory practices, persuasion and punishment, obligations and moral pressure.

Background

The non-observed economy, variously referred to as the underground, cash, hidden, black, or shadow economy, is monitored by governments worldwide with a view to ascertaining its size and curtailing its growth. The concern that governments express over the non-observed economy is based not so much on the fact that it exists, but on the percentage of Gross Domestic Product (GDP) it represents (Schneider and Enste, 2000; Bajada, 2002; Ott, 2002; Schneider, 2002).

If the non-observed economy increases substantially as a percentage of official GDP, governments are likely to see an erosion of their tax base, and a reduction in the revenue that they can expect to collect for the purposes of governance. Of further concern is the fact that the government's ability to plan future economic policy depends on reliable and accurate estimates of economic activity. Distortion in the estimates weakens the accuracy of statistical modelling of future economic performance.

Apart from making life difficult for government administrators, a thriving non-observed economy can signal systemic problems of governance. For instance, low public confidence in political and social institutions of governance has been linked with a shift in productivity from the official to the underground economy (Ott, 2002). Furthermore, a thriving underground economy provides something of a haven for serious criminal activity (Organisation for Economic Cooperation and Development, 2002). Within its fold lie a raft of activities including the avoidance of tax (indirect or direct) and government regulation, defrauding government social security and health care systems, and the illegal production of goods and services forbidden by law (such as terrorism, drug trafficking or people smuggling).

Little consensus exists about how the non-observed economy should be defined or measured. The handbook of the Organisation for Economic Cooperation and Development (OECD) (2002) on *Measuring the Non-observed Economy* identifies four components: (a) underground production (activities that are legal and productive, but concealed from public authorities); (b) illegal production; (c) informal sector production; and (d) production of households for their own final use. The size and impact of the components will differ across countries, and not surprisingly, different countries (and researchers) adopt different definitions of what components should be measured, and what the best method of measurement is likely to be given the context (see, for example, Schneider and Enste, 2000; Bajada, 2002; Ott, 2002; Schneider, 2002).

In spite of these difficulties, some progress has been made toward 'sizing' the non-observed economy worldwide. Table 5.1 presents figures from the work of Friedrich Schneider, tracing the growth in what is referred to as the shadow economy in 21 OECD countries over a ten year period. While the average for OECD countries is estimated as having reached the 16 per cent mark, the best estimates available for developing countries and countries in transition are substantially higher (41% and 38% respectively).

Explaining Growth in the Non-observed Economy

Understanding growth in the non-observed economy involves answering a set of complex and interrelated questions about economic activity of different kinds at different levels. In order to piece together the entire puzzle, understanding of one kind of activity at one level may require following quite a different path from understanding activities at other levels. This chapter therefore tackles only one small piece of the puzzle. The focus is on the activities of ordinary citizens

Table 5.1 Size of shadow economy in per cent of GDP for 21 OECD countries using currency demand method

OECD countries	Per cent estimate			
	Average 1989/90	Average 1991/92	Average 1999/2000	Average 2001/2002*
Australia	10.1	13.0	14.3	14.1
Austria	6.9	7.1	9.8	10.6
Belgium	19.3	20.8	22.2	22.0
Canada	12.8	13.5	16.0	15.8
Denmark	10.8	15.0	18.0	17.9
Germany	11.8	12.5	16.0	16.3
Finland	13.4	16.1	18.1	18.0
France	9.0	13.8	15.2	15.0
Greece	22.6	24.9	28.7	28.5
Great Britain	9.6	11.2	12.7	12.5
Ireland	11.0	14.2	15.9	15.7
Italy	22.8	24.0	27.1	27.0
Japan	8.8	9.5	11.2	11.1
Netherlands	11.9	12.7	13.1	13.0
New Zealand	9.2	9.0	12.8	12.6
Norway	14.8	16.7	19.1	19.0
Portugal	15.9	17.2	22.7	22.5
Sweden	15.8	17.0	19.2	19.1
Switzerland	6.7	6.9	8.6	9.4
Spain	16.1	17.3	22.7	22.5
USA	6.7	8.2	8.7	8.7
Unweighted Average	13.2	14.3	16.8	16.7

* Preliminary figures.
Source: Schneider (2002).

working for and purchasing services on a cash-in-hand basis. Cash-in-hand services, in this research context, fall predominantly into the category of legally productive activity that is transacted in a way as to avoid tax and/or government detection.

Research Goals

The purpose of this chapter is to focus on the behaviour of individuals and to ask why some people in a country like Australia find their way into the cash economy, while others do not. The data were obtained from the *Community Hopes, Fears and Actions Survey* (Braithwaite, 2001; Braithwaite, Reinhart, Mearns and Graham, 2001) conducted in 2000 and the *Australian Tax System: Fair or Not Survey* (Braithwaite and Reinhart, forthcoming) conducted in 2001-2002. The surveys were based on a stratified random sample of Australians selected from publically available electoral rolls. In 2000, the response rate was 29 per cent (n = 2040) (see Braithwaite, Chapter 2, this volume for further details). In 2002, 1160 of these respondents were successfully contacted and completed a further survey.

The data on cash economy activity were collected through a self-report methodology in which respondents were asked about their actions, both as a purchaser of services on which tax is not paid and as a supplier of services on which tax is not paid. While the method is not without its problems or limitations, self-reports have proven to be surprisingly useful across a range of criminological research contexts (Junger-Tas and Marshall, 1999).

The survey findings are presented here in two parts. First, we examine the social demographic profile of those who do not participate in the cash economy (neither as a supplier nor purchaser) and those who do, and examine the likelihood of people moving into and out of such activities over an 18 month period. Next, we test five hypotheses about cash economy participation. All are derived from a social rift analysis of regulatee responsiveness (Braithwaite, Braithwaite, Gibson and Makkai, 1994; Braithwaite, 1995). The central idea of the social rift model is that individuals control the distance they place between themselves and an authority in order to psychologically minimise the threat the authority poses and the influence the authority can have over their behaviour (see Braithwaite, Chapter 2, for a description of motivational postures). As individuals distance themselves from an authority, they may also perceive weaknesses in the integrity of the authority. A perceived lack of integrity may make it easier to devalue the authority. This process has been discussed by others in terms of self-justification or rationalisation of the ways in which one departs from or fails to satisfy social expectations, laws and rules (Sykes and Matza, 1957; Thurman, St John and Riggs, 1984). Part of the process of distancing and devaluing may involve finding social support for the position one is taking. Through finding like-minded others, a shared social identity may emerge that gives members credibility and confidence in their opposition to the authority (see Taylor, Chapter 4, this volume). In certain regulatory contexts, however, the distancing and the devaluing may be rather private undertakings, given that individuals may be reluctant to expose supposed misdemeanours to public gaze. With social distance and justification for the distance in hand, the individual is psychologically free to behave in ways that are not necessarily to the authority's liking. In these circumstances, the individual will not necessarily engage in non-compliant activities: The opportunity and the incentive need to be present. But given opportunity and incentive, non-compliant activity becomes an option, once psychological freedom from authority influence has been achieved.

Hypothesis Development

Motivational postures reflect the degree to which individuals are accepting of a tax authority in terms of its goals and ways of operating and the degree to which they are sympathetic to the enterprise and open to its influence. Two postures, capitulation and commitment, are sympathetic postures, the former because resistance to authority seems useless, and the latter because paying tax is seen to be a noble action. Three other postures represent the placing of greater distance between the tax office and taxpayers. Resistance reflects the posture of those who are within the system but object strongly to the way it is operating, disengagement reflects the posture of those who have cut themselves off completely from the system and want nothing more to do with it, and game playing reflects detachment with effective defiance. Those who adopt the game playing posture relax the social distance constraints to the point where they can obtain the information they need to beat the tax office at its own game. Game playing is about tax avoidance, that is, finding ways of legally using law against the tax authority and sidestepping the obligation to pay tax (see McBarnet, Chapter 11, this volume).

Involvement in the cash economy, at least as a supplier, does not involve playing with or misunderstanding law, but rather it involves knowingly engaging in illegal activity. For this reason, one might expect to encounter disengagement more often than normal in this group, with commitment being displayed a little less often. Thus, we hypothesise that the motivational postures most likely to be related to being involved or not involved in the cash economy are disengagement and commitment, with disengagement increasing the likelihood of participation, and commitment decreasing participation (Hypothesis 1).

Those who break the law through cash economy activity are likely to be able to justify their behaviour. Justification can take many forms and may vary from individual to individual depending on experience and circumstances. A justification, however, that is likely to be systematically expressed by those involved in the cash economy is the rather broadly based one that the tax office lacks integrity. By this we mean that the tax authority lacks soundness of purpose in the goals it pursues, and the way it pursues them. Thus, we hypothesise that cash economy activity will be higher among those who believe that the tax office displays low integrity (Hypothesis 2).

The psychological purpose of distancing from and dismissing the integrity of an authority is to gain a sense of well-being. In theory, personal well-being involves creating one's own sense of security outside the reach of the authority.

This may be with like-minded others in one's social network or it may be through one's own assemblage of beliefs and observations about how the world operates and one's place in it. We thus propose three hypotheses associated with self-protection from sanction, shame or guilt: (a) Cash economy activity will be higher among those who do not anticipate being caught or punished by the tax office (Hypothesis 3); (b) cash economy activity will be higher among those who anticipate feeling no shame or guilt in the event of being caught by the tax office (Hypothesis 4); and (c) cash economy activity will be higher among those who do not identify with the group called 'honest taxpayers' (Hypothesis 5).[1] Once constraints on behaviour have been relaxed through removing concerns about being caught and/or fined, through eliminating feelings of shame and guilt, and through re-interpreting so called wrongdoing to make it acceptable, the path has been cleared for participation in illegal activity.

Research Findings

The first task was to find out the social demographic characteristics of those who were involved in cash economy activity in *both* 2000 and 2002, those involved in 2000 but not 2002, those not involved in 2000 but involved in 2002, and those not involved at either time. The analysis was carried out for suppliers and purchasers of labour. In order to find out who was a supplier, respondents were asked: 'Have you worked for cash-in-hand payments in the last 12 months? By cash-in-hand we mean cash money that tax is not paid on' (response categories were 0 indicating no and 1 indicating yes). Purchasers were classified according to their answer to the following question: 'Have you paid anyone cash-in-hand payments in the last 12 months for work or services they provided to you? By cash-in-hand we mean cash money that tax is not paid on' (response categories were 0 indicating no and 1 indicating yes).

Moving In and Out, and Staying Put

Of the 1119 people who provided answers to the questions about supplying cash-in-hand work or services in the 2000 and 2002 surveys, we found that the vast majority claimed not to be involved at either time (90.4%). The remainder comprised 2.0 per cent (N = 22) who were supplying labour in 2000 and 2002, 3.9 per cent (N = 44) who were supplying labour in 2000 but not 2002, and 3.7 per cent (N = 41) who were not supplying labour in 2000 but were in 2002. These figures suggest that among those who are involved in the supply of labour, there is considerable movement in and out of the shadow economy (79% are involved at one time, but not the other). Such a pattern implies that the drivers of cash economy participation are not stable but change as the individual's life space changes. Within this frame, it is worth noting that between the 2000 and 2002 surveys, a goods and services tax was introduced in Australia, allegedly making it harder for small businesses to operate successfully within the cash economy.

When attention is turned to those who purchase cash economy work or services, again we find the majority of survey respondents uninvolved at both times, although the percentage claiming non-involvement in purchasing is substantially lower than the percentage claiming non-involvement in supplying (75.4%). The remaining 25 per cent are distributed evenly across the remaining three options for involvement: 7.5 per cent were involved in both 2000 and 2002, 8.0 per cent were involved in 2000 but not 2002, and 9.2 per cent were involved in 2002 but not 2000. Again, purchasers tended to move in and out of cash economy activity across the 18 month to two year period, with 70 per cent involved at one time, but not the other.

The numbers involved in the cash economy from this community survey are on the smallish side for purposes of statistical analysis, but given the rarity of data of this kind, some insights may be gleaned from examining the characteristics of those who are repeat players, transitional players and non-players.

We considered it likely that type of involvement as a supplier or purchaser would be related to a range of social demographic characteristics such as age, sex, marital status, number of children, family income, education, work status, occupation, work sector, and country of birth (Australian versus non-Australian). On the supply side, few of these variables were relevant to cash economy involvement. The significant relationships[2] to emerge were as follows. Younger people aged 18 to 30 were more likely to be supplying labour in the cash economy (and were also the age group most likely to move out of this kind of work from 2000 to 2002). Those owning their own business had disproportionately high involvement in supplying labour in the cash economy. The relationship between education and cash economy labour supply was most notable among those with diplomas. A diploma, and to a lesser extent a tertiary qualification, indicating the possession of skills of a specialised kind, increased the likelihood of cash economy involvement. Being a supplier of labour in the cash economy at some time was also more likely among those with a personal income, or a family income, in the middle range of A$19 000 to A$47 000.

Being a purchaser of cash economy labour had several links to social demographic characteristics. Purchasers were more likely to be in the middle age group (31 to 55 years), married, to have a university degree and a professional or managerial occupation, to work full-time, and to be among the highest personal income and family income group (that is, a personal or family income of A$48 000 to A$250 000). Purchasers were also more likely to work in their own businesses.

Testing the Motivational Postures Hypothesis

To supply labour in the cash economy, or more specifically, to fail to declare payment received on one's tax return, is to evade tax. Given that this is a commonly known form of tax evasion (Braithwaite et al., 2001), it was hypothesised that the motivational postures that would be dominant in the cash economy worker would be high disengagement from and low commitment to the tax system. The data on the motivational postures for each group of taxpayers is presented in Table 5.2. Scores on each posture range from 1 to 5, with higher scores indicating more of the attribute being measured. Table 5.2 shows that the hypothesis was confirmed: Disengagement is higher and commitment is lower among those involved in supplying labour in the cash economy in 2000 and 2002 compared with those who had never been involved in such activity. The scores of transient cash economy workers fell between those of the repeat players and non-players.

The purchase of services in the cash economy was related to motivational posturing in unexpected ways. Those who had never purchased services in the cash economy had relatively higher game playing scores, a finding that makes sense given that game playing provides a legal avenue for avoiding taxes, whereas the cash economy does not. The absence of a relationship between being a purchaser in the cash economy and the motivational postures of disengagement and commitment suggests that there is not a moral or legal consciousness coming into play to prevent people purchasing services in the cash economy. The data suggest that people can be committed to the tax system on the one hand and pay for services in the cash economy on the other. This is consistent with the weak but significant relationship in Table 5.2 showing purchasers as being relatively high on commitment to the tax system. The purchaser-supplier relationship appears to be one where the purchaser provides the temptation and opportunity, while the supplier carries the moral responsibility for tax evasion.

Testing the Integrity Hypothesis

Integrity, defined in an institutional rather than individual sense, describes unity and soundness of purpose (see Braithwaite, Chapter 13, this volume). Soundness of purpose refers to holding goals and standards that are in keeping with principles of democratic governance, and that are willingly and openly defended in these terms. Unity of purpose means that there is a reasonable level of consistency and connectedness between ideals, operating principles and actions from the micro-level of taxpayer-tax administrator interaction to the macro-level of government-to-government interaction.

Tax system integrity is conceptualised in terms of five different, but interrelated dimensions: (a) collection of taxes in such a way that all groups are paying their fair share; (b) the use of taxes for the public good; (c) genuine consultation with taxpayers about the tax system; (d) respectful treatment of taxpayers; and (e) granting taxpayers the status of trustworthiness in the absence of information to the contrary.

These five dimensions were measured using a set of attitude scales, some of which have been used in other contexts and some developed specifically for taxation (see Braithwaite, 2001, for further details). Generally, responses on these scales comprised ratings that indicated different levels of agreement or disagreement with a set of statements. The important point to note about these measures is that they are all concerned with external integrity, that is, how outsiders perceive the tax office and tax system performing on the five dimensions.

Table 5.2 Mean scores and significant differences on motivational postures for four groups defined by cash economy activity in 2000 and 2002

Motivational postures	Group 1 Both '00 and '02	Group 2 Neither '00 nor '02	Group 3 In '00 out '02	Group 4 Out '00 in '02	F Value
Suppliers					
Commitment	3.55 [2, 4]	3.90	3.76	3.86	3.86**
Capitulation	3.25	3.43	3.29	3.40	1.87
Resistance	3.27	3.15	3.25	3.14	0.87
Disengagement	2.60 [2]	2.25 [3, 4]	2.41	2.42	5.57**
Game playing	2.60	2.39	2.37	2.50	1.30
Purchasers					
Commitment	3.99 [3]	3.87	3.79	3.90	2.10
Capitulation	3.35	3.43	3.34	3.40	1.42
Resistance	3.18	3.15	3.21	3.12	0.56
Disengagement	2.23	2.27	2.38	2.26	1.51
Game playing	2.27 [2]	2.42 [4]	2.41	2.25	3.35*

* $p < .05$ ** $p < .01$

Note: Significant differences among the four groups for each posture were tested using one way analyses of variance, with between groups means tested using the least-significant difference method. A superscript next to a mean score indicates that that particular mean is significantly different from the group defined by the superscript.

The question of internal integrity (what actually happens within the sanctuary of the tax office) is equally important, but needs to be addressed through a different methodology.

The extent to which the collection of taxes is perceived as being fairly shared across social groups (the avoidance of a free-rider effect) was measured using an index developed by Kinsey and Grasmick (1993). These authors argued that an individual's perceptions of unfairness in contributions to the tax system could be inferred from the degree to which citizens rated groups of taxpayers differently on the question, were they paying their fair share of tax. Kinsey and Grasmick's method is a useful one, but their measure is reliant on a small number of taxpayer groups. After all, the amount of dispersion or unfairness detected will be totally dependent on the nature of the groups rated by respondents. In order to resolve this problem, we decided to focus on groups that would give us maximum variation in occupational status from the very rich to the ordinary worker. Differences in the treatment of the rich and powerful and the average working person have caused considerable dissatisfaction with the tax system in Australia (see Taylor, Chapter 4, this volume).

Respondents in the present study were given sets of occupations that fell into the following categories: (a) top earning professionals and CEOs of corporations; (b) small business owners and farm owners; and (c) trades people and low income wage and salary earners. Ratings of fairness of tax contributions were averaged for each group and the standard deviation of these scores was used as an index of unfairness in contributions. The greater the standard deviation, the more the respondent perceived differences in the fairness of tax contributions from high to low status groups.

The use of tax for the public good was measured in terms of citizen satisfaction with government. First, we asked: 'Overall, how dissatisfied or satisfied are you with the way the government spends taxpayers' money?'. We then asked two questions that formed the fair deal index: (a) Do you think that the tax you pay is fair given the goods and services you get from the government? and (b) Would you prefer to pay less tax even if it means receiving a more restricted range of goods and services? (reversed scored).

Consultation was a special purpose scale made up of the following items: (a) The Tax Office consults widely about how they might change things to make it easier for taxpayers to meet their obligations; (b) The Tax Office goes to great lengths to consult with the community over changes to their system; (c) The Tax Office is more concerned about making their own job easier than making it easier for taxpayers (reverse scored); and (d) The Tax Office listens to powerful interest groups, not to ordinary Australians (reverse scored).

Treating taxpayers with respect was based on the work of Tom Tyler (1997) and asked respondents to indicate level of agreement with: (a) The Tax Office respects the individual's rights as a citizen, and (b) The Tax Office is concerned about protecting the average citizen's rights.

The scale to measure treating taxpayers as if they are trustworthy was taken from the work of Braithwaite and Makkai (1994): (a) The Tax Office treats people as if they can be trusted to do the right thing, and (b) The Tax Office treats people as if they will only do the right thing when forced to (reverse scored).

Finally, the Australian Taxation Office (ATO) has a Taxpayers' Charter that delineates 12 standards for how taxpayers should be treated (see Braithwaite, Chapter 1, this volume for a description). Respondents rated the ATO on their performance on each standard (Braithwaite and Reinhart, 2000). These responses were summed to give a Taxpayers' Charter score which corresponds well with the concept of procedural justice, that is, the degree to which the tax office employs fair and reasonable processes in its dealings with taxpayers (see Wenzel, Chapter 3, this volume).

Together, these measures represent tax office integrity. In Table 5.3, the different kinds of involvement in the cash economy are related to each of the integrity measures, first for suppliers, then for purchasers. With the exception of the first measure (rich not paying) which is a dispersion measure, the integrity scale scores range from 1 to 5, with a higher score indicating more of the attribute being measured.

Table 5.3 Mean scores and significant differences on integrity measures for four groups defined by cash economy activity in 2000 and 2002

Integrity	Group 1 Both '00 and '02	Group 2 Neither '00 nor '02	Group 3 In '00 out '02	Group 4 Out '00 in '02	F Value
Suppliers					
rich not paying	0.94	0.81	0.90	0.85	1.36
dissatisfaction	3.77	3.53	3.39	3.73	1.17
fair deal	2.89	2.95	2.95	2.84	0.25
consultation	2.66	2.72	2.63	2.67	0.31
respect	2.93 [2]	3.30	3.20	3.26	1.66
trustworthiness	3.04	3.25	3.03	3.21	1.51
enact Charter	3.17 [2]	3.60	3.54	3.38	2.78*
Purchasers					
rich not paying	0.93 [2]	0.79 [3]	0.90	0.81	3.83*
dissatisfaction	3.53	3.48 [3, 4]	3.74	3.75	3.14*
fair deal	2.90	2.95	3.13 [4]	2.87	1.67
consultation	2.51 [2]	2.74 [3]	2.55	2.70	4.35**
respect	3.08 [2]	3.31	3.17	3.26	2.48
trustworthiness	3.22	3.24	3.23	3.15	0.43
enact Charter	3.31 [2, 3]	3.60	3.61	3.53	2.88*

* $p < .05$ ** $p < .01$

Note: Significant differences among the four groups for each integrity measure were tested using one way analyses of variance, with between groups means tested using the least-significant difference method. A superscript next to a mean score indicates that that particular mean is significantly different from the group defined by the superscript.

These findings provide limited support for the integrity hypothesis when applied to suppliers, and broader support for the hypothesis when applied to purchasers. The major differences between the groups involved those who had never been involved in the cash economy and those who were involved on both occasions in 2000 and 2002.

Suppliers who were repeat players in the cash economy were less likely to perceive the tax office as having respect for taxpayers and as enacting the principles of the Taxpayers' Charter. These were the only integrity measures related to being a supplier of labour in the cash economy.

Purchasers who were repeat players had more doubts about the integrity of the tax office in terms of its adherence to the Charter, its consultation record and its respect for taxpayers. They also complained more about disparities among groups in the payment of a fair share of tax. Those who had never been involved in purchasing in the cash economy were significantly more satisfied about the way the government spent taxpayers' money than were those involved in purchasing in the cash economy on a transient basis.

Testing the Sanctioning Hypothesis

Sanctioning was broadly conceived as an external or internal stimulus that would be interpreted by an individual as a disincentive for taking part in the cash economy. The external stimulus was the likelihood of getting caught. The measure involved asking the respondent to imagine that they had failed to declare $A5 000 for work they had done outside their regular job. The estimated probability of getting caught was recorded on a five point scale where 1 meant 0 per cent and 5 meant 100 per cent. In addition we tested a full deterrence term that captured perceptions of consequences and the seriousness of these consequences if indeed one was caught. The deterrence term was calculated as the product of the likelihood of getting caught *X* the likely severity of punishment *X* concern about punishment (following Braithwaite and Makkai, 1991). From Table 5.4, suppliers and purchasers were least likely to anticipate being caught and had the lowest deterrence score. The group most likely to anticipate being caught and to rate deterrence high were those who had never been engaged in the cash economy.

The internal stimulus hypothesised to be at work to curb cash economy involvement is commonly referred to as conscience, represented here by shame acknowledgment (Ahmed, Harris, Braithwaite and Braithwaite, 2001). Respondents were asked to indicate the degree to which being caught for not declaring A$5 000 for work done outside one's regular job would make them feel: (a) that what they'd done was wrong; (b) bad about the harm and trouble they had caused; (c) let down the family; (d) angry with self; (e) guilty; (f) embarrassed; (g) humiliated; (h) concerned to put things right; and (i) ashamed. Scale scores ranged from 1 to 5, with higher scores indicating higher levels of shame acknowledgment. In addition, respondents were asked about whether or not it was important to be a member of the group called honest taxpayer and whether or not they felt a sense of pride in being a member of this group. Together these two questions formed the honest taxpayer identification index with scores ranging from 1 (low identification) to 7 (high identification). The hypothesis was that conscience measured through feelings of shame and guilt or through one's ties to the social group called honest taxpayers (see Taylor, Chapter 4, this volume) would act as an internal constraint on cash economy activity. In Table 5.4, those who have never been involved in the cash economy, either as suppliers or purchasers, value their social identity as honest taxpayers more highly. Moreover, they score more highly on shame acknowledgment when they are asked to imagine themselves being caught for not declaring additional cash income on their tax return. Overall, sanctioning of either an external or internal kind is most likely to be recognised as an inhibitor of wrongdoing by those least likely to be involved in the cash economy.

Table 5.4 Mean scores and significant differences on sanctioning measures for four groups defined by cash economy activity in 2000 and 2002

	Group				
Sanctioning	1 Both '00 and '02	2 Neither '00 nor '02	3 In '00 out '02	4 Out '00 in '02	F Value
Suppliers					
prob. caught	2.27 ^{2}	3.13 ^{3,4}	2.60	2.63	6.67**
deterrence	111.09 ^{2}	174.27 ^{4}	143.93	130.33	4.93**
acknowledgment	2.63 ^{2}	3.15	2.94	2.96	4.53**
honest taxpayer	5.62	5.99 ^{3}	5.51	5.68	4.12**
Purchasers					
prob. caught	2.51 ^{2}	3.24 ^{3,4}	2.69	2.46	19.52**
deterrence	123.22 ^{2,3}	181.15 ^{4}	157.06	130.72	11.83**
acknowledgment	2.86 ^{2}	3.19 ^{3,4}	2.94	2.94	8.40**
honest taxpayer	5.81	6.02 ^{2,3}	5.50	5.77	6.82**

$^{**}p < .01$

Note: Significant differences among the four groups for each sanctioning measure were tested using one way analyses of variance, with between groups means tested using the least-significant difference method. A superscript next to a mean score indicates that that particular mean is significantly different from the group defined by the superscript.

Conclusion

Several concepts central to the social rift model of regulation have been shown to predict cash economy activity. The model proved particularly useful in differentiating those who were repeat players in the cash economy over a two year period and those who had never been involved.

Suppliers of cash economy labour were more disengaged from the tax system and expressed a relative lack of commitment to the system. They downplayed the prospects of getting caught more than others, and expressed less concern, shame and remorse for tax evasion than non-participants. Furthermore, they were more likely to believe that the tax office was lacking in procedural justice, through failing to meet their obligations under the Taxpayers' Charter and failing to respect taxpayers. In social demographic terms, suppliers tended to be younger, to have been educated along a vocational training path, to have family incomes falling into the middle income range, and to be running their own businesses.

Purchasers who were repeat players displayed a different style of engagement with the tax system and the cash economy. Like suppliers, when asked to imagine a scenario where they were caught evading tax, they expressed less fear of being caught and of the consequences. Interestingly, they did not distance themselves from the honest taxpayer identity nor did they express a lack of commitment to the system. As purchasers they apparently felt they could simultaneously be supporters of the tax system and the cash economy. Nevertheless, they were critical of tax office performance in terms of treating taxpayers with respect, consulting with taxpayers and abiding by the Charter. Purchasers also perceived greater disparity among occupational groups in the extent to which they paid their fair share of tax. Demographically, purchasers were among the more privileged in our society. They belonged to high income families, they were well-educated, employed, had professional or managerial occupations, were married and were in the middle age range. Purchasing cash economy labour was also more common among those with their own businesses.

Thus, purchasers and suppliers in the cash economy are not too much alike, apart from the fact that both are more likely to be found among the self-employed. Suppliers are the less successful group according to standard indicators: They are not as rich as purchasers, they are younger, less settled and less well educated. Moreover, they have placed themselves at a greater distance from the tax authority, expressing doubts about the office's procedural fairness and little concern about the impact of sanctions. Suppliers show signs of placing themselves beyond the reach of regulators, more so than appears to be the case for purchasers.

These findings are only the beginning to understanding how individuals become caught up in cash economy activity. Even so, there is evidence here to support some of the main ideas that economists have been touting in their analyses of growing cash economies at the macro level. For instance, sanctioning and the perceived chances of being caught have emerged as a strong and consistent predictor of cash economy activity for both suppliers and purchasers. Future work by our research group will explore the experience of sanctioning and whether or not this intervention discourages future cash economy activity. While deterrence theory is clearly relevant to the management of individual participation in the cash economy, so too are notions of tax system integrity and procedural justice. As Ott (2000) and her colleagues have observed in transitional economies, the cash economy provides an escape for people who have lost confidence in government and what it purports to represent within democratic society.

The surprising, and very important outcome of our research to date is that issues of integrity, in the sense of adherence to the Taxpayers' Charter, social fairness and citizen inclusiveness, are more important in predicting the future behaviour of purchasers than suppliers, and purchasers do not, it appears, exist on the margins of our society. They are more often than not found among the privileged ranks of our social order: High income earners, the well educated, professionals, managers and business owners, married and in the prime years of their lives. They have the credentials for being 'masters of the universe' to borrow a phrase from Tom Wolfe's (1987) *The Bonfire of the Vanities*. The question is: Are they also driving tax evasion in the cash economy?

Notes

1 While it would have been interesting and more directly relevant to ask about identification with the category, 'dishonest taxpayer', we were concerned about the reliability and validity of responses to this question in a general population survey. Such a question is better suited to populations with a known and proud history of resistance to taxation.

2 The four types of involvement in the cash economy were cross-tabulated against the social demographic variables (each expressed as a categorical variable) and each relationship was tested for statistical significance using the chi-square test of independence.

References

Ahmed, E., Harris, N., Braithwaite, J. and Braithwaite, B. (2001), *Shame Management Through Reintegration*, Cambridge University Press, Cambridge.

Andreoni, J., Erard, B. and Feinstein J. (1998), 'Tax Compliance', *Journal of Economic Literature*, vol. 36, pp. 818-60.

Bajada, C. (2002), *Australia's Cash Economy: A Troubling Issue for Policymakers*, Ashgate, Aldershot.

Braithwaite, J. and Makkai, T. (1991), 'Testing an Expected Utility Model of Corporate Deterrence', *Law and Society Review*, vol. 25(1), pp. 7-40.

_____ (1994), 'Trust and Compliance', *Policing and Society*, vol. 4, pp. 1-12.

Braithwaite, V. (1995), 'Games of Engagement: Postures within the Regulatory Community', *Law and Policy*, vol. 17, pp. 225-55.

_____ (Chapter 1, this volume), 'A New Approach to Tax Compliance'.

_____ (Chapter 2, this volume), 'Dancing with Tax Authorities: Motivational Postures and Non-compliant Actions'.

_____ (Chapter 13, this volume), 'Tax System Integrity and Compliance: The Democratic Management of the Tax System'.

_____ (2001), 'The Community Hopes, Fears and Actions Survey: Goals and Measures', *Centre for Tax System Integrity Working Paper No. 2*, The Australian National University, Canberra.

Braithwaite, V. and Reinhart, M. (2000), 'The Taxpayers' Charter: Does the Australian Taxation Office Comply and Who Benefits', *Centre for Tax System Integrity Working Paper No. 1*, The Australian National University, Canberra.

_____ (forthcoming), 'Preliminary Findings from the Panel Survey, Australian Tax System: Fair or Not?' *Centre for Tax System Integrity Working Paper Series*, The Australian National University, Canberra.

Braithwaite, V., Reinhart, M., Mearns, M. and Graham, R. (2001), 'Preliminary Findings from the Community Hopes, Fears and Actions Survey', *Centre for Tax System Integrity Working Paper No. 3*, The Australian National University, Canberra.

Junger-Tas, J. and Marshall, I. H. (1999), 'The Self-report Methodology in Crime Research', in M. Tonry (ed), *Crime Justice: A Review of Research*, The University of Chicago Press, Chicago, pp. 192-367.

Kinsey, K.A. and Grasmick, H.G. (1993), 'Did the Tax Reform Act of 1986 Improve Compliance? Three Studies of Pre- and Post-TRA Compliance Attitudes', *Law and Policy*, vol. 15(4), pp. 293-325.

McBarnet, D. (Chapter 11, this volume), 'When Compliance is not the Solution but the Problem: From Changes in Law to Changes in Attitude'.

Organisation for Economic Cooperation and Development (2002), *Measuring the Non-observed Economy:A Handbook*, OECD, Paris.

Ott, K. (2002), 'The Underground Economy in Croatia 1990-2000', Paper presented at the 58th Congress of the International Institute of Public Finance, 26-29 August, Helsinki.

Richardson, M. and Sawyer, A.J. (2001), 'A Taxonomy of the Tax Compliance Literature: Further Findings, Problems and Prospects', *Australian Tax Forum*, vol. 16(2), pp. 137-320.

Schneider, F. (2002), 'The Value Added of Underground Activities: Size and Measurement of the Shadow Economies of 110 Countries All Over the World', Paper presented at the Centre for Tax System Integrity Workshop on Economic Integrity in the Tax System, The Australian National University, 17 July, Canberra.

Schneider, F. and Enste, D. (2000), 'Shadow Economies: Size, Causes and Consequences', *Journal of Economic Literature*, vol. 38(1), pp. 77-115.

Sykes, G. and Matza, D. (1957), 'Techniques of Neutralization: A Theory of Delinquency', *American Sociological Review*, vol. 22, pp. 664-70.

Taylor, N. (Chapter 4, this volume), 'Understanding Taxpayer Attitudes Through Understanding Taxpayer Identities'.

Thurman, Q.C., St John, C. and Riggs, L. (1984), 'Neutralization and Tax Evasion: How Effective Would a Moral Appeal Be In Improving Compliance to Tax Laws?', *Law and Policy*, vol. 6(3), pp. 309-27.

Tyler, T.R. (1997), 'The Psychology of Legitimacy: A Relational Perspective on Voluntary Deference to Authority', *Personality and Social Psychology Review*, vol. 1, pp. 323-45.

Webley, P., Robben, H., Elffers, H. and Hessing, D. (1991), *Tax Evasion: An Experimental Approach*, Cambridge University Press, Cambridge.

Wenzel, M. (Chapter 3, this volume), 'Tax Compliance and the Psychology of Justice: Mapping the Field'.

Wiegand, B. (1994), 'Black Money in Belize: The Ethnicity and Social Structure of Black-Market Crime', *Social Forces*, vol. 73(1), pp. 135-54.

Wolfe, T. (1987), *The Bonfire of the Vanities*, Bantam Books, New York.

PART II
THE COMPLIANCE MODEL AS CHANGE AGENT

Chapter 6

Short-term Experience with Responsive Regulation in the Australian Taxation Office

Jenny Job and David Honaker

In the closing decades of the 20th century, public administrators in many Western nations faced growing demands to restructure their traditional approaches to service provision and law enforcement. In some areas of public administration this was coupled with challenges to fundamental legitimacy. The new demands and attacks on the legitimacy of public administration emerged in a context of considerable intellectual debate over the efficacy of alternative approaches to state regulation. The net result of controversy and debate were fundamental changes in how public agencies do business. Nowhere was this more apparent than in the area of taxation administration, and developments in Australia are illustrative. The Australian Taxation Office (ATO) moved from its long established style of command and control administration and tax enforcement to a program of responsive regulation. It did so even as it faced the added challenge of implementing an unprecedented and sweeping program of taxation reform.

This chapter examines staff perceptions of and early experiences with the ATO program of responsive regulation. It begins with brief comments on the changing political, popular and intellectual environment of public administration at the dawn of the new millennium. This is followed by a review of how the ATO responded to the increasingly challenging environment of taxation administration and a brief explanation of the objectives of this investigation. An outline of the methods employed in our research is then presented. Drawing from interviews with ATO personnel, the bulk of the chapter is a discussion of what was learned about the implementation process and its reception by field level personnel. The chapter concludes with summary conclusions that may be useful for both the ATO and other public agencies contemplating or facing a shift to responsive regulation.

Background

Commencing in the 1980s, public administration came under growing state and public demands to become more market-focused, service-oriented, open and efficient (Hughes, 1994; Sparrow, 2000). Many of the management strategies and practices espoused by critics were borrowed from private enterprise. They focused on 'service, customers, quality, and process improvement' instead of 'compliance management, risk control, or structuring the application of enforcement discretion' (Sparrow, 2000, p. 2). They required a shift from 'rigidity' with its focus on 'equity and due process' to 'flexibility' with a focus on 'results' (Hughes, 1994, p. 259; Gregory, 1999, p. 63). Change of this magnitude can be difficult, particularly for public agencies whose principal role is not service delivery but regulation or enforcement. Taxation agencies, for example, faced the challenge of implementing these reforms while simultaneously delivering obligations for compliance with taxation regulations (Sparrow, 2000).

Coupled with new demands on public administration generally were challenges to the legitimacy of tax systems. In some countries this began with reports of citizen or business outrage at abuses of power by tax administrations. In the United States, citizens charged that personnel of the Internal Revenue Service (IRS) were 'rude, abusive, or unhelpful', and also that 'the IRS retaliates against those who criticise it' (Report of the National Commission on Restructuring the Internal Revenue Service, 1997, pp. 1-2). There were complaints, moreover, that the IRS was 'reactive' rather than 'proactive', that customer satisfaction was low, and that the public believed the quality of IRS service was 'deteriorating' (1997, p. 11). As a result of these attacks, the National Commission on Restructuring the Internal Revenue Service was created and charged with recommending 'changes to the IRS that will help restore the public's faith in the American tax system' (1997, p. v).

The IRS did not stand alone as a target of citizen criticism, however. In the 1990s the Australian media increasingly drew attention to poor ATO practices and excessive use of power. There were charges of ATO harassment of 'small fry' to pay small amounts of money they owed while 'big debtors' were let off the hook (Sydney Morning Herald, 1996a, 1996b; The Age, 1996a, 1996b). ATO staff were accused of being 'bloodhounds' (Dobbie, 1993), who 'monstered' and 'tormented' taxpayers, and who launched 'covert attack' on them (Australian Financial Review, 1997; Anonymous, 1997a, 1997b, 1997c; Hunt, 1998). Accusations of excessive and unfair use of power (Gumley and Wyatt, 1996) were balanced with claims that the ATO was 'out of touch' and 'lacked understanding' of 'commercial reality' (Anonymous, 1997a, 1997b, 1997c). There were suggestions that the ATO's actions were 'morally wrong' (Sydney Morning Herald, 1996a, 1996b) and that poor ATO use of penalties 'threatened the integrity of the tax system' (The Age, 1996a, 1996b). Newspapers highlighted unacceptable internal ATO practice and sarcastically mocked ATO wastage of taxpayers' money (Sun Herald, 1996). Criticism and demands for change came from the community and government alike. These demands challenged the 'traditional' social order within the ATO and taxation administrations that operated in similar fashion.

Challenges to the practices and the legitimacy of public administration occurred against a backdrop of significant policy developments in the movement to enhance citizen and corporate compliance with regulatory rules (Parker, 2000). In the preceding decades, the dominant approach to compliance assurance was one referred to as 'enforced compliance' (Shover, Clelland and Lynxwiler, 1986) or 'command and control regulation' (Aalders and Wilthagen, 1997; Dodd and Hutter, 2000). As seen by its supporters, this approach to regulation parallels the way criminal justice agencies and personnel typically approach their work. Drawing from the assumptions and principles of deterrence theory, advocates of command and control regulation call for precise and narrowly drawn rules, threatened penalties for non-compliance, and punishment for violators (Reiss, 1984; Grabosky, 1995; Dodd and Hutter, 2000). Critics, however, charged that command and control regulation builds on mistaken notions about business firms and the meaning of non-compliance, and these flaws make it unreasonable and ineffective in practice (Bardach and Kagan, 1982; Grabosky, 1995; Paternoster and Simpson, 1996; Aalders and Wilthagen, 1997; Vaughan, 1998). Deterrence based regulation, they said, could not accommodate what was learned about the nature of non-compliance; its 'one size fits all' conception of threats and punishment seemed poorly suited to the empirical realities of the matter.

Controversy over the merits of enforced compliance and other approaches to regulation prompted a synthesis known as 'responsive regulation' (Braithwaite, 2002). This is regulation that is 'responsive to industry structure in that different structures will be conducive to different degrees and forms of regulation' and also one that is 'attuned to the differing motivations of regulated actors' (Ayres and Braithwaite, 1992, p. 4). This style of administration is knowledgeable about and takes into account the problems, motivations, and conditions behind non-compliance. Strong emphasis is placed on educating firms about rules and assisting them in efforts to comply, while programs that rely principally on threats and the mechanical imposition of penalties are de-emphasised. The ATO adapted and extended the Ayres and Braithwaite approach to responsive regulation to include individual taxpayers and other entities, as well as the owners of firms. The ATO assumption was that different types of taxpayer have differing motivations and taxation structures and that regulating taxpayers responsively may encourage voluntary compliance.

Programs of responsive regulation legitimise and make available to officials a range of options when responding to compliance problems (Gunningham and Grabosky, 1998). The fundamental assumption is that a substantial proportion of taxpayers will self-regulate with minimal external monitoring so long as they are treated fairly by regulatory officials and are met with understanding and assistance should they encounter problems doing so (Tyler, 1990; Makkai and Braithwaite, 1996). For citizens and businesses that fail to comply despite appeals and cooperative actions, officials may escalate their responses and sanctions in proportional fashion. As the seriousness of infringements and the wilfulness they represent increases, officials may employ less conciliatory responses.

The ATO Compliance Model

In response to political questioning and regulatory policy debate, the ATO adopted several measures intended to make it more open and sensitive to the concerns of taxpayers. The most important of these measures, unquestionably, was its decision to develop and implement a program of responsive regulation for tax administration. This took the form of the ATO Compliance Model, which the Commissioner of Taxation publicly announced on 22 April 1998 (see Braithwaite, Chapter 1, this volume for further description of the Compliance Model). In the weeks preceding the announcement, face-to-face training sessions were conducted for all senior ATO staff to explain the Compliance Model, and in September 1998, a team of four ATO staff was established to raise awareness and understanding of it for all ATO personnel. As a member of this team, the senior author helped conduct formal training throughout the ATO for a twelve month period. Eventually, approximately 3000 ATO staff received face-to-face training in the Compliance Model by this team.

Objectives and Method

Although environmental pressures of the kind sketched here may help to create policy change in organisations, often they are not sufficient to ensure these will be institutionalised and become significant constraints on organisational direction and decision-making (Mitchell and Larsen, 1987). As Douglas (1986, p. 45) has noted, the 'entrenching of an idea is a social process', the outcome of which may be unpredictable. In the remainder of this chapter we examine some of the early challenges that adoption of the ATO Compliance Model posed for field level ATO staff whose work brings them into contact with taxpayers.

Between December 1998 and July 1999, the senior author conducted semi-structured telephone interviews with a sample of ATO staff who had completed the Compliance Model training course. These interviews explored the attitudes and perceptions of ATO staff towards the Compliance Model in the nine to eighteen month period following its introduction. They also explored the degree to which the Compliance Model and its underlying assumptions were gaining acceptance and use within the organisation. More specifically, answers were sought to the questions: (a) did staff see the Compliance Model as relevant to taxation administration generally and to their work in particular?; (b) were staff using its principles in their work, and did they think it was finding acceptance in the organisation?; (c) what changes, if any, had they seen in staff perspectives and practices?; and (d) what are some apparent sources of both support for, and resistance to, use of the Compliance Model?

Time was made also to pursue the concerns and contributions of respondents. Some shared their doubts about the Model, others recounted success using it, and several pointed to aspects of the organisation which hindered its acceptance and efficacy. Others shared stories of counterproductive behaviour in past years by ATO staff which they now recognised as being contrary to the principles of the Compliance Model. The interviews ranged from 10 minutes to approximately one and a half hours, with an average of about half an hour. During and immediately following the interviews, the senior author took notes on responses to questions and other information volunteered by the respondents.

An effort was made to talk with a variety of other staff as well, including some who had not yet attended the training course. In all, 46 staff from 22 different branch offices, covering all Australian states and the Australian Capital Territory, were interviewed. They ranged from junior level operatives to the upper levels of middle management. The majority of respondents, however, were employed as staff in branch offices where ATO personnel have most day-to-day contact with taxpayers.

Research Findings

Perceived Legitimacy

To be accepted, a new administrative approach must be perceived as legitimate or reasonable in that it meets the goals of both the organisation and its staff (Mitchell and Larsen, 1987). The legitimacy of a new regulatory approach in part is based on its efficiency and effectiveness. Does it facilitate accomplishing the substantive goals defined by the organisation's political mandate while also maintaining a working atmosphere for staff in which learning, resourcefulness, and pride in accomplishment flourish? Staff must come to believe that the new approach is 'a potential solution to the problem' and that the shift to it can be accomplished without excessive turmoil' (Mitchell and Larsen, 1987, p. 550). To the extent a new approach gains legitimacy, it gains strength as a constraint on decision-making. The interviews conducted for this study suggest the Compliance Model instituted at the ATO was seen as legitimate and superior to command and control administration by a majority of the staff interviewed.

ATO staff members interviewed indicated that they wanted and were prepared for a change that promised increased efficiency. They readily acknowledged they wanted to be less reliant on the 'cut and dried' rules and guidelines they had worked with for so long. Independently, they had come to question the merits of command and control policies, particularly since they had failed to ensure compliance by some taxpayers. Many thought that in difficult cases of taxpayer non-compliance, the Compliance Model could be an effective solution. They saw promise in it, in part because it gave them ideological support for tailoring agency responses to suit individual cases. As one respondent put it:

> The Compliance Model gives staff a mandate to deal with taxpayers in the most appropriate way for that taxpayer. This was not the case before. Previously, audit staff had to concentrate on getting in the dollars and on doing those cases which were the most extreme and would reap the greatest dollar benefit for the ATO.

The legitimacy of the Compliance Model for some respondents also evolved from the way it reduced their uncertainty and fear when they creatively adapted agency resources to address difficult cases. They enjoyed the new latitude and 'breathing space' afforded them by the increased capacity to customise responses to the case at hand, that is, to use their discretion as Black (2001) describes. Some staff, moreover, spoke of the new feeling of security and validation they gained from regulating responsively:

> [The Compliance Model] justifies and protects ATO staff. Staff get comfort from knowing they have other options [than audit and prosecution].

They recounted how they benefited from the reinforcing qualities of an 'action plan' that structures and guides the resourcefulness called for by the Compliance Model:

> In the past after a review was done, officers were left with no path to follow. The Compliance Model shows a complete compliance program. It gives staff a path to follow.

> The Compliance Model gives the basis for making cultural change. The desire to make this change is not just the rhetoric of the leaders. The Model gives us a different framework for dealing with any activity in the future.

Such comments suggest that staff felt empowered and personally reinforced by the Compliance Model. During the period in which the transition was made from a formal approach based on definitive prescriptions for forcing compliance to a less formal approach based on creative use of resources to encourage compliance, feeling empowered can be critical for agency success. With the command and control model, staff felt powerless to make change when policies were not effective. Much of the time, they had no avenues by which to gain compliance other than through the use of threats. The Compliance Model, in a very real sense, gave them permission to 'think on their feet', which helped to develop their capacity for making judgments on a case-by-case basis.

For some, then, the legitimacy of the Compliance Model was bolstered by belief that it is more rewarding to staff personally to encourage user-friendly compliance than to impose mechanically the penalties prescribed by command and control administration. One manager told us that his team members were 'happy working this way, because it is a better, nicer way and they are seeing a changed response from the public'. He also said that the relationship between the ATO and the industry group he was working with had improved. Communication was enhanced because 'working this way builds a greater rapport with the taxpayer'. Consequently, he felt 'much happier working this way'. Respondents, moreover, appeared to realise that when both parties to a transaction are happy with the results, future transactions become much easier to negotiate.

Adoption and use of the Compliance Model also contributed to increased job satisfaction for some staff. Respondents suggested, for example, that it improved the quality of communication when compliance issues were raised with management. Respondents reported that staff were talking about the Compliance Model and its principles during meetings with management and were pointing to how it 'said' certain factors must be considered. One team leader made the point that 'staff are trying hard' to embrace the Model and change the way they work for the better. He also said that he had 'seen an improvement in sharing best practice, sharing stories in meetings, and an increase in discussion [among staff] about cases'.

This officer had noticed a decrease of the old 'audit culture' that had supported the use of punishment driven compliance and an increase in the ability of ATO staff to develop new strategies. His team had regularly discussed the Compliance Model and had used case studies to practice using its principles. These are examples of learning and confidence building via practice and staff discussions, which are tools that have been found to be very helpful in learning to regulate responsively (see Braithwaite, Chapter 9, this volume; Shearing and Ericson, 1991; Sparrow, 2000).

By improving staff communication, the Compliance Model also improved inter-staff relationships. One person commented that the team she worked in was thinking not only about how the Compliance Model fosters better communication between ATO staff and taxpayers but also between staff members themselves. She believed this change in thinking had occurred because of the 'support' and 'encouragement' of their manager, and that the team had received effective training in the use of the Compliance Model. She added that the team enjoyed doing the training because it was 'interactive' and that there was talking afterwards within the team about the training and what it meant for their work. As a result of the increased quality of staff interactions, many interviewed staff reported being happier with the quality of their work and with the response they were getting from taxpayers.

Overall, the interviewed staff perceived implementation of the Compliance Model as a legitimate goal for the ATO. The strong points of the Compliance Model were reported to be that it encouraged staff creativity and sensitivity to the needs of individual taxpayers. It provided guidance for staff as they developed taxpayer specific plans of action, it developed the capacity of individual staff for making judgments or 'thinking on their feet', it increased job satisfaction among the staff, it improved communication between staff members and between staff and management, and it improved ATO/taxpayer relationships in many of the more difficult cases.

This is not to deny, however, that difficulties inevitably emerge which must be faced when putting in place new policies. This may be true particularly when efforts are made to do so in large organisations, where both organisational and individual level barriers or constraints may prove difficult to surmount. Our interviews suggest this was the case at the ATO.

Organisational Barriers

When implementing far reaching programs like the Compliance Model in a large bureaucracy like the ATO, research has shown there can be resistance to change. Kanter (1989) found that 'in the traditional bureaucratic corporation...narrowly defined jobs constricted by rules and procedures also tended to stifle initiative and creativity' (p. 280). Some of our respondents noted how this tendency to play by the rules or maintain the status quo in the organisation manifested itself in various structural barriers to full implementation of the Compliance Model.

An important barrier arose from the fact that communication, networking, and mutual support can prove difficult in a large, segmented organisation that also serves a vast geographic region. At the time the interviews were conducted, the ATO employed 19,000 staff split into 12 divisions, with 34 separate offices spread out over a country of 7,692,030 square kilometres (Commissioner of Taxation, 2000; The Europa World Year Book, 2001). The result can be a sense of operational and individual isolation. The impact of this on some offices in this structure is that 'staff memory' tends to be more local than organisational. In other words, issues of concern to the bureaucracy as a whole may not be salient for offices and staff in far flung parts of the ATO's jurisdiction. The implementation of an innovative idea like the Compliance Model in a hierarchical and segmented organisation like the ATO required the institution of procedures at all locations that ensured effective leadership, good communication between management and staff when problems arise, and creation of staff opportunities for mutual support and knowledge sharing sessions when needed.

Another barrier to implementation stems from staff being presented with unfamiliar tasks caused by adoption of the Compliance Model. Interviewed staff who had focused for many years on the same type of work faced new challenges when learning to regulate responsively. These challenges varied from case to case, from person to person, and from office to office, making differing demands on each staff member's particular skill set. In some cases there appeared to the respondents to be a single skill, single focus mind set that served to limit acceptance of the new approach:

> There is a definite understanding that the Compliance Model is applicable to the ATO generally, but not necessarily to [a staff member's] work in particular.

> Staff are not looking at the connections between the Compliance Model and what they do in their work...there is a lack of feeling that it is a 'whole thing'. People are just focusing on bits of it.

Another respondent told us that 'too many people have stayed in the one job for too long and now find it difficult to change'.

Our interviews suggest that acceptance of and the ability to make use of the Compliance Model depended somewhat on the type of work staff performed; thus, specialisation and having a defined skill set constrained the ability of some staff to take a broad, organisational view of compliance. The ways in which activities like audit and help and education could be related was not clear to them, and this caused confusion. Some respondents held the view that staff with a 'rulebook mentality' were most likely to resist taking on the responsibility of thinking for themselves. For example, those whose work traditionally focused on long-term investigation of past taxpayer activities were less accepting of the future-oriented activities of the Compliance Model. One interviewee showed his lack of interest in the model when he stated:

> The Compliance Model is irrelevant in ninety five per cent of dealings with clients. We should start again...go back to audit and refine the way we do audits. We could have refined the audit process. [Instead] we just said it wasn't working.

By July 1999, a feeling had grown in some ATO branch offices that:

> The Compliance Model is on everyone's mind, but there are different perceptions of what it means. There is an element of it not getting through...the assimilation of help and advice as part of what we do. Staff still compartmentalise activities. The reason is that different skills are required and many staff do not have the skills to do the help and education work.

Acceptance of and ability to use the Compliance Model seemed to come more easily in those parts of the organisation that did client contact work aimed at helping taxpayers. One manager of a team with a client contact focus commented that his team thought the Compliance Model was simple and easy to grasp. He and his staff viewed this as a positive thing because it helped them readily develop their own thoughts on help and education. On the other hand, staff whose work had a long-term and in-depth investigative focus reportedly were unaccustomed to 'thinking on their feet'. Such skills are required by an eclectic administrative style like the Compliance Model, which integrates several formerly separate approaches.

One barrier noted by the interviewed staff was the existence of an 'entitlement culture' at the ATO in which some managers and staff do not routinely question the relevance or feasibility of a new idea that administration puts before them. In this situation, staff did not do things for themselves or initiate action on a problem but instead wait for others to make the needed changes. In addition, management can buy into this status quo mode of thinking and influence staff members to accept the way things are. For example, one staff member commented that using the Compliance Model was not easy because a senior manager in his branch office had 'views' about staff using personal judgment rather than following policy and established guidelines. This example highlights Black's (2001, p. 14) comments on the role of leadership in 'defining' organisational culture. A manager's world view has a strong influence on the approach staff take to their work, and the acceptance or otherwise of a change in the way they work.

In sum, organisational barriers to implementation of the Compliance Model at the ATO that were noted by our respondents include inherent constraints on communication in a large, segmented organisation spread out over a vast area, the unfamiliarity or newness of the tasks presented to staff by the adoption of the Compliance Model, the lack of experience of some divisions with people-oriented activities, and the existence of a culture at the ATO in which staff do not attempt innovation, but rather wait for others to make changes to established routines.

Individual Level Barriers

Other barriers to be faced in the implementation of a new administrative style arise not from organisational characteristics, but instead from individual level concerns. For instance, resistance or political activity by powerful individuals or small groups may serve to block or limit the change (Mitchell and Larsen, 1987). Interviewed staff indicated that both these problems occurred in the ATO in the early days of transition to the Compliance Model. Resistance was manifested in abstinence from action by sympathetic staff and a resulting tendency toward the status quo. Some staff perceived that auditors and other groups with high status were acting, albeit passively, to block the changes.

Many of those interviewed spoke of their enthusiasm about and their attempts to use the Compliance Model. However, one problem noticed by those interviewed was that some individuals simply seemed afraid to embrace the new model. They were afraid to change 'old rules', or to experiment with something new because they did not want to make a mistake. Others lacked confidence in their ability to take on something new; they feared losing their skills and status if they 'looked stupid'. Still others were afraid of being reprimanded for mistakes or oversights when they tried something new. Staff members in this group did not personally pursue implementation of the Compliance Model; they preferred simply to work the way they always had. One respondent noted that:

> Many staff are scared of change. They are scared of making a mistake. It is safe to keep doing what you have always done because you know you won't make a mistake and you won't get into trouble.

Our respondents noted that for some, fear of change manifested itself in criticism of academics and their theories. Some ignored the Compliance Model, saying it was just theory that had not been tested in the taxation arena. One person suggested that there was 'an anti-intellectual bias in the organisation and anything intellectual is mockingly dismissed'. This cynicism seems to have disguised a fear of change, highlighting what Kanter (1983, p. 92) called the reinforcement of a 'culture of inferiority'. In a very real sense, 'outsiders' who come into an organisation, suggest new ideas and achieve success, can serve to make 'insiders' depressed about their abilities. In such a situation, there are few opportunities for change for the better.

Some respondents had noticed that fear of change seemed to manifest itself in a lack of confidence for some staff members, which was accompanied by discomfort when asked to work with the Model. This problem seemed to be one of inexperience, as staff were not used to applying the higher levels of personal judgment asked of them by the Compliance Model. Two respondents talked of this discomfort among the staff:

> [After having] developed a friendly relationship with a taxpayer, they can't now get tough. It's like dobbing in a mate. Before the Compliance Model, staff came from a strong position or base when going to a taxpayer's premises to do an audit. There was no personal relationship...staff need greater clarity about what the lower level of the Compliance Model is all about.

> It is hard to be soft one time and tough the next...[It is] hard to be all things.

For some, to be both 'soft' and 'tough' was to exhibit 'questionable behaviour'. Rather than appear to be clumsy implementers, some staff appear to have used a 'corporate myth' to rationalise protecting command and control administration at the ATO and the way they had always worked. Such myths have been found to warn group members away from 'unacceptable' behaviour (Douglas, 1986). In this case, the myths helped some staff to rationalise that it was best to uphold the clear cut rules of the 'enforced compliance culture'.

We were told that some staff feared the undesired consequence of a loss of status because their specialised role perhaps would no longer be valued, due to the new focus in the ATO. Hollander (1964) described this individual barrier as feelings of lack of security. Much of this concern about loss of status appeared to some respondents to be due to mistaken interpretations of the Model. Many auditors were found to have the mistaken impression that the Compliance Model meant they and other auditors should be doing 'help and education' work, as audits had become a thing of the past.[1] Still other auditors believed there were simply no other options for them to be anything but tough and impersonal. Some perceived no need to try and understand the taxpayers they were dealing with. Typical were the two respondents who said:

> By the time a taxpayer gets to the auditors, they are all crooks. [Auditors] have to be tough; [auditors] can't be nice or soft.

> Staff can't do both help and audit work...that's changing hats midstream. Why do I want to distribute pamphlets? I have tertiary qualifications. Half of the help and educate staff don't have tertiary qualifications.

Thus, the ATO's adoption of the Compliance Model was perceived by some staff as undermining revered positions that had the 'superior' skills of auditing and legislative drafting. Other staff reportedly avoided becoming victims of this all or none mentality and, as a result, were able to develop an understanding of the holistic nature of responsive regulation (see Hobson, Chapter 7, this volume for a description of working within the model).

A related personal barrier some staff had to surmount was belief that the Model required use of skills they did not have and did not value, such as the 'people' skills required to educate and provide assistance to taxpayers. The issue for them was not the 'specialist versus the generalist' argument discussed above. Rather it was whether they had the ability to 'mesh' what they do with the prevailing desired organisational goals or outcomes. Additionally, some auditors believed that having to do other types of work would contribute to the loss of their specialised skills and the loss of ability to maintain the quality of their auditing work.

Other individual level barriers to implementation noted by the respondents revolved around the degree to which leaders endorsed and visibly practiced the Compliance Model. Successful implementation of a new approach requires not only effective management but also leadership. 'Leadership and management differ in that management is designed to promote stability or to make the organisation run smoothly, while the role of leadership is to promote adaptive change' (Wood, Wallace, Zeffane, Schermerhorn, Hunt and Osborn, 1998, p. 524). Leaders can serve as role models for those less sure of how to proceed. On the other hand, lack of leadership can prove to be a powerful constraint on implementation efforts. Some of our respondents believed this occurred at the ATO, as lower level staff looked to senior staff for 'permission' to adopt the new approach. One told us that 'those at the lower levels might be aware and understand, but they will not do it. They will wait until told by their managers to do it'.

A recurrent theme in our conversations with ATO staff members who had received training and who had experience using the Compliance Model was belief that staff do not buy into a new approach as readily when management does not meaningfully involve them in decision-making. Researchers have consistently found that one of the basic requirements for effective implementation is communication and consultation with those affected (Hollander, 1964; Argyle, 1972; Wood et al., 1998). Staff participation in management decision-making has been linked with positive worker attitudes, organisational loyalty, and feelings of security and job interest among workers (Hollander, 1964). The Compliance Model training sessions were a positive contribution to implementation for some staff in that they signalled that management was giving them an opportunity to understand where the organisation was going. For others, the training sessions had a negative effect on their attitudes toward the Model and their feelings of security within the organisation. This may have been partly because their participation was not active and they perceived the sessions as simply a 'token', sometimes 'contrived' to get staff to do what management wanted (Hollander, 1964, p. 41). Indeed, some respondents believed they had little or no real input in the implementation process:

> ATO staff are tired of talking about it. They put ideas up to management and never hear of any action, so they lose enthusiasm.

> Staff just get it done to them...there is reduction by stealth. Staff had no opportunity to provide input to these things. They were just told it was happening.

Perceptions of token efforts by management can have multiple negative effects on staff (Hollander, 1964). For some staff, disappointment at lack of participation in decision-making during the implementation stage developed into accusations of lack of support in general and a questioning of management honesty:

> [Senior] management is too hard to understand. They either give too much detail or not enough. Managers need to be honest and show that staff ideas and input are valuable. Managers need to lead by example...Too many managers leave staff to take the blame and do not support them.

The respondents frequently expressed the view that before staff would fully adopt the Compliance Model their managers had to demonstrate their acceptance of and enthusiasm for its principles. This need for managers to lead by example was also characterised as the need for them to 'walk the talk'. The respondents believed a manager's behaviour should visibly model the principles of the Compliance Model. If it did not, efforts to implement a new administrative approach can be severely compromised:

> Much depends on team leaders. They need to talk about the [Compliance Model with staff].

> Staff have to see managers at all levels doing it.

> Team leaders must be supportive.
>
> If a manager is negative, staff will be negative. They won't speak up and will drift with the others.

There was the perception of some staff that 'middle management is one of the main blockers' and that some managers had not bought into the Compliance Model to the point they were actively pursuing it in their divisions:

> Managers and directors are not fully responding despite all the work that has gone into them.
>
> Senior people know and understand the Compliance Model but are just paying lip service to it. They can get away by just referring to it in documents without having to do anything else.

Some staff commented that their managers were 'too busy' to be actively thinking about implementing the Compliance Model. Other staff noticed evidence of passive resistance by leaders who represented special areas of interest. Commenting about one group of specialist staff who were viewed as leaders, one respondent said:

> If we are about change and doing things differently, they will come along for the ride, [but they will] be passive, [they will be] blockers. They filter information, and they have a position of power, and they can use it wrongly [because] they want to be comfortable. They create the environment for lower level staff.

Several staff commented that it was the Compliance Model itself, which was providing leadership to the ATO by setting direction and setting up avenues of support for both management and field staff. Some believed that if they used the principles in the Compliance Model, managers would offer more support for how they did their job. If a manager is only paying lip service to or is passively resisting the Compliance Model, then the inspiration and direction it can provide for the organisation cannot be utilised. One person stated that:

> There has been some lack of direction from the top in the past. Staff felt that management were just going around in circles and doing the same things over and over because they didn't know where [else] to go. No one knew where they were. Staff did not know where they stood. [We are] starting to get a feeling amongst staff now that leaders are getting it a bit more consistent. Everyone needs to know where they stand at all times.

A final barrier to implementation that was noted by our respondents was that some managers might lack the interpersonal skills needed to stimulate, inspire, and encourage staff in innovative initiatives. The groups with managers that have such 'people skills' may be the most likely to experience success with the innovative Compliance Model. In the words of one respondent:

> A manager makes the section. [They make] a big contribution, [so] the ATO should look at managers' personalities and see if they are suitable to be managers who will take on change and encourage others to do so...[It] needs to identify the personalities and plant them in the right place...spread them around.

Some staff expressed the belief that the ATO should actively recruit these social skills necessary for the implementation of the Compliance Model:

> Give them a problem to solve and look at how they do it...the way they think...the processes they use to solve the problem...See if their attitudes reflect the type we want in the ATO.

Staff comments suggest that a manager with technical skills aplenty but few social skills or a manager that is too busy to actively pursue innovation may not be the best candidate to lead, aid, and inspire implementation of the Compliance Model. For many of those interviewed, the implementation of a user-friendly, people-oriented program like the Compliance Model requires a communicative leader with good social and verbal skills. Leaders who lack these attributes impede organisational efforts to reform or change.

In sum, it appears that many individual level constraints acted to circumscribe the effectiveness of efforts to implement the Compliance Model. They include: (a) passive resistance to the model by some individuals in positions of power; (b) staff member's fear of making mistakes when changing long established rules and procedures; (c) lack of trust or faith in academic theories; (d) a staff member's discomfort with the idea of using higher levels of personal judgment in dealings with taxpayers; (e) a staff member's fear of loss of status or job security due to specialised roles no longer being valued; (f) lack of effective, innovative leadership by some managers; (g) lack of management inclusion of staff participation in decision-making during the early stages of implementation; (h) lack of management acceptance of, and enthusiasm for the Compliance Model; and (i) management not possessing the social skills required to inspire and encourage innovation.

Summary and Conclusion

The changes required if the Compliance Model was to find acceptance and use by staff of the ATO were cultural, organisational and personal. Taken together, they amount to a need for revamping the way the organisation 'thinks' (Douglas, 1986). Change was required in formerly routine practices, in the way tasks were accomplished and in the way tax officers interact with taxpayers, colleagues and managers. More open communication and negotiation at all levels of ATO staff were needed. The promised payoffs would include continuous learning, smarter regulatory practice, and improved performance in managing compliance.

Organisational and individual responses to mandates for change, however, are constrained significantly by the 'meaning, which different groups attach to [it]' (Silverman, 1987, p. 183). Not surprising, therefore, the authors found that the introduction of responsive regulation met with dissatisfaction and resistance from some ATO staff. They saw the approach as neither a solution to important problems nor a preferred alternative. Their stance was grounded in belief that it did not meet either personal or collective goals. Unpersuaded by or uncommitted to the Compliance Model, they feared losing specialised skills and status. For them, the Compliance Model created nothing so strong as uncertainty and anxiety.

Whilst some feared the consequences of adopting and using the Compliance Model, they were more than balanced by others who welcomed it. These staff members saw that it could be made to serve practical ends for ATO personnel and taxpayers alike. It appealed cognitively to nearly all those we interviewed; it 'made sense'. Some staff were enthusiastic about the Model and enjoyed sharing stories of success using it. They reported changes in attitudes, understanding, and work practices. The majority believed that the Compliance Model furthered personal and collective goals whilst it also provided legitimacy and direction for the future.

Those who reacted favourably to adoption of the Compliance Model and subsequent training believed they had gained an increased awareness of developments in the ATO. They were more willing to take on new ideas and wanted to keep up to date with what was happening in the organisation. This also indicated a need within the ATO for more talking and sharing of experiences, which is an integral part of learning to regulate responsively. Many realised that the Compliance Model had given them the opportunity to make suggestions about new ways of working and to participate in decision-making. It is noteworthy that staff wanted rewards for their ideas, suggestions, and their attempts to adopt the Compliance Model. For many of those we talked with, it was not financial reward which was important but intrinsic rewards such as praise and gratitude (Kanter, 1983). As King (1990, p. 19) notes, '[f]eedback and recognition from supervisors have been found to play an important role...[and] appropriate feedback...[is] an important facilitator of creativity...while one of the obstacles...is lack of appreciation of creative accomplishment'.

To facilitate adoption of the Compliance Model, ATO staff need to be given the time and encouragement to practice the skills of responsive regulation, using story telling, problem solving, and the design of new methodological tools. Staff reported an awareness of these needs. Our interviews reveal clearly that they believed they did not have all the skills they needed to work with the Compliance Model. Lack of appropriate skills among staff can be detrimental to change and reinforce the old culture. Thus, one staff member pointed out that:

> There is an issue around skilling and retention of skills. Those with field audit skills have left the ATO or are not using these skills. When people are unskilled the way they handle a tough taxpayer is by using nasty behaviour. It is hard to get them to step back and be objective.

ATO staff welcome acquisition of new skills of report writing and the interpersonal skills they will need to work with and negotiate effectively with taxpayers. They recognise, moreover, that change is a long term process.

Note

1 Audit work 'traditionally' has been regarded [by auditors within the Australian Taxation Office] as the 'real' work of a taxation administration. Auditors had a particular status within a tax office and were seen as members of an elite club. In the days when much of a taxation administration's work was transactional, audit staff possessed specialised skill sets, often developed formally as well as on the job. Auditors competed amongst themselves to raise revenue. The auditor raising the highest amount of revenue during the year received organisational recognition, and a 'god-like' reputation.

References

Aalders, M. and Wilthagen, T. (1997), 'Moving Beyond Command and Control: Reflexivity in the Regulation of Occupational Safety and Health and the Environment', *Law and Policy,* vol. 13, pp. 415-43.

Anonymous (1997a), 'Carmody and the Critics', *Taxation in Australia*, vol. 32(4), pp.188-92.

_____ (1997b), 'The Critics', *Taxation in Australia*, vol. 32(4), pp. 193-4.

_____ (1997c), 'Monstering the Tax Minimisers', *Taxation in Australia,* vol. 32(6), pp. 286-8.

Argyle, M. (1972), *The Social Psychology of Work*, Pelican Books, Harmondsworth.

Australian Financial Review (1997), 'Tax Office Accused of an Attack in Trusts', 14 November, H. van Leeuwen, Dow Jones Interactive, http://ptg.djnr.com/ccroot/asp/publib/story.asp.

Ayres, I. and Braithwaite, J. (1992), *Responsive Regulation*, Cambridge University Press, Cambridge.

Bardach, E. and Kagan, R.A. (1982), *Going by the Book: The Problem of Regulatory*

Unreasonableness, Temple University Press, Philadelphia.

Black, J. (2001), 'Managing Discretion', Paper presented at the Australian Law Review Commission Conference, 7-9 June, Sydney.

Braithwaite, J. (2002), *Restorative Justice and Responsive Regulation*, Oxford University Press, New York.

_____ (Chapter 9, this volume), 'Large Business and the Compliance Model'.

Braithwaite, V. (Chapter 1, this volume), 'A New Approach to Tax Compliance'.

Commissioner of Taxation (2000), *Annual Report 1999-2000*, Commonwealth of Australia, Canberra.

Dobbie, M. (1993), 'Bloodhounds Called to Heel', *Financial Forum*, vol. 2(11), p. 1.

Dodd, N. and Hutter, B.M. (2000), 'Geopolitics and the Regulation of Economic Life', *Law and Policy*, vol. 22, pp.1-24.

Douglas, M. (1986), *How Institutions Think* (1st ed), Syracuse University Press, New York.

Gumley, W. and Wyatt, K. (1996), 'Are the Commissioner's Debt Recovery Powers Excessive?', *Australian Tax Review*, vol. 25(4), pp. 186-201.

Grabosky, P.N. (1995), 'Regulation by Reward: On the Use of Incentives as Regulatory Instruments', *Law and Policy*, vol. 17, pp. 257-82.

Gregory, R.J. (1999), 'Social Capital Theory and Administrative Reform: Maintaining Ethical Probity in Public Service', *Public Administration Review*, vol. 59(1), pp. 63-75.

Gunningham, N. and Grabosky, P. (1998), *Smart Regulation: Designing Environmental Policy*, Clarendon, Oxford.

Hobson, K. (Chapter 7, this volume), 'Championing the Compliance Model: From Common Sense to Common Action?'.

Hollander, E.P. (1964), *Leaders, Groups, and Influence*, Oxford University Press, New York.

Hughes, O.E. (1994), *Public Management and Administration*, Macmillan Press, Houndmills.

Hunt, R. (1998), 'Tormenting Tax Debtors', *Taxation in Australia*, vol. 32(10), pp. 528-36.

Kanter, R.M. (1983), *The Change Masters*, Simon and Schuster, New York.

_____ (1989), *When Giants Learn to Dance*, Simon and Schuster, New York.

King, N. (1990), 'Innovation at Work: The Research Literature', in M. West and J. Farr (eds), *Innovation and Creativity at Work*, John Wiley and Sons, Chichester, pp.15-59.

Makkai, T. and Braithwaite, J. (1996), 'Procedural Justice and Regulatory Compliance', *Law and Human Behavior*, vol. 20, pp. 83-98.

Mitchell, T. and Larsen, J.Jr. (1987), *People in Organizations: An Introduction to Organizational Behavior*, McGraw-Hill, New York.

Parker, C. (2000), 'Reinventing Regulation within the Corporation: Compliance-oriented Regulatory Intervention', *Administration and Society*, vol. 32, pp. 529-65.

Paternoster, R. and Simpson, S.S. (1996), 'Sanction Threats and Appeals to Morality: Testing a Rational Choice Model of Corporate Crime', *Law and Society Review*, vol. 30, pp. 549–83.

Reiss, A.J.Jr. (1984), 'Selecting Strategies of Social Control Over Organizational Life', in K. Hawkins and J. M. Thomas (eds), *Enforcing Regulation*, Kluwer-Nijhoff, Boston, pp. 23-36.

Report of the National Commission on Restructuring the Internal Revenue Service (1997), *A Vision for a New IRS*, National Commission on Restructuring the Internal Revenue Service, Washington, D.C.

Shearing, C.D. and Ericson, R.V. (1991), 'Towards a Figurative Conception of Action', *British Journal of Sociology*, vol. 42, pp. 481-506.

Shover, N., Clelland, D. and Lynxwiler, J.P. (1986), *Enforcement or Negotiation? Constructing a Regulatory Bureaucracy*, State University of New York Press, Albany.

Silverman, D. (1987), *The Theory of Organisations: A Sociological Framework*, Gower Publishing, Aldershot.

Sparrow, M. (2000), *The Regulatory Craft*, Brookings Institution Press, Washington D.C.

Sun Herald (1996), 'Tax Money is Being Wasted', 28 April, A. Mitchell, Dow Jones Interactive, http://ptg.djnr.com/ccroot/asp/publib/story.asp.

Sydney Morning Herald (1996a), 'Tax Office Move on Claims "A Grab For Dollars"', 25 March, A. Lampe, Dow Jones Interactive, http://ptg.djnr.com/ccroot/asp/publib/story.asp.

_____ (1996b), 'Double Inquiry Into Tax Office', 1 October, D. Stott, Dow Jones Interactive, http://ptg.djnr.com/ccroot/asp/publib/story.asp.

The Age (1996a), 'Large Jump In Tax Complaints', 19 September, P. Chamberlin, Dow Jones Interactive, http://ptg.djnr.com/ccroot/asp/publib/story.asp.

_____ (1996b), 'Tax Office Accused Of Leniency To Big Debtors', 19 November, P. Chamberlin, Dow Jones Interactive, http://ptg.djnr.com/ccroot/asp/publib/story.asp.

The Europa World Year Book (2001), *The Europa World Year Book* (Vol. 1), Europa Publications, London, p. 519.

Tyler, T.R. (1990), 'Why People Obey the Law', Yale University Press, New Haven.

Vaughan, D. (1998), 'Rational Choice, Situated Action, and the Social Control of Organizations', *Law and Society Review*, vol. 32, pp. 23-57.

Wood, J., Wallace, J., Zeffane, R., Schermerhorn, J., Hunt, J. and Osborn, R. (1998), *Organisational Behaviour: An Asia-Pacific Perspective*, John Wiley and Sons, Brisbane.

Chapter 7

Championing the Compliance Model: From Common Sense to Common Action?

Kersty Hobson

> A 'champion' has status or clout and advocates on behalf of others. Champions, in fact, help legitimise the idea originator, serving as a bridge or translator between the sometimes unconventional originator (ideator or inventor) and the more traditional organization (Rosenfeld and Servo, 1990, p. 54).

> When you're pioneers, it's always difficult and you feel as if you're up against it or you're walking on quicksand. But when it all happens, it all just clicks into place, and my belief is it will click into place. It's just a matter of finding that switch that will make it happen (quote from ATO champion interview).

This paper examines change 'champions' in the Australian Taxation Office (ATO). Specifically, it explores why certain ATO staff members have become the champions or advocates of the ATO Compliance Model, a tax compliance innovation introduced into the ATO through collaboration with researchers at the Australian National University. It seeks to understand why ATO champions chose to become the 'translators' of the Compliance Model, as the above Rosenfeld quote suggests, and why, despite many barriers, they had faith that change would prevail, as the second quote suggests. Specifically, this paper seeks to examine how these individuals understood and made use of the Compliance Model; and what this can tell us about how the ATO might take the Model forward.

Why focus on the ATO Compliance Model champions? First, the presence of motivated individuals who advocate and advance new ideas is believed central to operationalising positive change within an organisation (Bouwen and Fry, 1991; Rogers, 1995; see Job and Honaker, Chapter 6, this volume; Shover, Job and Carroll, Chapter 8, this volume). Much has been written about the personalities and practices of these innovators. Yet most research has taken place in the corporate sector where innovation and profit margins are key operational and behavioural drivers (Damapour and Gopalakrishnan, 2001). The public service has remained a relatively uncharted area of inquiry, yet employs a significant proportion of the workforce (see Australian Bureau of Statistics, 2001), who are charged with delivering timely, effective and efficient public policy through large-scale organisational structures.[1] Therefore, studying champions in the ATO offers a rare glimpse of how individuals innovate in a public service department.

Second, research often focuses on the adoption of new ideas that have been generated *within* an organisation (West and Farr, 1990). By contrast, the Compliance Model was informed by independent academic research, that was developed within the ATO context (see Chapter 1 for details of the history and development of the Compliance Model). Studying the ATO Compliance Model offers an opportunity to examine how such an externally generated model is adopted and translated into meaningful practice by individuals within an organisation – a process that may become important to understand further as partnerships between universities and public organisations grow in the face of changing knowledge climates.

Finally, there is the type of innovation that the ATO Compliance Model represents. Innovations normally pertain to either changes in *products* or changes in *processes* (Damapour and Gopalakrishnan, 2001). A product is goods or services offered to a client, whilst a process is the mode of production or delivery of goods or services. The majority of literatures about innovation and change in organisations focus around the introduction of new technologies or systems of production in industry (see Rogers, 1995). By contrast, the Compliance Model is both a product and a process – a 'soft' (ways of thinking, ATO philosophy) and 'hard' (routine practices, services, publications) form of change (Harrisson, Laplante and St-Cyr, 2001). The rationale of the model is to encourage ATO staff to treat taxpayers as individuals who are embedded in specific contexts. This perspective affects processes, whilst also making ATO staff think pre-emptively about how to write and target their literatures, affecting products. As a result, it is an 'outward-looking' innovation that cuts across organisational boundaries, and has ethical and value implications for its practitioners and for taxpayers. This makes it an unusual form of organisational innovation and one worthy of further investigation.

Studying ATO Compliance Model Champions: Epistemological Approaches to Change

How then is change or the effects of the introduction of the ATO Compliance Model to be studied? The scope of conceptual frameworks to choose from is vast. Possible perspectives include looking at the ways in which the types of organisational structures and procedures in the ATO promote or stifle innovation (Kanter, 1983; Bouwen and Fry, 1991; Harrisson et al., 2001); or examining the salient characteristics of the ATO Compliance Model, to assess its 'adoptability' (Rogers, 1995; Damapour and Gopalakrishnan, 2001). Also possible is studying how factors external to the ATO promote innovation within the organisation (Hollingsworth, 2000); the key practices or characteristics of champions (Rogers, 1995; Hooper and Potter, 1999); or different stages in the process of creating and adopting the Compliance Model (King, 1990; Rogers, 1995). Thus, the innovation, the organisation, the context, or the personalities involved are all potential subjects of study, either in isolation or as cause-and-effect variables.

Yet taking a contrasting epistemological approach could potentially be highly beneficial when asking questions about individual understanding and translation of an abstract concept such as the ATO Compliance Model. Welford (1998) has argued that organisational researchers are too quick to adopt the prevailing epistemologies of contemporary management theory, thus limiting the questions that can be asked about organisational change. Change processes and outcomes can be studied using the tools of mathematical modelling (Visser, 2000), psychology, and systems (King, 1990), to name but a few. Yet, it is important to understand that underpinning the above body of research are implicit assumptions about the functioning and structuring of organisations and individuals. For example, organisations are normatively mapped out as structural entities, which are:

> Rational collectivities of social actors engaged in purposive goal-oriented activities within the domain of a clearly defined boundary (Boden, 1994, p. 15).

This positivist approach could tell the following story of ATO Compliance Model champions. The ATO Compliance Model appeals to certain ATO staff's values and attitudes. These values are either changed or evoked, and are then translated into altered behaviour, as long as personal or institutional barriers do not stand in the way (see Fishbein, 1993; Terry, Gallois and McCamish, 1993). Although this is a gross simplification of the positivist story, it is worthwhile asking if there is another story to tell and whether the ATO Compliance Model, being the type of innovation it is, benefits from the adoption of a different epistemological approach. This paper takes the position that indeed there is another approach worth taking as the Compliance Model is not a discrete or bounded innovation whose effects can be tracked through indicators such as increased output or product quality alone (although these factors could offer some information on the impact of the Compliance Model on the ATO). Instead it is an idea about ways of acting and thinking, whose translation requires turning it into meaningful practices, set within the everyday contexts of the ATO. In this sense, it is 'below the line' of most organisational change studies. This means it requires treating champion's ideas, thoughts and experiences of the ATO Compliance Model as instrumental to its enactment, not merely as incidental or anecdotal to the 'real' changes taking place. It therefore warrants an approach that places individual social practices as a central part of a conceptual framework.

Organisational Change and the Critical Social Sciences: The Road Less Travelled?

Despite a slow uptake of this approach in the academy, critical social sciences can be highly informative in unravelling organisational practices and change (see Stubbs, 2000; Harrisson et al., 2001). Rather than casting organisations as static, structural entities within which workers slot into immutable roles, organisations are instead viewed as *on-going processes*, constantly re-created through norms, values and expectations (Kanter, 1983; Hollingsworth, 2000). This position comes under the broad framing of social constructionist or anti-reductionist approaches (Sibeon, 1999), which posit that investigating how people think and behave requires addressing values, beliefs and cultural assumptions, and how these all relate to cultural meanings (Reser, 1995). These relate not only to the organisational context of investigation but also to the broader social contexts of the individual actor (see Edwards, Ashmore and Potter, 1995; Burningham and Cooper, 1999).

One theory that is very useful in understanding this approach is Anthony Giddens' structuration theory (1984). Structuration theory focuses on the on-going processes of social life and their role in constituting patterns of ordering at all levels of society. Giddens basically argues that recursive and routine actions (a form of knowledge called practical consciousness) and awareness or knowledge that is verbally or cognitively expressed (called discursive consciousness) form the bedrock of social life. What we all know about how to 'go on' in everyday life and what we can give discursive vent to are not incidental to how society is structured and functions. Rather, they are the very processes that shape our 'here and now', and future practices. This approach places human knowledge at the centre of social processes. The theory postulates that through on-going practices, the consequences of actions feed back into social reproduction across periods of time, creating sets of social conditions that are beyond the intentions and remit of particular actions.

To give an example, a tax officer may carry out sets of routine practices on a day-to-day basis that are based on a great deal of 'hidden' knowledge (practical consciousness). This may include sending out letters to taxpayers or entering data onto a computer system. Taken-for-granted knowledge is expressed in these actions, some of which may be verbally shared and recreated with other ATO staff (discursive consciousness) through informal conversations and team meetings. These practices have set intentions (such as to collect revenue and promote compliance) but they also have other outcomes that are not directly intended, perhaps affecting taxpayer's views of the ATO and institutionalising certain practices through their constant use. The combination of intended and unintended outcomes sets the scene for, and both constrains and enables, the future conditions of action.

This framework is pertinent to asking questions about the role of the ATO Compliance Model champions. How Giddens (1984) constructs social ordering and the issues that the ATO Compliance Model aims to address are closely related.

They both place as central the need to understand what individuals know and how they act, and the effects of these actions on others. This framework, or epistemological outlook, will be used here to examine the champions' understandings and rationality, to unravel the forms of knowledge they bring to their work with the Compliance Model, and also to examine the implications of the champions' actions for the ATO.

Research Methods

The above epistemological stance presupposes the use of certain research methods and forms of analysis that are qualitative. This research was conducted using one-to-one interview methods as part of an on-going investigation by researchers at the Centre for Tax System Integrity (CTSI) into the impact of the Compliance Model on the ATO. Interviewees were selected using a 'snow-balling' method. That is, key individuals known to the ATO team implementing the Compliance Model were interviewed and in the process were asked to recommend others who might be interested to talk about the model, whether their outlook was positive or negative. This resulted in 22 ATO officers being interviewed (17 male, 5 female).[2] The managerial scope of interviewees ranged from the most senior levels to Australian Public Service (APS) 6 (one level below junior middle management), although the majority were clustered around the rank of senior management and top middle management (see Job and Honaker, Chapter 6, this volume for a different perspective, that is, the view 'from below').

All interviews were semi-structured, to allow data comparable to other CTSI Compliance Model research to be drawn, whilst also allowing interviewees the space to talk openly. Questions asked included interviewee's understanding of the Compliance Model, any positive and negative experiences they had of trying to implement the model in the ATO, other ATO staff's understanding and support of the model, and also how implementation of the model might be improved in the future. All interviews were taped and transcribed. This paper is based on a process of open coding, which aimed to enable the key themes to emerge from the data (see Strauss, 1987 for further discussion of this process).

Research Findings: 'Understanding' the ATO Compliance Model

Moscovici (2001) argues that when examining others understanding of an idea, such as the ATO Compliance Model, the question should not be whether they are 'right' or 'wrong' but rather how their understanding has come about. That is, research is not about testing to see if subjects have the 'correct' information. Rather, it should concern how this information has been formulated into knowledge or meaningful representations (Ehrlich, Wolff, Daily, Hughes, Daily, Dalton and Goulder, 1999). This is a transformation from the abstract into the actionable, and implies a *process* of moving information to knowledge, which is not simply about information retention but involves meaningful translation (Hinchliffe, 2000).

To explain this point further, many champions could not recall thoroughly the contents of the ATO Compliance Model, although all stated they felt they had a good 'understanding' of it. How it had been explained and represented to them in meetings and presentations was often referred to vaguely as 'that triangle'. Some seemed surprised they could not recall a concept that had become important to their work or felt concerned that they may have got it wrong, saying:

> I hope my understanding of the Compliance Model is the right one.

The contradictions this threw up in the interviews were interesting. In one, the individual gave a thorough and multi-faceted explanation of their understanding of the ATO Compliance Model:

> So I see the model gives quite clear levels and responses and it lets you take into account individual's personal circumstances, so people at the end of the day feel they are being properly treated. They have been listened to, they have had an opportunity to debate the issue. At the end of the day they might feel that they don't like the answer but they think they had a proper hearing...But on the other side too, I think it's about understanding industries and individuals and the drivers within an industry to help us know how to target our approaches and educational material, or enforcement activity or the balance of those sorts of activities. So it's really about...an individual interacting with the system – treat them in a professional, personal way, but also enable the ATO to understand the various business sectors.

Yet, later the same interviewee said, when asked what the CTSI can do to help the ATO:

> Well, I would think just helping understand it more deeply...maybe a refresher course or a refresher discussion that would actually help. Because everyone gets very busy focused on outcomes and things.

This contradiction could be interpreted as the champions being those who have paid the model the loudest lip service. Or, maybe the ATO Compliance Model had become such a part of their thinking, straddling the boundary of practical and discursive consciousness, that the central tenets of the Compliance Model were now part of their taken-for-granted knowledge. This latter reasoning is a feasible conclusion to draw, and is discernible by taking a closer look at what the ATO Compliance Model represented to champions.

The ATO Compliance Model: Common Sense Distilled

Many interviewees stated that their initial reaction to the Compliance Model was that it made intuitive common sense:

> It all fell into place.

> And so it was just very intuitive to me.

> I just thought it was common sense. I liked the fact that it brought a lot of things together I suppose. That here is a model, and you need to be able to place your client on that pyramid, but before you did that you needed to understand what he's on about in that context of the BISEP.[3] I thought it was sort of tidy, sort of academic but at the same time it looked very practical to me.

This emphasis on 'common sense' and intuitive reasoning is noteworthy. It suggests that for these individuals, the ATO Compliance Model had an internal logic that is immediately self-evident. It created an almost immediate sense of recognition. This recognition occurred because the messages of the Compliance Model were in strong accordance with the individual's ideas and hopes about how the ATO should or could be operating. Some said that it was a crystallisation of their own, often disparate, aims and plans, and that by harnessing all the model had to offer, they could build upon previous work, or at least head in favourable directions:

> And the thing that struck me was that, it was funny but I don't know what was new about it. That was always my attitude, all the way back but I just said 'right, they have finally formalised it and that's the way to go now' which is great. Our whole team were pretty keen on it.

Thus, on one level the Compliance Model appealed, as it brought together the ideas and ideals that seem to have been part of these champions' practical consciousness for a long time. It not only brought them to the awareness of individuals, but also enabled connections to be made between often-scattered ideas and bits of knowledge. This is an important process as:

> Pointing out connections between previously isolated bits of people's assumptions can create both greater awareness of those bits and new cognitive links among them (Strauss and Quinn, 1997, p. 40).

For some, there was almost a 'Eureka!' moment, where a sense of clarity was gained about their own knowledge. However, the ATO Compliance Model is more than just an idea that appealed to champions because it legitimised their worldview.

It also provided them with a new discursive tool that they hoped would help bring about changes in the ATO.

The Discourse of the ATO Compliance Model

Over a quarter of interviewees directly stated they saw the ATO Compliance Model as a form of *philosophy*, a *framework* or a *touchstone*, which they could use to inform their outlook and guide their practices:

> At the end of the day the ATO Compliance Model is really a qualified philosophy, principles as to how you want to behave.

The introduction of the Compliance Model into the ATO was timely as it fitted neatly into ongoing discourses about reshaping the tax system and how it is administered. This discourse, which is commonly defined as a form of argument or 'group of utterances which seem to have a coherence and a force to them in common' (Mills, 1998, p. 7), is directly related to the introduction of the Taxpayers' Charter. The Compliance Model also resonated with the recently released Public Service Code of Conduct (see Public Service and Merit Protection Commission, 2000) and other tax reforms that had taken place within the ATO over the previous few years (see Shover et al., Chapter 8, this volume). In line with these initiatives, the Compliance Model embodied ideals that the ATO should do more than collect revenue by concerning itself with building community confidence and partnerships. Thus, the ATO Compliance Model was very much:

> In full alignment with the Taxpayers' Charter. We are clear that we are dealing with the individual taxpayer, and the circumstances of taxpayers need to be examined and not just put all in one big group – and say 'everything is the same, everything applies to that group'.

> The last two years the Compliance Model has been specifically mentioned in our corporate plan in different contexts, and it's particularly compatible with the Taxpayers' Charter goals. In the early days when we were communicating the Compliance Model to staff we had a lot of success linking it with the Taxpayers' Charter and using it to support its goals.

Thus, the Compliance Model fitted the general direction in which ATO managers and business planners wished to head. However, the discourse of the Compliance Model was not only in-keeping with conceptual currents in the ATO. It also provided new ways for the champions to think about and create 'space' within the ATO, in which they could do things differently.

The ATO Compliance Model was a new way of talking and communicating with others. For example, one interviewee called the Compliance Model a 'tool to talk'. Another interviewee stated how it had given space, or 'permission' to those who wanted to air views about how to do their jobs differently. Another saw it as giving staff a 'bit of paper' to overtly show how they were taking the community into account, in adopting an ethical stance in interactions with taxpayers. Thus, it was not only what the model represented that was important, but also the institutional space it afforded champions to rethink their practices and future direction. Where once staff's cries of 'we should do things differently' may have fallen on deaf ears, champions now had a hook to hang their beliefs on – 'the Compliance Model says…' – which legitimised their positions and gave them the green light to try different approaches:

> We were certainly open to trying new things and looking for new ways of operating because we had been doing the same thing for so long. It was really along some of the lines we've been heading or trying to head anyway, but it probably just put some structure around that.

For those who had worked hard at trying to 'sell' the principles of the Taxpayers' Charter within the ATO, the Compliance Model was a new bow to their arrow:

> And what the model did was gave me a way of telling stories.

It also presented the opportunity, if not the outcome, for the ATO to reach a common 'lexicon of language', in terms of understanding and sharing common principles and practices. In this way, the ATO Compliance Model can be framed as a 'social representation', which is a form of shared knowledge that is produced and communicated through social processes, moving from the abstract to common sense or common dialect, through interaction (Kruse and Schwarz, 1992; Billig, 1993; Moscovici, 2001). Although there is not the space to develop this argument further here, Lalli's (1999) assertion that social representations reconstruct common sense in local (everyday) situations and can therefore be seen as the 'local operators of common sense' is an interesting one that merits future consideration in relation to organisational innovation.

The Compliance Model also positioned champions and the ATO in broader business discourses. Senior staff were only too aware of the trends occurring in international management practices, and felt that the ATO Compliance Model allowed them to take their place in this arena. Again, this is a sense of legitimation, of being an international 'player', shown by the many references made to how other countries were working with these issues and how using the Compliance Model put the ATO 'ahead' in terms of being pro-active and forward-thinking:

> I can recall we had some visitors from the UK last year and I remember at the end of the week and a half he said it was one of the best and most exciting things he'd seen, the Compliance Model. So he was taking it back to the UK.

The fact that the Compliance Model is based on research from outside the ATO made it exciting to some champions, and enabled them to feel they are part of 'something' beyond the boundaries of the ATO:

> When I spoke to some staff and to others, you were able to say 'This is not just the ATO saying this, this has come from worldwide research of regulatory practices!'.

This process appeared to allow staff to feel more comfortable with themselves and their social role. Instead of being the dreaded tax collector, commonly perceived as making unreasonable demands on honest people, they instead felt that the ATO Compliance Model allowed them to help taxpayers and some have experienced members of the community warm to them as they do. In sum, they felt more liked and happier in their jobs:

> I must say that it is far more pleasant work to do than actually go through someone like a dose of salts.

Examples were given in the interviews of how changing simple procedures had made their jobs more tolerable, such as altering the tone of lodgment letters, as referred to in the following quote:

> Not only did we get better lodgement outcomes but, more significant when I think what we got, was that when people rang up they were nice. They didn't ring up and abuse you for sending them a nasty letter, they rang up and they were nice.

This enabled ATO staff to adopt discourses that may previously have seemed incongruous coming from a tax officer. For example, interviewees talked about bringing to their workplaces practices based on the concepts of human dignity, openness and respect, in keeping with the tenets of the Compliance Model.

Adopting the Compliance Model also helped to reshape the public face of the ATO, according to the champions. One interviewee talked of how working with the Compliance Model required staff with different personality traits and outlooks than the old command and control style of auditing. As a result:

> I know there's a certain number of jobs that we have advertised in the last 12 months or so in the preparation for the GST workload that have explicitly included within the selection requirements those sorts of traits.

Several other interviewees commented on how recruitment candidates were now tested for their understanding of the ATO Compliance Model in the selection process. This appeared to give the champions the feeling that they were no longer just recruiting auditors and administrators but that there was something special and different about the new staff coming into the ATO. As a result, it was at least hoped that these new people and new outlooks would gradually change the face and the feel of the organisation.

Thinking About and Thinking With the ATO Compliance Model

The above argument is not intended to portray the ATO Compliance Model as a way of talking that was adopted by champions in a distanced, self-interested sense, to simply get what they want. Rather, the adoption of the discourse of the Compliance Model, for all its attendant benefits, was part of the process of *internalisation*. That is, there was a subtle but important distinction in the Compliance Model interviews between those who thought *about* the Compliance Model and those who thought *with* it.

As already discussed above, it appeared that those who had a deep understanding of the ATO Compliance Model could not always remember much about its abstract form. This did not denote a lack of comprehension, as interviewees displayed an understanding of the Compliance Model that went beyond merely repeating its contents, to grasping its complexity, ambiguity and potential ramifications. This was because they viewed the model dynamically. Indeed, it was applied dynamically and was adapted into various useable guises. For example, one interviewee talked about having used the Compliance Model as an educational tool to talk to taxpayers:

> When I was doing real time reviews, as part of an explanation to the taxpayer, I used to explain the Compliance Model. I'd just draw a little triangle, fairly basic and I explained it from a soft angle to them. And a lot more people after that explanation would accept the fact that even if they were audited there's a reason behind it.

Most champions did not use the model in such an overt way, as they had internalised it as 'another way of thinking'. For example, one interviewee described how they used the ideas of the model on ATO staff, such as to inform approaches to internal training. Indeed, some champions believed that it was only when they had stopped making overt reference to the model, when it had been digested and had become second nature, that they had truly understood it:

> It's not a model that you can pick off the shelf sometimes and use, it's more just a part of the way we do things. So I think we would consider it to be a success if we had all the elements of the model embedded in our work practices without calling it a model any more.

This is because:

> It's not a set of rules, it's a philosophy.

Thus, these champions were suggesting that the Compliance Model had become embedded in their practices, making it 'a cultural thing', as one interviewee referred to it. Or:

> It's not so much the model or anything but it's just been accepted as a way we actually go about doing things now.

This differed from those who thought *about* the Compliance Model. From this second perspective, the Compliance Model triangle was used to locate individual positions in the ATO, to understand where their work practices fitted in and where taxpayers sat. This, however, caused no end of confusion, as it suggested a static interpretation of the model. As the following quote suggests, when the model was presented to some staff:

> The understanding of the model was not always good and we did get a lot of people who thought what it meant was you didn't respond appropriately to non-compliance. People tended to think statements like 'we treat people as honest unless we know otherwise' meant that even though the overwhelming evidence was that they'd been diddling and telling fibs, we would have to accept them as honest. That, I think, is an area where the subtleties of the model are not always well understood.

This distinction was well made by one interviewee. He compared staff who had to use the model to plan business (and therefore had come to understand the Model through 'playing' with it) with ground staff who had 'mapped' themselves onto the model and used it to locate where they were in reference to others in the ATO:

> So at the rank and file level people map themselves on a model – which I suppose is a human tendency to find where I fit. They don't see it as sort of dynamic – that if you fit here, that's where I live and that's where I am staying and that there isn't a role upwards or downwards in it.

As the Compliance Model is shaped like a pyramid, some ATO staff appeared to think it suggested all ATO compliance work should be located at the bottom, at the 'soft' end of the Model, forsaking prosecution for education. In this way, they saw the Compliance Model as providing the ATO with a:

> Visual sense of proportion as to what the ATO wants and where we'd like to go.

In one sense this is true. The Compliance Model does encourage ATO staff to use the tools of education and persuasion with taxpayers. However, this reading also meant that many ATO staff did not see the model as applicable to them. Others saw it as a threat to the work they did:

> A lot of people see it as the Compliance Model moving from an audit environment to a help and education environment and a lovey-dovey rose coloured glasses situation. But again, if you step back, it's not that at all, if you really understand what it's all about.

This 'thinking about' reading of the model created a whole host of problems. Because interviewees had tried to apply the principles of the Compliance Model in a rigid way, not adapting it but sticking to its original abstract format, they had great difficulty matching it up with their everyday realities within the ATO. In this sense, these individuals (a few of the champions, but mostly reportage from champions about others) talked about using the Compliance Model as if they were laying siege to the ATO. The interviewees with this outlook talked as if they were pushing an idea against great resistance, continually 'belting it over the head' to try and get the message across. This kind of 'pioneer spirit', adventurous as it may appear on the surface, was a rather impoverished translation of the Compliance Model in comparison to those who had made it actionable through the internalisation processes. The distinction between these two ways of seeing the ATO Compliance Model is sketched out in Figure 7.1, which presents this argument mapped onto a simplified version of the ATO Compliance Model (see Chapter 1 for a more complete diagram of the Compliance Model).

The first figure on the left shows an interpretation of the ATO Compliance Model that is one-dimensional, the 'I am here' or the 'taxpayer is here' reading of the model and its behavioural implications. The second figure on the right shows how champions who have internalised the ATO Compliance Model as a way of thinking saw it as multi-dimensional. This was not about using the model to position oneself in the ATO (that is, I am at the soft/hard end) but rather thinking 'inside' the model about how their practices affect outcomes, in reference to both temporal and contextual factors.

To explain the right-hand side of Figure 7.2 further, the implications of the Compliance Model were seen as spanning a wide array of contexts, which affect each other incrementally. This applied both to ATO staff practices, in terms of actions and material, as well as to a wide array of social relations, both personal and professional. One interviewee talked about how ideas embodied in the ATO Compliance Model were used by some staff to think about how they might alter senior manager behaviours in relation to their acceptance of the model. This

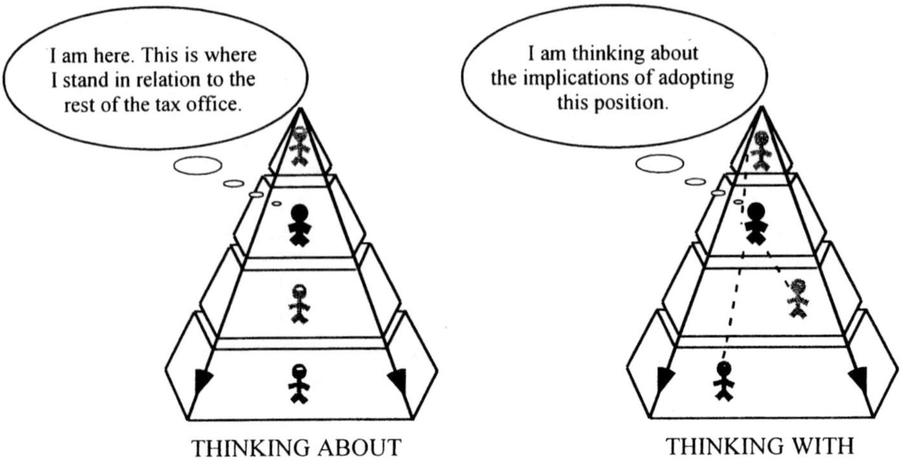

Figure 7.2 'Thinking about' and 'thinking with' the Compliance Model

resulted in the formulation of a strategy for dealing with managers' outlooks, which was based on the principles of the model. As another interviewee aptly stated:

> We work inside the model. Now, if we interpret the model as one dimension, we could have a self-fulfilling prophecy. We prosecute them, they get angry, they don't lodge. It's a catch-22, it's a circular argument. So by looking at the compliance model a little bit more strategically, you can add that extra dimension where at the moment it doesn't work.

This was about seeing how contexts or spaces are interconnected across time. Interviewees who had been thinking *with* the Compliance Model saw it as encouraging a middle-term perspective, in terms of the ramifications of ATO practices. For example, one interviewee suggested that rather than interpreting the model as suggesting the ATO should not prosecute as much, it was rather a way of seeing the effects of prosecutions on future actions, not just on individual taxpayers but also on Australian society as a whole. With this perspective, the aim was not to reach a general consensus on what to do or how to enact the ATO Compliance Model by being given step-by-step instructions. Rather it was about being part of an on-going dialogue about where to go now. As one interviewee commented:

> I don't think you'll ever get consensus. I think genuine commitment is what I think is essential.

Where did these differences in outlook stem from, between those who thought with and those who thought about the Model? One of the key factors creating these differences were individual experiences of the model, both in terms of attempts to implement it, as well as how their position in the ATO affected their personal outlook.

'The View From Up Here': Considering the Lifeworld of ATO Champions

Although the management and business lines of the champions in the ATO vary in the way they saw the Compliance Model, they appeared to share some sense of 'vision' in terms of future directions of the ATO. In this way, the model appealed as 'intuitive business common sense', as one interviewee put it, as a way to increase compliance and thus increase revenue. Yet, this stance was not only about roles in the ATO, but also about how work, and experiences in work, affected lifeworlds. 'Lifeworld' here refers to the idea that understanding the Compliance Model was not solely contingent upon narrow work-defined or isolated cognitive processes. Rather, it was related to significant life-experiences, which are given meanings through new forms of learning and experience (Finger, 1994). Interviewees' positions in the ATO did not just entail performing sets of tasks and adopting a work persona in a detached manner (in comparison to Goffman, 1969; Pruzan, 2001). Instead, their heterogeneous knowledge and experiences (see Latour, 1993; Murdoch and Clark, 1994) contributed to how they saw the Compliance Model. For example:

> I think there's certainly a better appreciation of what the model is at senior management level than there is further down. So, I suppose, the level of understanding is still cascading through the organisation. I think there's been more education at the senior level because they are people who are planning our business so they're getting to see the concepts of the model. Like education will teach you about the model, but they actually have to do it and I find models hard until I play with them. I think a lot of the senior management might be the same. When you start looking at business strategy through concepts that are consistent with a model like that then you actually get to see how it can operate and what it's about.

In contrast to this:

> I mean we have an area called Special Investigations. We work on taskforces with the National Crime Authority and the National Federal Police, basically auditing drug dealers, money launderers, people involved in illegal occupations. So there you see the

> worst of the world. So that's more painful. With some of our staff who have grown up doing tax audits – that's what they did for years, got rewarded for doing tax audits more quickly and producing more revenue – they've found it quite hard.

Therefore, it was not only their experiences of the tax system but also experiences of the ATO Compliance Model itself that made a difference to how it was internalised and operationalised. As one interviewee aptly observed:

> People have some resistance to the concept until such time as they personally experience it or see the results.

The interviews supported this assertion time and time again. Some champions may have intuitively reacted 'we already do that' when first seeing the model, but others suggested that only through 'getting in there' had they come to understand it:

> I guess it's one of those things that intuitively you have difficulty disputing and we have had that response right through when we have been publicising the model in the ATO. People are saying 'yes, we already do that' and I suppose that demonstrates our superficial understanding of what it was really about, and I suppose my initial views were that it wasn't that much different to what we were doing, but the more I explored it and the more I sought to understand it, the more I realised how we weren't really doing those things at all. We were imposing our own will on the market segments that we had created rather than understanding their needs. And instead of looking at what *they were* doing we were looking at what *they should* be doing.

Even those who were sceptical when first seeing the model had their opinions altered when they had worked with the model in their everyday practices:

> My first reaction was 'what's this shit?', not in terms of what the model was trying to say, it was just the language, it was in academia. It wasn't until we started using it at the first conference, when we started playing with some of the ideas in it, that I started to understand it. So I guess for a person like me the worst thing to do was to get me to read something about it. The first thing to do is not even tell me that there's a model. Just start doing some things.

Thus, how the Compliance Model was viewed was dependent upon how life experiences in the ATO had shaped individual perceptions of both tax issues and human nature. For example, champions often stated that tax systems are about 'doing the right thing', not only from the taxpayers' perspective but also from the ATO's:

> My philosophy is that a big percentage of the taxpayers will do the right thing if you just help them do the right thing.

When asked about the role of the ATO in general, two-thirds of interviewees stated that they believed it was about collecting revenue in a fair and reasonable way, and enabling the government to carry out equitable practices of redistribution:

> Yes, we do have a huge social obligation and we have to make a social contribution, so the way we raise revenue has to be a legitimate form – and we fit within social justice, redistribution of wealth.

Half of these respondents also added that the tax system encompassed issues of community ownership, and confidence that the ATO would be fair, just, and listen to an individual's concerns. Indeed, when asked to summarise the strengths of the Compliance Model, just under half said it enabled them to better understand the taxpayers' lives and contexts, enabling them to treat taxpayers more personally, not only with the aim of increasing compliance but also because that is 'how it should be'. This, therefore, was not a neutral or detached position to take on the responsibilities of ATO officers. It was instead one bound up with moral and ethical issues beyond the ambit of simply collecting revenue. The ideas represented by the Compliance Model, being abstract, moral and instantly recognisable, were parts of the champions' worldview. As one interviewee stated:

> It just made sense of the world where I live.

Some interviewees even reported that they, or other staff members, had applied the Compliance Model to their personal relationships with great success!

However, this is not to give the impression that all champions were in agreement about the place that morals and values have in the ATO. Some felt that it was essential that staff now bring their values to work with them, and think beyond the office door. Others felt this was a dangerous move, as who judges what is a worthy or right value? Some ATO staff felt justified in trying to 'get' those rich and famous Australians who, in the public eye too, were not paying their fair share of tax, although they were not doing anything illegal *per se*. This was not a tax judgment but a moral one, seemingly based on principles of 'fair play' that are believed to be enshrined in the tax system (see Braithwaite, Reinhart, Mearns and Graham, 2001 for data on public perceptions of tax in Australia). Ultimately it appeared that champions at least hoped the ATO Compliance Model could lead the way through this ethical minefield. That is, by bringing tax administration and procedural fairness together, through encouraging staff to think about the implications of their practices not just from a revenue perspective but also from a contextual one, the ethics of 'fair play' would become a natural part of ATO behaviour. In short, they could persuade members of the public to pay their tax, rather than having to force them to pay.

Barriers to Action: The ATO and the Structure of Practices

This section considers some possible implications that the champions' ideas may have for future ATO practices. There were without doubt multiple barriers to actualising the ATO Compliance Model, which stem partially from translating it from the abstract into action. These barriers were also caused by staff-management relations, administrative structures and the tax system as a legal entity (see Job and Honaker, Chapter 6, this volume; Shover et al., Chapter 8, this volume). There is also no doubt that champions believed the Compliance Model was good for the ATO and that its use should become more widespread within the organisation. The question was how to translate this good idea into practice.

Lower level staff members did not have the luxury of being able to 'play' with the model in their everyday work, as many of the champions have done to come to grips with it. To make up for this lack of direct experience, some champions believed the way forward was to keep pushing the message of the Compliance Model on staff until they finally 'got it':

> I would say people are aware of it and people understand the principles, but need on-going encouragement to continue to do it – because it takes time for these things to become automatic – so we need to keep working at it so that it becomes automatic.

Indeed, this assertion seemed to be pretty realistic, as positive change rarely happens overnight. Other interviewees were more strident, suggesting that staff needed to be *inculcated* and taught to *adhere* to the ATO Compliance Model. This language of submission and erosion should come as no surprise considering the structuring principles that have framed the ATO for so long (Grabosky and Braithwaite, 1986; Boucher, 1993). The ATO has a long history of rigid work practices, of collecting revenue by set means and seeing the taxpayer as the enemy that needs to be outwitted – a mentality that still prevails in some sections according to these interviews (especially audit and prosecution). The ATO Compliance Model ultimately requires that this rigidity be transgressed. This means a change in both attitudes and actions. Some champions suggested that a change in attitudes *was* taking place:

> My observation is that our people feel a greater sense of fulfilment and value through management putting faith and confidence in them being involved in the decision-making process.

However, these changes were often reported by champions as not working 'on the ground' or 'in the field'. Those working more closely with field staff suggested that changes were not really happening on a day-to-day basis because:

> It doesn't work within the public service delegated authority type regime very well.

Interviewees were clear that to get over these barriers and have the Compliance Model fully accepted there needed to be a 'culture' change in the ATO. This was not an easy task to undertake:

> It takes time. You're stepping over the boundaries a little bit that currently exist and that is a real mind shift, for that to occur.

> You do see general support. There's probably reluctance though, in stretching the boundaries more so than we've got at the moment. We need to break down some of those paradigms and say 'Well, what does it mean for us in the new environment?', and there needs to be space for that thinking and there also needs to be a level of support to take in that work.

Yet, is it really feasible or possible to talk about changing an organisational culture by getting staff to rethink their values? For one, the literatures on resistance to behaviour change strongly suggest that giving individuals information on a personal and social problem, and expecting them to then simply change their core beliefs, does not work (Prochaska and DiClemente, 1986; Prochaska, DiClemente and Norcross, 1992; Rollnick, 1996; Wardle 1996). That is, telling people to change their values and beliefs is, to all purposes, a non-starter, especially if done in a manner that even hints at coercion and lack of consultation (see examples in Job and Honaker, Chapter 6, this volume).

One of the reasons for this, at an organisational level at least, may be that institutions are not merely constituted through disembodied ethics, which can simply be changed as required. Many professions have codes of conduct, such as those factored into the *Australian Public Service Act 1999*. These pertain to standards of behaviour that are respectful of others and forward best practice, which can be carried out by individuals who do not necessarily hold certain values but who can professionally undertake actions that embody these values. However, having these service values differs considerably from a Chief Executive suddenly proclaiming 'this is how we are now going to think and react from here on', in the expectation that all desired change will then follow (in comparison to Pruzan, 2001). In everyday life, and also epistemologically, there is no separation between values and actions. That is, the 'culture' of the ATO, which interviewees refer to on many occasions, is embodied and perpetuated through individual and collective routine practices, be it the way officers talk to taxpayers, or the way information is processed.[4]

The champions who *thought with* the ATO Compliance Model were able to see this potential 'catch-22'. They did not simply call for structures or values to be changed but recognised that they are all inextricably linked in indecipherable complex ways:

> I mean the trouble is with an organisation – at a level where you start looking, at the whole people system – everything's damn well integrated. It's the identity, it's the culture, it's the kind of way that leaders lead, it's all that stuff. I find that all a bit daunting.

Indeed, daunting it is. A parallel example can be made from the environmental change literature. Some environmental researchers suggest that changing behaviour without changing values is adequate (this is called Applied Behaviour Analysis: see Geller, 1989). A second view is that technology and the processes of widespread ecological modernisation have the answers (see Cohen, 1998). A third approach argues that values of 'deep ecology' have to be nurtured before wide-scale environmental improvements can be seen (see Pepper, 1996). The ATO faces a similar issue but on a smaller scale. That is, how to create the widespread acceptance of a new way of thinking and acting that is fundamentally moral? If Giddens is used constructively, it can be suggested that changing practices is the best way forward. As one interviewee suggested:

> I think it's just about keeping it fairly simple to start with. Just starting with some fairly simple sorts of changes. We ran some fairly small pilots that were able to actually demonstrate some changes that it made. I guess it's about actually making it practical for staff. It just clicks with people. That one message. If you started with that you've gone somewhere, you've gotten somewhere with it – and then if you come back again and you talk about 'let's do something else', you just get that gradual change I suppose.

Thus, altering practices so that they embody the ATO Compliance Model ideas seems to be the most practicable way forward. This assertion can be supported by research the author carried out into individuals taking part in a sustainable consumption behaviour change program in the UK, called *Action at Home* (Hobson, 2001a, 2001b). Over a six month period, it was found that many participants of *Action at Home* only changed a few small, seemingly mundane practices, such as turning off the taps when brushing their teeth or switching lights off when leaving the room. However, what was significant were the changes in personal outlooks that resulted from participants thinking about the social and environmental implications of their previous habits, and their reconsiderations of the types of attitudes these previous practices embodied. Issues such as water and energy use were brought from the practical to discursive consciousness, making individuals ask themselves why they carried out certain actions the way they did, and what the ramifications of their actions might be. The resultant magnitude of behaviour change may not appear significant. However, it seemed to leave behind a 'lens of difference'. This means that participants were left with a residual awareness of the issues that *Action at Home* discussed. They had not become converted to being 'green' but had internalised a consideration for the environment that touched and subtly affected the way they viewed the world and their own behaviour.

The same could be argued for the ATO. By altering small practices, ATO staff can experience the Compliance Model in action, and can carry out the principles of the Compliance Model without having it overtly enforced. This is a small but important step forward in getting ATO staff to rethink their practices. It is not about trying to create new values, but rather put into action the ideas of the ATO Compliance Model through small changes to practices.

Examining briefly the processes through which the Compliance Model appears to have made an impact in the ATO supports this assertion. For one, there are the 'above the line' examples, such as embedding it into ATO recruitment strategies. Making the Compliance Model part of staff's everyday thinking is partially a result of these official stances. For example, the need for strong leadership in the ATO was stressed time and time again in reference to making the Compliance Model work (see Bouwen and Fry, 1991; Hooper and Potter, 1999; Job and Honaker, Chapter 6, this volume; Shover et al., Chapter 8, this volume). Yet, there appear to be other processes involved – ones 'below the line' of official managerial practice – that are equally important and hinge upon the ATO Compliance Model being translated into everyday behaviours for staff, either by champions involved in training or through the informal 'mentoring' of staff. As champions were able to think with the model, they clearly saw that the translation process of the model from the abstract into the everyday requires tapping into the knowledge and language of ATO staff, not simply expecting them to jump 'cultures' as the result of one presentation or meeting.

For example, one interviewee talked about how the language of the Compliance Model had been changed to enable it to resonate with ATO staff:

> Originally we used to have some delineations within the compliance pyramid that showed education advice here and then audit here and people love to box things so they kind of saw it was a static kind of model. So, when I introduced it to people the first thing you had to do is – when it had that language on it – was take it all off. Let people use their own words and let them write their own words on the model so that then they could be engaged.

Another champion told of how she used stories to translate the model into reality. Through detailing to other staff her own personal experiences of the ATO, in trying to correctly lodge her personal tax returns and feeling that she was treated as guilty until proven innocent by the ATO, she was able to bring the model to life for staff. In training sessions:

> I read them the letter[5] and they said 'Oh'. So practically I could say 'see, this is what's happening'. So I was able to use that story. That story worked wonders.

The same interviewee later explained why telling stories of actual experiences, using ATO language and processes, works:

> But when you actually say in their language 'well you know when you do blah blah blah procedure? Dah, dah, dah happens'. As soon as you say that, you've got them hooked because they think 'She's one of us!'.

The importance of making these initial connections with the Compliance Model cannot be underestimated as many champions reported how staff switched off from the model in presentations, saying it had nothing to do with them and their line of work. Therefore:

> It's really about taking it from a model and making it real for people, which was the important step.

Being able to make this initial connection then enabled staff to understand and work with the Compliance Model, to get *into* the model rather than feeling they had this rigid entity into which they must squeeze their work. As one interviewee put it:

> Instead of chipping away, these things could just be like a snow-ball running down the hill, it would really feed on itself.

There were signs that a snow-ball effect was happening, as many champions were positive that the Compliance Model was making an impact on the ATO, although there are still many barriers to overcome. The key point to make is that changes were happening through staff using the model, talking to others about it, and seeing its positive benefits for themselves:

> When I first went around the country to talk to my teams, I got the same response – 'It's just a waste of time. All taxpayers are cheats'. But fortunately when team members actually have gone out and applied the concept or used this strategy, they personally see the result that comes of it. Therefore, there's a change in mind-set, to be more accepting of the concept.

These can be seen as processes of social learning and social diffusion. Rogers (1995) argues that an individual's adoption of innovations stems not just from reading about an innovation but from listening to and witnessing how other individuals in their social network have evaluated the innovation (see Flinn, 1997 for further discussion of social learning). Talk between ATO staff and others, be it informal or formal, is important as change is achieved through communication and negotiation, as well as through simply watching others. This is social learning. The adoption of new ideas can rarely be imposed from the outside (Harrisson et al., 2001) but instead takes place along 'learning-action' networks (Clarke and Roome, 1999), which cut across formal organisational hierarchies and boundaries. This is social diffusion. Thus, bringing the ATO Compliance Model to life is not about individuals singularly adopting the Compliance Model internally and then putting it into action in tandem with others. It is instead a process of 'joint action' (Shotter, 1993a, 1993b), facilitated through different processes of learning.

De Young's (1993) typology of behaviour change processes makes this point. He suggests that both tangible and intangible processes of behaviour change exist. Examples of tangible forms are feedback, material incentives and legal mandates, whilst intangible forms can be direct experience, personal insight, self-monitored feedback, and a sense of confidence and commitment. The point to be taken from this is that adoption of the Compliance Model in the ATO should not be about employing just one of these forms of change. Instead, it requires a mixture of leadership, support, information, policy reworking, personal experience, commitment to change, and broad thinking. The Compliance Model champions appear to embody and encompass this broad array of behaviour change processes, enabling them to think with the model, and offering interesting insights into how change might be forwarded in organisations such as the ATO.

Conclusion

This paper has sought to address why certain individuals in the ATO can be considered Compliance Model champions. It has attempted to offer an alternate story from positivist approaches, by examining how these individuals talked about the ATO Compliance Model and its place in their lifeworld. Through this 'below the line' approach the themes of experience, social learning and interaction have emerged as positive aspects of change. Yet the departing message of this research should not be read as advocating all tax staff adopt 'touchy-feely' approaches, as several interviewees put it. The ATO has to administer tax laws across a large and diverse country, a task that requires procedures and systems able to cope with vast quantities of information and assessments. The messages are rather that the lifeworld of many tax officers is such that the Compliance Model would not have immediate resonance in relation to their everyday experiences. Thus, the process of translation is important. Often this translation is believed to involve either changing the wholesale 'culture' of the ATO or turning the Compliance Model into a step-by-step rulebook. This research advocates a more middle-ground approach from the lessons the champions have to offer, by examining how small practices embody the central tenets of the ATO Compliance Model. As a result, it encourages the taking of a gradual, iterative approach to change.

This research can also reflect on implications for how taxpayers are treated. In the spirit of reflexivity, it is hoped that organisations like the ATO might conclude that their own staff's rejection or disengagement from the abstract form of the Compliance Model might give some insight into how the taxpayer struggles with tax returns. Do tax officers speak to the 'world where they [taxpayers] live'? Why should the taxpayer comply with a set of regulations or practices that do not take into account the constraints and lack of adequate infrastructure in their everyday lives, when some tax officers feel exactly the same way about the Compliance Model? Funnily enough, this argument brings this research full circle, back to the Model itself. The fact that this research supports a 'below the line' approach to encouraging changes in practice can be seen as offering support to the central tenets of the Compliance Model. That is, by understanding the consequences of one's actions and the messages embodied in practices, we can begin to understand and positively affect others' practices and bring them into a more supportive and compliant environment, whether we are talking about tax office staff or the taxpaying community at large.

Notes

1 For example, the ATO seeks to maximise revenue through efficient operational structures, similar to private industry. It differs in its role of administering tax law and being directly implicated with issues of procedural and distributive justice.

2 Interviews were carried out by members of the CTSI and the Regulatory Institutions Network, Australian National University. Interviewers were Brenda Morrison, Kristina Murphy and Declan Roche.

3 BISEP represented the idea that to understand the compliance of an individual or group, one needed to understand the lifespace in which they operated. The initials of this acronym stand for B = Business profile, I = Industry factors, S = Sociological factors, E = Economic factors and P = Psychological factors.

4 For example, several interviewees made reference to the way current information technology systems did not allow them to access information required for a 'complete picture' of individual taxpayer's circumstances and history. Yet understanding history and circumstances is at the heart of implementation of the ATO Compliance Model.

5 This letter was received by the interviewee from the ATO after she had failed to lodge correctly. The interviewee felt the tone of the letter made the assumption that she was trying to cheat on her tax payments.

References

Australian Bureau of Statistics (2001), *Labour: Characteristics of Employment*, Australian Bureau of Statistics, Canberra.

Billig, M. (1993), 'Studying the Thinking Society: Social Representations, Rhetoric and Attitudes', in G. M. Breakwell and D.V. Canter (eds), *Empirical Approaches to Social Representations*, Clarendon Press, Oxford, pp. 41-62.

Boden, D. (1994), *The Business of Talk*, Polity Press, London.

Boucher, T. (1993), 'Risk Management on a Market Segmented Basis', in P. Grabosky and J. Braithwaite (eds), *Business Regulation and Australia's Future*, Australian Institute of Criminology, Canberra, pp. 231-44.

Bouwen, R. and Fry, R. (1991), 'Organisational Motivational and Learning', *International Studies in Management and Organizations*, vol. 21(2), pp. 37-51.

Braithwaite, V., Reinhart, M., Mearns, M. and Graham, R. (2001), 'Preliminary Findings from the Community Hopes, Fears and Actions Survey', *Centre for Tax System Integrity Working Paper No. 3*, The Australian National University, Canberra.

Burningham, K. and Cooper, G. (1999), 'Being Constructive: Social Constructionism and the Environment', *Sociology*, vol. 33(2), pp. 297-316.

Clarke, S. and Roome, N. (1999), 'Sustainable Business: Learning-Action Networks as Organizational Assets', *Business Strategy and the Environment*, vol. 8, pp. 296-310.

Cohen, M. J. (1998), 'Science and Environment: Assessing Cultural Capacity for Ecological Modernisation', *Public Understanding of Science*, vol. 7, pp. 149-67.

Damapour, F. and Gopalakrishnan, S. (2001), 'The Dynamics of the Adoption of Product and Process Innovations in Organizations, *Journal of Management Studies*, vol. 38(1), pp. 45-65.

De Young, R. (1993), 'Changing Behavior and Making it Stick: The Conceptualisation and Management of Conservation Behavior', *Environment and Behavior*, vol. 25(4), pp. 485-505.

Edwards, D., Ashmore, M. and Potter, J. (1995), 'Death and Furniture: The Rhetoric, Politics and Theology of Bottom Line Arguments Against Relativism', *History of the Human Sciences*, vol. 8(2), pp. 25-49.

Ehrlich, P.R., Wolff, G., Daily, G.C., Hughes, J.B., Daily, S., Dalton, M. and Goulder, L. (1999), 'Knowledge and the Environment', *Ecological Economics*, vol. 30, pp. 267-84.

Finger, M. (1994), 'From Knowledge to Action? Exploring the Relationship Between Environmental Experiences, Learning and Behaviour', *Journal of Social Issues*, vol. 50(3), pp. 141-60.

Fishbein, M. (1993), 'Introduction', in C. Gallois, M. McCamish and D.J. Terry (eds), *The Theory of Reasoned Action: Its Application to AIDS-preventive Behaviour*, Pergamon Press, Oxford, pp. xv-xxv.

Flinn, M.V. (1997), 'Culture and the Evolution of Social Learning', *Evolution and Human Behavior*, vol. 18(1), pp. 23-67.

Geller, E.S. (1989), 'Applied Behavior Analysis and Social Marketing: An Integration for Environmental Preservation', *Journal of Social Issues*, vol. 45(1), pp. 17-36.

Giddens, A. (1984), *The Constitution of Society: Outline of the Theory of Structuration*, Polity Press, London.

Goffman, E. (1969), *The Presentation of Self in Everyday Life*, Penguin, London.

Grabosky, P. and Braithwaite, J. (1986), *Of Manners Gentle: Enforcement Strategies of Australian Business Regulatory Agencies*, Oxford University Press, Melbourne.

Harrisson, D., Laplante, N. and St-Cyr, L. (2001), 'Cooperation and Resistance in Work Innovation Networks', *Human Relations*, vol. 54(2), pp. 215-55.

Hinchliffe, S. (2000), 'Performance and Experimental Knowledge: Outdoor Management Training and the End of Epistemology', *Environment and Planning*, vol. 18, pp. 575-95.

Hobson, K. (2001a), 'Talking Habits into Action: An Investigation into Global Action Plan's "Action at Home" Programme', Unpublished Doctoral Dissertation, University College, London.

_____ (2001b), 'Sustainable Lifestyles: Rethinking Barriers and Behaviour Change', in M.J. Cohen and J. Murphy (eds), *Exploring Sustainable Consumption: Environmental Policy and the Social Sciences*, Pergamon, London, pp. 191-209.

Hollingsworth, J.R. (2000), 'Doing Institutional Analysis: Implications for the Study of Innovations', *Review of International Political Economy*, vol. 7(4), pp. 595-644.

Hooper, A. and Potter, J. (1999), 'Take it From the Top', *People Management*, vol. 5(16), pp. 46-9.

Job, J. and Honaker, D. (Chapter 6, this volume), 'Short-term Experience with Responsive Regulation in the Australian Taxation Office'.

Kanter, R.M. (1983), *The Change Masters*, Simon and Schuster, New York.

King, N. (1990), 'Innovation at Work: The Research Literature', in M.A. West and J.L. Farr (eds), *Innovation and Creativity at Work*, Wiley, Chichester, pp. 15-60.

Kruse, L. and Schwarz, S. (1992), 'Who Pays the Bill? The Language of Social Representation', in M. von Cranach, W. Doise and G. Mugny (eds), *Social Representations and the Social Bases of Knowledge*, Hogrefe and Huber, Lewiston, pp. 23-29.

Lalli, P. (1999), 'New Challenges for Social Communication about Health', *Alcologia: European Journal of Alcohol Studies*, vol. 2, pp. 1-11.

Latour, B. (1993), *We Have Never Been Modern*, Harvard University Press, Cambridge.

Mills, S. (1998), *Discourse*, Routledge, New York.

Moscovici, S. (2001), *Social Representations: Explorations in Social Psychology*, New York University Press, New York.

Murdoch, J. and Clark, J. (1994), 'Sustainable Knowledge', *Geoforum*, vol. 25(2), 115-32.

Pepper, D. (1996), *Modern Environmentalism*, Routledge, London.

Prochaska, J. and DiClemente, C.C. (1986), 'Toward a Comprehensive Model of Change', in W. Miller and N. Heather (eds), *Treating Addictive Behaviours: Processes of Change*, Plenum Press, New York, pp. 3-28.

Prochaska, J.O., DiClemente, C.C. and Norcross J.C. (1992), 'In Search of How People Change: Application to Addictive Behaviours', *American Psychologist*, vol. 47(9), pp. 1102-14.

Pruzan, P. (2001), 'The Question of Organizational Consciousness: Can Organizations Have Values, Virtues and Visions?', *Journal of Business Ethics*, vol. 29(3), pp. 271-84.

Public Service and Merit Protection Commission (2000), *Australian Public Service Values*, http://www.psmpc.gov.au/publications/values.htm.

Reser, J.P. (1995), 'Whither Environmental Psychology? The Transpersonal Ecopsychology Crossroads', *Journal of Environmental Psychology*, vol. 15, pp. 235-57.

Rogers, E.M. (1995), *Diffusion of Innovations*, Free Press, New York.

Rollnick, S. (1996), 'Behaviour Change in Practice: Targetting Individuals', *International Journal of Obesity Related Metabolic Disorders*, vol. 20(1), pp. 22-6.

Rosenfeld, R. and Servo, J.C. (1990), 'Facilitating Innovations in Large Organizations', in M.A. West and J.L. Farr (eds), *Innovation and Creativity at Work*, Wiley, Chichester, pp. 151-64.

Shotter, J. (1993a), *Cultural Politics of Everyday Life: Social Constructionism, Rhetoric and Knowing of the Third Kind*, Open University Press, Buckingham.

_____ (1993b), *Conversational Realities*, Sage, London.

Shover, N., Job, J. and Carroll, A. (Chapter 8, this volume), 'The Compliance Model in Action: A Case Study of Building and Construction'.

Sibeon, R. (1999), 'Anti-Reductionist Sociology', *Sociology*, vol. 33(2), pp. 317-34.

Strauss, A.L. (1987), *Qualitative Analysis for Social Scientists*, Cambridge University Press, New York.

Strauss, C. and Quinn, N. (1997), *A Cognitive Theory of Cultural Meaning*, Cambridge University Press, New York.

Stubbs, M. (2000), 'Action, Knowledge and Business-Environment Research: A Case for Grounded Constitutive Process Theories and a Sense of Audience', *Business Strategy and the Environment*, vol. 9, pp. 24-35.

Terry, D., Gallois, C. and McCamish, M. (1993), 'Reasoned Action and Health Care Behaviour', in D.J. Terry, C. Gallois and M. McCamish (eds), *The Theory of Reasoned Action: Its Application to AIDS-preventive Behaviour*, Pergamon Press, New York, pp. 1-28.

Visser, B. (2000), 'Organizational Communication Structure and Performance', *Journal of Economic Behaviour and Organization*, vol. 42, pp. 231-52.

Wardle, J. (1996), 'Obesity and Behaviour Change: Matching Problems to Practice', *International Journal of Obesity Related Metabolic Disorders*, vol. 20(1), pp. 1-8.

Welford, R.J. (1998), 'Corporate Environmental Management, Technology and Sustainable Development: Postmodern Perspectives and the Need for a Critical Research Agenda', *Business Strategy and the Environment*, vol. 7, pp. 1-12.

West, M.A. and Farr, J.L. (1990), 'Innovation at Work', in M.A. West and J.L. Farr (eds), *Innovation and Creativity at Work*, Wiley, Chichester, pp. 3-14.

Chapter 8

The ATO Compliance Model in Action: A Case Study of Building and Construction

Neal Shover, Jenny Job and Anne Carroll

In 1996, the Australian Commissioner of Taxation formed a Task Force comprised of representatives from industry, community groups and government to develop an understanding of the cash economy and potential responses to it. After the Task Force issued its initial report, in July 1997 the Australian Taxation Office (ATO) launched a series of initiatives aimed at the cash economy. They specifically targeted cash transactions by small firms in several industries, including building and construction. Several months later, these cash economy initiatives were augmented by an ATO decision to adopt a new approach to tax enforcement, one that incorporates principles of responsive regulation (Cash Economy Task Force, 1998). Known as the ATO Compliance Model, it reflects considerable research into regulatory processes and is touted as a more effective approach to compliance assurance (see Job and Honaker, Chapter 6, this volume). Shortly after adopting the Compliance Model, in April 1998, the Commissioner of Taxation announced that the ATO would begin using it in programs aimed at the building and construction industry and others also where evidence suggested there were significant cash transactions. Eventually, some 200 ATO personnel were assigned to the Cash Economy Building and Construction Project (CE/B&C project). Organised in teams of some 10-15 members each, they were located in major metropolitan areas throughout Australia.[1] The research reported here examines the reception given the Compliance Model by front-line supervisors and personnel assigned to the CE/B&C project and its short-term impact among small building and construction firms.

This chapter begins with a brief description of the objectives of our research into the implementation and impact of the CE/B&C project. We next introduce and define the concept of *organisational capacity*, which is followed by presentation of the underlying assumptions of our investigation and a description of key aspects of the ATO Compliance Model as it was applied to the small building and construction industry. The research findings are presented next, drawing from analysis of the experiences and perspectives of ATO field-level personnel and the owners of small building and construction firms. The chapter concludes with a discussion of the lessons of this research.

Research Objectives and Methods

This research commenced some eighteen months after the Compliance Model was adopted by the ATO leadership and was added to ongoing initiatives aimed at the cash economy. It was premised on awareness that reformers cannot assume that their intentions and plans will meet with committed and faithful implementation. The reasons for this are several, but it is well recognised that bureaucracies charged with implementing reform policies can show highly varied capacity for the job at hand:

> Policy ideas that sound great in theory often fail under conditions of actual field implementation. The implementation process has a life of its own. It is acted out through large and inflexible administrative systems and is distorted by bureaucratic interests. Policies that emerge in practice can diverge, even substantially, from policies as designed and adopted (Bardach, 2000, p. 25).

Doubtless it was recognition of this that led the ATO's Cash Economy Task Force to emphasise as constraints on the implementation and impact of tax reform 'attributes of the tax regime,' including both 'its administration, and ATO cultural factors' (Cash Economy Task Force, 1997, p. 6).

Because the Compliance Model posits complex and slow-developing long-term relationships between the behaviour of enforcement officials and the responses of taxpayers, it was recognised at the outset that an adequate evaluation of the CE/B&C project would require collection of data over several years. At inception, our objective was a retrospective *process analysis*. Process analysis is used in evaluation research as a way of understanding *how* reforms are implemented and brought to bear in the day-to-day work routines of managers and employees (Weiss, 1998). It can lay bare how organisational realities and dynamics constrain reforms adopted in other circumstances for reasons often unknown to or unappreciated by those charged with implementing the policy. Typically, process analysis includes use of interviews and observation as a way of interpreting the statistically observable consequences of a new policy or program.

We planned to collect a variety of data on the ATO's implementation of the Compliance Model as well as evidence of some of its short-term impacts. We assumed that by using a variety of methods and collecting a variety of data, findings gained from multiple methods or sources to some extent would compensate for their individual shortcomings. Twenty months after its inauguration, however, the impending arrival of fundamental tax reform (the Goods and Services Tax, or GST) caused a substantial reduction in personnel and resources committed to the CE/B&C project. This also caused us to scale back our original research plans and to shift our focus somewhat to examination of the ATO's capacity for effective implementation of the Compliance Model.

Data were collected over a ten month period (August 1999 through May 2000). We began by interviewing fifteen ATO managers or employees, some face-to-face and others by long-distance telephone. These conversations, which averaged approximately 25 minutes in length, helped familiarise the senior author with the ATO and provided an opportunity to talk with several managers who played important roles in the field-level implementation process. This was followed in November-December 1999 by visits to five ATO field offices where significant CE/B&C project initiatives were underway (Sydney CBD, Parramatta, Penrith, Box Hill, and Dandenong). We interviewed 26 field-level managers and operatives about their experiences with and opinions of the Compliance Model in building and construction. The semi-structured interviews followed a topical guide and averaged approximately 35 minutes each. All were tape recorded and transcribed for subsequent analysis. Following these interviews, in May-August 2000, a survey instrument was e-mailed to all ATO personnel who at any time were assigned to the CE/B&C project. After two follow-up reminders to the 260 persons who were sent surveys, 32 per cent were returned to us.[2]

During May-June 2000, we interviewed the owners of 27 small building and construction firms in Melbourne and Adelaide. The semi-structured interviews, which were tape recorded for subsequent transcription and analysis, averaged approximately 30 minutes and explored respondents' experiences with and beliefs about the ATO and its operations. The interviews focused primarily on respondents' contacts with the ATO in the years immediately before and after introduction of the Compliance Model in 1997. Although we had planned to interview equal numbers of firms/owners with varying degrees of contact with the ATO in the preceding two years, a variety of difficulties left us unable to do so. Among them, we were unsuccessful in obtaining telephone numbers for many firms listed in ATO files, and a substantial majority of those we did talk with declined our request for an interview. We estimate that not more than five per cent of all firms that were contacted agreed to and completed an interview. As a result, the sample of businesses almost certainly is tilted toward those who comply with tax requirements and have no particular reason, therefore, to be wary of sharing their experiences with and opinions of the ATO. As one of our subjects told us:

> I think if a company is fair dinkum and up-front, they shouldn't be worried about the ATO, you know. If you're doing the right thing you've got nothing to worry about.

In the language and logic of the Compliance Model (see Figure 1.1 in Chapter 1), these firms and their owners are located near the bottom of the enforcement pyramid, and our findings are limited to the population they represent.

In addition to interviews with ATO personnel and the owners of small building and construction firms, we also interviewed an executive of the Department of Public Prosecutions and a representative of the Master Builders Association of Victoria. These interviews also were tape recorded. We recognise that the short follow-up period we employed and the limitations of our samples substantially diminish confidence in our research findings and the degree to which they can be generalised to other times and locales.

Organisational Capacity and Responsive Regulation

Organisations are constrained by a variety of characteristics and conditions that affect their capacity to adopt and to implement reform initiatives. Organisational capacity is the extent to which an organisation possesses the mandate, requisite resources, determination and facilitative environmental conditions to implement reform policies with fidelity to the goals envisioned by reformers. It also includes routinised organisational procedures for monitoring the short-term consequences of reform initiatives.

Our data collection and analysis were guided by three assumptions about the short-term changes one should reasonably expect if the ATO possessed or acquired appropriate and sufficient capacity to implement successfully the ATO Compliance Model. First, there should be evidence that top leadership of the ATO supported and invested in the reform policy. Absent this condition, there is little reason to believe that mid-level managers, their field-level counterparts and front-line staff will take seriously its prescriptions and change their behaviour accordingly. There should be evidence, moreover, that leadership has planned for and put in place from the outset mechanisms for monitoring early implementation and subsequent evaluation of the initiative. Doing so ensures the intelligence needed to assess progress or the lack of it and to make short-term corrections to the implementation process.

Second, the reform policy, as defined and presented to supervisors and front-line personnel should neither conflict with nor be cognitively incongruent with their current perspectives and practices. There should be evidence, moreover, that as they were trained and acquired experience with the new policy, ATO staff moved in the direction of increased understanding and support for it.

Last, the context and times should be permissive of, if not conducive to reform. Whilst probably few reforms are undertaken in placid times – typically there seems little reason for change in these circumstances – a calm environment lends itself to the deliberate and self-reflective decision making that can nurture and sustain through the precarious early days. Reforms undertaken in times of turbulence and tension by contrast may not permit personnel to focus on the job at hand or to reflect upon and make use of evaluations. Times of turmoil do not lend themselves easily to careful, deliberative decision-making. In sum, assuming that staff understand and are committed to reform, that sufficient organisational resources are invested in it, and that environmental conditions are hospitable, there is reason for optimism. Absent one or more of these conditions, it is doubtful a new policy can be instituted without serious departures from the vision of reformers.

Small Building and Construction Industry

In addition to legitimising and making available to officials a range of options when responding to compliance problems, programs of responsive regulation highlight the importance of understanding the characteristics and contexts of regulated industries and the variety of factors that make firms either compliant or non-compliant (Gunningham and Grabosky, 1998). It is taken for granted that a host of economic, sociological, cultural and psychological factors condition the ways typical firms see and interact with regulatory agencies and personnel.

Where the ATO is concerned, this constellation of industry-specific factors, known as BISEP,[3] shape firms' capacity and inclination to comply with taxation requirements. The use of BISEP materials enables the ATO and other regulatory agencies to make use of industry-specific information which might require a particular strategy. It also strengthens awareness of both current and future challenges and permits the ATO to plan for them in a way that meets both its needs and the needs of the industry.

The conduct of business by small firms in the building and construction industry is filled with uncertainties. Business owners tend to be a fairly casual lot who, while they are prepared to take risks, are also content to remain as small businesses. Business relationships are characterised by informality; written contracts are eschewed, and a great deal of advertising is by word of mouth. Trade regulation is minimal, and licensing requirements vary. Owners of small building and construction firms are independent people who like to manage their own show. Nearly half of these business owners are sole traders, and nearly a third are in partnerships, commonly with their wife. The overwhelming majority of them use the services of tax agents, but few maintain on-going relationships throughout the year. The business records are maintained by the wives. This industry is often faced with economic uncertainty and pressures from international competition, inflation, fluctuating interest rates, and inclement weather. Barter is common, as is the use of cash. The industry norm is that weekend work is paid for in cash that is not declared as income. The industry ethic is very much one of looking after each other. Relationships in the industry are competitive but close, and the high level of union membership illustrates this. There is a strong belief in the 'level playing field', meaning that everyone should have an equal chance to make a living. The industry is dominated by males with low literacy levels and variable skill levels, many of whom come from non-English speaking backgrounds. Distrust of government and fear of the ATO are common. Generally it is considered OK not to pay tax, and peer pressure contributes to many taking the risk of cheating on their taxes. This description highlights the need for ways of communicating with the industry and with constituent firms other than by form letters couched in the language of officialdom.

Enforcement Technology

Every approach to regulation features a somewhat distinctive technology of compliance assurance. Audits are a key component of command and control tax regulation. The audit process highlights the importance of monitoring individuals and business entities in order to uncover violations of law. Audits can require months to complete. Those found to be non-compliant are assessed penalties, which presumably serve to remind them and others as well that compliance is the best way to go. Accusation and confrontation are unavoidable by-products of the technology of command and control enforcement. Not surprisingly, agencies that operate in this fashion frequently are seen as high-handed adversaries by citizens and firms subject to their programs (Braithwaite, Walker and Grabosky, 1987). Historically, the ATO operated this way; it generated large numbers of prosecutions, the bulk of which were directed at taxpayers of modest means (Grabosky and Braithwaite, 1986).

Adoption of the Compliance Model caused the ATO to develop and train its staff in a technology of compliance that contrasts in several ways from the one they used previously. Whilst maintaining audits as part of the compliance-assurance arsenal, the Compliance Model, as developed and applied by the ATO, features a technology called 'Real Time Reviews' (RTRs). The objectives here are more ambitious than a search for violations and assessment of penalties. Whereas audits typically require detailed examination of a firm's records over a period of months or even years, RTRs generally are limited to examination of business records and activities for the preceding three-months period. They require less time than traditional audits. RTRs have a strong educative focus; they are employed not only to uncover evidence of non-compliance but also to increase understanding of proper bookkeeping practices and future compliance. Taxpayers are treated according to their individual circumstances. Where significant discrepancies are identified, they are advised and invited to review and amend their previous taxation returns. The focus is on increasing the odds of compliance in the future. This technology also allows ATO field officers to refer cases for audit or prosecution when wilful or egregious non-compliance is detected. The use of RTRs allows field staff to achieve greater coverage and visibility in the business community and also garner intelligence about specific industries (Australian Taxation Office, 1999a, 1999b).

Research Findings

To what extent were our assumptions about organisational capacity for change matched by conditions in the CE/B&C project during the first few years of its operation? Did it have or acquire the resources to suggest that over a longer period of time the expected results of responsive regulation would be realised?

Leadership and Staff

Doubtless few would dispute the assumption that committed and supportive executives are critical to an organisation's capacity for faithful implementation of reform policies. One way this can be demonstrated is by providing the level of fiscal and staffing resources required. Ample evidence suggests that strong and ongoing support was given by senior ATO managers. This support came from the highest levels of the ATO, particularly from the Commissioner, the Deputy Commissioner of the Small Business area, the Assistant Commissioner responsible for managing the cash economy initiative, and the Project Leader for Building and Construction. They sponsored and provided resources for training in the Compliance Model for all staff on the CE/B&C project, and they visited and provided encouragement. When the initial training program was begun, senior ATO managers signalled their support by attending and participating in the training course. They discussed the direction the ATO was moving in and how the Compliance Model complemented it. They emphasised that ATO practices and procedures were important issues in building and maintaining community confidence in the ATO and its ability to administer the taxation system. None of the personnel we interviewed faulted ATO executives for failure to support or to provide sufficient resources for the CE/B&C project.

Survey findings were not strongly one sided, however. Thirty-five per cent of our survey respondents indicated that at some time they were responsible for supervising other ATO personnel as part of the CE/B&C project. They ranged from team leaders to mid-level managers. All survey respondents, former supervisors and operatives alike, were asked to indicate their agreement or disagreement with the statement: 'The leadership of the Australian Taxation Office failed to devote sufficient resources to implementation of the Compliance Model'. For supervisors, 33.3 per cent of respondents agreed or agreed strongly whilst 40.7 per cent disagreed or disagreed strongly. For respondents who were not supervisors, the results are 34.6 per cent and 36.5 per cent respectively. Taken together, our interview and survey findings suggest that proportionately few supervisors and operatives perceive a failure by ATO executives to provide adequate fiscal resources and personnel for the CE/B&C project.

Here and in other ways as well, support for the Compliance Model by ATO executives was not lost on field-level staff. When asked for his opinion about the Compliance Model, one ATO operative spoke with apparent conviction about the importance of treating taxpayers with 'understanding', 'respect' and 'compassion'. As the interview progressed, however, and he was asked to reconcile seemingly contradictory statements, he said that his earlier comments reflected belief that ATO executives are committed to the Compliance Model, that they expect field-level staff to get on board, and that they would be watchful for signs of weak commitment and follow through. Only then did he acknowledge that his earlier characterisation of the model masked considerable doubt about its efficacy at the coalface.

This is not to say the Compliance Model was welcomed by all or even by most staff. Some saw it as a hopelessly abstract approach that was developed by academics and then adopted by ATO executives:

> Let's face it: the Compliance Model was an academic model adapted to the tax situation. It was developed by,...I think, people outside of [ATO]. ATO saw it as the way we should be moving,...and I'm not disagreeing. I think they're right. But it was done at the more senior level by people who are inclined that way [toward consultative approaches] anyway.

For most field-level personnel of the ATO, adoption of the Compliance Model for the small building and construction industry apparently came out of the blue.[4] For those we interviewed, there was limited awareness of how the decision was made combined with some disappointment and cynicism:

> I'm an employee of the Taxation Office, and this is an instruction that's put to me. I've no input into its adoption whatsoever. I'm not asked whether, you know, this is a good

> idea. Should we go this way, or whatever? You're an experienced taxation officer. You've been in this place for [more than 25] years, what have you found in that period of time about, you know, compliance in taxation?

> This was imposed certainly. No two ways about it. We were given two days to provide feedback...It was like, okay, 'we've made a decision, but we should get something from the people in the office to make them think that they're having some feedback into it'. [W]e didn't feel we were part of it at all...[T]he decision was made before we even were given a chance to offer feedback. I think they ended up – so many people complained – they gave us another week to give feedback, but it was still basically we felt that they just threw it away or put it in a corner and basically came out with the model they wanted.

For these reasons, perhaps, a mid-level manager who helped implement the Compliance Model told us that:

> It wasn't universally welcomed in the ATO, or in the project [CE/B&C project] anyway, which is probably representative of the ATO. I think the majority of people in the ATO thought straight off 'oh, yeah, now we're going soft on everyone', you know. I think that was the quick interpretation of it, that 'oh, now we just pat them on the head and tell them to be good in the future and walk away', you know.

The respondent noted further that apparently little thought was given to 'the ability of people' (staff) to shift to the new approach, adding that 'it's a huge jump for some'.

Whatever their initial reactions, however, successful implementation of a reform is enhanced if staff take on as their own its fundamental assumptions. Consequently, in our survey we asked current and former CE/B&C project personnel to comment retrospectively on their expectations about the ATO Compliance Model at introduction and after they gained experience using it. Responses to this series of questions suggest that the subjects fall into three groups. Nearly ten per cent (9.8%) indicated they were very sceptical about the Compliance Model when they were introduced to it whilst 4.7 per cent were equally enthusiastic about it. The remaining 85.6 per cent of respondents ranged from somewhat sceptical to somewhat enthusiastic. Although few of those who held strong opinions about the Compliance Model at introduction changed their assessment with experience, for those in this large group with less extreme opinions a majority (54.1%) became more positive about it. Our interview data are consistent with this pattern.

> Q: So, you have had two years experience now with the Compliance Model?
> A: Yes.
> Q: And what's your assessment of it now?
> A: I like it. I like it. It has a greater impact, because previously you were only dealing, you know, [one-on-one] and had no impact on the industry. But now, bringing in the various associations and what have you and getting the publicity, it has a wider impact. So it is more one-to-many, which I like. A lot more flexibility, a lot more choice, which I like.

> [O]riginally…it was seen as 'oh, this is going to be Mickey-Mouse type of activity that they're going into. When will they get back to doing actual work?'. And things like that. After a while of going through it, they could see the advantages of doing some of the alternative type of work as well as the audit activities. But I think it was only when they could see that there was room for the two.

Growing field-level support for the Compliance Model does not extend to an unqualified endorsement of it; staff beliefs about and experience with tax enforcement have left many ambivalent about the long-term consequences of responsive regulation. On one hand, many prefer real time reviews to audits. Generally the latter are triggered by suspicion or evidence that something is amiss with the tax behaviour of a business. The resulting detailed examination of financial records can be both adversarial and confrontational. They can be difficult both for operatives and for the targets of their efforts. Several of the ATO operatives we interviewed commented spontaneously on their dislike for the audit process, which puts a premium on being able to act assertively. For example:

> While I was an auditor I hated it. When I was doing my degree I always wanted to be an auditor, and it's like, you know, you get there and you think, 'this is horrible'. So I didn't like it. I didn't like the aggression that came along with auditing. It was more than assertive, it was probably aggressive…And it was like, let's see what we can get, how we can intimidate this person, that sort of thing…So I really learned to hate it a lot. When the Building and Construction Project came along, and we saw the methodology was real time reviews, we didn't know what it meant. But when we saw that it was a lot softer than an audit, a lot faster, and less intimidatory, and probably more helpful, I liked it. I preferred that way of doing things.

On the other hand, former CE/B&C project staff members tend to be rather cynical about the sources of tax compliance. Asked, for example, whether 'fear of penalties is more important than conscience and the obligations of citizenship' as reasons for tax compliance, 71.8 per cent of our survey respondents agreed or agreed strongly. Clearly, they believe that a strong threat is fundamental to the compliance assurance process. Not surprising, therefore, one of their most frequently mentioned concerns was whether the ATO would maintain the level of prosecutions needed to make it work. Put differently, they wonder whether the 'benign big gun' will be employed sufficiently often to maintain an acceptable level of tax compliance.

The enforcement technology at the heart of the Compliance Model does not end with real time reviews; responsive regulation highlights the importance of involving community and industry groups in efforts to maintain or improve overall tax compliance. This means that ATO staff now are expected also to contact and work with these stakeholders in order to improve awareness of and support for the tax system. This requires work routines and personal skills different from audits and penalties, the traditional mainstays of tax enforcement. Early on in the CE/B&C project, the Project Leader visited the senior management of the Master Builders' Association and the Housing Industry Association in Canberra. He explained that the project would be using the principles of the Compliance Model, and outlined the benefits its use would bring to the ATO and to the building and construction industry. Similar meetings were held with the management of comparable associations around Australia. The new efforts bore fruit; the Master Builders' Association announced its support of the work the ATO was doing in the industry and its willingness to work with the ATO to ensure cash economy practices were ended (Australian Taxation Office, 1999c).[5] It is premature to examine the effects of these complex and indirect effects of responsive regulation, but field-level ATO personnel who responded to our survey were notably positive in their assessments of how well this process proceeded and the payoffs from it. Specifically, they were asked to indicate their degree of agreement or disagreement with the statement: 'During the time I worked in the Cash Economy Building and Construction Project, I witnessed substantially improved trust and cooperation between trade associations and the Australian Taxation Office'. A majority of respondents (60%) agreed or agreed strongly whilst 26.5 per cent were undecided, and the remainder disagreed or disagreed strongly.

Whilst the broad principles of the Compliance Model are endorsed by subjects, this begs the question whether their increasing support for it in the abstract reflects detailed understanding of its principles and whether they in fact changed their work routines accordingly. Concern about these matters is heightened by comments we repeatedly heard to wit: it is 'just common sense' or 'it's what we've been doing all along'. This suggests that the more arcane aspects of the Compliance Model may have been missed by a substantial proportion of those assigned to the CE/B&C project. A team leader told us:

> [I]t's really interesting. When we did our one-to-one session, and even afterwards, one of my team members said to me [that] he wished he knew about this Compliance Model previously. Because it's not just a tool you can use in your work environment, it's a tool you can use in real life, you know, in your relationships with other people. I mean you give people a chance before you go heavy with them. It's what we've always done but all you've done now is put a name to it. You call it a Compliance Model. It's what we always used to do.

Context and Timing

We noted that favourable environmental conditions can play a critical part in an organisation's capacity to change policy directions and to construct viable new structures and practices. Use of the Compliance Model was added to an ongoing series of initiatives begun in 1997 that were aimed at increasing citizen trust and reducing cash transactions in several industries. These initiatives came in the midst of what seemed to some of those we interviewed as a period of torrential changes, nearly all of which necessitated change in work routines and skills. To this was added later the inexorable approach of the GST. By mid-1999, when we interviewed ATO operatives, expressions of anxiety and fear of being overwhelmed were commonplace.[6] For example:

> Our workload has increased. Our responsibilities have increased...The knowledge that you require to do your job properly is increasing...The biggest change in the ATO I've

> seen [however] is because of technology, not because of the Compliance Model...I'm not the best person when it comes to technology. It's going too fast for me...and I'm more reluctant to change...Now we've got the new tax system, and it is coming on top of everything else. And I just don't want to know about it yet. I really don't. I don't want to know anything about GST.

The subject is not alone in his perceptions and anxiety. Responding to twin imperatives of the push for improved efficiency provided by rapid technological change and new tax policy, the result is a marked increase in workload and efficiency by ATO personnel (Commissioner of Taxation, 2000, pp. 13-14). Along with outsourcing of work formerly carried out by government employees, hoteling or 'hot desking' has changed forever the nature of operatives' work and their interaction with supervisors and headquarters; a great deal of this now takes place electronically. For many front-line employees, one of the principal consequences is a sense of mistrust and anxiety to which the rapid approach of the GST was a major contributor.

Evaluation

The ATO evaluated its cash economy projects and reported evidence that things are working (Australian Taxation Office, 1999c, 2000). Evidence of two kinds is cited in support of this conclusion: gains in income and reported taxes by building and construction firms, and the results of an on-going series of surveys in which citizens are asked their perceptions of the ATO and its operations (Commissioner of Taxation, 2000, pp. 35-36). Both are reasonable and appropriate measures of program impact, the former because use of the Compliance Model clearly is meant to increase taxpaying and the latter because the new ATO, in time, should be seen by citizens as a more helpful and less threatening arm of government.

No data or evidence used or cited to this point as evidence of success can stand cursory methodological scrutiny, however. Although reported income is up, this increase must be seen against the backdrop of economic improvement and the upward trend in tax revenues. 'For most of the past decade, total and company tax collections have grown at a rate greater than GDP' (Commissioner of Taxation, 2000, p. 9). Since December 1996, the ATO has conducted biannual surveys to measure community perceptions of the organisation. Whilst citizen perceptions of some aspects of ATO operations have improved modestly over the past three years, 'the results to date have remained fairly constant' (Commissioner of Taxation, 2000, p. 49). Studies of samples drawn from the building and construction industry have been more promising, but failure to examine the possible influence of other factors limits confidence in these findings. The short period of time (three years) is not sufficient to warrant more than cautious optimism.

Business Owners and the 'New ATO'

Underlying our interviews with the owners of small building and construction firms is the assumption that if the Compliance Model is on the right track, there should be evidence that the word is getting out to those at whom the policy is aimed and evidence also that they are changing their perspectives. Specifically, we reasoned that if any short-term impacts of the CE/B&C project were to be apparent after less than two years duration, it should be present in the experiences and opinions of business owners who had direct contact with the ATO during this time.

Before moving to an examination of this issue, it is noteworthy that very few of those we interviewed expressed opinions of unfairness about the taxation system generally. One respondent, however, told us:

> [T]he thing that you'll find in the building industry is that they are particularly hostile to the taxation department because they sit there and they watch multinational companies paying no bloody tax at all [whilst] they are being screwed into the ground. That's where the hostility comes from. That's where a lot of the cash economy comes from, because there...is resentment...The rates are too high, [and] multinationals will not pay their taxes. And not only multinationals, there are others too. But generally the wealthy don't pay their bloody taxes, and that's where the resentment comes from.

> Q: What...could ATO do to soften this perception of unfairness in the taxation system?
> A: Charge multinational companies exactly the same rate of tax that we pay, and don't let them write off losses that everybody knows are fake. Everybody knows that these losses are paper losses. The money's being shipped out overseas. We know that, the Government knows that...But they never touch them. It is time – all over the world – if the multinationals could be pulled into line because if they pay their share, everyone else will have to – we'll all of a sudden find that everything's down to a reasonable rate. I mean, these people deal in billions of dollars not in, you know, $50,000 a year or something like. They deal in billions of dollars.
> Q: So you think the tax system generally is simply unfair?
> A: It's grossly unfair. The rich pay nothing.
> Q: *Grossly* unfair?
> A: Grossly unfair. It's to the point of nearly being highway robbery. The middle and lower income earners are paying for everything. The rich at the top they don't. They write it off on schemes. They can afford fancy accountants and all the rest of it. The rest of us can't...It's ridiculous.

This subject was virtually alone in his charge that the taxation system is distributively unfair.

Most business owners were less critical of the taxation system overall and directed their criticism at the ATO specifically. They were mistrustful and cynical about it and its policies. A substantial proportion believe that little good and potentially a great deal of trouble and lost production time can come from contacts with the ATO. One remarked:

> Q: How often does ATO come up – I realise these are unusual times because of GST coming in, right – but if you can go back to six months ago, before everyone started to worry about GST, how often does ATO come up in conversation on the job?
> A: Hardly ever...
> Q: When it does come up, what is the general tenor of comments about the ATO?
> A: Fear. ...Probably it's the fear of the unknown, you know. We all reckon that public

servants are arrogant pricks anyway that really don't know what they're doing, and the only reason they're there is because they couldn't make it in the real world...That's the sort of attitude because when – if you talk to anybody that's met them, that's how they come over. It's like a policeman standing there...and everybody fears a policeman, don't they? Doesn't matter whether you're not doing anything or whether you were, you know...[Y]ou think, 'what have I done wrong?'. And you get the same sort of thing when they mention the ATO or the tax department. 'What in the hell have I done wrong now?'. And that's the reason – they're not there to help you, they're there to nail you.

Another and unusually clear representation of this was given by a plumber who was interviewed along with his business partner and mate on their job site:

I mean, it's all too hard: that something that should be so simple is made so hard. On top of going to work and making a living, we're expected to work all our tax out and everything else out, and it's that bloody complicated. Chartered accountants can't work it out who are trained to do that. And yet they want us to do it. I mean, like, how many of those guys can come and put up gutters and dig trenches and lay plumbing? Fucking none of them! But they expect us to be able to do it – to keep our books in – in absolute perfect order.

The Tax Office is very inflexible when it comes to listening to any reasons why – it's not like dealing with anybody else. I mean, it's basically, 'You were due to pay that on the 21st'. And this one young lady...I spoke to her and I said, 'Look, you know, can I have, you know, two weeks [to meet tax obligations]?'. (And I had never defaulted on my taxes.) She said, 'No, I've got a record here that you paid late the last two months'. And I said, 'Yes, but I *have* paid, and I am finding it really hard at the moment'. She said, 'No, you will pay like immediately or I'll start fining you tomorrow, and you're going to get' – I can't remember what she said – some sort of record as a problem payer...And I thought she was a very hard woman...So...yes, I lost it. I couldn't even talk to her. I hung up. Anyway, she rang me back a couple of days later, and she was a little bit nicer. But...– it had got to the point where [our business] was really struggling.

Q: What is your impression of how small business owners like yourself generally see the ATO?
A: How do we see it?
Q: Yes. Does this ever come up in conversation between you and your mates?
A: Not really, no. The consensus is everybody hates it, you know. The ATO is there to rob us of any chance of making any profit for anything, and that's it, and I think that's the consensus with most people.

Another subject commented simply that 'the public perceives them to be just a bully'.

Wariness and cynicism were not universal, however; a minority of the respondents noted that the ATO merely carries out policies enacted and modified periodically by 'politicians' (i.e., Parliament). Consequently, a subject told us: '[I]f you need any advice, then who better to go to than the ATO – apart from your own accountant. [If] there are some little things that you might want to know...the ATO will be able to tell you. So it's best to go there'.

One of the principal objectives of the Compliance Model is improved business perception of the ATO and a more cooperative culture among business owners. No one expects this will be accomplished quickly, but the Model rests on an assumption that over the long haul, its use will produce effects of this type. Our interviews focussed principally on subjects' experiences with and perceptions of the ATO over the past five years. Few of the building and construction owners were aware that the ATO had launched the Compliance Model, but a much larger number reported they had personal contacts with the ATO during this time. One of the most striking characteristics of the responses we received was the large proportion who spoke positively of the way they were treated in these contacts. A man whose business records were audited by ATO staff some ten years ago commented on the contrast between that experience and a real time review conducted by ATO approximately one year before our conversation:

> Q: You mentioned a few minutes ago that, historically, the building and construction industry is one where – you didn't say it this way, but I think this is what you meant – people are suspicious of, a bit wary, of the Australian Taxation Office?
>
> A: Years ago, yes...Up until the last few years, you know. I must admit the first time I ever got audited that they treated me like a common criminal, you know, until you're proven innocent. And consequently I had a shocking attitude to the taxation department because I just thought all they were trying to do is put you out of business...I must admit I had a shocking attitude towards them...But I think that the people that have contact with them now understand that they've got their job to do and that they are trying to be user-friendly as much as possible...I must admit, my attitude's been changed completely.

As impressive as these comments are, they and others like them are subject to a host of interpretations other than the tempting one that business owners are changing their perceptions as a result of ATO's use of the Compliance Model. The respondent was asked, for example:

> Q: Do you think getting a little bit older also has anything to do with this?
>
> A: Most certainly. Most certainly.
>
> Q: How would you interpret that?
>
> A: I just think that when you're younger you're a little bit more gung ho sort of thing...but I think as you get older you start to become a little bit wiser and start to understand, you know, they've [ATO] got their job to do and, consequently, we need to pay taxes to have all the benefits that everybody needs. You do have that [attitude]...when you're young. And that's when most companies are starting – they just want to go full on trying to get their businesses up and running, and if anybody comes in – it doesn't matter if it's the taxation department or anybody else – to interrupt what they're trying to achieve then they would try to dismiss them...And I think most people that run their businesses are inclined that way...They just don't like to be pulled up...They just want to go for it.

Our cautious interpretation of what we were told, however, should not obscure the fact that this respondent was not alone in noting that he has seen a change in the ATO. Responding to a question, another business owner commented:

> Q: Has this [most recent] contact [with ATO] in any way changed the way you think

about them?

A: Absolutely. Absolutely. Like I said...it was, first of all it was nice to see that it was actually a human being that worked for the ATO. Because as far as I always thought, they weren't humans anyway. Yes, it was nice to have somebody you could look at and actually speak to, and, yes, he was a nice guy.

Q: But when we began talking, you used some of the words that [others] have used to describe them: 'rude', 'arrogant'...

A: That's right. Yes. And that was from speaking over the phone [with them]. And...when I had this meeting with them some time ago, that was exactly the way that I'd always thought of them. Especially from that initial time [several years previously]. Yes, my perception definitely changed after having this guy here a couple of weeks ago. Like I said, he was nice, he was understanding. He explained, you know, what we wanted to know...It was good to be one-on-one and see one of these guys.

It is well to recall again that the sample of firm owners we interviewed is made up almost entirely of those with a record of compliance. This should temper our readiness to interpret these findings as indicative of success for the ATO Compliance Model. They are strongly suggestive, however.

Lessons

This research began with two overarching questions: (a) to what extent did the ATO have or acquire during the initial two years of operation of its CE/B&C project capacity to implement the ATO Compliance Model with a reasonable chance of success; and (b) what can be learned from the CE/B&C project initiative that could be useful now that the Compliance Model has been extended throughout the Australian Taxation Office?

Regarding the former, there is strong evidence that ATO executives supported the Compliance Model and provided adequate resources for its trial implementation. There is evidence also, albeit considerably weaker, that field-level staff gradually warmed to the approach although they continue to harbour ambivalence about it and reservations about its long-term impact. The Compliance Model was adopted by the ATO during a time of considerable external change and uncertainty, and it can be extremely difficult to isolate and determine the effects of new policies under conditions such as these. The ATO was powerless to maintain for the CE/B&C project an environment in which it could function smoothly and reflectively. The problems, however, are not confined to the absence of stable environmental conditions; the Compliance Model was adopted at a time of change and uncertainty within the ATO as well. Management initiatives to increase employee productivity coupled with changes in employee work routines contributed to pervasive uncertainty and stress.

For reasons presumably diverse and complex, some conditions important for achievement of reform initiatives did not materialise, however. Plans for evaluating the CE/B&C project were not built in and were hampered in any case by shortcomings in routine data collection and management capabilities. The ATO's Case Management Reports and Analysis system (CaMRA) is a case in point.

CaMRA was designed for reporting in the area of withholding tax, and only later was modified for use in other areas of taxation. The modifications, however, were stop gap in nature, and the finished product was unsatisfactory. When applied to the CE/B&C project, the resulting system of data and case management was of limited utility both for ATO personnel and for those who would use it to examine the implementation and effectiveness of the ATO Compliance Model. It proved unreliable as a guide for drawing our sample of firms with variable intensity of contact with the ATO during the preceding two years, and even efforts to determine how many RTRs were conducted during the same period yielded inconsistent numbers. Despite indications of considerable organisational capacity for responsive regulation, the ATO probably will not know with any degree of confidence how well the program operated.

What lessons can be drawn from the CE/B&C project that may be of value now that the ATO has extended the Compliance Model to all areas of compliance assurance? Clearly, new policies and procedures for evaluating them should be launched at one and the same time. This was not done when the ATO moved to responsive regulation of the small building and construction industry. One possible consequence of this is limited gain in knowledge of how to implement and make work soundly new policies. An interview subject told us:

> I think the biggest problem in the office is that we always go – we don't have balance. We go all or nothing. So, we go Compliance Model…'This is the be all and the end all, and it's happening today, and everybody will live and breathe it'. And that was the message that was put out: 'You will live the Compliance Model'…It should be – and I am not sure how to achieve it – a more subtle thing; it should be built, and it shouldn't just be bang, thrown on the table and 'here, take it away. This is what you have got to do'. We do a lot of things that way. The Office seems to always work that way; if it is going to start something it doesn't pilot it, it doesn't test it, it goes for it.

Although this subject may be unaware of it, his comments on the importance of testing new programs carefully and rigorously is disputed by few policy analysts. Not only should they be tested, but procedures for doing so and a clear understanding of the specific kinds of data to be collected should be built into the program from the outset. Decisions about the kinds of evidence that will be taken as a sign of success or failure should be reflected in routine record keeping. Whether or not the turbulent environment conditions in which the ATO has operated in recent years and its own unsettled internal worlds would have made possible anything more than was done is unknown, but the ATO's evaluation studies and the results of this research are cause for modest optimism.

Notes

1 Several months before it adopted the ATO Compliance Model, the ATO issued the Taxpayers' Charter (Australian Taxation Office, 1997). Seen as a covenant with taxpayers, it spells out their rights and obligations and the options available to them should they be dissatisfied with their treatment by the ATO.

2 This low response rate leaves us unable to assume confidently that those who returned the survey are representative of all who took part in the CE/B&C project. Although we can only speculate as to the reasons for it, the timing of the survey was unfortunate; by the time it was mailed to ATO personnel, the CE/B&C project had been scaled back substantially. The Compliance Model no longer was a salient issue or focus of work routines, and many ATO staff may have stopped caring about their experiences using it. In addition, the volume of e-mail field-level personnel receive daily is both sizeable and increasing, and this may make it easy to overlook or ignore messages which clearly do not require a response. The average age of the 84 survey respondents was 42.6 years, and the average length of time they were assigned to the CE/B&C project was 22.6 months. Women comprise 21 per cent of the respondents. When asked if they had worked as a supervisor at any time during the project, 34.6 per cent of the respondents answered affirmatively.

3 BISEP represented the idea that to understand the compliance of an individual or group, one needed to understand the environment in which they operated. The initials of this acronym stand for B = Business profile, I = Industry factors, S = Sociological factors, E = Economic factors and P = Psychological factors.

4 Some may see irony in the fact that the ATO Compliance Model, which highlights the importance of and the payoff from consultation, education and cooperative relationships, was adopted and implemented in a top-down, command and control fashion within the Australian Taxation Office.

5 The one building and construction industry representative we interviewed was quite positive in his comments about responsive regulation as he had experienced it. He was impressed particularly by the willingness of ATO personnel to attend meetings of their organisation, to do presentations as part of the meeting program, and afterwards to answer questions posed by builders in attendance.

6 In 30 years research, the senior author rarely has encountered the level of unease and anxiety expressed in interviews with ATO field-level personnel. Whether this results from unfamiliarity with academic investigators or from the pace of change in their work day, many of those we interviewed seemed unusually jittery.

References

Australian Taxation Office (1997), *Taxpayers' Charter*, Australian Taxation Office, Canberra.

_____ (1999a), 'Introduction to Real Time Reviews: Facilitation Guide', Eastern Building and Construction Team, Canberra.

_____ (1999b), 'National Quality Assurance Program for Building and Construction Work (Real Time Reviews)', Small Business Line, Canberra.

_____ (1999c), 'Building and Construction Project Evaluation Report', Compliance Assurance, Small Business Line (December), Canberra.

_____ (2000), 'Final Report Following Early Closure of Project (Painters Sub-industry, NSW)', Australian Taxation Office, Canberra.

Bardach, E. (2000), *A Practical Guide for Policy Analysis,* Chatham House, New York.

Braithwaite, J., Walker, J. and Grabosky, P. (1987), 'An Enforcement Taxonomy of Regulatory Agencies', *Law and Policy*, vol. 9, pp. 322-51.

Cash Economy Task Force (1997), 'Compliance Model: An Hierarchical Approach to Tax Compliance', Australian Taxation Office, Canberra.

Cash Economy Task Force (1998), *Improving Tax Compliance in the Cash Economy*, Australian Taxation Office, Canberra.

Commissioner of Taxation (2000), *Annual Report 1999-2000*, Commonwealth of Australia, Canberra.

Grabosky, P. and Braithwaite, J. (1986), *Of Manners Gentle: Strategies of Australian Business Regulatory Agencies*, Oxford University Press, Oxford.

Gunningham, N. and Grabosky, P. (1998), *Smart Regulation: Designing Environmental Policy*, Clarendon, United Kingdom.

Job, J. and Honaker, D. (Chapter 6, this volume), 'Short-term Experiences with Responsive Regulation in the Australian Taxation Office'.

Weiss, C.H. (1998), *Evaluation* (2nd ed), Prentice-Hall, Upper Saddle River.

Chapter 9

Large Business and the Compliance Model

John Braithwaite[1]

Setting the Scene

In April 1998 the Cash Economy Task Force (1998) produced an influential Australian report entitled *Improving Tax Compliance in the Cash Economy*. *Improving Tax Compliance in the Cash Economy* proposed a new Compliance Model for the Australian Taxation Office (ATO) with four elements: (a) understanding taxpayer behaviour; (b) building community partnerships; (c) increased flexibility in ATO operations to encourage and support compliance; and (d) more and escalating regulatory options to enforce compliance. During late 1998 and early 1999, the question was asked whether or not the Cash Economy Compliance Model was relevant to tax compliance for the large business market segment. At the time there were doubts.

This chapter opens up some issues for consideration about applying the model to the ATO's compliance work on large business. Preliminary examination revealed that the four elements of the model mentioned above all have relevance to large business, though a different kind of relevance than in the case of the cash economy. This chapter is structured around considering each of these elements in turn. The spirit of the chapter is to identify a number of policy ideas that might give meaningful content to the model in the large business context.

The Compliance Problem in Large Business?

'Compliance means that taxpayers are meeting their obligations in accordance with the *Income Tax Assessment Act*, regulations and court decisions.' This is the definition adopted by one influential ATO large business report on 'Staff Perceptions of the Compliance Behaviour of the Top 100 Companies Audited Under the Large Case Program' (Australian Taxation Office, 1995). The report went on to show that in the large corporate domain ATO staff adopted a more purposive view of compliance than the somewhat literalist view in the above definition. That is, ATO staff working on the Large Case Program were looking for compliance with the spirit of the law or the policy purpose intended by the parliament. Doreen McBarnet's (1992) British work (see McBarnet, Chapter 11, this volume) has shown that large corporates themselves tend to be literalists because their modus operandi is to choose, depending on their interests, among five options: (a) comply with the intention of the law; (b) compromise by negotiating how a particular law works under particular circumstances and making a deal on how it will be applied; (c) comply with the letter of the law in such a way that the declared objectives of the law may not be met (McBarnet calls this compliance in form); (d) transform the legal rules, through lateral thinking, into positive routes for tax avoidance; and (e) break or ignore the law and hope not to be caught. This could include the preparation of secondary accounts to cover any tracks (Williams, 1995). McBarnet (1992) found that large corporations tended to pursue a strategy of compliance in form to achieve two things:

> If successful, it allows taxpayers to escape tax...But at the same time, whether successful in that first goal or not, it allows them to escape any risk of stigma or penalty (p. 334).

In light of the above, an ATO compliance objective could be *compliance with the purposes of tax law, while working to increase the certainty with which those purposes can be applied in practice.* An alternative objective would focus on 'dollar-based information...as potentially ambiguous risk management data rather than unambiguous taxpayer compliance data' (Wickerson, 1993, p. 7). Such an objective that bypasses the concept of compliance might be *reducing risks to the revenue while upholding the requirements of tax law and increasing the certainty of that law.*

Enforcement

Although this chapter will argue that the ATO Compliance Model provides a valuable framework for large business compliance work, the concepts and enforcement strategies through which one escalates in a large corporate compliance pyramid will be found to be quite different from those in a cash economy compliance pyramid. For example, at the peak of the ATO's Compliance Model enforcement pyramid, the ATO confronts disengagers from the tax system using a prosecutorial strategy. Many individual taxpayers and small businesses do opt out of the tax system altogether. Even some larger businesses that we call organised crime (but that in reality is rather disorganised) do this. They do not play the game, sometimes because they are so cynical or disenchanted about it, sometimes to evade it in a calculative way. But some large businesses, on the other hand, are quintessential game players. At the peak of the large business enforcement challenge are the most entrepreneurial of the players of the tax planning game. Disengagement is not a major source of non-compliance here.

There is no problem with adapting the ATO Compliance Model to this reality of large corporate compliance. The idea of a compliance pyramid is that all compliance staff will discover a content for it that is relevant to the context in which they work. It is not a recipe book but a model to guide strategic thinking.

The deeper question about the model for the compliance of large businesses is that it tends to assume that the majority of taxpayers want to comply and as we move up to more and more serious tax evasion, there are fewer and fewer taxpayers in this category. Evidence on individual taxpayers suggests that this assumption is fairly accurate. For example, US audit evidence has been used to conclude that about two-thirds of individual taxpayers intend to pay the right tax (some of them inadvertently cheat), but only a third of individual taxpayers actually set out to cheat in a significant way (and then to varying degrees) (Andreoni, Erard and Feinstein, 1998, p. 820).

With large corporations in Australia, it is clear that many more than two-thirds of taxpayers intend to comply with the letter of the law, or at least to have a 'reasonably arguable position' that they have done so most of the time. However, it seems equally clear that there are many who do not intend to comply with what the ATO regards as the policy purposes of the parliament's tax laws. The evidence for this is that more than half of them pay no tax, some for many years, which is certainly not parliament's intention.[2] Australia collects more than the Organisation for Economic Cooperation and Development (OECD) average in company tax as a proportion of all tax revenue and as a proportion of Gross Domestic Product (GDP) and is one of the few countries in the late 1990s that saw corporate tax revenues increase at a faster rate than the increase in company profits. The corporate tax collection crisis is not distinctively an Australian one.

From these known patterns of taxpaying, the fact that compliance policy must confront squarely is that while the pattern of individual compliance is broadly pyramidal, the pattern of large corporate compliance is egg-shaped, with most taxpayers playing for the grey (see Figure 9.1). Large corporate compliance strategy might be conceived as pushing the large grey bulge in the middle of the egg downwards into the white zone – so that the egg becomes a pyramid.

It is hard to make compliance strategies work when compliance behaviour is egg-shaped. As corporate compliance behaviour takes on more of a pyramidal shape, the compliance policies discussed in this chapter will progressively become more effective. The task is more daunting than for tax collection with small business and individuals because the reality of the challenge is majority non-compliance with the policy purposes of the law (at least as they are conceived by many officers of the ATO). The argument to be made here is that law reform is the first of three key circuit breakers to move that grey bulge down into the white. Two further circuit-breakers are proposed in this chapter: One is for the compliance debate to take a more democratic turn, the other is for it to take a more international turn. This chapter seeks to show that once these three circuits are broken, there are a number of more specific policy options for improving compliance.

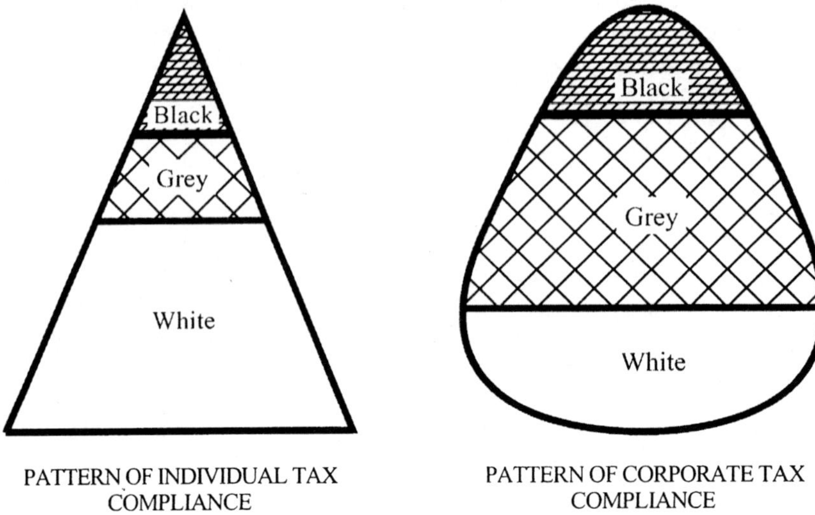

Figure 9.1 Patterns of individual and corporate tax compliance

Tax Compliance in a Democracy

The Australian people increasingly believe that large corporations and high wealth individuals do not pay the share of tax that the law says they should (Braithwaite, Reinhart, Mearns and Graham, 2001). A June 1998 community survey of 1000 Australians, commissioned by the ATO, found that only 32 per cent believed that 'Tax laws are effective in making sure large companies pay their share of tax' declining to 27 per cent for 'very wealthy people'. Only 20 per cent believed 'The ATO does a good job of stopping tax avoidance by large companies', falling to 15 per cent believing 'The ATO does a good job stopping tax avoidance by very wealthy people' (see also Wirth, 1998).

Such perceptions are a major risk to voluntary compliance by individual taxpayers. The reason is that there is evidence that individuals are more willing to pay their taxes honestly when they perceive most others to be honest; this evidence suggests that the direction of causality here is that when citizens perceive most others to be cheating, they are more likely to cheat themselves (Levi, 1988; Scholz, 1998; see also Cowell, 1990).

Perceptions are so entrenched that it is past the point of government trying to pretend to the Australian people that all large corporations are paying a share of the tax burden commensurate with the share of Pay-As-You-Go (PAYG) taxpayers. The better way to manage this risk to the revenue is to be open with the Australian people about the depth of the problem. This means explaining to them that it is not that companies are cheating in large numbers. It is that some large corporations are aggressively planning their way around Australian law and moving profits and losses around the globe to limit tax liability.

The Judiciary in a Democracy and Tax Compliance

Of equal importance, a full and frank public debate about the nature of the problem is the way to begin to bring the Australian judiciary to an understanding of their central importance to solving the problem. The behaviour of the judiciary in the aftermath of tax reform is ultimately the most critical risk in the new ATO environment. History teaches us that when judges are literalist in the way they interpret tax law, legal entrepreneurs will open up more and more loopholes in the law. Yet because judges are properly independent of the executive government, it is not appropriate for the ATO to 'tackle' the judiciary when they fail to interpret tax law in a more purposive way.

So another path is needed. Most Australian judges believe in the sovereignty of parliament or the sovereignty of the Australian people or both. A tax compliance debate that engages the parliament with the desire of its people, openly expressed, that the law be interpreted to require large corporations to pay the share of tax the law intends is the best way to seek to move judges who believe in a sovereign parliament responding to a sovereign people. The judges understand that a literalist approach to tax adjudication can survive while tax law remains arcane to the people; equally, they understand that judicial repute suffers in the democracy when this approach is later discredited in the eyes of the people and their parliament, as happened to the Australian judiciary in the 1980s (Levi, 1988). In the long run, court cases like the recent Packer saga, which led to Australia's richest person being accused in the press of paying virtually no tax, are corrosive of respect of the people for the law and the courts.[3] The more open the public debate on tax law, the more clear it will be to the judiciary why this is so, and the more pointedly will they grasp the necessity and propriety of their being more purposive and less literalist readers of tax law.

Margaret Levi's (1988) analysis of the 1983-85 tax reform debate is that it engaged the Australian people in a way that increased their preparedness to comply with the tax laws. Part of this accomplishment was that they did see the Barwick (literalist) era of judicial interpretation in tax matters, of which they came to disapprove, come to an end.

Understanding Taxpayer Behaviour

Perhaps this first element of the compliance framework should be conceived more broadly as 'Understanding the Tax System'. The ATO Compliance Model does take a broad view of what understanding taxpayer behaviour means, that is, understanding individual and business behaviour in the context of an industry, macroeconomic and sociological environment. This is what is referred to as BISEP[4] in the ATO Compliance Model. The key addition for the large corporate sector is understanding compliance in an international environment. There needs to be understanding, for example, that the taxpaying behaviour of a Japanese transnational corporation in Japan is different from its taxpaying behaviour in other countries.

The ATO approach to understanding taxpayer behaviour is risk management of a tax system. The ATO has been influenced by voluntary Australian Standard 4360, which identifies the stages in risk management in Figure 9.2.

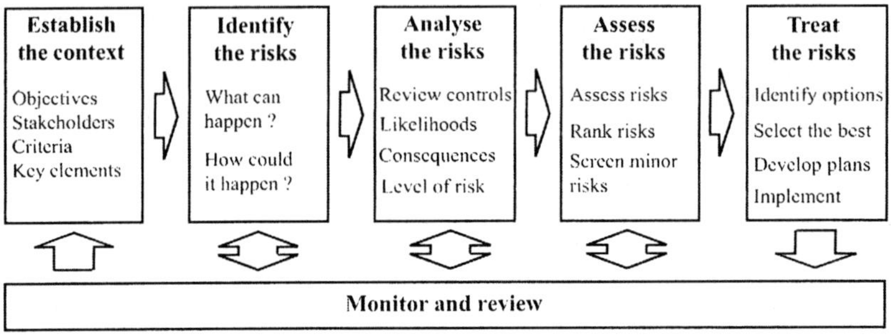

Figure 9.2 Stages of risk management (from Grey and Cooper, 1998)

The ATO generally has done a good job of the first four stages of this process, particularly at a strategic and organisational level, but is only beginning to do a good job on the fifth stage (Treat the Risk), and is still doing a poor job on the final stage (Monitor and Review). In establishing the context, identifying the risks and analysing the risks, the ATO has the advantage of being an unusually knowledge-rich organisation. It takes research seriously. While there are gaps in this knowledge which need to be filled, the bigger challenge is to find existing knowledge and synthesise its implications.

While ATO staff are increasingly on top of risk analysis and assessment, mostly they do not operate by searching and seizing opportunities to leverage those risks. Ask in a large business industry segment in the ATO whether they have assessed and ranked risks and they will pull out a document that shows where they have done that. This is genuinely impressive. But ask fieldwork or management staff to tell you the best stories of how they have leveraged each of those risks and only some will enthuse with their triumphs.

Risk leveraging is a creative activity. It requires creative staff. It is a bad idea to provide a formula for how to do it because advisers will soon learn that formula. Continuous reinvention of risk leveraging is what will keep them guessing and therefore complying. A culture of continuous reinvention of risk leveraging seems to us to require taking storytelling more seriously within a tax authority. The ATO has begun to move away from being a business run according to a procedures manual (see Job and Honaker, Chapter 6, this volume). At the level of informal staff interaction, ATO culture is no longer just a rulebook, it is also a storybook.

Some staff see ATO management culture, in contrast, as a thicket of models (an observation also made by Job and Honaker, Chapter 6, this volume). The challenge is to value stories that make sense of models and models that provide a conceptual scheme for generating better stories. One staff response to the roll-out of the ATO Compliance Model was: 'Oh no, not another model. Now a [ATO] Compliance Model to add to Risk Assessment,...System Analysis and Planning, Strategic Direction, Performance Management, Business Systems models, Accountability and Governance, and on and on'. Our suggestion is that the approach to moving the ATO risk management model beyond risk assessment to risk leveraging is to create a framework for storytelling about compliance successes. Some leading corporations, such as 3-M, have come to the conclusion that an excess of abstraction is their problem and have taken the remedy so far as to write their strategic plan in storytelling fashion (Shaw, Brown and Bromiley, 1998). The rationale for the storytelling approach lies in optimising human capacity for not only digesting information but also acting on it.

> Stories are central to human intelligence and memory. Cognitive scientist William Calvin describes how we gradually acquire the ability to formulate plans through the stories we hear in childhood. From stories, a child learns to 'imagine a course of action, imagine its effects on others, and decide whether or not to do it'...Cognitive scientists have established that lists, in contrast, are remarkably hard to remember...(Shaw, Brown and Bromiley, 1998, p. 42).

There are two interconnected staff morale rationales for considering a storytelling culture. One is that staff grapple with many models that are often presented to them abstractly rather than as stories. The second is that there is the feeling that those who are playing an aggressive game are winning. Hence, a framework for storytelling *with stories of success* that bring to life models, such as the ATO risk management model, are needed. A suggestion is therefore that parts of the ATO that are not already doing so conduct regular informal workshops which give staff a platform to share their latest success stories. This means a different kind of best practice workshop than sometimes happened in the past, one that is less oriented to concepts and models of best practice and more oriented to stories of best practice (from which an understanding of models flows). Each ATO large business segment would then select its best success stories and the ones that supply lessons of more general applicability for best practice workshops. A consequence of such a culture change would be that 'heroes' of risk leveraging success stories would be noticed in a way that would percolate into their performance reviews.

Our analysis, in summary, is that the abstractness of ATO risk assessment might be a roadblock to the contextual staff creativity that moves into risk leveraging. In the next stage of the development of a compliance framework, one suggestion would be for a document more dotted with success stories than this one. Perhaps that is an imprudent suggestion given the difficulty in rendering large business stories anonymous. Perhaps it would be more appropriately cautious about confidentiality to sustain storytelling only as an oral tradition for those staff dealing with large business tax compliance. But at the least, our recommendation would be that it be a more deeply institutionalised oral tradition – a proliferation of storytelling best practice workshops that illuminate broad strategic issues.

A move to institutionalising ATO culture more as a storybook (Shearing and Ericson, 1991) than a rulebook or a model-book is not to downplay the importance of rules and models. Internal rules and models will be more sensible when they connect with a more bottom-up process of reflection on accumulations of success stories. Risk leveraging occurs at two levels. One is at the level of clinical analysis of cases of single corporations – for example, diagnosing patterns of imbalance among corporate PAYG receipts and wages paid, Goods and Services Tax (GST) receipts and income tax to inform a risk leveraging prognosis to heal the ailing taxpayer. The second level is cross-case leveraging through more quantitative analysis of strategies (see Braithwaite, Pittelkow and Williams, Chapter 10, this volume).

The risk leveraging skill at the first level is the skill of the clinician who heals one patient. That is the level most informed by storytelling. The second level requires the skill of the medical researcher who finds generic therapies that will be valuable for curing many patients. That is the level most informed by number crunching.

Tax authorities worldwide develop statistical models akin to a regression equation. For example, given what is known about the income of this company, the proportion of its activities based offshore, the industry sector it is in, movements in its stock price, the various ratings it has received by ratings agencies, and certain other pieces of known information, is it paying less company tax than the model predicts or more? Those that are paying a great deal less tax than the model predicts can then be approached to seek explanation and possibly be audited.

Watching an industry or other group of taxpayers can also be done to diagnose risk with the techniques of the detective, akin to the clinical skills of the doctor discussed earlier. The officer scans the horizon for information on industry developments that might have tax implications. A new subsidiary is opened in the Bahamas. Three industry leaders have a secret meeting in which they agree not to compete on tax planning; they will all pay around 10 per cent so that they have enough for their franking credits. A new CEO with a reputation for aggressive tax planning is appointed to a formerly conservative company. Detection of these developments leads to real time enquiries (as opposed to an audit years later) that prevent tax losses before they occur.

Building trust is and should be a fundamental value of tax authorities. When a relationship of trust is built with a particular client, this can be drawn on to leverage compliance. Once there is trust, that trust is a resource that has benefits to both sides (Ayres and Braithwaite, 1992, Chapter 2). Those benefits imply a cost to breach of trust. Good tax office staff learn how to use their relationships to make judgments as to when they can rely on that trust to leverage risk (just ask that it be done), when it is best to 'trust but verify', and when it is best to withhold trust. We should never forget that cooperative relationships are the best source of evidence of what is going on in the business world. Even the best detectives are trusted by a lot of criminals. More importantly, however, the evidence from the research program of the Australian National University research group on business regulatory compliance is that when regulators treat regulatees as trustworthy, they actually behave in a more trustworthy fashion (Braithwaite and Levi, 1998). More specifically, treating business as trustworthy does increase their subsequent compliance with the law (Braithwaite and Makkai, 1994).

It would be a mistake to see the regression-, detective-, and trust-based risk leveraging approaches as only about the targeting of taxpayers. If regression analyses show that all 30 of the clients of a particular adviser are way below the regression line, it may be more efficient to target enforcement against one adviser than 30 taxpayers. The same point applies with detective- and trust-based analyses of intelligence. So there may be virtue in considering a strategic intelligence matrix of the form illustrated in Table 9.1.

Table 9.1 Illustrative matrix of regression-based, detective-based and trust-based leveraging of risks posed by imaginary taxpayer, agent and adviser to that taxpayer

	Taxpayer	Agent	Adviser
Regression	Below line	Average	90% of clients below line
Detective	No intelligence	No intelligence	Rumoured to be promoting a new dubious scheme
Trust	Trust but verify	Trustworthy	Breach of trust with ATO in past

An intelligence assessment of this table quickly leads to the conclusion that this taxpayer is not a good target for audit or some other form of monitoring. Nor is the agent who submits the taxpayer's return. However, the adviser this taxpayer uses is a prime target for risk leveraging, one reason being that our presently honest taxpayer may be at risk of being tempted by the adviser's dubious new tax planning scheme. For certain kinds of compliance strategies (e.g. a letter to request that a certain matter has been checked), the trustworthy agent may be the better target precisely because they have a stronger interest in maintaining their reputation with the ATO as trustworthy than does the taxpayer. There is a growing literature on when it is better to target gatekeepers and when it is better to target principals (Kraakman, 1984; Braithwaite, 1997). Our main point here is that the 'Understanding Taxpayer Behaviour' element of the ATO Compliance Model should be conceived broadly to include an understanding of the behaviour of gatekeepers to taxpayers.

Evidence Based Tax Administration: Learning from Medicine

It was not until 1914 that in the average encounter between a doctor and a patient the patient was more likely to come away better off than worse off. Unfortunately with law enforcement, we have probably not yet reached 1914. If we put more police into a neighbourhood, we are just as likely to increase the crime rate as to reduce it. The reason is that, like doctors with leeches, police do a lot of things that make crime worse (as well as a lot that makes it better).

Law enforcement needs to learn two things from medicine. One big step medicine took toward making us healthier early this century was a research investment in randomised controlled trials of its risk leveraging strategies. If it believed a particular therapy or a particular pill would outperform existing therapies, it would randomly assign a large group of patients to the new treatment versus the old. In effect, this meant tossing a coin to decide whether patients got the currently popular therapy or the new one. With a large enough sample, the miracle of randomisation delivered two groups that were exactly comparable in every way other than the treatment. If fewer patients died under the new therapy, then we could be fairly sure that the therapy was the reason. This was the big advance over the old science that allowed quacks to delude themselves into believing that when patients got better after being treated with leeches that it was the leeches that cured them. Or when they died that the leeches had not been applied early and often enough.

As more and more therapeutic advances increased our life expectancy, medicine's new problem was of *too much* knowledge. Most doctors were not up-to-date with what science was finding. So a new evidence-based medicine movement to get the results of science through to doctors in a digestible form began: A science of diffusing science through soft networks of revered peers. The nation that ventures into an evidence-based tax administration comparable to evidence-based medicine is likely to become the cutting edge. Evidence-based tax administration will be much cheaper than evidence-based medicine and much less fraught with ethical dilemmas.

Imagine a tax authority comes up with an idea for a new auditing product, which it believes will improve compliance at lower cost. Some people think they are wrong, others that they are right. A new evidence-based Commissioner sees that there are some good arguments on both sides. Moreover, they both have equally good arguments as to why their approach would be procedurally fairer and cheaper for taxpayers, so there are no ethical arguments against experimentation. There are resources available for 200 audits where this kind of audit is relevant. So the Commissioner requires that a risk analysis select the 200 most suitable targets for audit. A random number generator then assigns 100 of these cases to the new audit product and 100 to the old audit.

Where there are one or two extremely large or atypical corporations these might be excluded from the experiment on grounds that if both ended up in the same group, this would skew the results. Or the randomisation can block on them, so that it is guaranteed that one will go into the experimental group, the other into the control group. Absent such extraordinary lumpiness, the laws of probability prove that randomly assigning two hundred companies or two hundred individuals is almost certain to produce two groups with almost identical breakdowns on average income, age, sex, in fact anything we can measure and check (and everything that we cannot measure and check). The only reason for a difference in tax paid by the two groups is that one gets the old style audit rather than the new style audit. There is no need for complicated multiple regression analysis. Tax officers just count how much money comes through the door from the new audit group compared to the old audit group.

An even better research design will require a risk assessment to identify the 300 best targets for auditing. Then the computer will assign 100 to the new audit, 100 to the old audit, 100 to no audit. It might be that even though the new audit brings in more tax than the old audit, over a three year follow up, neither group outperforms the 'no audit' group. The reason might be that the 'no audit' group are afraid of an audit in years two and three, while the audit groups believe they get a free kick for those two years.

Under both research designs it is possible to test which is the cheaper process to run without having to contend with doubters who say the new process was cheaper only because it was tried out on less complicated audits. Randomisation will have assured that on average the new and old groups are of equal complication.

In few areas of problem-solving could randomised controlled trials be more viable than in tax administration. It has been necessary to the advancement of medicine to randomly assign sick patients to a placebo (an inert pill) or to no treatment when they might have been helped. While many of us are alive today because this was done, it raised awful ethical dilemmas. There is not this level of ethical dilemma in randomly assigning a high risk taxpayer to miss out on an audit. There would be in a world where the community regarded it as just that all high risk taxpayers should be audited. The world of tax is not such a world – the supply of compliance work is always less than the need for it; a high risk company that is randomly assigned to no audit this year can always be purposively assigned to audit next year or the year after or both. However high their risk, a tax authority cannot afford to audit them every year.

Many other kinds of compliance initiatives have the same character as audit in these regards. Consider, for example, an interesting initiative of simply writing to companies in the manufacturing sector that have paid no tax for three years to say that the ATO is concerned about this situation and requests them to write with an indication of whether they think their circumstances will change such that they will be paying some tax next year. The hypothesis is that the fear that they are being monitored in some special way will cause them to pay more tax in the next year. 100 companies could be randomly assigned to no letter and no audits; 100 companies to the letter and X audits for those who fail to reply with an indication that they expect to pay tax next year; 100 to no letter and X audits; 100 to the letter and no audits. This design would enable an assessment of whether the (practically costless) strategy of getting the computer to send a hundred letters increases tax receipts even without backing them up with audits for those who ignore them. Or whether this would only work when coupled with a commitment to do something if tax did not come in.

A major advantage that tax has in enabling randomised controlled trials in comparison with medicine is that it has the entire population of taxpayers on the computer, so randomisation with high external validity can be done at low cost. Most people who do not have experience of randomisation doubt that with corporations you would get an experimental group and a control group that would be identical on relevant characteristics. A needed confidence-building measure is to ask the doubters to name the variables on which the experimental group might end up different from the control group. The data would be collected to show that the two groups had the same value on average for these measures.

Building Community Partnerships

Building community partnerships is the second element of the ATO Compliance Model. Indeed this model itself was the product of a community partnership, with active and constructive participation by business, non-government organisations (NGOs) and professions.

In the next section on increasing the flexibility of tax office operations we consider the idea of not only co-designing compliance strategies with industry in the way this is already being done, but also using external stakeholders as 'test pilots' of the new designs when they are first put into the field. Partnership with the judiciary is out of the question from a separation of powers perspective. However, as argued in the early part of this chapter, there is a need for a richer dialogue among community-ATO-parliament, carried forward at public conferences and in the media, to which the judiciary is exposed and chooses to respond as it sees appropriate.

A dilemma of business-industry partnership is that business norms are not pro-tax, but anti-tax (witness the egg-shape of compliance in Figure 9.1). A risk of partnership, therefore, is that the tax office will be captured by an anti-taxpaying culture. One idea for a new paradigm of community partnership to respond to this change of capture would, we suspect, be premature until some of the other strategies in this chapter were given more time to work. This is the idea of the government negotiating with the business community a *compliance-tax-rate-spiral*. The reason it may be a bad idea at this time is that there are too many corporations presently paying no tax who therefore have no interest in trading off higher compliance for lower company tax rates. However, floating the possibility of a *compliance-tax-rate-spiral* as something that might work in future could encourage public-regarding business taxpayers to see that in the long run there is much that Australian business could gain from a more cooperative compliance culture.

So how would a *compliance-tax-rate-spiral* work? The tax authority would set say five quantitative corporate compliance benchmarks. They would be benchmarks that involved an estimate of the extra dollars brought in by improved compliance. As each benchmark was met, the government's promise would be to reduce company tax rates by 2 per cent. If all five corporate compliance benchmarks were surpassed, the company tax rate would fall by 10 per cent. The compliance benchmarks would be set so that the aggregate increase in revenue from increased tax and increased penalties on non-compliers at each benchmark would be calibrated at the cost of a 2 per cent tax cut. It would be highly desirable to incorporate tax penalties into the formula because this would give community-minded businesses an incentive to lend political support to higher penalties for non-compliers (that would be returned to compliers in lower tax rates). Business partnerships might be built on reversing the existing reality where non-compliers do not pay and compliers make up for it, with a mechanism where non-compliers pay monies that are channeled directly to compliers.

While the government would generate no extra revenue by giving back all the gains from higher compliance and higher penalties in lower tax rates, it would generate a little extra revenue as the compliance rate moved up between benchmarks. Both business and the ATO would benefit from lower tax administration costs as the system moved to a more cooperative, less combative, compliance regime. But most importantly, business and government would both benefit from the higher income that a low tax, low litigation, high compliance compact would bring.

The idea for the moment would be to do no more than introduce this into the debate. Not something that seems plausible, but something that signals the kind of world that might one day be possible if only we can learn how to forge a more meaningful business-community-government partnership toward a decent tax system.

Why call this a *compliance-tax-rate-spiral*? We assume two things. First, once the difficult challenge of achieving the first compliance benchmark had been met and the first tax cut delivered, momentum toward achieving the second benchmark would be easier – a virtuous circle that would feed upon itself. Once cooperative businesses had tasted the benefits of an initial 2 per cent tax cut, they might even lobby for higher tax penalties (all of which would be returned to them) to deliver more quickly the next 2 per cent cut. Increased compliance would not depend upon industry associations compelling their members to improve their compliance. It would depend on: (a) changing the nature of the social bargain between business and government (Levi, 1988) so that business actually wanted to comply with the law; (b) changing business culture so that business leaders disapproved of their business colleagues who did not comply with the law (as free riders on the rest of the business community and obstructers of national economic growth); and (c) business leaders politically supporting higher tax penalties and other measures to enforce the law against the grey economy (such as providing intelligence on dubious tax planning schemes to the ATO).

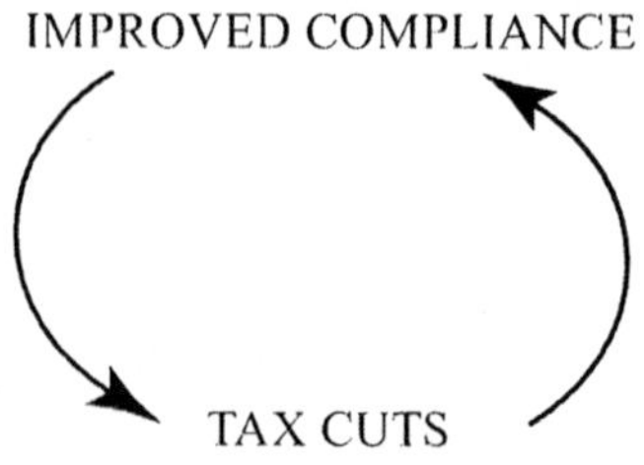

Figure 9.3 The Compliance-Tax-Rate-Spiral

There is also an economic analysis of why the idea advanced here is a *compliance-tax-rate-spiral.* There is empirical evidence that as tax rates fall, compliance becomes economically rational for more individual taxpayers and voluntary compliance increases (Friedland, Maital and Rutenberg, 1978; Clotfelter, 1983; Baldry, 1987; Alm, Jackson and McKee, 1992; Williams, 1995; Joulfaian and Rider, 1996; Andreoni, Erard and Feinstein, 1998; but see Feinstein, 1991; Alm, Bahl and Murray, 1993). Hence the virtuous circle is set up (see Figure 9.3). A cut in the tax rate increases voluntary compliance and the increase in voluntary compliance moves the system down the path to the next 2 per cent tax cut.

Increased Flexibility in ATO Operations to Encourage and Support Compliance

The approach of the ATO Compliance Model values flexibility, showing that there are many ways of delivering on compliance and objectives of the Taxpayers' Charter. Institutionalising a storytelling culture is one way of fostering flexibility. Success stories that grab people's interest will be stories of innovation, of more flexible responses than have been attempted in the past.

A growing source of flexibility is to take problems to international forums. The Advance Pricing Arrangement (APA, called Advanced Pricing Agreements in many countries) is one approach to locking in higher tax receipts from transnational corporations (Killaly, 1996). APAs are negotiated arrangements between the ATO and corporations on transfer pricing methodologies negotiated at the OECD, which result in an appropriate allocation of income and expenses between related parties that are selling goods or services between different countries. Negotiating APAs is painstaking work, but because they lock in higher returns than audits do and because they shift the rules of the game to more cooperative ones with business, the investment is well justified.

On the other hand, the ATO needs to monitor the cost of keeping APAs up to date in the face of company-, product- and time-specific changes that make the parameters of the APA obsolete. In addition, there was a worry that only 'squeaky clean' companies would ask for APAs, hence skewing ATO activity to areas of low risk. Initially, companies were reluctant to enter into APA negotiations because they feared this may have revealed tax liabilities going back over many years. However since then APAs have become widely used. The kind of flexibility of ATO response that could be examined is for the ATO to consider granting an amnesty on tax liabilities going back more than two years as part of the incentive for entering into negotiations. International tax competition can cause compliance problems that can only be addressed through international cooperation via forums such as the OECD and multi-lateral APAs. The same international imperatives apply with tax havens, E-commerce and a variety of other questions.

The real power to increase flexibility does not lie with senior managers so much as with fieldworkers who are daily at the coalface (Sparrow, 2000). Fieldworkers must be the key risk identifiers. Their performance reviews should give high priority to evidence of identifying wider risks in the course of their fieldwork, documenting them and following through to ensure that the risks are analysed and treated. In the view of some, this follow through is not their job. Their job is to report the risks they identify to their immediate boss so that management can take care of it. This is neither our view nor that of senior ATO management involved in large business compliance work. The ATO needs more leadership from below. Fieldworkers can often report risks to Segment Managers who can be too busy to follow through on them. It is often more efficient for the fieldworker with the direct experience of the risk to chase it up through the bureaucracies, to participate in the senior discussions there on what can be done to treat it and then to offer to be a 'test pilot' for the treatment – to report back whether the treatment is working with the initial kind of risk they identified. Better still, the fieldworker might recruit one of the clients they work with to be an external test pilot as well, and also participate in the discussion at senior levels concerning the problem they have decided to own.

If tax professionals at all levels of the ATO from fieldworkers up are encouraged to be leaders (see Job and Honaker, Chapter 6, this volume), to own risks with a commitment to follow through all the stages of risk management, then loop closing will improve. Most critically, the law reform loop will respond faster, and fieldworker morale will improve compared to a situation where they sit on their hands and grumble about management dropping the ball. What follows is that the tax authority storytelling culture needs to be about stories of junior employees being rewarded in performance reviews for following risks right through to treatment and evaluation. In few areas is this more important than law improvement.

Flexible Adjustment of Tax Law

In the midst of the wave of tax law reform currently being experienced in Australia we must remember that it is naïve to believe that we can ever reform tax law and get it right in a way that will remain right for long. Nothing is more important to improving corporate tax compliance than law reform. But the reality is that as soon as the new law is in place, there will be legal entrepreneurs who will be at work to open up loopholes in it, and globalisation will over time deliver changes that will make it progressively obsolete. So law reform is not the task of an historic moment, but a continuous process.

The ship of tax reform needs to be continually rebuilt at sea as legal entrepreneurs open up one leak after another. Every decade or so the accumulation of extra pieces added to the ship to plug these holes will start to weigh it down with an excessive burden of complexity. The ship then has to be taken into dock and rebuilt from the ground up in a more simplified way. The most crucial assessment of the health of the system must involve a sophisticated group looking periodically at the ship to assess whether the overall pattern of its complexity justifies such a systemic legal refit. Plugging holes at sea and periodic simplifications of the whole structure are both recurrently necessary because an accumulation of new rules to plug old loopholes can be a resource for opening up new loopholes. Complexity favours the legal entrepreneurs. The objective is to give the judges only as much detail as they need to apply the policy purposes of the law with as much certainty as is possible for the contrived uniqueness of the circumstances with which they are continually presented (see McBarnet, Chapter 11, this volume).

The job of fieldworkers is to be the antennae that detect those risky new contrivances as early as possible. A good auditor has the ability to see that an issue that has come up in an audit will be a risk to the revenue in many other cases unless the law is clarified or improved. Provision exists for auditors to identify risks on case files that are available for computer analysis to group problems that are looking for common solutions. The culture change needed is one where writing down the risk is just the beginning of a process for the fieldworker of following the risk through to ensure there is a ruling or litigation to clarify the case law, an actual change in the law, or a principled decision to let the risk sit there until the next comprehensive reform of the law. At every stage the fieldworker has a role as a reality tester for the lawyers, as an antenna to detect the latest manoeuvre of the other side and as a test pilot for the proposed legal remedy.

Tax law will become more certain and effective when fieldworkers are engaged with the daunting challenge of continuous improvement of a living law rather than the narrow challenge of enforcing a static law. It will become even more certain and effective if fieldworkers engage the public-regarding side of large business at the coalface, where the problem in the law breaks out, to help repair the law in the public interest. Law reform in the past has been too top-down and insufficiently continuous. Also, as argued at the beginning of the chapter, it has not engaged the people of Australia in public discussion and understanding often enough. The ATO needs to persuade the people of Australia that more equitable and certain enforcement of the tax law is something they can reasonably demand of their institutions – the parliament, the judiciary and the ATO. By articulating forcefully to the Australian people that the ATO does not want to be let off the hook for tax integrity, it makes it harder for the parliament and judiciary to be allowed off the hook (which to a significant extent they have been in the past).

It is doubtful that any amount of synoptic brilliance in re-configuring tax law at one point of history can deliver Australia a high integrity tax system. Rather, what is required is for us to be more pre-emptive through a continuous improvement process of simplification-clarification-resimplification-clarification. This iterates endlessly. Commitment to excellence in the pre-emptiveness and responsiveness required for continuous improvement of tax law is the key. Australia can have a high integrity tax system, but only if the ATO, the parliament and the judiciary jointly end the buck-passing. My plea is that the ATO publicly put up its hand and force the hands of the other institutions.

Flexible Dispute Resolution

Improved disputing can improve compliance considerably. The reason is the now substantial evidence that when people and companies believe they have experienced fair procedures, they are more likely to comply with the law (Lind and Tyler, 1988; Tyler, 1990, 1998; Tyler and Dawes, 1993; Makkai and Braithwaite, 1996). The Large Corporate volume of the ATO Professionalism Survey does show procedural fairness to be a concern of large corporates with ATO staff (Donovan Research, 1998).

Adversarialism arises often in tax fieldwork. Procrastination as an alternative to resolving disputes commonly uses delaying tactics such as manipulating the administrative privilege of accountants, Freedom of Information requests, administrative law hearings, holding back on assistance with providing requested records, providing only parts of the information requested, and failing to attend meetings. Good tax office practice is to refuse to tolerate failure by either party to resolve disputes. Otherwise the agency hands victory to the people who practice 'Defer, Delay, Defeat'. Headbutting or delay that is obstructing resolution can be dealt with by widening the circle involved in the dispute. Some large businesses are alert to this option themselves as they regularly go over the head of fieldworkers to their superiors. Experience demonstrates it to be a good option for the large business fieldworker as well (and so does theory, Braithwaite, 1997). If a matter is important enough, the fieldworker's senior manager can write to the CEO saying, in effect, 'We need you to supply this information in a timely fashion so we can settle this matter. We can use our powers to compel you to do so and stand ready to go to court to enforce this. But this is not the way we like to do business. Can we meet and exchange the information we need to get this dispute over with?'. At lower levels, an auditor having difficulty with the tax manager of a company can ask for a meeting with the tax manager and his boss together, and then with the boss's boss if that meeting accomplishes no reconciliation.

The rationale for this path to flexible dispute resolution is that large businesses are full of many adversarial people and many cooperative people. The trick is to move up the organisation through various layers of adversarial managers until the tax officer reaches a cooperative manager who insists that the matter be settled rather than take up more of everyone's time. Actually, the grounds for optimism that this works are even stronger than suggested so far. Even the most adversarial of executives have a cooperative, socially responsible self as well as a combative self (see Braithwaite, Chapter 2, this volume). The gifted tax officer has the ability to treat clients with a respect that persuades even the most combative of them to put forward their socially responsible self. If she has a bad day where she fails to pull this off, she knows how to retreat, widen the circle for another day on which she hopes to catch the new player when his socially responsible self is to the fore. Moving up the organisation until a more senior cooperative person is found who will instruct the junior obstructionist to cooperate can be time-consuming. But it is less time-consuming than escalating prematurely to setting up an arbitration or litigation, or leaving the problem to fester.

More and Escalating Regulation Options to Enforce Compliance

The ATO has in recent years made considerable movement down this path recommended by the ATO Compliance Model. Following the external evaluation of the Large Case Program[5] (Pappas, Carter, Evans and Koop, 1992), the ATO moved from full audit as a more or less standard single compliance product to a suite of audit products: roll-over audits, pre-lodgment audits, last year lodged audits, specific issues audits, loss tracking audits, new legislation/ruling reviews and record retention audits. Industry watching briefs and tax strategy reviews (which are risk assessments rather than audits) also became important fieldwork tools. The suite of products provide greater choice and flexibility to better target risk treatments; and taxpayers, subject to enforcement, can experience varying types of fieldwork contact, making them more careful in their tax affairs. Even if they have a full audit in one year, they cannot rule out some special purpose audit in the next year.

The ATO Compliance Model is a compliance pyramid, with cooperative and educative compliance options at the base escalating to progressively more enforcement-oriented and punitive options as we move up the pyramid. The philosophy is to consider cooperative strategies first and only escalate up through each layer of the pyramid as each lower level of the pyramid fails to deliver compliance. This raises the question of why not try reward at the base of the compliance pyramid.

Some ATO staff and corporates considered it improper to reward large business for what was seen as meeting their legal obligations. This concern seems especially apt in light of experience with other areas of regulation where financial incentives to meet legal obligations have engendered some perverse incentives to deliver the form, but not the substance, of what is intended to be rewarded. The ATO, however, can make a special effort to give a service 'beyond the call of duty' to clients who have an exemplary record on compliance and cooperation in making the tax system work. For example, they could be given extra quick turnaround of advisings. Indeed, it might only be as particularly trustworthy taxpayers that they could be given this: Mutual trust enables an advisings process to be transacted more time-efficiently. The time-efficiency can be achieved by increasing ATO preparedness to accept the corporate's tax analysis and relying on verification of selected key components of that analysis. The service of the Key Client Manager, an officer dedicated to one corporate taxpayer, could also be viewed in this light. Indeed, in light of the desirability of rewarding greater compliance with better service where this is a principled thing to do, Key Client Managers could be allocated to the largest 100 corporate *taxpayers* in the country, measured by amount of tax paid over the past five years, rather than to the largest 100 corporations in *income*.

The Canadian Audit Protocols (Revenue Canada, 1996) are not just about a move to real time and better coordinated audits; they are also about building cooperative relationships. Negotiated Protocols offer the potential to reduce compliance costs for business and increase compliance effectiveness for the ATO. This might involve scheduling visits by different areas of the ATO so that disruption to business is minimised, holding concurrent audits, and assisting business with knowing in advance the form in which financial records might be kept to avoid double handling. The key idea is that a tax administrator and participating large businesses can jointly produce a written framework that establishes guidelines and standards for building and maintaining a relationship for managing compliance.

While financial rewards that are identified as rewards for compliance can be dangerous in the signal they give, this is not true of the informal rewards of praise and giving credit where credit is due. Moreover, most people underestimate how important these are to assisting business regulatory compliance. In Makkai and Braithwaite's (1993) study of Australian nursing home regulation, the use of informal praise by government inspectors was associated with improved compliance over the next two years after controlling for other causes of compliance. An activity that could be underestimated in its value is a letter from the Commissioner to a large corporation that has moved from an obstructionist to a cooperative approach to compliance. Such a letter could thank the relevant executives of the corporation for the cooperation they afforded to ATO staff in doing their job and for the reasonableness they displayed in assuring that agreement could be reached on a just tax assessment. On all manner of smaller things, thank-you letters by more junior ATO staff and face-to-face expressions of appreciation are important compliance activities.

Large businesses that have exemplary corporate compliance systems and governance processes especially merit positive recognition both verbally and/or in writing. In a storytelling regulatory culture, success stories should not be restricted to good things tax officers do; they should include stories of best practice among large business, such as corporate compliance systems and governance processes put in place by corporates. This can be institutionalised by nurturing tax compliance professionalism in the way the Australian Competition and Consumer Commission has done with Trade Practices professionalism (through establishing the Association of Compliance Professionals in Australia) and consumer affairs (through initiating the Society of Consumer Affairs Professionals in Business).

Informal recognition in the form of expedited service (e.g., advisings), praise and recognition as a public-regarding corporate citizen (as by involvement in the co-design of ATO policies) are therefore possible at the base of a compliance pyramid (see Figure 9.4). They can be combined with educative measures, the most important of which is advice and encouragement to establish credible corporate compliance systems. Accreditation is one path to nurturing tax compliance professionalism (or risk self-assessment).

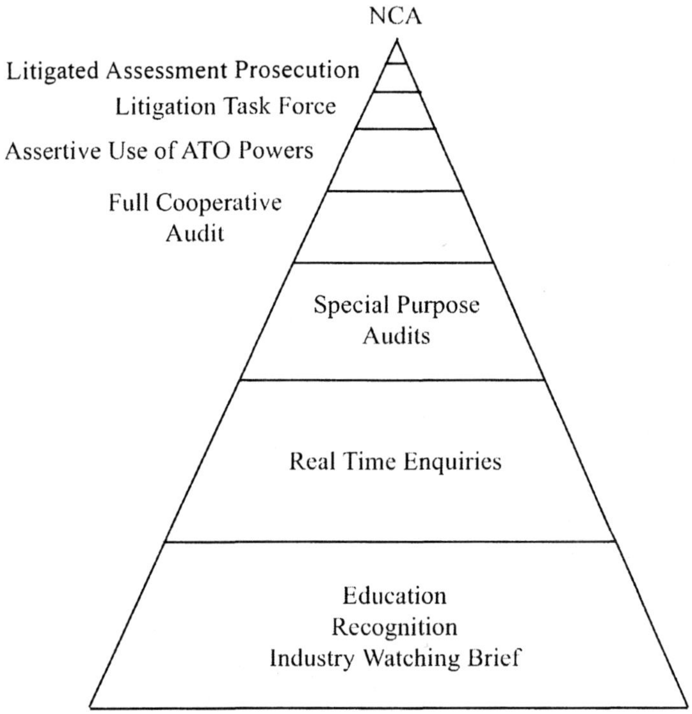

Figure 9.4 One illustration of a large business compliance pyramid

The first step up a large business compliance pyramid might be a Tax Strategy Review that checked directors' minutes, working papers, accounting and tax manuals, audit files, financial planning files, budgets/forecasts and the like. This is a small step up the pyramid for a large corporation. It is hardly an enforcement step at all, merely a risk assessment exercise. Nevertheless, it is a good first step to take when perhaps all that is required is a signal that the tax authority is reviewing the affairs of the business.

The second step might be Real Time Enquiries to clarify a concern; the third a Special Purpose Audit or other low-intensity cooperative audit; the fourth a Full Cooperative Audit (see Figure 9.4). When escalated cooperative audits meet with repeated obstructionism, escalation to what might be called 'Assertive Use of ATO Powers' could be deployed with little hesitation. This means use of formal powers to demand documents and answers to questions, and surprise visits to premises to demand access to documents where this is necessary. Escalation from cooperative audit to assertive use of ATO powers should not normally occur until there has been opportunity for an ATO senior manager and the CEO to discuss cooperative dispute resolution options.

When both obstructionism and reasonable suspicion of serious non-compliance exists, a Litigation Task Force might be put on the case (see Figure 9.4). The litigation task force would be multidisciplinary, including a lawyer who would liaise with the Director of Public Prosecutions. The obligation of the head of the litigation task force would be to ensure that the necessary evidence was collected to pursue prosecution and other penalties. This is not to say that maximum legal action would be pursued; rather, the objective would be to make it clear that this was inevitable unless the taxpayer moved the relationship down the pyramid to more cooperative problem resolution. There has been a view that the evidence rarely exists to warrant higher penalties or for prosecution to be successfully pursued. Doubts exist about this assumption. Rather, an alternative view is that a large corporation which has escalated this far up the pyramid will be vulnerable somewhere in its complex of activities to false and misleading statements having been made, among other vulnerabilities. In part, this view on tough enforcement may itself stem from a perceived lack of support from ATO managers, the ATO itself and even the Director of Public Prosecutions. The use of a litigation task force could help crystallise this support and more tangibly signal to the staff and the taxpayer involved that swift and sharp enforcement will be taken.

The next rung in the compliance pyramid will be assessments/penalties that trigger litigation by the taxpayer and/or prosecution by the Director of Public Prosecutions (see Figure 9.4).

The final rung of the compliance pyramid could be referral to the National Crime Authority (NCA).[6] This occurs rarely at the moment, a situation that should continue. The NCA's superior powers and criminal enforcement capabilities should not be employed even on the most hardened criminals, but only on uncooperative hardened criminals who are believed to be major tax evaders.

The pyramid in Figure 9.4 is an illustrative pyramid that may be useful in navigating the compliance options available in large business compliance at this point in time. No compliance pyramid can be effective without changing over time, with context, and in response to research findings from evidence-based risk leveraging. Nor should this compliance pyramid, or any other, be prescriptive. They are no more than a guide to compliance decisions that should never be allowed to trump contextual wisdom. It should never be a criticism of an officer that they are not following the ATO pyramid. It should be cause for praise when the idea of the pyramid is used flexibly to display an utterly original array of innovative risk leveraging strategies through which the ATO might escalate in dealing with a tough case (as Job and Honaker, Chapter 6, and Hobson, Chapter 7, argue in this volume). Rather than slavish implementation of 'the Model' we should want success stories of innovation in pyramidal thinking about leveraging compliance.

By thinking pyramidally about the enforcement options available, the tax officer engenders confidence and motivates cooperative compliance through showing a willingness to escalate up the pyramid. A regulator who believes that her pyramid is credible and who is willing to escalate up it if necessary rarely actually finds it necessary to escalate far up the pyramid. Confidence about the authority of the pyramid of enforcement capabilities projects an image of invincibility to the corporation that is the subject of tough enforcement. This rarely fails to engender cooperative compliance at low levels of the pyramid, enabling de-escalation to even lower levels. The effective regulator is cooperative and trusting at first, tough if that trust is abused, tougher and tougher if it is still abused, but forgiving if trust and cooperation is finally restored (Ayres and Braithwaite, 1992, Chapter 2). It does not matter that escalation at lower levels of the pyramid has very little bite with large corporations; at that level the objective is to *signal* escalation rather than cutting deeply into the corporate's interest. The crunch is whether the tax authority is willing to escalate until it does reach something that bites.

For the pyramid to work, fieldworkers must be confident that they will get senior management backing if they escalate. They have that confidence because they do not escalate or threaten escalation of a particular type unless they get backing at a level that can support that level of escalation. Fieldworkers would not escalate to an enforcement option and would not initiate assertive use of ATO powers without getting the backing of their leaders in advance. Fieldworkers, however, should not assume their leader's support when they want to escalate to assertive use of ATO powers and beyond. They must be able to count on their backing when the fieldworker and leader agree in advance on the circumstances of the escalation. Once a litigation task force is established, control passes out of the fieldworker's hands into the hands of the head of the task force (usually a lawyer). Assurance that at some point the lawyers take over as a matter of policy adds to the confidence and authority of the fieldworker who can say: Look, unless we can sort this out, the conflict will escalate to the point where ATO policy requires that it be taken over by a Litigation Task Force. Near the peak of the pyramid, no promises of escalation would be made without the backing of the Commissioner.

Of course, many of the strategies in Figure 9.4 will be deployed for risk management reasons rather than out of any desire to give a signal that the behaviour of the taxpayer is causing their case to be taken more seriously. Sometimes when escalation up the pyramid is occurring, the circumstances will warrant a jump up several rungs of the pyramid. The pyramid represents a preference for resolving matters at lower levels, not a rule to do so. Starting at the base of a pyramid and moving up progressively is a presumption that can be overridden by compelling evidence, for example, of criminal behaviour or aggressive tax planning, that this is a case that should go straight to the peak of the pyramid. But we should be extremely reluctant to do that.

It is a challenge to educate people that there is no single or correct pyramid, but that there is virtue in having the professionalism that comes from having thought through the range of responses through which a regulator can escalate when faced with non-cooperation. For example, one way to meet the challenge could be to build various compliance pyramids that deal with access to information. A workshop would get a group of fieldworkers who confront a similar group of clients with similar access difficulties to co-design their own pyramid of escalated response to denial of access. In the course of the workshop, they would be shown the compliance pyramids designed by other access workshops. Seeing their differences would both give them ideas and assurance that they could design their own. Indeed, there would not have to be agreement at the workshop. Different participants could go away with different pyramids that suited their contexts. The objective would be that each participant would develop a pyramid that she thinks would work for her and that she could get her supervisor to back her on.

Conclusion

The four elements of the ATO Compliance Model: (a) understanding taxpayer behaviour; (b) building community partnerships; (c) increased flexibility; and (d) more and escalating regulatory options have been found to have relevant meanings for large business tax policy. This is so even if it is the case that improving compliance is a less satisfactory way of planning large corporate tax objectives than reducing risks to the revenue and increasing legal certainty. There is a long way to go before large business tax enforcement achieves problem-focused flexibility informed by bottom-up storytelling and top-down demands for evidence-based risk leveraging. The field has a long way to go before it is genuinely a regulatory craft (Sparrow, 2000). An egg-shaped form of compliance behaviour where most enforcement effort is directed at grey areas of avoidance rather than evasion makes the challenge especially difficult. It also makes it a challenge where law enforcement and law reform must be integrated instead of separated functions. My argument is that a combination of escalated responsive enforcement integrated with responsive law reform has some hope of shifting much of the grey bulge of tax avoidance into tax compliance.

Notes

1 This is a revised version of a longer paper by John Braithwaite and Andrew Wirth, 'Towards a Compliance Framework for Large Business Tax Compliance', Centre for Tax System Integrity, Working Paper No. 24, The Australian National University, Canberra.

2 In a 29 May 1998 presentation to the NSW Annual State Seminar of the Taxation Institute of Australia, LB&I (Large Business and International, ATO) reported that 'almost 60 per cent' of its companies were non-taxpayers. Consolidation would doubtless reduce this proportion substantially because one large corporate group might include a number of entities that pay no tax and others that pay large amounts.

3 Kerry Packer's taxpaying behaviour has been subject to public scrutiny on a number of occasions. See, for instance, House of Representatives Select Committee on the Print Media Inquiry (1992) and *The Australian* (2000), 'Packer Sues over Internet Tax Ads', 5 September, A. McGilvray and A. McKenzie, p. 1.

4 BISEP represents the idea that to understand the compliance of an individual or group, one needs to understand the environment in which they operate. The initials of this acronym stand for B = Business profile, I = Industry factors, S = Sociological factors, E = Economic factors and P = Psychological factors.

5 The Large Case Program focused ATO audit activity on the largest corporate taxpayers and was conducted during the later half of the 1980s and early 1990s.

6 This is a body akin to Crime Commissions that have special evidence-gathering powers against serious organised crime in a number of countries. Indeed the National Crime Authority in Australia is in transition to becoming a National Crime Commission.

References

Alm, J., Bahl, R. and Murray, M. (1993), 'Audit Selection and Income Tax Underreporting in the Tax Compliance Game', *Journal of Development Economics*, vol. 42, pp. 1-33.

Alm, J., Jackson, B. and McKee, M. (1992), 'Estimating the Determinants of Taxpayer Compliance with Experimental Data', *National Taxation Journal*, vol. 45, pp. 107-14.

Andreoni, J., Erard, B. and Feinstein, J. (1998), 'Tax Compliance', *Journal of Economic Literature*, vol. 36, pp. 818-60.

Australian Taxation Office (1995), 'Staff Perceptions of the Compliance Behaviour of the Top 100 Companies Audited Under the Large Case Program', Paper presented to the Compliance Improvement Committee, Australian Taxation Office, 12 December, Canberra.

Ayres, I. and Braithwaite, J. (1992), *Responsive Regulation: Transcending the Deregulation Debate*, Oxford University Press, New York.

Baldry, J.C. (1987), 'Income Tax Evasion and Tax Schedule: Some Experimental Results', *Public Finance*, vol. 42, pp. 357-83.

Braithwaite, J. (1997), 'On Speaking Softly and Carrying Sticks: Neglected Dimensions of Republican Separations of Powers', *University of Toronto Law Journal*, vol. 47, pp. 1-57.

Braithwaite, J. and Makkai, T. (1994), 'Trust and Compliance', *Policing and Society*, vol. 4, pp. 1-12.

Braithwaite, J., Pittelkow, Y. and Williams, R. (Chapter 10, this volume), 'Tax Compliance by the Very Wealthy: Red Flags of Risk'.

Braithwaite, V. (Chapter 2, this volume), 'Dancing with Tax Authorities: Motivational Postures and Non-compliant Actions'.

Braithwaite, V. and Levi, M. (1998), *Trust and Governance*, Russell Sage Foundation, New York.

Braithwaite, V., Reinhart, M., Mearns, M. and Graham, R. (2001), 'Preliminary Findings from the Community Hopes, Fears and Actions Survey', *Centre for Tax System Integrity Working Paper No. 3*, The Australian National University, Canberra.

Cash Economy Task Force (1998), *Improving Tax Compliance in the Cash Economy*, Australian Taxation Office, Canberra.

Clotfelter, C.T. (1983), 'Tax Evasion and Tax Rates: An Analysis of Individual Returns', *Review of Economic Statistics*, vol. 65, pp. 363-73.

Cowell, F.A. (1990), *Cheating the Government: The Economics of Evasion*, MIT Press, Cambridge.

Donovan Research (1998), 'Australian Taxation Office Professionalism and Service Standards Research, Volume 5: Corporates', Australian Taxation Office, Canberra.

Feinstein, J.S. (1991), 'An Econometric Analysis of Income Tax Evasion and its Detection', *Rand Journal of Economics*, vol. 22, pp. 14-35.

Friedland, N., Maital, S. and Rutenberg, S.M.A. (1978), 'A Simulation Study of Income Tax Evasion', *Journal of Public Economics*, vol. 10, pp. 107-16.

Grey, S. and Cooper, D. (1998), *Australian Taxation Office Large Business and International Business Line: Risk Management Process Definition*, Cambridge Broadleaf Capital International, Cambridge.

Hobson, K. (Chapter 7, this volume), 'Championing the Compliance Model: From Common Sense to Common Action?'.

House of Representatives Select Committee on the Print Media (1992), *Report from the House of Representatives Select Committee on the Print Media News & Fair Facts: The Australian Print Media Industry*, Commonwealth of Australia, Canberra.

Job, J. and Honaker, D. (Chapter 6, this volume), 'Short-term Experiences with Responsive Regulation in the Australian Taxation Office'.

Joulfaian, D. and Rider, M. (1996), 'Tax Evasion in the Presence of Negative Income Tax Rates', *National Taxation Journal*, vol. 49, pp. 553-70.

Killaly, J. (1996), 'Advance Pricing Arrangements: The Australian Position: Practical Issues Relating to Australia's APA Program', *Organisation for Economic Cooperation and Development, Working Paper No. 6*, Organisation for Economic Cooperation and Development, Paris.

Kraakman, R.H. (1984), 'Corporate Liability Strategies and the Costs of Legal Controls', *Yale Law Journal*, vol. 93, pp. 857-98.

Levi, M. (1988), *Of Rule and Revenue*, University of California Press, Berkeley.

Lind, A.E. and Tyler, T.R. (1988), *The Social Psychology of Procedural Justice*, Plenum Press, New York.

Makkai, T. and Braithwaite, J. (1993), 'Praise, Pride and Corporate Compliance', *International Journal of the Sociology of Law*, vol. 21, pp. 73-91.

_____ (1996), 'Procedural Justice and Regulatory Compliance', *Law and Human Behaviour*, vol. 20, pp. 83-98.

McBarnet, D. (1992), 'The Construction of Compliance and the Challenge of Control: The Limits of Noncompliance Research', in J. Slemrod (ed), *Why People Pay Taxes: Tax Compliance and Enforcement*, University of Michigan Press, Ann Arbor, pp. 333-45.

_____ (Chapter 11, this volume), 'When Compliance is not the Solution but the Problem: From Changes in Law to Changes in Attitude'.

Pappas, Carter, Evans and Koop (1992), *Review of the Large Case Program*, The Boston Consulting Group, Boston.

Revenue Canada (1996), *Revenue Canada 4024 The Audit Protocol*, Revenue Canada, Ottawa.
Scholz, J. (1998), 'Trust, Taxes and Compliance', in V. Braithwaite and M. Levi (eds), *Trust and Governance*, Russell Sage Foundation, New York, pp. 135-66.
Shaw, G., Brown, R. and Bromiley, P. (1998), 'Strategic Stories: How 3M is Rewriting Business Planning', *Harvard Business Review*, vol. May-June, pp. 41-54.
Shearing, C.D. and Ericson, R.V. (1991), 'Culture as Figurative Action', *British Journal of Sociology*, vol. 42(4), pp. 481-506.
Sparrow, M.K. (2000), *The Regulatory Craft*, Brookings Institution, Washington D.C.
Tyler, T.R. (1990), *Why People Obey Law*, Yale University Press, New Haven.
_____ (1998), 'Trust and Democratic Governance', in V. Braithwaite and M. Levi (eds), *Trust and Governance*, Russell Sage Foundation, New York, pp. 269-94.
Tyler, T. and Dawes, R.M. (1993), 'Fairness in Groups: Comparing the Self-Interest and Social Identity Perspectives', in B.A. Mellers and J. Baron (eds), *Psychological Perspectives on Justice: Theory and Applications*, Cambridge University Press, Cambridge, pp. 87-108.
Wickerson, J. (1993), 'Measuring Taxpayer Compliance: Issues and Challenges Facing Tax Administration', Australian Taxation Office, Canberra.
Williams, R. (1995), 'Behavioural Research Synopsis', Australian Taxation Office, Canberra.
Wirth, A. (1998), 'Public Perceptions and Expectations of the Australian Taxation System', Australian Taxation Office, Canberra.

PART III
BEYOND THE COMPLIANCE MODEL

Chapter 10

Tax Compliance by the Very Wealthy: Red Flags of Risk

John Braithwaite, Yvonne Pittelkow and Robert Williams

The issue of detection of tax evasion and avoidance is no small challenge for tax authorities. Oftentimes detection depends on extensive auditing. The ambiguity and difficulty of the task has led tax authorities to devise risk management strategies so that they can dedicate their limited resources to detection exercises that are likely to uncover instances of evasion or aggressive avoidance. The process of identifying a set of red flags that alerts tax officers to aggressive tax planning is the focus of attention in this chapter. We illustrate how a statistical methodology can be deployed with subjective estimates of risk made by expert analysts and more objective data in the form of dollars at risk.[1]

The High Wealth Individuals (HWI) Taskforce

In 1996, the Australian Taxation Office (ATO) established a High Wealth Individuals (HWI) Taskforce to enhance compliance management for HWIs. It did this in a way no other tax authority in the world has done before to our knowledge. Traditionally, tax authorities treat individual persons and corporate entities (partnerships, trusts, corporations) as separate taxpayers in their case management. The innovation of the HWI Taskforce was to treat the individual return of a HWI and the entities they control as a single case. In the first year of operation, 180 HWIs received a questionnaire about the groups of entities they controlled, or from which they received income. These were formalised in subsequent years into expanded returns, called Current Year Data Collection (CYDC) returns. In 1997 and 1998, 285 HWIs (142 rated as medium overall risk and 143 high overall risk) were required to complete expanded returns for their 2371 and 2599 associated companies, trusts, partnerships, or individuals. The level of these individuals' wealth, and the amount of tax they paid, to qualify for this level of scrutiny is confidential. However, all those completing expanded returns are extremely wealthy.

The HWI program seems to have increased the amount of tax paid by HWIs. In 1994 and 1995, the two years before the program was set up, private companies controlled by individuals in the program paid 17 per cent and 12 per cent less tax than non-HWI companies respectively. Afterward, HWI companies paid 23 per cent more than non-HWI companies in 1996 and 20 per cent more in 1997

(Braithwaite, 2001, p. 13). It is believed that this is because HWIs are generally more cautious with their tax affairs when they are under the microscope of the HWI program:

> It's the constant surveillance of being on the program that causes compliance...Part IVA is of indeterminate width. It might be applied more aggressively in future. So I advise clients to be careful.
>
> Asking the question and getting them to focus their mind on where everything is had an impact.
>
> (HWI advisers quoted in Braithwaite, 2001, p. 10.)

Another adviser suggested that 'the more information he's [the Commissioner] got, the less aggressive they will be in their tax planning'. What was meant by this comment was that through notifying the Commissioner of 'X' in 1998, taxpayers reduced their degrees of freedom to re-configure their 1999 affairs in such a way that not-X appeared to be the case in 1999. Changes from year to year will be noticed, so HWIs must keep their affairs consistent with the underlying truths of earlier declarations. Also the more holistic approach of HWI program surveillance means there is a need to work harder at keeping the story about one HWI entity's tax affairs consistent with that of another (Braithwaite, 2001, p. 11).

The Risk Ratings

The data in this chapter are based on risk ratings of 207 potential risk issues identified from 1997 and/or 1998 tax returns for 235 individual HWIs and the entities they control.

ATO analysts might examine as many as 100 expanded returns from all the entities controlled by a HWI, and then in theory rate each of the 207 potential risk issues from 0 to 10. These ratings are estimates of indications of risk; that is, there is no guarantee that there really is a high risk. Usually an audit would be needed, sometimes even litigation, to establish if the risk was a reality.

As with all risk ratings, the rating estimates used as the basis for this report were checked by a supervisor who may have revised them. For the highest risks, senior taskforce staff would also meet to discuss the analyst's assessment.

Most of the potential risk issues were not recorded or rated for each HWI. In fact more than half the HWIs in the database had less than ten rated issues. The maximum was fifty-one, and the minimum was one.

This chapter is concerned with high risk ratings. A rating of 1-3 was defined by the taskforce as a low risk, 4-7 as medium, and 8-10 as high. The defining features of a score of more than 7 in the instructions to analysts are indications of aggressive tax planning 'like significant loss creation', followed by a list of other types of aggressive tax planning or 'further information desirable and would suggest audit action'. Judgments about what is aggressive tax planning are controversial and subjective[2] and there are many reasons to suspect risk ratings as unreliable.[3] In the first part of this chapter we accept these subjective judgments at face value and use them to predict several criteria of overall risk of the HWI and the entities they control. We then test if the 'objective' criterion of dollars at risk adds any additional information to the more 'subjective' assessment of risk.

The list of 207 potential risk issues used in this analysis has been until now highly protected. While not all issues are identified specifically, it is now possible to release results that reveal at least the issues that turned out to be important in these analyses. The collection of risk ratings, which are the basis of these analyses, has now been suspended and superseded, so the definition of issues discussed in this chapter does not provide useful information to tax advisers. Even at a more conceptual level, some of the issues, which we find to be serious risks for 1997-98, are no longer risks as a result of tax reform.

Our objective with this research is not to revise a list of 207 risk issues that have already been revised, but rather to seize the unique opportunity the data provides and to explore the kinds of risk factors that predict the existence of the highest levels of overall risk. That is, what are the issues which, when rated as an indication of high risk, are a red flag for the existence of many other high risks to the revenue?

What are the Most Common High Risks for HWIs?

Analysts rated risks in comparison with other HWIs, not general taxpayers. If this were not the case, virtually all HWIs would have attracted a large number of high risk ratings based simply on their wealth, income levels, and the complexity of their business dealings. This outcome would have been unproductive for determining where the greatest risks lay. As a result, and because not many issues were rated by analysts, it is rare for a HWI to be given a risk rating over 7 on one of the 207 issues.

Table 10.1 shows the 13 issues most commonly given a rating greater than 7. In addition, the ratings of the 235 HWIs on each risk have been averaged and appear in the second column alongside the number of HWIs scoring in the extreme categories. While these statistics suggest a somewhat different ordering of risk, priority tends to be given to use of extreme categories rather than average rating. Tax authorities are more interested in the extreme risks than in average risks, as they only have the resources to deploy audits and other strategies against the highest risks.

The most common risk issue, rated over 7 in only 12 cases, was the utilisation of revenue losses (as opposed to capital losses) through transfers within the HWI's group of entities – moving losses to a taxable entity to save tax for that entity (Issue 1, Table 10.1). The second most common high risk was the use of an offshore entity (company, trust, partnership) in an unlisted (that is, low taxed)[4] country (Issue 2, Table 10.1).

There are seven instances of revenue loss creation via research and development (R&D) deductions (Issue 5, Table 10.1). R&D investment receives a concessional tax treatment and has traditionally been used in tax minimisation arrangements (Issue 6, Table 10.1). There are seven instances of 'taxable distributions to a loss entity', which is the inverse of transferring a loss to a taxable entity. The term 'distribution' means it is limited to trusts in this instance.[5] If used unscrupulously a loss can be transferred a number of times and can be used in each entity it passes through. This is known as 'loss cascading' and has been considered a serious risk to the revenue.

There are eight cases of 'debt forgiveness/bad debts' (Issues 3, Table 10.1). This technique can be used to create a revenue loss within a group of companies. If one company fails to repay a loan, the company that made that loan can claim it as a bad debt for tax purposes. A bad debt is tax deductible, and, when deductions exceed income, a loss is created. An 'asset disposal' can create a capital loss if the asset is sold for less than the purchase price. Purchase price can be manipulated when the same person ultimately owns the company that is selling the asset and the company that is buying the asset. In this way an artificial, and tax deductible, capital loss will be created within the group with no corresponding economic loss to the taxpayer. There are also eight instances of 'other significant deduction issues' (Issue 4, Table 10.1). These 'other issues' will be discussed later in this chapter.

Table 10.1 also shows the recorded mean dollars at risk (e.g., the dollars transferred within the HWI group) for each of the common high risk issues. The dollars at risk are the maximum dollars at risk in either 1997 or 1998. Note this is not the dollars at risk when the risk was rated over 7; this would be a higher number. The mean dollars at risk number is the mean dollars at risk for this risk across all ratings of risk from 1 to 10 (regardless of whether it was high or low). Note also that the mean dollars at risk will include zero entries if they are recorded. However the value of zero may mean no dollars were at risk or that the analyst did not know the dollar amount for some HWIs or the entities they control. The high value of $46 million for those placed in the miscellaneous 'other' category is significant and will be interpreted later in this chapter.

Table 10.2 shows the issues with the highest mean dollars at risk across all 207 issues (as opposed to just the highest risk issues). Transfer of trading stock has an average of $379 million at risk. This could be indicative of a transfer pricing issue, but there are only three HWIs with recorded dollars at risk for this issue. In general, the estimates of the mean dollars at risk should be treated with caution. For example, if an entity is only partially controlled by a HWI there is a possibility that the analyst has included only a portion of the actual risk.

Table 10.1 Most common high risk issues

Issue	No. HWIs with risk rating > 7	Mean risk rating	Mean dollars ar risk ($AUS)
Revenue loss utilisation via intra group transfer (1)	12	4.12	$4 328 670
Use of offshore entity in an unlisted country (2)	8	4.40	-
Revenue loss creation via debt forgiveness/bad debts (3)	8	4.21	$5 416 922
Miscellaneous income and deduction items – other significant deduction issues (4)	8	4.04	$4 540 784
Revenue loss creation via research and development deduction claims (5)	7	5.76	$3 332 722
Trust distributions – taxable distributions to a loss entity (6)	7	4.14	$5 492 180
Other miscellaneous items – disposal of significant capital item in review period (non-assessable profit) (7)	7	3.93	$15 843 564
Evidence of value shifting or unusual transactions – means of minimising income tax in group (8)	6	5.22	-
Other miscellaneous items – other (9)	6	4.27	$46 153 472
Evidence of value shifting or unusual transactions – means of minimising capital gains tax in group (10)	5	5.62	-
Group restructure due to significant new ventures (11)	5	4.24	-
Trust distributions – distributions from capital profits reserve (12)	5	4.63	$3 315 175
Trust distributions – capital distribution in cash (to the HWI) (13)	5	4.73	$1 196 229

Table 10.2 Issues with highest mean dollars at risk

Issue	No. HWIs with risk rating > 7	Mean risk rating	Mean dollars at risk ($AUS)
Related party transactions with an entity in an unlisted country – transfer of trading stock	0	7.00	$379 333 333
Other miscellaneous items – other	6	4.27	$46 153 472
Other miscellaneous items – finance/treasury issues	2	6.25	$34 848 766
Capital loss creation via cost base manipulation	0	5.33	$22 782 914
Related party transactions with an entity in an unlisted country – transfer of assets/property	1	4.20	$21 222 264
Evidence of dividend streaming within group companies	0	3.67	$17 485 377
Related party transactions with an entity in a listed country – granting of guarantees	0	1.00	$17 382 600
Trusts – use of beneficiary loan accounts (loan source unknown)	3	4.28	$16 152 070
Other miscellaneous items – disposal of significant capital items (non-assessable profit)	7	3.93	$15 843 564
Companies – use of shareholder loan accounts (loan source is HWI)	4	3.19	$10 579 077
Capital loss creation via property development/industry	1	3.26	$10 318 261
Significant franking credit surplus in group	0	3.33	$9 464 742
Related party transactions with an entity in an unlisted country – interest income	1	2.57	$9 186 641

Predicting High Overall Risk

The initial objective was to use a cluster analytic procedure on the HWI risk factors to show which risks went together, in hope of revealing systemic risk factors that were underpinning a variety of seemingly unrelated risks. It was thought that risk clusters might be particularly useful in targeting types of specific purpose audits. For example, risk cluster A should get audit product X; risk cluster B, product Y; and so on.

Unfortunately, it eventuated that cluster analysis was inappropriate because, as described above, high-risk ratings are rare events with joint occurrence of any two specific high risks being even lower. In fact there are only two pairs of issues on which four HWIs are both rated as a high risk; all the other pairwise combinations have fewer HWIs sharing a high risk on both issues.

Thus, cluster analysis and other pattern finding methodologies are inappropriate for this data set where the emphasis is on high risk. Empirically this suggests that if a 'risky' taxation strategy is measured as a combination of issues assessed as high risk, then these strategies tend to be unique to each HWI or rather shared by very few HWIs.

Due to this finding, the analysis shifted to identifying specific risks that are the best red flags for high overall risk. A 'high' overall risk assessment is defined with a clear action orientation. It means the analyst and their supervisor agree that, all things considered, the application of some kind of audit product is justified. Being placed in the high overall risk category is still a rare event. This characterised only thirty-three HWIs (14%). There were six HWIs who were not assessed as being in either a high, medium or low risk category. They were treated as not a high risk and included with medium and low risk HWIs for the purpose of the following analysis.

Table 10.3 shows the summary from a logistic regression analysis predicting high overall risk. The independent variables in the model are the 207 issues coded as 1 for a high risk (that is a rating greater than 7) and zero (that is a rating of 1 to 7). Issues coded like this are referred to as flags to differentiate them from rated issues. Because of the interest in choosing a minimum set of 'flags' we chose a stepwise algorithm, which selects the best predictor of likelihood from amongst the 207 flags, then the second-best after the first-best has been included, and so on. The stopping criterion is when the addition of further flags does not sufficiently increase predictability of membership into the correct risk group to warrant the added complexity. A scree slope test based on the percentage correctly predicted was used to define this stopping point. Thus we attempted to balance statistical and practical significance.

The first predictor of high overall risk is being rated over 7 in the 'other miscellaneous items – other' category (Issue 9, Table 10.1): The potential meaning of this finding is discussed in the next section.[6] The issue rated over 7 with the next most predictive value in this model is 'use of an offshore entity in an unlisted country' (Issue 2, Table 10.1). We might assume that ratings over 7 will mostly be incurred when there is concern that the unlisted country is a tax haven. The third most useful predictor is 'trust distributions – capital distributions in cash (to the HWI)'[7] (Issue 13, Table 10.1). Various other analyses were undertaken to confirm the stability of these results, and this flag also turned out to be important in these supplementary analysis. For example, 'trust distributions – capital distributions in cash (to the HWI)' is the top predictor in a model predicting the sum of all risk ratings (0-10) across all 207 issues. Indeed all three flags in Table 10.3 are recurrently useful and statistically significant predictors across different types of analyses. Column two in Table 10.3 shows the Likelihood Chi-square statistic for the inclusion of the flag at each step of the model building process. Beyond this set of flags, the increase in correctly predicted high risk HWIs was small (even though other flags subsequently entered into the model were statistically significant).

The percentage in the fifth column of Table 10.3 shows that with information about whether or not each of these three issues is rated over 7 (and with no other information about the case), we can correctly classify the case as High or not-High 91.9 per cent of the time. Of the 202 HWIs in the low to medium risk group, 201 were correctly predicted. Of the 33 HWIs in the high risk group, 15 were correctly classified into the high risk group.

Table 10.3 Predicting high overall risk with flags* using logistic regression analysis

Step	Chi-square	df	Sig.	% Correctly Classified	Flags
1	24.557	1	0.000	88.5%	Other miscellaneous items – other
2	21.402	1	0.000	90.6%	Other miscellaneous items – other Use of an offshore entity in an unlisted country
3	14.894	1	0.000	91.9%	Other miscellaneous items – other Use of an offshore entity in an unlisted country Trust distributions – capital distribution in cash (to the HWI)

* A flag is a risk from a list of 207 possible risks that an analyst rates over 7 on a risk scale from 1 to 10.

While it may seem obvious that these would be crucial issues, there may be any number of sets of completely different issues that would generate the same reaction. The question is which of the 207 risk issues we really would have selected as the top three predictors of overall risk. In our experience, auditors have hunches about red flags of risk that are in no way confirmed by these data. Some auditors believe that the use of a company controlled by a wealthy person to own a luxury yacht, a holiday home, or a racehorse is a red flag. Although there is some support for this view from the data, knowledge of risk on any of these items classifies only two HWIs in the high risk group. Given the time it takes to get on top of the complexity of cases such as these groups of HWI entities, even very senior analysts may have a remarkably narrow scope of experience. While their supervisors might have greater breadth of experience built by approving the analyses of others, they lack the depth of experience of the analyst who has pored over the case. Hence a method that takes at face value that depth of experience, but aggregates it over the breadth of (235) cases, is valuable. Although less obvious, use of statistical reasoning can also produce results which are important though less intuitive.

Proxy Analyses for High Overall Risk

Although the three flags shown in Table 10.3 are statistically significant and useful in correctly predicting about half the HWIs in the high risk group, it is important to test if alternative sets of flags work equally well. There are many methods of looking for subsets. The method employed here is to remove the most significant from the potential set of flags used to predict high risk and to repeat the analysis. Then the most significant flag from this analysis is removed from the potential pool of flags as well, and so on. This iterated method also identifies the best predictors of high risk when used on their own as the first step in the analysis. Further, there is the advantage of excluding the 'other miscellaneous items – other' issue (Issue 9, Table 10.1) from the potential pool of flags, since having a miscellaneous 'catch-all' issue as the best predictor of high risk can be difficult to interpret.

When 'other miscellaneous items – other' was excluded from the potential pool of flags, 'use of an offshore entity in an unlisted country' (Issue 2, Table 10.1) became the top predictor, followed by 'other significant deduction issues', a subheading of 'miscellaneous income and deduction items' (Issue 4, Table 10.1). Interestingly, a slightly more specific catch-all issue has been substituted for another category of catch-all issues. 'Trust distributions – capital distributions in cash (to the HWI)' (Issue 13, Table 10.1) remained the third most significant predictor once these other flags were included (see Table 10.4). When 'other miscellaneous items – other' and 'use of an offshore entity in an unlisted country' were excluded from the pool of potential flags, 'trust distributions – capital distributions in cash (to the HWI)' became the top predictor, followed by 'miscellaneous income and deduction items – other significant deduction issues' (again) and another issue that looks like a proxy for 'use of an offshore entity in an unlisted country', that is, 'evidence of funds coming onshore irregularly' (as opposed to 'regularly'). This is not one of the most common high risk issues and therefore does not appear in Table 10.1.

When 'trust distributions – capital distributions in cash (to the HWI)' was removed from the pool of potential flags the 'utilisation of revenue losses via intra group transfers' (within the group of HWI entities) (Issue 1, Table 10.1) became the top predictor.[8] This means moving losses from one entity controlled by the HWI to wipe out or reduce the profits recorded in another entity that it controls (or vice versa), so that tax does not have to be paid on these profits.

Three new 'other' issues became the next best predictors of high risk: 'group structures – use of multiple entities (other)', 'group structures – evidence of value shifting/unusual transactions in group (other)' and 'other miscellaneous items – disposal of significant capital items (non-assessable profit)'. In our first proxy analysis an 'other' variable is replaced by a different 'other' variable. When this second 'other' is deleted from the analysis, two different kinds of 'other' variables are prominent in alternative sets 2 and 3. In short, as we delete one 'other' variable, another keeps popping up across all the proxy analyses. There is a stable 'other' effect.

Given also that Tables 10.1 and 10.2 show that the amount of money at risk in these 'other' issues is high, there is too much evidence to ignore this 'other' effect in an analysis of high risk and we need to consider whether there is some potentially explanatory meaning behind their significance. The four best predictors of overall high risk on their own (without entering other flags into the analysis) are 'other miscellaneous items – other', 'use of an offshore entity in an unlisted country', 'trust distributions – capital distributions in cash (to the HWI)', and the 'utilisation of revenue losses via intra group transfers'.

Table 10.4 Predicting high overall risk with flags* using proxy analyses

Alternative set 1 with 91.1% correctly predicted	Alternative set 2 with 90.6% correctly predicted	Alternative set 3 with 89.4% correctly predicted
Use of an offshore entity in an unlisted country (Issue 2)	Trust distribution – capital distribution in cash (to the HWI) (Issue 13)	Revenue loss utilisation via intra group transfers (Issue 1)
Miscellaneous income and deduction items – other significant deduction issues (Issue 4)	Miscellaneous income and deduction items – other significant deduction issues (Issue 4)	Other miscellaneous items – disposal of significant capital items in review period (non-assessable profit) (Issue 7)
Trust distribution – capital distribution in cash (to the HWI) (Issue 13)	Evidence of funds coming onshore – irregularly	Group structure – use of multiple entities (other)

* A flag is a risk from a list of 207 possible risks that an analyst rates over 7 on a risk scale from 1 to 10.

Other Risks and the Evolutionary Ecology of Tax Planning

As would be expected with more than 200 possible risk labels, the number of HWIs rated above 7 in the 'other miscellaneous items – other' category is very small – only six HWIs. But all six have been assigned to the high risk group. This is very high when the probability of being in the high risk group for the whole data set is only 0.14. The Chi-square test of independence has a significance of less than five in a million that this result would have occurred by chance. One source of error in this calculation is that two HWIs who were related were both rated high for seemingly the same issue and thus independence is questionable. However, the test would still remain very significant with the removal of either one of the relatives. Examination of the data also showed that the two HWIs who had the highest number of 'other miscellaneous items – other' type issues rated as a high risk were the two HWIs who also had the two greatest numbers of high risks. Overall 8 per cent of the 207 issues were labelled as 'other' type issues and they were rated as a high risk 11 per cent of the time.

It is surprising that when more than 200 issues have been created to define the most important risks, some of the most worrying fall outside that list. This could be due to limitations in the type of risks included on the original risk identification form, or to the way analysts complete the form. For instance, they may have been confused by the way that their instructions conjoin 'further information desirable' with 'and would suggest audit action'. If insufficient information were available to properly assess an unusual issue they would be obliged to rate it as a high risk. Yet perhaps this unexpected outcome is not so surprising given the very nature of aggressive tax planning. Tax planning at its most aggressive is also at its most creative and entrepreneurial. The strategies that everyone, particularly the ATO, knows about will not be the most lucrative. When everyone is into the same aggressive tax planning strategy, the strategy will be highly visible and will draw the fire of the ATO. This will cause the smart money to move into more boutique strategies, and is a similar effect to the evolutionary ecology of predation in nature. While there are certain strategies of predation that can each inhabit a strong niche for predation, if all predators jumped into the same niche some would perish. It is thought that a new predation strategy is more likely to persist if it is different from that already used by other predators competing for the same resource (Cohen and Machalek, 1988). That is, under this scenario, the most successful strategies are the most idiosyncratic. Similarly with tax planning, the best tax planners are game players who are always coming up with new angles or games.

There is no single best strategy that all the smart money gravitates towards. ATO analysts commonly identify a set of strategies, which could be conceived in an evolutionary ecology of tax planning as standard niches, each of which support a lot of players. In Australia in recent years these have included: (a) redefining income as capital by the use of multiple trust structures that conceal a common controlling mind; (b) creating artificial losses (e.g., by acquiring companies or trusts with accumulated losses); (c) disguising distributions to HWIs and family members as loans and other non-taxable benefits; (d) using off-shore trusts; (e) converting activities undertaken for private pleasure into tax losses (e.g., pleasure craft, horse breeding and racing); and (f) using charitable trusts to disguise benefits to HWIs and their families. Aggressive tax planning is to a degree recurrent and patterned into the above standard forms.

However, it is also true that its leading edge is about finding new niches that are maximally lucrative because no one else is exploiting them and no law enforcers are watching them. At its most sophisticated, this leading edge involves engineering completely new financial products, mutations that are not covered by existing tax law (Tanzi, 2000). Faced with this evolution of tax planning, the belief that most aggressive tax planning in Australia is patterned into such stable and predictable niches could lead analysts to miss tax planning niches which pose the highest risk to the revenue. This could explain why a high risk under 'other miscellaneous items – other' would be both predictive of high risk overall and associated with maximum dollar amounts.

Is there evidence from the case files to support the notion that the 'other miscellaneous items – other' category, when rated as a high risk, indicates an innovative strategy, or was it rather that the analyst 'sensed' a risk not adequately covered by the predefined issues? Two cases were picked up by Penny Gilson of the HWI Taskforce with narratives identifying risks that could have (perhaps should have) been classified under one of the 207 risk categories. Without going back to the analysts and asking them to reconstruct their reasoning it is hard to be sure that they did not see an important additional risk that was not adequately captured by the pre-defined risk issues. One case narrative has, on the face of it, a jumble of concerns that seem over-rated and that suggest a lack of information more than systemic risk. Examples are:

> Overseas borrowing – group entity claimed deduction of $218 000 for interest paid to a Swiss financier.
>
> Share trading – a group trust received substantial number of company X shares in float. Media reports indicate HWI made substantial profits through the sale of company X shares. Trust accounts do not reflect this amount.

While the first example involves a small amount of money we do not know whether the analyst knows something about this financier that causes the high risk rating. Perhaps the second example represents a kind of turning over of a seemingly inoffensive rock where something dangerous lurks. Perhaps the whole list of ten 'other' concerns conceals a detective's intuition about an inchoate underlying pattern of risk. We cannot be sure either way.[9] For example, the HWI Taskforce staff suggested that in trying to make sense of losses, analysts might well say: 'There's a big loss but I'm not sure of the source. I'll put losses down as a risk. There is something else going on so I'll record it in the 'other' risk category. The case looks like a high risk overall. I'll get to the bottom of it when I audit them'. At the very least, we should read the strong predictive power of 'other miscellaneous items – other' as a caution about relying wholly on pre-defined risk issues for identifying aggressive tax planning. Rather, it encourages intuitive detective work to follow risks that fall between the cracks.

Predicting the Total Number of High Risk Issues

An alternative definition of high risk is the number of issues where the 1 to 10 risk score exceeds 7 for a HWI. The question then becomes: if a particular risk issue is rated over 7, how many risk issues in total will be rated over 7? This is just another way of testing whether the existence of one kind of risk is a red flag for many different risks. We use a similar algorithm to that used for predicting high risk. The estimation procedure is ordinary least squares, and residual analysis was carried out to test the validity of assumptions important in this situation. Since the dependent variable in the model is a composite of all the potential independent variables (the flags) there is no attempt to use the statistical tests commonly associated with this type of modelling. The issue which when rated greater than 7 accounts for the most variance in this alternative definition of risk is included in the model first. Then the flag that accounts for the greatest proportion of the remaining variance is included, and so on until the amount of additional variance explained does not increase much relative to that already explained. The size of this change is determined by a scree slope test using R^2.

The top predictor with this flag analysis is 'capital loss creation via by asset sales' (see Table 10.5). The second predictor is 'trust distributions – taxable distributions to a loss entity' (Issue 6, Table 10.1), another trust distributions issue. One of these issues is about creating losses and the other about shifting losses. This is the game of creating or buying losses and then avoiding tax by shifting value that would otherwise be taxed into an entity that has losses, thereby cancelling out their value. The number three predictor of the model in Table 10.5 is 'group restructures – significant new ventures' (Issue 11, Table 10.1). This will often be rated as a risk because when new ventures are undertaken new entities are created that may be significant in terms of scale or in terms of moving offshore, or new in terms of being a new type of business for this group. Analysts may see reasons to worry that they may be connected to an aggressive tax planning scheme in the particular case.

Table 10.5 Predicting the total number of high risks with flags* using ordinary least squares regression analysis

Model	R^2	Flags
1	0.38	Capital loss creation via asset sales
2	0.55	Capital loss creation via asset sales
		Trust distributions – taxable distributions to a loss entity (Issue 6)
3	0.67	Capital loss creation via asset sales
		Trust distributions – taxable distributions to a loss entity (Issue 6)
		Group restructures – significant new ventures (Issue 11)

* A flag is a risk from a list of 207 possible risks that an analyst rates over 7 on a risk scale from 1 to 10.

When proxy analyses are used with this alternative definition of risk, the conclusion is that little additional insight is afforded. 'Investments held off-shore in a listed country' is the top predictor if 'capital loss creation via asset sales' is removed from the potential flags. Unfortunately it may not be of practical significance as a red flag since only one HWI was rated a risk (greater than 7) on this issue. However not only was this HWI rated a high risk, they had the highest number of high risks (31); just over one and a half times their nearest competitor (19) in terms of the number of high risks!

The three best predictors when used on their own are 'capital loss creation via asset sales', 'bank accounts and investments held in a listed country' and 'trust distributions – taxable distributions to a loss entity', each accounting for approximately the same proportion of variance in the dependent variable.

Using Dollars at Risk on a Specific Issue to Predict High Overall Risk

A comparison of Tables 10.1 and 10.2 shows that the most common high risks are not the most costly high risks necessarily. Consequently, instead of using flags, the next set of analyses use dollars at risk (see Table 10.2) on each of the 207 specific issues to predict high overall risk and number of high risks. Table 10.6 shows the significant issues included in a model using dollars at risk to predict the probability of an overall high risk. As before, a forward stepwise logistic regression algorithm is used. However, issues were added to the predictive set until the likelihood ratio test for their inclusion was not significant. The analysis includes the implicit assumption that no dollars are at risk if a value is not recorded. This may not always be correct. The logistic model including the dollars at risk for the issues in Table 10.6 correctly predicts approximately 95 per cent of the HWIs into their overall risk group. If we used a scree test slope as was done earlier, only three issues would have been shown and the percentage correctly predicted would have been 90.2.

Most of the issues that make it into the final model at the conclusion of this chapter (see Table 10.8), based on the subjective risk ratings, do get some support from the more objective risk ratings data in Table 10.6. Having involvements in an offshore-unlisted country has multiple entries in Table 10.6. Trust distributions also feature in Table 10.6. 'Trust distributions – capital distributions in cash (to the HWI)' is the second highest objective predictor.[11] 'Utilisation of revenue losses via intra group transfers' is also present. Capital loss creation does not appear nor does 'other miscellaneous items – other'. Dollars at risk recorded in 'capital loss creation by asset sales' and 'other miscellaneous items – other' are actually significant predictors of high overall risk, but they are not as important as some of the others, nor are they as important in adding additional predictive information once some of the other issues are included in the model. All the HWIs who were given a *high* risk rating on 'other miscellaneous items – other' had zero or no dollars recorded, so it is not surprising this issue is not amongst the best.

There is interest also in issues from the list of 207 that crop up in the dollar-based analysis that are not in the top predictive sets for the subjective rating analyses. The number three predictor in Table 10.6, 'property held offshore in a listed country – real estate', is an interesting one. It was also one of the best independent (stand-alone) predictors of high risk when measured as the number of risks greater than 7, but it did not outweigh the other predictors in Table 10.7.

Table 10.6 Predicting high overall risk with dollars at risk using logistic regression analysis

Step	Chi-square	df	Sig.	% correctly classified	Dollars at risk for issues
1	15.622	1	0.000	87.7%	Trust beneficiary loan accounts – credit balance and no draw-downs[10]
2	12.540	1	0.000	88.5%	+Trust distributions – capital distributions in cash (to the HWI) (Issue 13)
3	9.977	1	0.002	90.2%	+Property held offshore in listed country – real estate
4	9.408	1	0.002	90.6%	+Trust distributions to charitable trust
5	7.790	1	0.005	90.2%	+Utilisation of revenue losses via trading activities
6	5.348	1	0.021	90.6%	+Related party transactions with an entity in an unlisted country – royalty/ license income
7	5.037	1	0.025	91.1%	+Use of company shareholder loan account – repayments by HWI
8	4.909	1	0.027	91.5%	+Related party transactions with an entity in an unlisted country – provision of finance
9	9.422	1	0.002	93.2%	+Revenue loss creation via debt forgiveness/bad debts (Issue 3)
10	5.262	1	0.022	93.2%	+Trust distributions – capital distribution in cash (to group entity)
11	11.708	1	0.001	94.9%	+Utilisation of revenue losses via intra group transfers (Issue 1)

Why would the dollar value of offshore real estate investment not in a tax haven in a listed country help to predict overall risk? Firstly we need to consider the data. There are only two HWIs with dollar amounts ever recorded for offshore real estate investment in an *un*listed country (a tax haven), so it is not surprising that this issue was not an important predictor. There were not enough cases to pick up any effects. Real estate in tax havens might have. However, there are thirteen non-zero recorded dollar amounts for the issue 'property held offshore in a listed country – real estate' (twenty-eight HWIs were rated on this issue with two being rated as a high risk). The two largest dollar amounts were both HWIs where overall they were rated a high risk. This issue then, manages to capture just a few more of the high risk group over and above the first two issues in Table 10.6. On its own, or as is sometimes said, as a direct effect, it is only marginally significant with fifty other issues being more useful. Therefore, although the dollars at risk for this issue adds additional predictive power to the model after the first two issues are included, it is not particularly useful in the predictive sense on its own. How far to speculate an explanation of the predictor is not a simple question. Usually, if the purpose of modelling is explanatory, then theoretical considerations would be used in defining a model rather than an algorithmic approach as used here. That said, it may be reasonable to hypothesise a relationship of some sort between the finding that large real estate investment in a listed country is a high risk, and the earlier finding that a high risk rating for bank accounts and investments held in a listed country were two of the four best independent predictors of the total number of high risk issues. Christopher Skase, the major Australian corporate criminal who fled to Spain, is not included in these analyses. But he is a well known case with large real estate investments and bank accounts in a listed country.

The fourth predictor shown in Table 10.6, 'trust distributions to charitable trust', is also not included in Tables 10.3 or 10.4. In Table 10.7, where we use dollars at risk to predict the total number of high risk issues, another issue – neither in Table 10.3 nor 10.4 – crops up, that is, 'revenue loss creation explained by negative gearing'. The HWI with the largest dollars on this issue, approximately $50 million, was also rated overall a high risk, had the second largest number of high risk issues, and was rated high on 'other miscellaneous items – other'. Taking all this data together, although interesting, is likely to be indicative of the boutique strategies mentioned earlier, rather than useful for identifying red flags of more general predictive value.

When we spoke to HWI Taskforce staff about these issues, their reaction was the same as ours: 'Analysts would not think this was a risk in itself'. However, there is the interesting question of whether tax planners exploit this reasonable kind of expectation. It may be that if you want to move an amount of money that is too large to hide, it is best to make it visible through a vehicle that makes it appear unexceptionable. Hence, it could be that having offshore real estate is not a risk factor, but placing huge amounts of money into these vehicles should put analysts on the alert. While negative gearing is a perfectly legitimate and normal commercial practice, extraordinarily large losses created by negative gearing may give reason to be watchful, though one would expect even aggressive players to exhaust legitimate deductions like negative gearing before moving on to more doubtful techniques.

Table 10.7 reports the predictor issues whose dollars at risk predict the number of high risk issues. One reason for these analyses is to see how well the dollars at risk for the different issues predict high risk, and which ones are the best predictors. Another reason is to provide a possible corrective for the subjective nature of the assessment of the ratings used in the first part of the paper. There is concern that there may be consistent analyst bias in the ratings data since both the aggregate estimates of risk (overall risk rating and number of high risk issues), and the estimate of risk on the issues, are a subjective assessment carried out by the same assessor and may be prone to the same bias. As a hypothetical example, consider the analyst who rates businessman X incorrectly high on certain issues because of bias or error; the same bias or error may result in the businessman being rated as a high risk overall. The role of the supervisor in these cases will eliminate some of the more obvious errors, but not all.

Table 10.7 Predicting the total number of high risks with dollars at risk for each issue using ordinary least squares regression analysis

Model	R^2	Adj. R^2	Flags
1	0.503	0.501	Revenue loss utilisation via intra group transfers (Issue 1)
2	0.612	0.609	Revenue loss utilisation via intra group transfers (Issue 1)
			Revenue loss creation via negative gearing
3	0.677	0.673	Revenue loss utilisation via intra group transfers (Issue 1)
			Revenue loss creation via negative gearing
			Trust distribution – capital distributions in non-cash (to the HWI)
4	0.712	0.707	Revenue loss utilisation via intra group transfers (Issue 1)
			Revenue loss creation via negative gearing
			Trust distribution – capital distributions in non-cash (to the HWI)
			Use of shareholder loan account – repayments by HWI
5	0.732	0.726	Revenue loss utilisation via intra group transfers (Issue 1)
			Revenue loss creation via negative gearing
			Trust distribution – capital distributions in non-cash (to the HWI)
			Use of shareholder loan account – repayments by HWI
			Trust distribution – capital distributions in cash (to the HWI family member)

It is difficult to know where to draw the line in our interpretations since often the number of cases is low, both in the number of issues where dollars at risk are recorded and the number of HWIs who are assessed as being a high risk. However the sparsity observed in this data set is very characteristic of rare events data. If the notion of an evolutionary ecology of tax planning with the occurrence of stable and new niches is apt, then the prediction of a small number of rare events is important to keep abreast of new strategies.

The only issue that is consistently listed in Table 10.6 and 10.7 and the earlier tables where risk ratings were used is 'utilisation of revenue losses via intra group transfers'. This is actually the top predictor for the total number of high risk issues (see Table 10.7). Since this is also recurrently predictive in the subjective analyses, 'utilisation of revenue losses via intra group transfers' was considered a definite contender for being a red flag issue. Of the 207 issues, it is also the one that most commonly has a high risk rating (see Table 10.1). This makes it a decidedly useful red flag for our final models.

Choosing Between Subjective and Dollar Risk

In practice it appears that the two types of analyses described, those using the estimates of risk rating and those using the dollars at risk estimates, are capturing different aspects of the risk prediction process.

Focusing on issues from the preceding tables, we examined the relationship between risk rating and dollar ratings. Although there is some evidence that the higher risks had higher dollars associated with them, it was by no means universal nor unambiguous as many issues had zero or low dollars associated with high risk and vice versa. Thus, we need to interpret the dollars knowing that low dollars at risk do not necessarily signify low risk in the view of the assessor. Dollars at risk for 'revenue loss creation via negative gearing' is also a good example of the disjuncture: Assessors rarely considered the issue a high risk but unusually large dollar amounts recorded for this heading was predictive of high risk.

This chapter focuses on the subjective ratings and their use in predicting high risk. It is therefore of interest to ask if the dollars at risk for any issue adds significantly to the prediction after the flags from Table 10.3 have been included. This was analysed several ways and the dollars at risk for 'property held in a listed (non-tax-haven) country – real estate' consistently added to the prediction of high overall risk after subjective ratings were included. From our analyses it would appear that the subjective, informed assessment of the analyst is a useful approach to detecting risk, with the quantitative data providing further clues to follow. This is contrary to the notion that the dollars at risk, being a more objective measure, would have superior predictive capacity to predict: Better to analyse subjective risk assessments first, then add some value with a diagnosis of unusually large dollar amounts.

Our experience of the regulatory craft (Sparrow, 2000) leads us to suspect that analysts need both the skills of a detective and those of an accountant. Nuance of judgment is needed; things have to pass the smell test. When the good analyst smells a rat, they are more likely to chase it down a hole than to further analyse numbers. While quantitative analysis provides clues, systemic wisdom must then be applied to the specific case. That case should be looked at through many different lenses, of which the quantitative lens is only one.

These data suggest to us that there might be a case for a two-step process with aggressive tax planning analysis. Step 1 is a qualitative diagnosis of returns and other intelligence surrounding the case that is informed by knowledge of red flags of systemic risk. Step 2 is a re-examination of objectively unusually large amounts of money that occur under labels that are not viewed as red flags, but that might become red flags when the dollars in them are extraordinary. Step 2 does not mean further interrogation of all extraordinary amounts. It means a harder look only when exceptionally large amounts occur under non-red-flag issues that the kind of analysis in Tables 10.6 and 10.7 reveal to be significant predictors of overall risk.

The analyses reported in this chapter only take us as far as making some practical suggestions for the identification of red flags for Step 1. Step 2 would only make sense to become a standard methodology after complementing the quantitative analyses in Tables 10.6 and 10.7 with qualitative intelligence on the operations of aggressive tax planners.

Final Red Flags Models

Having carried out the above analyses, our final task is to convert the results shown in Tables 10.3 to 10.7 into a more useful form for discussion and practical application. It is clear that most of our potential red flags were consistent with what we referred to as standard niches. Other issues appeared to be indicative of more boutique niches. It has further been demonstrated that the number of HWIs rated as high on any one issue was small, which means that single high risk issues are a narrow basis for selecting cases for audit.

Could the results be made more useful for auditors by aggregating some of the issues that rarely occur as high risks? Consider 'capital loss creation via asset sales'. When the risk under this issue is rated high, the number of other high risk issues (that is, the number rated over 7) averages 16 (compared to a mean of 0.86 when 'capital loss creation via asset sales' is not high). But there were only four HWIs with a rating over 7 on 'capital loss creation via asset sales', so the level of risk on this particular issue is sufficiently rare that it will be of limited value in audit practice.

Consequently, we created an aggregated issue of wider scope. This issue was 'capital loss creation' instead of the narrower (but more powerfully predictive) issue 'capital loss creation via asset sales'. The broader issue was a composite of nine different kinds of capital loss creation. Hence, if there was a rating of more than 7 for any single capital loss creation issue, the red flag was put up – whether the loss was created by asset sales, property development, debt forgiveness, bad debts, takeover/acquisition/merger, cost base manipulation, artificial loss duplication, related party transactions or some other explanation, or even if the capital loss creation was unexplained. Note, however, that it is not so broad as to include revenue loss creation; it is a capital loss creation variable only.

The second recurrently predictive red flag that we broadened was trust distributions. While 'trust distributions – capital distributions in cash (to the HWI)' was the most predictive red flag here, twenty different kinds of distributions from trusts were combined in the composite red flag. This included distributions in cash and non-cash to the HWIs themselves, to HWI family members, to group entities, to charitable trusts, to a loss entity, and from probate/deceased estates, related entities, and so on. There were *from* as well as *to* distributions. Finally we broadened 'other' to include all sixteen 'other' issues including 'other significant deduction issues'.

Table 10.8 shows the summary results from a logistic regression predicting high overall risk and an ordinary least squares regression predicting the total number of high risk issues (i.e., with a rating over 7) with our set of red flags which now include the broadened issues. What we are doing in Table 10.8 is a re-run of the analyses in Tables 10.3 and 10.5, but with 'other', 'capital loss creation' and 'group trust distributions' as broader red flags with many more high risk cases.

Table 10.8 Summary results of the final models predicting risk using original and aggregated red flags

Final red flags
Other categories (aggregated flag) Capital loss creation (aggregated flag) Group trust distributions (aggregated flag) Use of an offshore entity in an unlisted country (original flag) Utilization of revenue losses via intra group transfers (original flag)
Overall high risk based on logistic regression
92.8% correctly classified with 196 out of 202 HWIs in the low to medium risk group and 22 out of 33 HWIs in the high risk group correctly classified
Number of high risk issues based on ordinary least squares regression
An $R^2 = 0.90$ and an adjusted $R^2 = 0.82$

The adjusted R^2 for the final red flags regression model predicting number of high risks is an impressive 0.82.[12] Also these red flags, when used to predict overall high risk, yielded a slightly higher classification rate of 92.8 per cent (compared with the three predictors in Table 10.3). It is of note, however, that the final red flags model actually correctly predicts more HWIs into the high risk group but at the expense of incorrectly predicting some of the other HWIs as being high risk.

Nonetheless, we can conclude from these analyses that the final aggregated red flags, which are arguably better for auditing purposes, do as well or better than our previous sets of red flags. Therefore, there appears to be value for auditors in aggregating some of the issues that rarely occur as high risks.

Of the original set of red flags, two make a contribution in these final analyses, 'utilisation of revenue losses via intra group transfers' and 'use of an offshore entity in an unlisted country'. The former, although significant, is not particularly useful in predicting the high overall risk group, but it does significantly increase the amount of variance explained when predicting the total number of high risk issues for a HWI. Hence we have identified five final red flags for overall risk: (a) trust distributions; (b) capital loss creation; (c) use of an offshore entity in a country that may be a tax haven; (d) utilisation of revenue losses via intra group transfers; and (e) extraordinary risks that fall between the cracks of the other risks.

Further analyses showed that the five subjective red flags were of more importance in predicting high overall risk than any of the dollar amounts associated with the red flags. The only red flag where the associated dollars at risk added significant extra predictive information above that of the subjective ratings greater than 7 was 'utilisation of revenue losses via intra group transfers'. This was only the case for the model predicting number of risks greater than 7.

Conclusion

The five red flag issues are consistent with what many would regard as the fundamentals of aggressive tax planning. Fundamentals here is used in opposition to the idea that the best red flags would be telling symptoms of deeper problems (e.g., converting private pleasure activities into tax deductions – pleasure craft, horse breeding, racing deductions, for instance). The verified red flag issues are: (a) trust distributions (especially capital distributions in cash to the HWI); (b) capital loss creation (especially through asset sales, but not revenue loss creation); (c) use of an offshore entity in a country that may be a tax haven; (d) utilisation of revenue losses via intra group transfers (that is, within the group of entities controlled by the HWI); and (e) 'other' extraordinary risks that fall between the cracks.

The surprisingly robust results on the 'other' measures may suggest that we do not always know what the emerging fundamentals of the future may be. These results are not interpreted as anomalous, but rather as suggesting an evolutionary ecology of tax planning. Tax planning strategies that everyone, particularly the ATO, knows about will not be the most lucrative. While there will be recurrent predation strategies, the best new strategies will be those that are not crowded out by others who use a similar strategy. Minority strategies flourish. We therefore caution against the idea that we can settle in advance all risk categories for aggressive tax planning. We also highlight the importance of intuitive detective work to follow risks that fall between the cracks. This advice follows not only from the importance of the 'other' category, but also the result that the estimated 'objective' dollars at risk added little explanatory power to the ability to predict high risk above and beyond that provided by subjective risk ratings by ATO analysts.

An evolutionary ecology of tax planning implies that some successful players will seek new niches. Financial engineering of new derivatives never conceived before by tax law and global capital mobility make this more possible than in the past (Department of the Treasury, 1999). As the law adapts to close off new niches the change in the tax law environment may also create new niches for other tax strategies. Law makers are less and less able to control these unintended effects as tax law changes in other countries create new niches available to local aggressive tax planners. The aggressive tax planner benefits from both an expanding range of niches globally, and expanding technical capabilities for local financial engineering. The first four red flags listed here may cover the standard niches while the last one covers the new niches.

The analyses also suggest a subset of cases that should be examined closely to see if there is evidence of new and previously unseen strategies or niches. These are cases where extraordinary dollar amounts are seen under issues that are not normally red flags, especially in those instances where other red flags suggest systemic risk.

Some aspects of the red flags we have identified should cease being indicators of risk to the revenue in future as Australian tax reforms have been undertaken to specifically deal with some of these problems. To this extent, the findings suggest that tax reform was well directed. For instance, the new loss integrity measures should prevent the 'cascading' of losses and will address some, but not all loss creation issues. Corporate consolidation measures are intended to limit the 'trafficking' of losses from outside the company (but they will not affect the genuine transfer of losses as this is accepted as part of normal business practice).

The proposed entity taxation regime, if adopted, will tax non-fixed trusts as companies and treat trust distributions as dividends, which would remove much of the tax effectiveness of trusts. This regime, however, has been put on hold at the time of writing. While not such a recent development, the controlled foreign corporations law was introduced to deal with tax haven use. Initially payments to these countries decreased, but in its annual report, the ATO notes that transfers to tax havens have increased significantly since 1996 (Commissioner of Taxation, 2000). Perhaps some aggressive tax planners have found a way of circumventing this legislation. In any case it appears that tax haven use remains a high risk area (Tanzi, 2000).

In a dynamic ecology of aggressive tax planning enforcement, tax administrators must adapt to cut out old risk factors just as they must prepare for mutations into new ones. Some of the most recurrent forms of aggressive tax planning are variations on fundamental themes that have been with us for many decades. Yet many of the mutations that seem so new retain the character of those fundamental strategies. A clever new piece of financial engineering may be clever and new at the same time as it is just another way of shifting losses, even if it cannot be recognised at first as loss shifting.

Notes

1 The ATO acknowledges the comments made in this paper and notes that the conclusions reached are based on aged data. The practices employed by the HWI

Taskforce have significantly changed and the conclusion reached may not be the same if this analysis were undertaken today.

2 For instance, the ATO conceives of aggressive tax planning as techniques which: (a) undermine the policy intent of the law; (b) impact on the integrity of the tax system; and (c) erode community confidence in the fairness and the equity of the tax system. Characteristics which mark aggressive tax planning in the ATO's view include arrangements which: (a) are contrived and artificial in their method of execution; (b) are uncommercial from a business or economic perspective; (c) are not implemented as specified in contractual and other legal documentation; (d) involve round robin finance or circular movement of funds and loans paid off by future earnings; (e) involve fraud on the revenue; (f) involve permanent tax advantage as distinct from a timing advantage; (g) abuse a specific concessional or anti-avoidance provision contrary to the policy underlying the law; and/or (h) attempt to reduce the amount of tax properly payable and thus create a revenue risk.

3 For example, in some instances analysts have included a risk more than once simply because it is feasible that the risk could fall under more than one category.

4 The Income Tax Regulations include a 'list' of countries which are considered to have tax systems broadly similar to the Australian system. There are fifty-eight of these 'listed' countries. 'Unlisted' countries are all those that do not appear on the list. They have taxation systems that range from almost comparable to full blown tax havens. Hence 'use of an entity in an unlisted country' would imply that profits were somehow derived in a low taxed country, and that a reduced amount of tax would be paid on them.

5 Income from trusts comes in the form of a distribution: From companies it is a dividend.

6 The individual risks named in the data are loosely grouped under five broader risk categories. The broad risk categories are International, Losses, Group Structure, Miscellaneous Income and Deduction Items, and Other Miscellaneous Items. The broad categories in turn contain more specific risk categories. Each of the specific risk categories contains a catch-all variable named 'other' to accommodate the less common or less understood risks of that type. As the broad category 'other miscellaneous items' has itself the flavour of a catch-all category, one would expect the least common or least understood risks to appear under the label 'other miscellaneous items – other'. Oddly, this has turned out to be the most highly predictive variable.

7 In this sense 'capital' is the money contributed to set-up a business or keep it running. Unlike profit, it is not taxable when it is returned to the contributor (because it is assumed to have been taxed previously). There are obvious tax benefits to the HWI if they can re-characterise profit as capital.

8 It is also a top predictor when we predict the sum of all risk rankings (0 to 10) or the number of issues where the risk score exceeds 7.

9 One risk that was classified as 'other' that was more or less systemic was property developers treating building costs as deductible on the revenue account while treating income from sales as capital. This practice gives the advantage of immediate deductions for expenses but a concessional treatment of income. It is not allowed by the legislation, but it appears that taxpayers 'try it on' in the hope the ATO will not detect it. It has since emerged that it is widespread among property developers.

10 Loan accounts are often used by HWIs as a tax free source of cash to maintain their lifestyles. A credit balance in a loan account would suggest that there was another source of income and analysts could find this a cause for concern.

11 Note also the predictive power of the dollar amounts of 'trust distributions – capital distributions in non-cash (to the HWI)' in Table 10.7.

12 An R^2 of 0.82 means that 82 per cent of the statistical variance is explained.

References

Braithwaite, J. (2001), 'Through the Eyes of the Advisers: A Fresh Look at the Compliance of High Wealth Individuals', *Centre for Tax System Integrity Working Paper No. 22*, Australian National University, Canberra.

Cohen, L.E. and Machalek, R. (1988), 'A General Theory of Expropriative Crime: An Evolutionary Ecological Approach', *American Journal of Sociology*, vol. 94, pp. 465-501.

Commissioner of Taxation (2000), *Annual Report 1999-2000*, Commonwealth of Australia, Canberra.

Department of the Treasury (1999), *The Problem of Corporate Tax Shelters: Discussion, Analysis and Legislative Proposals*, Department of the Treasury, Washington D.C.

Sparrow, M. (2000), *The Regulatory Craft*, Brookings Institution Press, Washington D.C.

Tanzi, V. (2000), 'Globalization, Technological Developments, and the Work of Fiscal Termites', *International Monetary Fund Working Paper WP/00/11811*, International Monetary Fund, Washington D.C.

Chapter 11

When Compliance is not the Solution but the Problem: From Changes in Law to Changes in Attitude

Doreen McBarnet

A cooperative taxpaying culture is the ultimate goal of the Compliance Model of enforcement adopted, among other regulatory agencies (see, for example, Hawkins, 1984), by the Australian Taxation Office (ATO) (Cash Economy Task Force, 1998; Australian Taxation Office, 2000a). This volume, therefore, includes chapters on why people comply – or do not – and on the best way for enforcement agencies to secure compliance. Securing compliance is seen as the key, as the solution to the regulatory problem of making policy effective in practice. This chapter offers a different perspective. It asks: What happens to the Compliance Model when compliance is not the solution but the problem?

The Compliance Model focuses on the strategies adopted by those enforcing the law. They should be cooperative, understanding, focusing on fostering compliance rather than on leaping immediately to punishing non-compliance, with 'big stick' sanctions reserved for those recalcitrants who continue with non-compliance regardless (Ayres and Braithwaite, 1992). But choice of strategies is not the preserve of enforcement agencies. Different strategic responses can be adopted by those on the receiving end of the law too, and these translate into different approaches to compliance. Faced with a tax bill, people may choose to comply willingly. We might think of this as *committed compliance.* They may choose to comply unwillingly, complain but pay up nonetheless. We might think of this as *capitulative compliance.* They may invent false expenses, pack their cash in a suitcase and whisk it out of the country without declaring it, or simply operate in the cash economy, opting for *non-compliance.* Or, if they have the resources, they may set their lawyers to work[1] on the legal form of their activities to package or repackage them in ways they can claim fall beyond the ambit of *dis*advantageous, or within the ambit of advantageous, law. They can engage in *creative compliance.*

It is the essence of creative compliance that it can be defended as *not* non-compliance. Indeed, that is exactly how it is often presented, as 'not illegal', or more positively, in that well-worn phrase, as 'perfectly legal'. Nonetheless, just like non-compliance, the essence of creative compliance is that it escapes the intended impact of law. The creativity inherent in creative compliance involves finding ways to accomplish compliance with the letter of the law while totally undermining the policy behind the words. It is therefore when compliance takes the form of creative compliance that it becomes, for those vested with the task of enforcing policy, a problem not a solution.

Creative compliance devices abound in the area of tax, but are not confined to it. Far from it. Creative compliance will be found in any area of law in which those subject to it have the motivation and the resources (in terms of money and/or know-how) to resist legal control legally.

Recognising this will help those concerned with tax to realise that creative compliance is not a tax issue but a much more general law issue, and a fundamental one at that. Recognising that the issue goes beyond tax avoidance to law avoidance means we can try to learn from experience in other areas of law, in such areas, for example, as that first cousin of tax avoidance, creative accounting. Indeed, creative accounting is pertinent to tax not only as a parallel area of creative compliance, but as potentially integral to tax computation.[2] In the analysis that follows I draw not only on my own research on tax avoidance in the United Kingdom (UK)[3] and in Australia,[4] but on joint research on creative accounting[5] to draw out the challenges posed for effective enforcement by creative compliance.

Creative Compliance

Two factors contribute to the practice of creative compliance. One significant factor is the nature and operation of law itself. The law-making process leads to lobbying and compromise, legislators cannot address every contingency that might arise, drafting is fallible. More fundamentally, it is in the nature of law that it is open to different interpretations, and that its meaning and application are arguable.

Creative compliance, however, does not arise deterministically from the nature of law. It also requires a particular attitude to law, an attitude which, far from seeing law as an authoritative and legitimate policy to be implemented, sees it as a material to be worked on (McBarnet, 1984), to be tailored, regardless of the policy behind it, to one's own or one's client's interests. And it requires active legal work.

Law is open to alternative interpretations. Innovations in practice can leave law behind. But grey areas, alternative interpretations and innovative legal forms do not only arise 'naturally'. Rather, they may be motivated precisely by the desire to outflank the law. Creative compliance involves careful scrutiny of law in order to seek out material for and actively construct alternative and innovative arguments and legal forms. Creative compliance involves seeking out: (a) gaps facilitating the 'where does it say I can't do that?' argument; (b) the ex-files of law, expressing exemptions, exceptions, exclusions, with practices then restructured to fit within them; and (c) rules, the more prescriptive and rigid the definitions and thresholds involved, the better, with legal forms adopted to fit inside or outside their literal ambit (a practice of working to rule).

Regulators often express concern about uncertainties in the law being exploited,[6] but creative compliance operates particularly effectively in the context of a rule-bound regime, where the words of the law can be treated as recipes for avoidance.

How this works in practice can be readily demonstrated from research. When it was proposed in the UK that value added tax (VAT) should be levied on domestic fuel, hitherto exempt, there was extensive protest on the basis that the old and the poor would suffer. In the event, not everyone suffered. Some institutions, including university student residences, found a nice way to avoid the new costs involved in heating and hot water. They would sell their boilers, which of course remained exactly where they were in the institution's basement, to a separate company. The company would buy the fuel to heat the water. The company would have to pay VAT on the fuel but, as a commercial enterprise, could reclaim it. The company then sold the water to the institution. There is as yet no VAT on water so, hey presto, nobody pays any VAT. And the 'where does it say I can't do that?' argument, along with a quick referral to the rules, can be brought into play to justify it.

UK national insurance is currently being avoided in the North Sea oil industry by transferring UK staff to overseas agencies. Transnational tax avoidance by using tax havens or differential rules in different jurisdictions (for example, the 'Delaware Link' device (McBarnet, 1992)) is common practice. But avoidance can also be readily accomplished within a jurisdiction simply by working to, or playing with, the rules. For example, to avoid UK national insurance contributions (national insurance contributions being paid by employer as well as employee), a practice was developed in the financial sector of paying part of the salary in the form of large bonuses in shares. No national insurance contributions were payable on shares, though they had a clear monetary value and could be converted immediately into cash. To deal with this, the law was changed to impose national insurance on any payment in a 'traded commodity on a recognised exchange'. The result was a shift to payments in fine wine, also of clear monetary value, also amenable to immediate conversion to cash, but not traded on a recognised exchange.

Creative compliance is pervasive in corporate practice in many areas of law and has, over time, involved a vast array of techniques (see Griffiths, 1986, 1995). Take an example from my research with Christopher Whelan on creative accounting, one we have frequently cited because it demonstrates so clearly the problems posed by creative compliance. This specific example, the 'orphan subsidiary', was widely used in the 1980s to cosmetically enhance a corporate group's paper profits and assets, with knock-on effects for share prices, performance-related pay and borrowing capacity. A parent company must, under company law, produce accounts, which include the profits/losses and assets/liabilities of its subsidiaries. The idea is that it should provide the full picture for all the companies it controls, and not hide away poor performances or liabilities in a separate entity whose details it does not disclose. But what if parent company A sets up a company B which it controls, but which is nonetheless carefully structured to fall outside the legal definitions of a subsidiary? In this 'orphan subsidiary' it would have the perfect vehicle to use in ventures which involved high risk or high borrowings – such as a highly leveraged acquisition – without the losses or liabilities appearing, detrimentally, in its group accounts.

The statutory definition of a subsidiary under Section 736(1) of the *Companies Act 1985* involved two criteria. Company B was a subsidiary of company A if (a) A owned more than half B's equity capital, or if (b) A controlled the composition of B's board of directors. With a little creativity, both criteria could be readily circumvented. There were many ways of achieving this, one of the simplest being to set up two types of shares, ordinary shares and preference shares, 50 per cent of each. Company A would own the ordinary shares, while its bank would own the preference shares. Company A would not therefore own more than 50 per cent of the equity capital. Company A and its bank would each appoint half the directors. Company A would not therefore control the composition of the board of directors. But the directors representing the ordinary shareholder (Company A) would have two votes to the preference share directors' one. Company A would not control the composition of the board of directors, but it would control the board's votes.

These are typical examples of creative compliance at work, and they demonstrate how the material of law is actively used to circumvent legal control. The constructs that emerge are backed with legal arguments and the opinions of leading counsel and, if challenged, a case can be produced (however 'bullish' – see ahead) to claim compliance with the law. And these are merely examples. Creative compliance is not a practice operating at the statistical margins, or at the margins of society. On the contrary, it is pervasive, and pervasive among leading lights in the social and corporate world. The orphan subsidiary, for example, was just one of a vast range of creative accounting devices, used routinely in the UK by household name companies.

Creative Compliance and Non-compliance

That creative compliance *is* compliance is, of course, only a claim. Whether it is perfectly legal or not is an unanswerable question, until it has won or lost in court. Often it is a claim that succeeds simply because it is not contested. Even if it is successfully challenged, the fact that it is a case based on applying the law rather than ignoring it[7] provides protection from the sanctions and stigma associated with simple non-compliance. A tax planning device may fail in court without being branded a tax fraud.[8] It is an essential element and attraction of creative compliance that it can claim to be 'not illegal', to be quite distinct from non-compliance.

But the line between the two is not always so clear as that suggests (McBarnet, 1992). The Australian Commissioner of Taxation (2000) has recognised that aggressive tax planning can in practice slip over the line into evasion: 'The competition in the market has also stretched the boundaries of arrangements, with some edging to the fraudulent' (p. 5).

What is more, creative compliance and non-compliance can intertwine. There has recently been a furore over Australian barristers going bankrupt with one creditor, the ATO, to whom they owed debts in unpaid taxes to the tune of millions of dollars (Commissioner of Taxation, 2000, pp. 6-7). In this case the actual non-payment of tax would not appear to be a matter of creative compliance, but of simple non-compliance under tax law. But resort to a different branch of the law, bankruptcy, permitted escape from the sanctions of tax law. Of course no one can go into bankruptcy unless they have run out of assets. But the reason for the furore was concern that assets remained in the family, accessible to and enjoyed by the bankrupt, despite the bankruptcy and the protection it offered regarding the enforcement of tax law. In short, there was concern that bankruptcy law had been used creatively. Certainly, bankruptcy can be planned and creatively constructed. The ATO Auditor-General Audit Report (1999) observed (on a broader base than the bankrupt barristers mentioned in the press) that the individuals concerned 'are generally well prepared for bankruptcy' (Auditor-General, 1999, p. 113).

Tackling Creative Compliance: 'Big Powers'

How is creative compliance to be dealt with? In the ATO Compliance Model, if a taxpayer is not won over to compliance via gentle cooperative control, there is a next step – a shift of gear from gentle persuasion to legal force, from cooperation to sanctions. The Compliance Model has two sides. It involves not just cooperation but 'big sticks'. Despite the primary consensual approach, there is a need to remember the power of the punch behind this velvet gloved approach (Clayton Utz, 1997). In the Compliance Model, law and sanctions may be a matter of last resort, but they are there, and they are there to be used.

But what happens when it is the taxpayer who is resorting, as a matter of first resort, to the law, and using it, whatever the enforcement agency's view, to claim compliance? Big sticks are for dealing with non-compliance. How do enforcers bring in legal sanctions to deal with what is claimed to be legal compliance? In this situation the issue is no longer a matter of enforcement style, of the agency choosing whether to bring in the big sticks or not. The enforcement agency cannot bring in the big sticks until it contests the claim to compliance. The issue, in short, is no longer one of enforcement, but one of enforceability. Before big sticks can be brought into play, the claim to compliance must first be contested.

To challenge the foundations of creative compliance, then, one first needs 'big powers'. Big powers mean more than just new specific rules, which can result merely in a cat and mouse game of new creative compliance adapted to the new words of the new rule. Big powers need to be of a qualitatively different kind.

There have been attempts to produce big powers in a number of areas, including tax in the UK and Australia, and financial services and financial reporting regulation in the UK. In many ways the UK's new regime in accounting regulation, driven in particular by the wish to control creative accounting, has been at the cutting edge of the big power approach.

Key big power strategies have included: (a) a shift, in the form of regulations, from rules to principles; (b) a focus on the substance of practice, not just its legal form; (c) taking a conceptual approach to the construction of definitions; and (d) an emphasis on 'super-principles'. Each will be discussed in turn.

Rigid detailed rules have been recognised as providing too fertile a soil for creative compliance. Where regulations involve rigidly defined categories, they can be too readily avoided by repackaging activities into a form that falls outside the clear delineations. The orphan subsidiary or the national insurance examples given above are classic examples. Hence, the approach of the Australian Accounting Standards Board (1994) of trying to write its regulation for dealing with such matters as off-balance sheet financing (in the Accounting Standards Board's financial reporting standard known as FRS5) in terms of a simple general principle: companies should report the substance of their transactions. The Australian Review of Business Taxation (Ralph Report, 1999) has also advocated 'a system based on clearly enunciated principles' as the best way to 'ensure horizontal equity and to reduce tax avoidance and hence to improve the integrity of the system' (p. 15).

FRS5 not only set out its regulation in the style of a principle not a rule, but it clearly stipulated that it was substance, not form, that counted. This notion of substance over form is also at the heart of the UK's 'new approach' to tax avoidance, introduced through judicial doctrine in the 1980s in the cases of *Ramsay (WT) Ltd v IRC [1982] AC300* and *Furniss v Dawson [1984] AC474*. The Australian Review of Business Taxation has also proposed a focus on 'economic substance rather than legal form' (Ralph Report, 1999, p. 15), and recommended that 'transactions with similar economic substance should be taxed in a similar manner' (p. 14).

The orphan subsidiary was based on a very specific definition in the *Companies Act 1985*, as we have seen, including the criterion of 'control of the composition of the board of directors'. The *Companies Act 1989* changed that, by including a much broader definition that went for the essence of control regardless of its specific form. One 'entity' was the parent of another (its subsidiary) if it had a 'participating interest' in it, and 'actually exercised dominant interest' over it. This was seen as a 'catchall' definition that avoided the invitation in more specific rules to slip beyond the parameters they set.[9]

Another strategy is to set up 'super-principles' which cut through or override literal compliance with specific rules. Australia's General Anti-Avoidance Rule can be seen as an example. The idea of substance overriding form can also be seen in this light. In the UK the epitome of the super-principle is the 'overriding' requirement in company law that accounts should give 'a true and fair view'. There is also an express clause requiring directors to depart from, rather than comply with, specific rules, if following them will not result in a true and fair view (see Sections 226(5) and 227(6) of the *Companies Act 1989)*.

What all of these strategies are about is bringing into play big powers that undermine the material for, cut through, or override claims to compliance based on the letter of the law, rather than on what those producing or enforcing the law see as its spirit. But these big powers pose their own problems.

Problems

A number of problems arise where big powers involve basing regulation on principles rather than on specific detailed rules. One problem is how to sustain principles and prevent them from being converted or reduced to rules, which can then be used once again as material for creative compliance.

Sustaining Principles

This kind of reduction can happen in a number of ways. It may occur through demands for guidance on how principles will be applied in specific contexts. FRS5, the Accounting Standards Board's regulation requiring the reporting of the substance of transactions, not just their legal form, took nine years to reach the standards book. Demands for guidance produced detailed examples which some have certainly looked to as new rules and potential material for creative compliance (McBarnet and Whelan, 1999). What happens in effect is that we get rules about how principles can be used.

Lobbying may result in negotiated curtailment behind the scenes of what looks in the books to be big powers. After the 'new approach' in UK tax, for example, the Inland Revenue responded to lobbying and met with legal and accounting professional bodies to negotiate the parameters within which they would apply the new approach in practice.

Something similar can be found in the Australian context in the Ralph Report (1999). Australia's big power is the General Anti-Avoidance Rule (GAAR), but the Ralph Report has sought a clear statement that 'the GAAR will not apply to the mere use in a straightforward and ordinary manner of structural features of the law to best advantage'. A 'statement of policy should confirm the circumstances in which the GAAR could be applied and reduce the perception that valid business practices could unintentionally be subject to the application of the GAAR' (p. 241). It has recommended that there should be a board to review the application of the GAAR, including rulings on whether or not a practice is caught by the rule. It has argued the need for producing clarity without mapping the minefield (Ralph Report, 1999, p. 44). This unfortunately is not a solution but a restatement of the problem – just how to produce the clarity requested without mapping the minefield. There is a real danger that in pursuit of 'clarity', the big power of the GAAR may be limited to narrower parameters and reduced to rules, undermining its capacity to override rule-based avoidance.

This narrowing can also be produced through the courts, not just through the enforcement agency losing but through the process of decisions being made (whoever wins or loses), reasoning being set out, and new material being provided for those bent on exploiting creative compliance. In the context of the new approach to tax avoidance in the UK, new 'rules', and therefore material for creative compliance, were found by scrutinising the arguments used by the judges, even in the *Ramsay* case, which introduced the anti-avoidance principle of looking through form to substance.

The *Ramsay* case comprised a circle of 'self-cancelling' transactions used to create an artificial loss, not unlike the recent Australian 'investment schemes' (Senate Economics References Committee, 2001), though more complex. The transactions required two companies and a subsidiary controlled by the taxpayer, two companies controlled by the scheme promoters (the Rossminster group). It involved two loans, one share issue, the exercise of options on interest levels (the interest rate on one loan was changed from 11 per cent to 22 per cent, on the other from 11 per cent to zero), the sale of the 22 per cent loan to a company controlled by the scheme promoter, which then sold the loan to the subsidiary of taxpayer company B, two liquidations, loan repayments, and exchange of shares for loanstock in another promoter-controlled company. Yet it was, as the judges observed, 'all over by lunch'. What is more, these multiple deals had 'no business purpose'. These observations were seized upon and steps taken in subsequent tax avoidance schemes to factor in a business purpose (with 'careful minuting', as one interviewee put it, to record it) to build in gaps and contingencies, and to change the timescale.

Even without resort to courts, precedents build up. In the context of rulings on the application of the General Anti-Avoidance Rule, it has been observed that 'an important body of case law is building up' (Clayton Utz, 1999). Rulings or clearances may be sought informally whether there is a statutory right to them or not, and interviews with UK tax officials and accountants indicated frequent requests to the Technical Office of the Inland Revenue for informal advice on 'hypothetical' or 'no-names' transactions. Tax officials had an ambivalent attitude to such requests, preferring to avoid rulings on such a basis but finding the requests a valuable source of information on the latest creative thinking. Potential new material for creative compliance is also produced every time there is a decision on the part of the agency on how a principle should apply to a specific situation. Even a simple failure to challenge a practice can be treated as endorsement by default, and built upon.

Application

Big powers are only as big as their application, and application may in practice be curtailed by a range of factors. These can be illustrated by looking at the record of enforcement in the new UK accounting regime.[10] The body responsible for enforcement is the Financial Reporting Review Panel, which came into being in 1991, armed with the extensive new powers listed above; and with a big stick sanction in the background in the judicial power to make directors personally liable for all the costs of revising and reissuing accounts which were successfully challenged by the Panel, along with legal costs. The Panel announced that it would use the true and fair super-principle to stop creative compliance:

> Where we are firmly of the view that accounts are not true and fair, we will not be deterred from taking action by the fact that there is room for forensic argument as to technical compliance with the particular FRS [accounting standard] (Financial Reporting Council, 1992, p. 24).

In other words, the Panel would use the true and fair principle to override what it saw as creative compliance.

But to date this power has never been used for this purpose. Rather, the Panel has monitored those situations where companies have invoked the true and fair principle to override compliance with specific rules. Indeed, it has tended to require companies to adhere to the rules even where there is strong opinion that following the rules does not produce true and fair accounts. In doing so the Panel may indeed be damaging its big powers. It may be setting a precedent that following the rules is more important than following the principle of a potentially clashing true and fair view. The big power of FRS5, requiring companies to report substance not just legal form, has been used only once against a small company. No directors have had to face personal liability costs, because no cases have gone to court.

It could be argued, of course, that all this tells us is that creative compliance has died off in the face of the new regime. But there are still many instances of practices that others see as 'bullish', or 'sailing close to the wind' (Griffiths, 1995; McBarnet and Whelan, 1999), and there is some danger that by not addressing them the Panel is in fact legitimising them.

Why then has the Panel been so circumspect in its use of its big powers? For, although the Panel has big powers in the books, our interpretation of what was happening was that a kind of 'self-regulation' was taking place, in the sense that the enforcers themselves were limiting their invocation of the powers at their disposal. Indeed, reflecting on the position of the Panel, or any agency in the same position (the ATO with its General Anti-Avoidance Rule, for example), the fact is that putting big powers into practice is not as straightforward as it might seem. Indeed, there are risks in using big powers which can foster caution.

There is a risk of 'winning but losing' in court with decisions and reasoning used in unforeseen but very damaging ways. In the accounting context, the *Argyll* case in 1981[11] involved successful prosecution of company directors for including in their group accounts a company they had not yet fully acquired. They argued that they effectively controlled it, it was in substance a subsidiary, and including it would result in true and fair accounts. The Department of Trade followed the case with a statement, underlining the message that specific definitions in the law had to be strictly adhered to. The unintended consequence was the highly damaging device of the orphan subsidiary, with the case and the statement pointed to as a powerful basis for arguing not only that the practice was not illegal, but that directors had no legal alternative but to keep a company that did not meet the specific definitions of a subsidiary out of their group accounts.

More generally, going to court means losing control to the judges who may, whether in ways favourable to the enforcement agency or not, come up with approaches with complex implications for other instances. And of course there is a risk of losing, not only opening the floodgates to copycat cases of the same type, but encouraging avoidance more generally. 'A daft judge can kill a standard', as one of our UK accounting regulators put it (McBarnet and Whelan, 1999, p. 88). The ATO has had experience of this in the past in terms of judicial treatment of the General Anti-Avoidance Rule. After the new approach cases in UK tax, the Inland Revenue required tax inspectors not to invoke the *Ramsay* ruling without getting central clearance to do so. Inland Revenue did not want taxpayers challenging them in court on the reach of the new doctrine in the context of just any case; the new doctrine of 'substance over form' was too important not to keep it carefully controlled.

Small wonder then if the pragmatic approach is to avoid confrontation in court. Indeed, big powers may be stronger for not testing them in court. The (until recently) chairman of the Accounting Standards Board, David Tweedie, observed of the new principle-based regime:

> We're like a cross-eyed javelin thrower competing at the Olympic Games: we may not win but we'll keep the crowd on the edge of its seats.[12]

He was reflecting on the (continuing) uncertainty surrounding how effective the new regime can really be. But the comment also captures the power of uncertainty. Uncertainty over where the regulatory javelin will fall (both because the regime is new and because it is based on principles) may make for greater caution among the regulated in embarking on creative compliance.

From the perspective of the regulators we can use another metaphor, and think of the benefits of the 'Oz factor'. The power of the Wizard of Oz lay in projecting big powers without exposing the mere mortal behind the image. For enforcement agencies, the image of big powers, never used, may be more effective in securing control than actually using them and taking the risk that they may be revealed as less powerful in practice than the image suggests.

This becomes in fact, an argument for the compliance strategy of enforcement, albeit on a very different grounding from that propounded by the ATO. But that has its dangers too, since a big power never used can soon lose its deterrent effect, and the failure to invoke big powers, may be taken as tacit admission that there are doubts on their reach.

There are other restraints on the use of big powers: concerns over the possibility of compensation demands if, for example, the agency loses a case and a regulated company attributes to it damage to reputation and loss of share value. Since, as the ATO explicitly acknowledges, there is always room for 'disagreements or different views on the law and compliance' (Australian Taxation Office, 2000a, p. 6), this is always a possibility – the more so where the application in practice of broad untested principles is concerned.

There can also be a real concern that the powers are just too big. The then chairman of the Financial Reporting Review Panel, which actually enforces the new regime in accounting, described the powers available to the Panel as 'draconian'. If the big powers were little used for cutting through creative compliance, it reflected a concern on the part of the enforcement body itself, that, for example, the 'true and fair' principle is too 'blunt' an instrument, and indeed that it should not be used to counter something 'which Parliament, rightly or wrongly, wrote in' (McBarnet and Whelan, 1999, p. 226). An agency dealing with such powers may see itself as structurally vulnerable to judicial review, or these days in the UK, litigation under the Human Rights Act.

A regime based on big powers is always vulnerable to lobbying on the basis of a rule of law critique. Big power regulation (based on principles, on a capacity to override literal compliance with specific rules by invoking broader purposes, or on a general anti-avoidance rule) can readily be presented as too uncertain, as involving retrospectivity, as giving regulators too much power, or as opening the way to arbitrary decision-making. All of these points were made in the wake of the UK's new approach to tax avoidance, notably in a booklet published by a joint committee of solicitors and accounting professional bodies, the Special Committee of Tax Law Consultancy Bodies (1998).

The Ralph Committee's concern about uncertainty in the reach of the Australian General Anti-Avoidance Rule, has already been noted. The committee's general terms of reference included assessment of how far current arrangements 'meet the aims of', among other things, 'certainty of taxation treatment' and 'clarity of law' (Ralph Report, 1999, p. vi). The ATO has also experienced direct criticism of its recent attack on artificial investment schemes (see Griffiths, 1995; McBarnet and Whelan, 1999) on the basis of retrospectivity (Senate Economics References Committee, 2001). The Accounting Standards Board's FRS5 took nine years and four drafts to reach the standard book precisely because of vociferous criticisms that the principled approach was too vague, too uncertain, and too impractical.[13] The big power response to creative compliance can only too readily be presented as 'creative control' (McBarnet and Whelan, 1999, p. 272).

Small wonder that enforcement bodies are inclined to be circumspect with big powers. It is precisely because they are regulating or 'taxing democracy', as this book's title underlines, with all its inherent tensions between due process and effective control.

Attitude

Finally, big powers, far from destroying creative compliance, may still fall prey to it. Even big powers can be treated as 'material to work on'. We have already seen how the judicial reasoning in the UK's new approach tax cases was mined for 'rules' which could be used to argue that new tax avoidance schemes lay beyond the reach of the new approach.

Regulations, even regulations geared to principles or anti-avoidance doctrines, have to be expressed in words, and even the words expressing the big powers to curb creative compliance can be subjected to the creative and advantageous interpretation on which creative compliance is based. Consider the orphan subsidiary. We saw earlier how it was based on careful scrutiny of and adaptation to very specific definitions in company law. We also saw how the law was changed. Definitions of a subsidiary under new legislation included the 'catchall' requirement to include an 'entity' in group accounts if the parent company had 'a participating interest' in it (a far cry from 'more than half the equity capital') and 'actually exercised control' over it (much wider than 'controlled the composition of the board of directors'). Legislators set out definitions of a broader, more abstract nature, and refused to define them further, precisely (and they were quite explicit about this) in order to stop feeding creative compliance.

Yet creative compliance continued. Even big powers have exemptions and exceptions ('ex-file' clauses) which were sought out and used. But more significantly still, the words in the catchall definition were themselves scrutinised and responded to with the 'deadlocked joint venture'. This involved two companies forming a 50-50 joint venture in which, it was claimed, neither 'actually exercised control', so that it remained off the accounts of both.

The power to override compliance with specific rules in order to require compliance with the overarching principle of producing true and fair accounts, has itself been scrutinised and resisted on the basis that it is complied with if companies give the 'true and fair' version of their accounts in the *notes* but leave the *numbers*, in the same accounts, based on literal compliance with specific rules – even though it is accepted that compliance at this level does not give a true and fair view.[14] The numbers of course, are more important than the notes, not only because the significance of the notes may be lost on the less expert reader, but because the numbers are what are used in calculating market ratios such as leverage or gearing. These ratios, in turn, are what are used by analysts in assessing share value, by banks in lending covenants to stop excessive additional borrowing by management, or which, when they reach a certain level, oblige management to consult shareholders. The numbers are, in other words, the basis of legal controls on a number of fronts.

In short, even big powers designed to counter creative compliance may themselves be vulnerable to it if they meet with the same attitude to the law – an attitude that treats the law as merely a material to work on. It is not only how big powers are applied that determines their impact, but how they are received.

A Change of Attitude

Creative compliance, I suggested earlier, is the product of two factors: the nature of law and the attitude taken to it. The application of law *is* problematic, given to grey areas and alternative interpretations. But the problem posed by creative compliance depends on those on the receiving end of law actively working on and taking advantage of those intrinsic problems. The enhanced uncertainty associated with principles and general anti-avoidance rules is a genuine concern. Yet the resort to such measures is itself a response to active abuse of more specific rules. The drift of principles to rules I have designated a 'problem', but it would not be a problem if those rules were not likely to be actively seized on and used to escape legal control, and if there were not a culture which treated the law as fair game for such activity.

What this suggests is that changes in law, however sweeping, are unlikely, alone, to eliminate creative compliance and the problems it poses for law and enforcement. The second factor, the attitude to law, needs to change too. The ATO, and the Compliance Model of law enforcement itself, recognise the need to foster a cooperative taxpaying culture, and indeed recognise that it is not just law that has to change, but attitude: 'Changing attitudes to our tax system is the remaining element that can give a major impetus to achieving a genuine new tax system in its fullest sense' (Commissioner of Taxation, 1999, p. xiii). The ATO is currently working to counter non-compliance by fostering an image of tax as a positive contribution, not as a negative imposition. It seeks to relate tax payment to the provision of public services: 'Our tax system is important to our community. It is about education, health treatment, support for those in need and roads and other community assets' (Commissioner of Taxation, 2000, p. 8). The ATO, in effect, is appealing for tax compliance as a mark of responsible citizenship (see also Australian Taxation Office, 2000b). The UK's Inland Revenue has announced a similar approach. It will be promoting the payment of tax as a 'badge of good citizenship', 'explicitly linked to public goods'.[15]

But this chapter, and the larger bodies of work on which it draws, indicates that tackling the attitude to non-compliance, appealing for compliance, is not enough. Whether compliance is enough depends on how people are complying. Compliance can itself be a creative construct, and a mark of resistance to tax policy, not cooperation with it. In aiming to construct a culture of compliance, then, the aim must be not just a culture of compliance as opposed to non-compliance, but a culture of compliance with the spirit of the law, rather than creative compliance with its letter.

Creative compliance is not just a tax problem but a law problem. The ATO is working to change the general attitude towards tax. But if a change of attitude is required, it is not just in the attitude to tax, but in the attitude taken to law, policy and compliance. This is true not just for taxpayers, but for their professional advisers – the lawyers and accountants whose creative work lies at the heart of creative compliance. What needs to be fostered is a change of attitude to the law, in which it is seen not as a game of words, a material to be worked on to one's own or one's client's advantage, but as an instrument of legitimate policy to be respected, with the policy, not just the words, looked to as the measure of compliance. That, I know, is itself problematic in many ways. But without some shift in that direction, the concern must be that compliance will remain not a solution but a problem for tax policy and tax enforcement, and, indeed, for legal policy and legal control in general.

Notes

1 Or if they are lawyers, as in the celebrated recent cases of Australia's bankrupt barristers (Auditor-General, 1999), set themselves to work.

2 The more so where taxable profits and financial reporting profits substantially overlap. There is variability between jurisdictions as to how far this is the case. See, for example, Touche Ross (1989).

3 Funded by the Economic and Social Research Council and based on in-depth interviews with lawyers, accountants and regulators (including the Inland Revenue, Accounting Standards Board, Financial Reporting Review Panel, Australian Taxation Office), along with key players from business as relevant.

4 As a Visiting Fellow at the Centre for Tax System Integrity, researching the ATO Compliance Model of enforcement and issues posed for it by legal creativity.

5 With Christopher Whelan. Funded by the Jacob Burns Fund for Socio-Legal Studies and the European Commission. See McBarnet and Whelan (1999), on which this chapter draws.

6 See for example, Australian Commissioner of Taxation's reference to 'tax arrangements which seek to exploit deficiencies or uncertainty in the law' (Commissioner of Taxation, 1999, p. xiii).

7 The Ralph Report (1999) distinguishes tax avoidance as a 'mis-use or abuse of law rather than a disregard for it' (p. 243).

8 I have elsewhere described one of the functions of creative compliance as 'fraud insurance' (McBarnet. 1991).

9 Drawn from European law. See McBarnet and Whelan (1991).

10 This section draws on analysis based on joint research with Christopher Whelan (McBarnet and Whelan, 1999).

11 Unreported magistrates' court case, but very influential. Reported unofficially in Ashton (1986).

12 Hence the 'cross-eyed javelin thrower' of our book.

13 See McBarnet and Whelan (1991) for a deeper analysis of 'the discourse of resistance' in relation to both tax and accounting regulation changes.

14 There was a controversial debate over this in the 1980s between accountants David Tweedie and James Kellas, on the one hand, and Ralph Aldwinckle of the Law Society, on the other. Even after a change of statutory wording, the debate continues. See McBarnet and Whelan (1999, Chapter 15) for a detailed analysis.

15 *Financial Times* weekend 20-21 January, 2001, quoting Nick Montagu, chairman of Inland Revenue, who also argued that a similar approach had 'worked in the Netherlands'.

References

Accounting Standards Board (1994), *FRS5: Reporting the Substance of Transactions.*

Ashton, R.K. (1986), 'The Argyll Foods Case: A Legal Analysis', *Accounting and Business Research*, vol. 17(65), pp. 3-12.

Auditor-General (1999), *Audit Report No. 23 1999-00: The Management of Tax Debt Collection*, Auditor-General's Office, Canberra.

Australian Taxation Office (2000a), *Cooperative Compliance: Working with Large Business in the New Tax System*, Australian Taxation Office, Canberra.

_____ (2000b), *Strategic Statement 2000-03*, Australian Taxation Office, Canberra.

Ayres, I. and Braithwaite, J. (1992), *Responsive Regulation*, Oxford University Press, Oxford.

Cash Economy Task Force (1998), *Improving Tax Compliance in the Cash Economy*, Australian Taxation Office, Canberra.

Clayton Utz (1997), 'When the Commissioner Comes Knocking', *Tax Litigation Issues*, Issue No. 2, Clayton Utz, Sydney.

_____ (1999), 'Challenging Private Rulings', *Tax Litigation Issues*, Issue No. 3, Clayton Utz, Sydney.

Commissioner of Taxation. (1999), *Annual Report 1998-99*, Commonwealth of Australia, Canberra.

_____ (2000), *Annual Report 1999-00*, Commonwealth of Australia, Canberra.

Financial Reporting Council (1992), *Annual Report*, Financial Reporting Council, London.

Griffiths, I. (1986), *Creative Accounting*, Sidgwick and Jackson, London.

_____ (1995), *New Creative Accounting*, Macmillan, London.

Hawkins, K. (1984), *Environment and Enforcement*, Clarendon Press, New York.

McBarnet, D. (1984), 'Law and Capital: The Role of Legal Form and Legal Actors', *International Journal of the Sociology of Law*, vol. 12(3), pp. 231-38.

_____ (1991), 'Whiter than White Collar Crime: Tax, Fraud Insurance and the Management of Stigma', *British Journal of Sociology*, vol. 42(3), pp. 324-44.

McBarnet, D (1992), 'It's Not What You Do But The Way That You Do It: Tax Evasion, Tax Avoidance and the Boundaries of Deviance', in D. Downes (ed), *Unravelling Criminal Justice*, Macmillan, Basingstoke, pp. 247-68.

McBarnet, D. and Whelan, C. (1991), 'The Elusive Spirit of the Law: Formalism and the Struggle for Legal Control', *Modern Law Review*, 54(6), pp. 848-73.

McBarnet, D. and Whelan, C. (1999), *Creative Accounting and the Cross-eyed Javelin Thrower*, John Wiley, Chichester.

Ralph Report (1999), *A Tax System Redesigned: More Certain, Equitable and Durable*. Report of the Review of Business Taxation, Commonwealth of Australia, Canberra.

Senate Economics References Committee (2001), *Inquiry into Mass Marketed Tax Effective Schemes and Investor Protection: Interim Report*, Parliament of the Commonwealth of Australia, Canberra.

Special Committee of Tax Law Consultancy Bodies (1998), 'Tax Law After Furniss vs Dawson', The Law Society, London.

Touche Ross (1989), *Accounting for Europe*, Touche Ross, London.

Chapter 12

Through the Eyes of the Advisers: A Fresh Look at High Wealth Individuals

John Braithwaite[1]

Framework for the Study

The Problem

Australians have become more sensitive to the issue of high wealth individuals paying their fair share of tax. A June 1998 survey of 1000 Australians commissioned by the Australian Taxation Office (ATO) found that only 32 per cent believe 'tax laws are effective in making sure large companies pay their share of tax' declining to 27 per cent for 'very wealthy people'. Only 20 per cent believed 'the ATO does a good job of stopping tax avoidance by large companies', falling to 15 per cent who believed that 'the ATO does a good job stopping tax avoidance by very wealthy people'. It was this kind of evidence that caused the Keating government to make high wealth taxpayers an election issue in 1995 and that caused the Howard government to set up the High Wealth Individuals Taskforce after its election victory.[2]

The problem cannot be dismissed as a creation of political imagination: One adviser in this study said he had a wealthy client who had not paid any tax since 1987. Certain sophisticated tax planning strategies appear to have been widespread. These include: (a) redefining income as capital by using multiple trust structures that conceal a common controlling mind; (b) creating artificial losses, for example by acquiring companies or trusts with accumulated losses; (c) disguising distributions to High Wealth Individuals (HWIs) and family members as loans and other non-taxable benefits; (d) using offshore trusts; (e) converting activities undertaken for private pleasure into tax losses (for example pleasure craft, horse breeding and racing); and (f) using charitable trusts to disguise benefits to HWIs and their families.

Method

A useful model for this research was presented with Roman Tomasic and Brendan Pentony's 1990 study, 'Defining Acceptable Tax Conduct: The Role of Professional Advisers in Tax Compliance'. It was decided to undertake a more focused investigation of advisers of HWIs and to limit the range of policy issues discussed with them. To define the topics, the author, together with Alice Dobes (an ATO evaluator from outside the Taskforce), first conducted interviews with most senior managers of the HWI Taskforce in Canberra, Sydney and Melbourne, mostly meeting them one or two at a time. This led to a decision to pursue fairly unstructured interviews with advisers of HWIs organised loosely around a set of questions prepared in advance. The questions were designed to address three issues: (a) the compliance problems common among HWIs; (b) to seek advisers' criticisms of the taskforce; and (c) to harness their creativity in considering new and better ways of improving compliance and identifying deficiencies in the law.

The objective then was to test their criticisms and ideas against the policy thinking we had secured from the taskforce managers, focus groups that Alice Dobes conducted with taskforce fieldwork staff subsequent to the adviser interviews, and against what we know from the research literature on compliance (not a lot for High Wealth Individuals).

The Sample

The sample was strategic rather than random, with 27 HWI advisers interviewed, mostly alone, for one to two hours in 1999. All interviews were conducted face-to-face with the exception of one which was conducted as a tele-conference.

The strategic sample included: (a) individuals who senior taskforce management regarded as key HWI advisers; (b) advisers whose policy thinking might be sharper because they have a larger number of HWIs and/or many more contacts with the taskforce due to audit and information gathering activities resulting from higher risk ratings of their HWI clients; and (c) HWI advisers who were selected by professional bodies which were interviewed to represent the views of their membership.

This sample ensured we secured interviews with advisers from all the (then) Big Five accounting firms, some non-charter firms, some distinctive boutique firms and certain prominent lawyer-advisers. In addition to the advisers I also conducted interviews at the Taxation Institute of Australia, the Australian Society of Certified Practicing Accountants, the Institute of Chartered Accountants in Australia, and the Law Council of Australia. Each of these bodies had informally canvassed their members to elicit specific concerns and suggestions.

To secure interviews, initial contact was made by letter offering prospective participants the opportunity to speak with either myself as the author of this chapter, or to both Alice Dobes from the ATO and myself. Confidentiality was guaranteed and respondents were informed that while what was said would be used, it would not be attributed to them as individuals or to their firm. They were also assured that they were not required to divulge the names or details of their clients.

While one adviser was overseas for the period of the study, no advisers refused to be interviewed, and in only one case did an adviser opt for a complete absence of the ATO during the interview.

The High Wealth Individuals Taskforce

The HWI Taskforce was established in 1996 with an objective to enhance compliance management strategy for HWIs. In the first year of operation, 180 HWIs received a questionnaire about the groups of entities they control or from which they receive income. These were formalised in subsequent years into expanded returns, called Current Year Data Collection (CYDC) returns or expanded returns. In 1997 and 1998, 142 and 143 HWIs respectively completed expanded returns for 2371 and 2599 associated companies, trusts, partnerships, or individuals respectively.

The taskforce has also provided advice to government on options for legislative reform to address minimisation techniques used by some HWIs, as well as evidence to the Ralph Review of business taxation on the exploitation by some HWIs of structural deficiencies in the tax system (Ralph Report, 1999).

Since the taskforce was established, the Australian Government has introduced several legislative measures that may impact on HWIs including: (a) abolition of research and development syndication arrangements; (b) trust losses; (c) private company dividends disguised as loans; (d) misuse of charitable trusts; (e) franking credit trading and dividend streaming; (f) taxation of foreign source income; and (g) denial of artificially created capital losses.

Findings

Cost of Compliance

All but one adviser we interviewed found the cost of compliance to be high, and higher than they believed it needed to be. The cost estimate for the professional fees associated with completing the expanded tax return required by the program was in most cases in the range $20 000 to $40 000 per HWI. At least this was the estimate for the first expanded returns: views varied on how much costs fell with subsequent returns. Adviser fees to assist with HWI audits were also reported to be as high as 'more than $1 million'. In addition, the program was reported to impose substantial costs on the time of the HWIs themselves and their staff. It was a distraction when 'they want to keep their eye on the main game which is creating wealth for the benefit of Australia'. Other advisers suggested that the high costs of doing expanded returns for the first time were considerably reduced on subsequent returns and could be reduced further by electronic lodgment.

The main suggestions for reducing costs related to reducing the repetitiveness and increasing the selectivity of expanded return targeting. A HWI who controls sixty entities has to complete sixty special returns, which demand a considerable amount of information. Some advisers said that such burdens on HWIs created business for them, but more were of the view that it was a kind of business they did not want – 'drudgery' as one put it. Others said they would prefer to be helping clients build their business rather than putting their energy into compliance administration. Some said that they were not well geared with the kind of staff needed to fill out hundreds of pages of returns by hand.

> It's not the business we want to be in. We want to add value. We don't want to be putting numbers in boxes. It's not satisfying. And our clients don't want to pay big dollars for *that*.

Because compliance costs are such a big issue, they are also a lever. Getting off the program is seen by advisers as a major benefit they would love to be able to secure for their HWI. The opportunity is to take them off the program only when certain compliance outcomes have been delivered.

Many HWI staff have a different perspective from the majority analysis of the advisers. One common view was that self-assessment in the 1980s may have gone too far in respect of companies and trusts. It is now impossible to do a risk assessment on these returns without seeking additional information. The HWI expanded returns are seen as a remedy for this error of the 80s. This was also a minority view among advisers:

> I admired Trevor Boucher [former Commissioner of Taxation], but one of the worst things Boucher did was simplify the tax return, especially for corporates. You need a complex return for complex taxpayers...The expanded return questions are pretty good questions...Wealthy people should never be off that cycle. Once you've done the first year, the costs are not high.

This adviser then went on to suggest, contrary to the majority view that he would put more, rather than fewer, questions on the expanded return.

Conservatively, compliance costs of the HWI Taskforce, on the basis of the estimates provided in our interviews, would seem to be well over $10 million a year – that is, a more significant economic issue than the funding of the program (which costs less than $10 million). This conservative estimate is based on multiplying the number of expanded returns by the modal compliance cost estimate for completing expanded returns, and adding just the estimated audit costs in cases we were told about.

We found that some HWIs accepted these compliance costs as reasonable; others interpreted them as persecution. How ever the ATO resolves the policy issues here, it needs to communicate more clearly the reasons why HWIs do and do not stay on the expanded returns. Otherwise 'the client gets a feeling of persecution for being who they are'. Failure to communicate reasons for seeking expanded returns risks the reaction of one HWI described by his adviser as someone who had rejected perfectly conservative kinds of tax planning advice on grounds that he wanted to pay his fair share of tax. His reaction to being kept on expanded returns for another year was: 'If the ATO thinks I'm ripping the system off, maybe I should start doing it'.

A policy option here is that after a risk assessment has been undertaken on each expanded return, HWIs be advised that the assessment has been completed and given a general reason if they will be required to complete an expanded return in the following year. If they are not advised, our interviews suggest that HWIs and advisers assume that the ATO is not doing its job and has simply not got around to completing the risk assessment. While expanded returns should be maintained as a routine requirement for HWIs assessed as having a high or medium risk profile, there is a case for continuous improvement in simplifying the process. Continuous reduction in compliance costs might be considered each year by examining four paths to lower costs: (a) reducing the amount of information requested in expanded returns; (b) reducing repetition of information from year to year and form to form (for example allowing an 'unchanged since last year' response); (c) greater discernment (possibly based on something like a Tax Strategy Review) in assessing which individuals should complete expanded returns in the first place and greater clarity in signalling a path for exit from the expanded return program; and (d) further work to facilitate electronic returns.

Overall Effectiveness

We can divide interviewed advisers into three groups: (a) a group of more than a dozen advisers who accepted the HWI Taskforce, while feeling it was conceived in such a political way that its targeting was ineffective; (b) a group of six who aggressively rejected the very idea of the taskforce; and (c) another group of six who felt strongly that the taskforce was a sound initiative: 'There should have been a program targeting high wealth individuals long ago'.

Only a few advisers thought the activities of the taskforce had made any difference to their clients. However, a minority did say that they felt the existence of the taskforce was making HWIs generally more cautious because they are 'under the microscope':

> It's the constant surveillance of being on the program that causes compliance...Part IVA is of indeterminate width. It might be applied more aggressively in future. So I advise clients to be careful.

> Asking the question and getting them to focus their mind on where everything is had an impact.

In some cases this impact was bringing into the system business that was offshore, sometimes openly in a way that would be brought to the attention of the ATO, sometimes indirectly, in a way intended to make it difficult for the ATO to notice. Several advisers mentioned instances of voluntary disclosure of large amounts of income prompted not by audit, but simply by the fact of having to fill out the expanded returns.

One adviser was of the view that this aspect of effectiveness would be severely compromised if the expanded return was not universal for wealthy people with complex affairs:

> Corporate Australia would say you really should go at it hell for leather as soon as they are dropped off. That's what happened with the Large Case Program. The Large Case Program should never have been stopped. Corporate Australia learned the lessons from it; the ATO walked away from those lessons.

For this adviser, an even more important point was:

> The more information he's [the Commissioner's] got, the less aggressive they will be in their tax planning.

What this adviser was saying here was that notifying X in 1998 reduces the taxpayer's degrees of freedom to reconfigure his 1999 affairs in such a way that not-X appears to be the case in 1998. 'Changes each year will be noticed.' So HWIs must keep their affairs consistent with the underlying truths of earlier declarations.

Most advisers thought it would return more revenue for the ATO to shift its resources to the cash economy; some favoured targeting corporations in high risk industries rather than targeting individuals simply because they were wealthy. One argued very forcefully that the best returns would be achieved with low HWIs or sub-HWIs rather than high HWIs.

> Forget Kerry Packer and Rupert Murdoch. They are far too big. Their advice is too good. Go after some middle HWIs or lower. Their accountants are small fry, many of them.

A widely held view of the HWI advisers was that a life course of HWIs could be defined. HWIs were most aggressive when they were making their first million, before they became HWIs. They continued to be aggressive while they were building their empires. Then they often wanted to avoid trouble and to pay their fair share once they had made it. Unfortunately, the HWI program is seen as targeting a lot of people who are in this latter quiescent stage, while the real returns are among the younger wealth-builders. One adviser classified HWIs as 'the meek, the bold and the normal'. The meek, on this analysis, would be found disproportionately among older HWIs, the bold among wealth-builders and the normal among mid-career HWIs.

Another view was that the very wealthy, and very aggressive, are hard targets. The more realistic policy objective than working from the very wealthy down is over time to push up the level of wealth where tax planning can succeed in eliminating the need to pay tax – that is, moving from the wealthy up toward the very wealthy.

The strongest and most widely held basis for doubt about the effectiveness of the taskforce was the belief that it collected a lot of information and then did little or nothing with it. Doubts were widespread that anyone had even looked at the information in the returns they had put in, let alone subjected it to a rigorous risk assessment and followed up with audit where appropriate: 'It's a fishing expedition. They don't know what they're looking for'.

Risk Assessment

Another virtually universal reaction in the interviews was that the politicised beginning of the taskforce was a source of resentment. Former Treasurer, Ralph Willis, claimed that HWIs were avoiding $800 million a year in unpaid taxes during the 1995 election campaign. This was a frequently cited focus of resentment. In some cases, the Commissioner of Taxation was seen as a co-conspirator with the government in whipping up a 'witch-hunt' against HWIs. This then led to an attack on the way the initial targets were selected. Business Review Weekly's list of the wealthiest 200 Australians was widely seen as the basis of the initial targeting, and as a markedly inaccurate source. Some HWI advisers claimed they had other clients who were wealthier than the clients who were targeted.

Beyond the complaint about the initial basis for risk assessment, there was little complaint about the way subsequent risk assessment was tackled. In many cases, HWI advisers seemed to have very little knowledge of how risk assessment was done. But if risk assessment were a black box to them, it was not a source of complaint. Many advisers were of the view that the shift away from full audits to risk assessment followed by a suite of audit products was a sound move by the ATO. Others were cynical, believing that compliance was falling because the risk of audit had fallen and that this fact was widely recognised in the marketplace. There was general agreement, however, that the ATO was doing a more competent job of risk assessment:

> The general view in the accounting profession is that the ATO is better geared than it ever was to detect where the leakage is. Therefore it should be possible for the ATO to keep a clamp on the most aggressive activity. But it audits less, making that more difficult.

Fairness and Professionalism

While there were many concerns about the fairness of the program, views about the fairness and professionalism of the ATO staff with whom advisers had dealt were overwhelmingly positive. A number of advisers complained that they had little or no contact, but for those who did, only seven were critical of the experience. The strongest criticism was lack of technical competence. Only a handful of incidents were described where ATO staff was seen as less than fair or professional. One repeated complaint was the recording of a 'jaundiced view of taxpayers', their honesty or their lifestyle, in internal memoranda obtained under Freedom of Information and even in position papers. Given the frequency with which this kind of taxpayer will use Freedom of Information to gain more insight into the ATO analysis of their case, especially in the context of settlement negotiations, more consideration may be needed in expressing opinions about taxpayers.

Some of the assessments were very positive: 'He was very good, commercial, understood the realities of going offshore...Compared to other audits I've experienced, it's been very professional'. In response to the question, 'Can you think of any instances where the ATO has not honoured the Taxpayers' Charter in its dealings with your HWI clients?', there was only one specific complaint. In 26 out of 27 cases, the answer was no, though in some cases this was qualified by the concern that the general lack of communication in the program or aggressive assessments to bring the taxpayer to the negotiating table may be Charter issues. Generally, the Charter did not seem to mean a lot to these advisers. One was brutal about it: 'The Taxpayers' Charter is a motherhood document that is really bullshit in the marketplace'.

The generally positive results on fairness and professionalism are important because the literature of the social psychology of procedural justice shows that when people believe they are treated fairly, they are more likely to comply with the law (Tyler, 1990, 1998; Tyler and Dawes, 1993; Makkai and Braithwaite, 1996; Lind and Tyler, 1998). The fact that HWIs often have a sense of fairness that contributes to compliance, and therefore must be sustained, is illustrated by the following kind of request that advisers said they commonly received:

> I want a tax plan that will get my tax down to X per cent, say twenty. I want to pay my fair share. But not that much. Then others will say I want a total tax wipe-out and even pay a ridiculous amount of money to get it.

Some advisers were critical of a failure of taskforce staff to work with other sections of the ATO (for example Transfer Pricing, Small Business, an industry segment of Large Business and International) to avoid turning over the same issues with different sets of ATO people.

On the technical questions, one suggestion was that audit staff be more willing to call in more senior technical people when the issues got thorny, and in such cases, for the ATO technical expert to have sign-off on position papers. There are already three levels of sign-off on HWI risk assessments (analyst, team leader, manager/director), which are often applied to position papers.

On the other hand, sign-off rules may be too formal an approach to something that is fundamentally a cultural challenge for the taskforce. On all aspects of audit, communication is needed to improve quality. Getting position papers echnically correct is just a small part of this. The taskforce must be careful in its quality control not to end up with such a focus on avoiding errors in its written communications that it neglects quality assurance of bigger strategic issues that would remove the need for a written communication in the first place. One HWI manager, for example, said that one of the most valuable pieces of advice he regularly gives auditors is: 'I've seen this stuff before and I can tell you following it is not productive'. His view was that the essence of professionalism was not getting bogged down in pointless pursuits.

Training is important here as well. But perhaps formal training is the more important path to keeping technical skills up to date (training the mind), while informal discussion between masters and apprentices is the more important path to improving the wisdom of strategic audit judgment (training the nose). One HWI adviser argued that it takes 20 years for auditors in complex cases to acquire a nose for the right lead. In light of this, he was critical of ATO early retirement packages that were disproportionately taken up by precisely such experienced people. Balance, an ability to extrapolate, the gift of getting an inkling on what a transaction means, and where it might lead, without the full information, are virtues that might be nurtured more by a retention program than by early retirement packages for the people with these rare gifts. The learning process perhaps can also be facilitated by the old and the wise conducting best practice workshops for the young who do not yet know how to read the commercial signs.

When position papers involve difficult technical issues, there seems to be a need for the level of authority for sign off to be increased. The taskforce also needs to set expectations for hours of formal technical training that are realistic in relation to workloads, but well in excess of what is expected of fieldworkers in less complex areas. An ongoing identity that fosters a storytelling culture about how to find fertile leads and how to avoid infertile ones is an issue more systematically addressed in an earlier chapter (Braithwaite, Chapter 9, this volume). Such a culture is one where apprentices are constantly asking masters to relate stories of their experience on strategic decisions they are making. It is also a culture where masters do not tell apprentices what to do so much as volunteer stories from their experience when they see their apprentices about to repeat mistakes they have made in the past. Best practice workshops are needed nationally to assist with the development of such a storytelling culture that nurtures strategic wisdom.

Communication

> A bit of frank discussion goes a long way.
>
> Auditors need to understand that it is natural for me to talk to their head. That is a cultural change needed.
>
> Why can't we have a relationship of trust, a process, which starts with me saying 'here's my analysis of how things have changed since last year'.
>
> What about the Asian and English model of tax inspectors building relationships. Almost a personal thing in paying your tax. A more personal approach that seems to work. Then it's hard to avoid a big issue that arises on either side (professional association interview).

Since most encounters with HWI staff were seen in a positive light by HWI advisers, it is not surprising that most of them wanted more communication. They particularly wanted communication about where their client was up to in the program: 'Had he received a clean bill of health?'; 'When would she get off the program?'. Many HWIs were reported by the advisers as philosophical, that it was reasonable that people of their wealth might be targeted in this way. But there was also a widely reported view that their clients felt victimised by the program. In the view of the advisers, here was where more communication from the ATO would help. Some older HWIs worried about their tax affairs and were concerned to do what was necessary to get a clean bill of health quickly: 'They say it's only money and it's better to sleep at night'. There is an opportunity lost for both the ATO and the taxpayers to reach accommodation quickly when this is the situation. Many advisers wanted agreed timelines for expanded returns to be assessed, decisions made whether to take the case further or to drop their client off the program. And they wanted communication on how this was progressing.

A majority of the advisers specifically requested that there be a taskforce representative assigned to their case and that they meet them in advance of the expanded return being requested. What was most commonly favoured was a preliminary risk assessment by an analyst based on information provided by the HWI at an initial interview. This information would include how the structure of the entities controlled by the HWI had changed since the last assessment, financials, extraordinary transactions, a mud-map of the group structures and the tax reconciliation (from accounting to taxable income). Advisers repeatedly argued that in many cases advisers were in a position to convince an analyst why their client paid little tax even though they were very wealthy.

One adviser suggested that meetings of ATO staff with HWI advisers would assist the professional development of both. It would improve the understanding and clear up misunderstandings about how the ATO works, and discussions on technical issues would expose ATO people to the technical insights of advisers and vice versa. An adviser gave an example. There had been enormous conflict over a disagreement in interpretation of the law. This disagreement was fuelled by the belief on the part of the adviser that the ATO auditor was technically incompetent. In the wash-up, the adviser admitted that it had been his technical analysis that had been less sophisticated. The ATO's Tax Counsel Network (TCN) had been giving sophisticated advice to the auditor:

> They were ahead of us and we didn't know. We just assumed this was another case of this auditor getting settled law wrong. Probably, we should have been communicating directly with the Tax Counsel Network. Certainly if there had been some communication, even from the auditor, on where he was coming from, unnecessary confrontation would have been avoided.

Communication, advisers argued, would help working relationships in other ways as well:

> If an auditor reviews something and gives it a tick, it is good to communicate that back. We learn from that. It also stops us from wondering: Did they miss the issue or did they mull over it? If they did give it a tick, they missed the opportunity to tell us they have

> noticed this and decided to let it through, the opportunity to have us say: These guys have been pretty fair. Rather than saying they have not been on the ball as they missed it.

Given the propensity in this game for the players to be uncharitable toward their adversary, it is likely that in the absence of communication, the assumption that the ATO is incompetent is exactly what the adviser will take away from the encounter.

Similarly, how ever the ATO resolves the big policy question of whether it should be normal or exceptional for HWIs to stay on expanded returns year in year out, there is virtue in taking seriously the following suggestion of an adviser:

> Why not a letter of commendation on clearance. Thanks for your cooperation. You've got a clear bill of tax health.

Even if the HWI is to stay on expanded returns, presumably such a letter might say: 'Thank you for your cooperation. A risk assessment on your return this year has resulted in a decision not to include you in our current round of audits. However, you will be required to complete an expanded return again next year as our risk assessment also showed that you are likely to continue to have a high-risk tax profile. If you have any questions about this, feel free to get in touch with your case contact person, Mary Smith'.

Another adviser implied that competent ATO staff picked up useful risk assessment signals from communication with advisers. This was an adviser who said he dropped HWIs when they lied to him. He felt that through this kind of act, the ethical adviser gives a signal that the competent ATO staff member knows how to read.

Communication between advisers and ATO staff can help keep the ATO up to speed with the latest arrangements in a world where 'the better an idea, the shorter its shelf life'. Several advisers confessed to us that they had dobbed in tax planning arrangements used by their competitors, combined with their opinion on what its technical weaknesses were. Others explained this was widespread because there is 'a lot of jealousy' or 'a degree of bitchiness out there'. In one example, firm A developed a product with some bugs in it. Clients of firm B were approached about buying into the scheme. Firm B then reverse-engineered the scheme into an improved version and 'made noises to our contacts in the ATO' about the bugs in firm A's version.

Some advisers and some HWI staff did not see the need for the ATO to initiate communication. These advisers said their experience was that they could telephone the taskforce and discuss any question that was concerning them. A number of other advisers had not had this experience, however. They found great difficulty in securing the communication they felt they needed, and in some cases, any communication at all.

Another option for improving communication is suggested by the Canadian Audit Protocols (Revenue Canada, 1996). The Canadian Audit Protocols are not just about a move to real time audits; they are also about rewarding cooperative relationships between the tax authority and its clients with negotiated audit protocols that reduce compliance costs for business and increase compliance effectiveness for the tax authority. For example, scheduling visits by different areas of the tax authority so that disruption to business is minimised, conducting concurrent audits, and informing business in advance of the form in which financial records might be kept to avoid their double handling. The idea is that Revenue Canada and participating corporations jointly produce a written framework that establishes guidelines for the relationship and the audit process. When a HWI is targeted for an audit, it seems quite possible and sensible to give their adviser an audit plan, with the proviso that they might be advised at any stage that the plan has been modified. Indeed, we were told this is generally done with HWIs, though not always in a timely fashion.

Complexity

> Half the advice I see people give is wrong...McKinsey and Co showed some years back that the ATO's advice on the basic matters dealt with at the enquiry counter was right only thirty per cent of the time; thirty per cent of the time it was wrong; and forty per cent of the time it was useless and beside the point.

> I know twenty per cent of it by working twelve hours a day, six days a week for twenty years.

> The Commissioner would have to take two weeks off to get up to speed in what he is talking about in that trust stuff. And he should not have to. The Act should not be so complex that only those below him have the understanding of the law to run and control agendas.

There was consensus among advisers that the complexity of the law was keeping compliance costs high for HWIs and making effective enforcement difficult for the ATO. There was general support for the idea of discerning general principles in the law and disciplining specific elements of the law to be consistent with these general principles. The idea is that all components of business tax law should be derived from, and consistent with, a smallish set of general principles. There was also general cynicism that the wash-up to the Ralph Inquiry (Ralph Report, 1999) that was developing such principle-based reforms would be any more simplifying than the results from two decades of pronouncements about such efforts. Three years on from the interviews this cynicism has been vindicated, as there has been little of the principle-based reform advocated by the Ralph process.

Offshore Investment

Advisers said that clients came to them requesting that they help set-up offshore investments, accounts and credit cards. But only two said they got into assisting HWIs with this. Two others said this was a reason why clients went elsewhere. A number of advisers felt that few HWIs avoided taxes by using offshore strategies such as tax havens. However three advisers felt offshore tax avoidance was the main risk to the revenue by HWIs and some others saw it as a significant risk. One of these made the point that a higher proportion of Australia's most wealthy people are immigrants compared with most other countries, making offshore trusts a bigger issue for us.

Three advisers also felt that a strategy of the aggressive HWI was to have conservative domestic tax planning arrangements managed by a reputable adviser from a Big Five or second-tier firm, and then to have another set of investments offshore which are not disclosed to their conservative adviser. This strategy implies securing a favourable risk assessment by the ATO on the basis of the conservative side of their dual strategy, thereby protecting the offshore side of the strategy from scrutiny.

Even those who thought offshore tax avoidance was a major problem emphasised that not all HWIs could exploit it. Offshore strategies would be foolish for a HWI who was a resident of Australia and who ran no actual businesses offshore. In these circumstances, it is difficult to conceal the movement of funds as they leave the country. For HWIs who are non-residents or who have non-resident family members, funds can be passed to them and then shifted offshore to a destination unknown. The ATO only has direct access to the domestic tax affairs of non-residents. An Australian resident who is wealthy enough to actually run a business overseas also has a formidable capability for 'bleeding some funds out' into personal accounts protected by a tax haven.

No adviser recommended targeting offshore investments as a sensible shift in enforcement strategy for the taskforce. For some, this was because they did not believe HWIs were using offshore accounts to avoid tax on any large scale. For others who believed HWIs were doing so in a massive way, the belief was that these arrangements would be impregnable or very hard to find: 'You'd end up chasing a British Virgin Islands company where you can't find out who their directors are under their law'.

However, three advisers recommended an amnesty on bringing home or paying tax on offshore investments. One felt that, particularly with older HWIs who wanted peace of mind and a capacity to pass wealth on to their children without undue complication, an amnesty based on agreement to pay back tax and interest (but no penalty) would bring a lot of offshore income into the system. A second adviser felt this would not generate enough incentive to bring in the huge offshore investments which he said he knew were out there. His policy suggestion was that as long as offshore funds were actually brought back for investment in Australia and future taxing on-shore, all back taxes and penalties should be waived. Only the removal of the threat of back taxes, he believed, would see the repatriation of worthwhile amounts of tax and capital:

> Half a dozen merchant bankers who were my clients would have been happy to bring money back into Australia if they did not have to pay back taxes...If you didn't ask any questions, a huge amount of money would come.

The third adviser who recommended an amnesty commended the experience of the ATO overseas controlled trusts amnesty of more than a decade ago. He said most of his clients with overseas controlled trusts came clean about them (on his advice) as a result of this amnesty. In practice, he negotiated on behalf of his clients for more than waiving of penalties – that is, for considerable waiving of back taxes as well: 'My experience is that if the Commissioner will not negotiate, do deals, he will get less tax'. One of them suggested the ATO might also have to bluff HWIs into believing that there would be a major enforcement crackdown on offshore investments after the amnesty and that this was the once in a lifetime opportunity to avoid its fury.

In summary, in this project we have found evidence of some movement of multi-million dollar offshore investments into the system, some known and some unknown to the ATO, simply as a result of the questions that have been asked about them in the HWI expanded tax returns. We suspect this movement has been more than sufficient on its own to pay the costs of the taskforce. We have found little basis for optimism that a crackdown on offshore strategies would generate a lot more revenue. However, an amnesty of say twelve months to encourage both bringing offshore tax into the system and capital back to Australia is a policy option, albeit one with risks and substantial administrative costs. It would need to be combined with a public commitment to enforcement for those who failed to avail themselves of this opportunity, even though the enforcement would not be very effective. In the world of tax motivation described by advisers, where both 'inertia' and 'peace of mind' are important, an amnesty might overcome the inertia of leaving tax-protected offshore investments be, by offering the taxpayer the peace of mind of a clean slate. This motivational account might be particularly appealing to older HWIs who want to leave their affairs in a tidier state for their children. The amnesty need not be a discriminatory benefit made available only to HWIs; it could apply to any taxpayer with offshore funds. There are, for example, academics who receive payments for teaching while they are on study leave which they put in foreign banks.

The Power of Advice to Secure Compliance

> If I tell them [HWIs] it's not legal, they don't do it.

The large majority of HWIs, according to their advisers, want to avoid anything illegal, any litigation, anything that will make them a test case for the Commissioner. Consequently, advice by the adviser that a claim is illegal is enough to stop it, a finding Tomasic and Pentony (1990) also reported. This fact reinforces the need for good communication between the ATO and advisers, who are the agents of much of their voluntary compliance work.

For the same reason, we were repeatedly told of the power of a simple media release by the Commissioner to stop schemes in their tracks: 'The moment taxpayers see a negative statement [by the Commissioner] on a scheme, it doesn't happen. The Commissioner can close them overnight'. A number of advisers pointed out that the ATO should be responsible enough not to issue such releases unless they were accompanied by or followed promptly with a supporting technical paper.

Others were critical of the under use of this effective tool of compliance: 'The ATO sits on things it could kill off'. Sometimes this is because the ATO is slow to complete its technical analysis, sometimes because it does not yet have the resources or political will to attack or test a scheme (and it wants to maintain a reputation for keeping its promises). Sometimes it is slow to detect new schemes, though most advisers felt the ATO had become much more effective in this regard, often pointing to the potency of the strategy of Strategic Intelligence Analysis. Most felt it was possible to keep abreast of the new schemes through a combination of maintaining good lines of communication with their fellow advisers: 'They love to chatter. People have big egos and love to brag. If this fellow doesn't, the next fellow will'. Simply 'knowing what is being said from the rostrum of Taxation Institute conferences, which covers nine schemes out of ten' and following up the advertisements in the Australian Financial Review and Business Review Weekly can cover much of the field.

Analysis

Changing Lenses: The View from Middle Australia, 1985-1999

This research was undertaken in a different environment from Tomasic and Pentony's (1990) report on the attitudes of advisers. That was a time when tax advising was seen as a much more cautious and responsible business than it had been a decade earlier. The widespread belief, effectively promoted to the public by the Australian Treasurer at the time, Paul Keating, was that the paper schemes of the 70s and early 80s were dead, compliance had improved markedly, capital gains tax had collected more revenue than projected and the rich were paying a fairer share of the tax burden. As Margaret Levi's (1988) research suggests, confidence in the tax system (and compliance itself) did seem to improve substantially after the reforms following the 1985 Tax Summit. 1992 Organisation for Economic Cooperation and Development (OECD) data suggest that at the time, Australia was doing better than most developed economies in getting corporations to pay taxes: Only Japan and Luxembourg were being markedly more successful (Slemrod, 1996).

That confidence has sagged again. And for the reasons Levi (1998) articulated, voluntary compliance of ordinary taxpayers is again at risk as a result. This seems to be a normal phase in an ongoing cycle of reform/honeymoon/decay/repair/collapse-of-confidence/reform.

The aspects of the environment that were causing decay in confidence in the fairness of the tax system at the time of these interviews were the large increases in the income and wealth of HWIs in a decade and a half when Pay As You Earn

(PAYE) taxpayer compliance improved, but their income and wealth increased by a lesser amount than that of the rich. There is a belief, which has some foundation (Picotto, 1996), that the globalisation of commerce opens up new opportunities for the rich which are not available to low and middle income earners. There are other changes in the global environment which are beyond the comprehension of the average punter, such as the impact of the growth in derivatives: 'The same minds that figured out how to split a security into a multitude of different cash flows and contingent returns are now engineering products in which the tax benefits are split off from the underlying economics of a deal' (Novack and Saunders, 1998). In a way, the fact that the average person does not understand these things is the problem, and the reason they resort to a simple-minded analysis that the wealthy must be breaking the law and using their power to get away with it.

Moreover, some ordinary citizens are frightened by the implications for their share in the wealth of global competition for the capital of the rich. This particularly focuses on the liberalisation of trade, as evidenced by the populist political movements of the left and the right against globilisation. Many Australians believe their government wants to attract capital to Australia by giving those who own a lot a better tax deal than them. They believe income tax and company tax rates have come down more than their rates. And they believe PAYE makes them more effective payers of those rates than the rich. While few remember 85 per cent income tax rates on high wealth individuals under the Menzies government of the 1950s, they do remember the 60 per cent rates of the early 1980s and the death duties that used to be a significant burden for the rich. In 1985, commentators readily accepted the argument that compliance could be improved by cutting the top income tax rate to align it with the company tax rate. But a year after its introduction, this alignment collapsed as the company tax rate was cut substantially to meet downward competitive pressure on company tax rates led by the Reagan and Thatcher governments and the newly industrialising economies of the Asian region. Middle income earners contrast this reduced burden on corporates and high wealth individuals with the way bracket creep has pushed more of their income into tax rates which were supposed to be the preserve of the rich.

Australia is a society with an egalitarian ethos and for most of its history it has been objectively among the nations with the most egalitarian distributions of income. Unfortunately, one of the things that goes with this ethos is an uncharitable view of the rich. So if a wealthy person is revealed to be paying no income tax, most Australians tend to assume that he or she has cheated, probably broken the law and certainly bent it. The assumption is rarely the charitable one that the high wealth individual has claimed deductions or transferred losses that the law fully intends to be legitimate.

When something like the HWI Taskforce is set up in response to these perceptions in middle Australia, both sides may end up perceiving themselves as victims. While low and middle income earners may perceive themselves as fools to be honest taxpayers, high wealth individuals perceive themselves as victims of a witch-hunt grounded in unfair labelling of them as tax cheats. Both perceptions are unhealthy for tax compliance. The taxi drivers rationalise not paying tax by saying that Kerry Packer (Australia's wealthiest person) pays none; high wealth individuals rationalise not paying tax by citing the non-compliance of people such as taxi drivers who are paid in cash.

It follows that a useful way of framing the compliance challenge before the government might be to ensure all participants in the economy pay a share of the tax burden that most participants would view as fairer than the present distribution, to enable all participants to have a realistic perception of that distribution and why it is that way, and thereby to eliminate inaccurate perceptions that some sectors are cheating more than they really are. Such a shift in perceptions might improve compliance in middle Australia, in the cash economy and among HWIs. If such improvements were strong enough, they might allow a reduction in tax rates for all, thereby further strengthening perceptions of fairness.

It is in the context of this framing of the compliance challenge that we might take seriously the suggestion of one HWI adviser that the HWI Taskforce disclose to Parliament the aggregated accounting income of all entities controlled by HWIs, and then the aggregated adjustments listed for each reason for adjustment that reduces the accounting income to the taxable income. This means a breakdown of the reasons for the tax-gap between accounting and taxable income. His argument is that the top half dozen reasons would account for most of the reduced tax liability of HWIs. They would be reasons such as depreciation on property, research and development, franking credits and write down of stock to market value. Because the big-ticket items on this list would be small in number, they would be easy for Parliament to digest. Parliament and the people would then have a more realistic understanding of why HWIs pay the level of tax they do. It would be clear why law breaking does not need to be invoked as an explanation. The major reasons would be plain to see. Then governments and electors could make their judgments about whether the economic and other benefits of each reason for the draining away of revenue justify the documented loss of tax receipts. Economic policy decision-making would become more transparent. Confidence in the integrity of government and of HWIs might thereby be enhanced. The adviser's claim was that this would not be difficult for the taskforce to do: 'You just list the reasons for adjustment on an Excel spreadsheet and add in the numbers for each taxpayer'. In summary, this policy presumption is that the ATO disclose to Parliament the aggregated accounting income of HWIs, what percentage of this they pay in tax, and the aggregated adjustments responsible for reducing the accounting income to the taxable income, listed in descending order of importance. This would render transparent the share HWIs are or are not paying and why.

The following analysis shows why this suggestion might be taken seriously. It is based on the cycle of principled tax reform, followed by a honeymoon when citizens perceive the system as decent, an inevitable creeping of unprincipled elements into the package as a result of global, technological and legal change, followed by rising taxpayer cynicism that ultimately makes the next cycle of reform necessary. One reason the unprincipled elements corrode the system is that legislators do not get feedback on the costs to the revenue of their legislative mistakes. They only become aware of them when the hole is so catastrophic that no one needs an Excel spreadsheet to notice it. But by then the interests entrenched to defend it, the scale of the investments entered into on the assumption that it would continue, may be so massive as to make repair extremely difficult politically. So the rationale for this prescription is that it might extend the honeymoon of confidence and trust in the tax system not only because it would be more transparent but because the transparency would put governments under pressure from Parliament and the people to nip in the bud unjustified corrosions of the tax system before they became gaping holes capable of destroying confidence in the system. By keeping middle Australia's lens on the tax system clear, it will be slower to change focus from the confidence after reform to cynicism about a system seen as in decay.

The Limited Relevance of Deterrence to Protecting the Revenue

> If you can stand by your interpretation of the law, then the prospect of audit does not deter.

Most people think that compliance with regulatory laws is mainly secured by punishments imposed by the courts if the law is violated. Hence, their crude analysis of the HWI Taskforce would be that HWIs are almost never prosecuted criminally and are infrequently subject to tax penalties, so this is the reason why they pay such a low proportion of their wealth in tax. In most regulatory domains, this view is simple-minded or mistaken, but particularly so with tax compliance by HWIs.

The advisers told us that outright non-compliance is rarely a rational strategy even when detection risks are extremely low. Consider the following highly effective form of blatant evasion available to HWIs. It is loosely based on a real case:

> The HWI has a million dollars in profits. He gets a charitable deduction by donating it to a breast cancer research foundation he sets up in Geneva. The foundation then almost immediately lends it back to the HWI at an exorbitantly high interest rate. This interest rate enables the company that pays it to record a loss that the HWI can then write off against profits in another entity he controls. The HWI gets his million dollars back and two tax write-downs: A deduction on the way over to Geneva and a loss he can use to reduce taxes on the way back from Geneva. If he disguises the transactions effectively, it almost certainly won't be detected. If it is, the HWI has reputable people organised to testify that he always fully intended to repay the loan. He can actually do so before the matter goes to trial. The Director of the Breast Cancer Research Foundation will testify that they wanted to use the money well, to wait until a research proposal came along that would really produce a medical breakthrough. But while they were waiting they wanted to put their money to work. They knew that their benefactor, the HWI, knew how to do that better than they. And he was generous enough to pay an above-market interest rate to ensure that all the profits from his investment would be passed back to the Foundation. The ATO decides it does not want a case where a judge might vilify it for persecuting a businessman dedicated to such a cause.

While this kind of case has happened, it is not a kind of scam that in the opinion of HWI staff is widespread, not one of the major risks to the revenue among HWIs with the level of resources needed to exploit it. Why? After all it is highly profitable, simple enough to execute and almost guaranteed never to land the HWI in jail. The perfect crime. The answer according to our interviews is twofold. First, the HWI has too much to lose to risk even the remote prospect of the perfect crime unravelling. Second, there are other perfectly legal ways she can arrange her affairs to avoid having to pay tax on her million dollars without losing any sleep at night. So she prefers to pay an adviser to help her execute one of these latter strategies. The level of tax benefit in respect of her million dollars will depend on how competent and aggressive her adviser is, both being attributes in an adviser she can pay a premium to get.

All the government should or can do about the HWI who goes to the extraordinarily competent, yet conservative, adviser is to close off the biggest legal opportunities they exploit. For these conservative HWIs who pay little tax, deterrence is utterly irrelevant as a strategy for protecting the revenue. There is no need to deter the Geneva charity scam because this kind of option is unthinkable to them. It would be improper to deter them from exploiting the services of an unusually competent but law-respecting practitioner.

We now consider whether there is a place for a strategy of deterring the use of an unusually aggressive adviser.

Global Competition and the Hustling of Tax Advice

> The global tax situation is more of a risk than Australian schemes.

Two letters sent by the Big Five accounting firm, Deloitte and Touche, in late 1998 opened as follows (Novack and Saunders, 1998):

> Dear___
> As we discussed, set forth below are the details of our proposal to recommend and implement our tax strategy to eliminate the federal and state income taxes associated with [the company's] income for up to five (5) years ('the Strategy').

They were sent to two medium-sized United States (US) corporations asking for a contingency fee of 30 per cent of the tax savings from taking the tax liability to zero.

In Australia, our interviews suggested that the then Big Five did not touch the marketing of schemes with anything like this kind of aggression and that they did not operate on such a contingency fee basis.[3] The more aggressive shelters are marketed by non-charter firms, some by small law firms, others by financial advisers of a rather fly-by-night character ('they get $10 000 each from 200 people for their scheme and then they don't care what happens'). That may be, but there is a reality of the global market here. The fact is that in the US, the Big Five seem to have been able to increase their profits substantially through shifts toward such tactics. Individual staffers can secure bonuses up to US $400 000 for landing deals such as those pursued by the Deloitte and Touche letter. Ernst and Young and Deloitte and Touche reported a 29 per cent jump in revenues from tax services in the US in 1997. Since 1993 tax revenues for the Big Five have grown at twice the pace of audit revenues (Novack and Saunders, 1998). American Express is contesting their market in a formidable way. Something is changing in the risk environment here and it is probably global.

If it is about global change in financial engineering, Australia cannot resist it. Novack and Saunders (1998) argue that in the US 'it has taken a while for inhibitions to be shed and the most outlandish gimmicks to propagate'. But the inhibitions have shed under pressure from the aggressive marketisation of proactive as opposed to reactive advice. Today, as one adviser worried 'if you pay enough you can find a lawyer to write an opinion supporting anything'. The advice market, in Australia as well, decreasingly operates through advisers just reacting with specific strategies to cope with the needs of clients as they arise.[4] If advisers do not proactively market strategies to substantially reduce the tax liabilities of major clients, they can count on it that competitors will. Once the large accounting firms reach the conclusion, as they clearly have in the US, that they will lose business unless they match it with aggressively proactive promoters of shelters, a level of global sophistication in the engineering of proactive tax planning that is within the competence of the big firms comes into play.

Moreover, as the major accounting firms increase their proactiveness, a change can be expected in business culture on tax matters. 'Inertia', as one HWI adviser explained to us, is a major cause of tax compliance. If no one is pushing aggressive tax planning at a client, they do not feel incompetent for failing to do it. In Australia, there is a business ethos, and an ethos of the elite tax advisers, that 'if there is not an underlying business case for an investment, but only a tax case, don't do it'. The gradually growing clout of the general anti-avoidance provision of Part IVA of the *Income Tax Assessment Act 1936* is perhaps one reason for this.

However, it would be naïve to assume that global commercial pressures might not change it. Thanks to the GATS (General Agreement on the Trade in Services) agreement of the GATT (General Agreement of the Tariffs and Trade) – for which American Express (a heavy buyer of tax lawyers and accountants) and PricewaterhouseCoopers were the leading advocates, along with Citibank – the financial services market is now globalising. The consequence will be that if the Australian tax advice culture is seen by aggressive foreign firms as excessively conservative, they may view it as a market they should attack through a sales force that systematically works a distribution network to all HWIs. Globalised investment banks, with all their aggression, networks, expertise and reputational capital,[5] may be the biggest threats for ushering in this change. So even if it is the case that Australian business culture is more reactive than proactive on tax design, and that the tax departments of large corporations are not typically seen as profit centres in their own right (increasingly the case in American business culture), the capacity for Australian businesses to resist a globally-driven culture change must be in doubt. There is a kind of culture transformation and take-off with these things, as

Australia saw with the schemes of the 1970s: 'Once companies get a taste, they become more comfortable and continue to do it' (Novack and Saunders, 1998). A critical litmus test of the culture change is a growing belief in the business community that paying any significant amount of tax is a sign of weakness that might be criticised by shareholders.

So it may be that global financial services market pressures will progressively unsettle the inertia and conservatism that delivers a lot of HWI taxpaying at the moment. Moreover, the profits that the US accounting firms seem to be deriving from contingency arrangements at the top end of the market suggest that there is reason for promoters to move down the market offering proactive hustling of more engineering-intensive tax planning.

This seems a risk to the revenue that would run down from HWIs and large corporates to players of more intermediate levels of wealth. In addition, it would put at risk the culture of tax compliance at lower levels of the economy which has been reasonably strong in Australia by international standards. The worry is that if ordinary Australians become as cynical as Italians about the tax morality of the rich, we will be at risk of Italian levels of voluntary compliance, or even Colombian levels. As difficult as the Commissioner's job is, we should never assume it is incapable of getting a lot more difficult. One step that is a priority in Australia is to persuade tax professional bodies to set self-regulatory standards that prohibit contingency fees on reduced tax liabilities.

For these reasons, it seems necessary to guard against the risks from global competition in tax hustling by deterring aggression in tax advice. How can that be achieved? It is not against the law to give aggressive tax advice and nor should it be. Advice to break the law is sufficient reason to withdraw a licence to offer tax advice. But we have seen that this is not the real problem. Deterrence is largely beside the point at the moment because taxpayers who breach the law on the basis of a reasonably argued position supplied by a licensed adviser will not be subjected to any penalty tax; they simply pay the back taxes plus interest. This means that it can be rational to go to advisers who push their advice to the limits of what could conceivably be accepted as a reasonably argued position.

In the US context, Novack and Saunders (1998) express this rationality as follows: 'The IRS misses nine out of ten shelters. On the tenth, the company pays back taxes and the government agrees to no penalties'. In the Australian context, there appear to be two highly rational strategies if you are a HWI: One is to go to a conservative adviser respected by the ATO who will put you only into tax planning arrangements which have been approved by the Commissioner in a Private Binding or Public Ruling, and who will do that with maximum transparency to the taskforce. The taskforce is therefore likely to assess you as a low risk. But the other rational strategy may be to conceal a highly aggressive tax planning activity so it is most difficult for the ATO to find and then cover it with a (weak) reasonably argued position. If you are unlucky enough to be audited and have it detected, you roll over and pay up quickly so long as there is no penalty in the settlement, or a minimal one. An in-between strategy of a highly visible reasonably argued position, which would have a strong chance of success in the courts (but is rejected by the ATO) is not attractive because you risk the uncertainty, costs and notoriety from fighting the ATO on a test case.

The policy objective we wish to explore is deterring the second strategy so as to encourage the first. This cannot be accomplished through penalties because the probability of a serious penalty is too low when there is some sort of reasonably argued position in relation to a low visibility activity that is unlikely to be scrutinised by an auditor. It can be accomplished, however, by targeting audits and other forms of surveillance on HWIs who use the services of aggressive advisers or promoters. Among other things, these would be advisers and promoters whose clients are frequently found to have activities tucked away, which are defended by a weak reasonably argued position supplied by the adviser. They would have a track record of promoting arrangements that have been disallowed by the Commissioner or struck down by the courts. The idea of this strategy is that clients who wish to avoid the risks and direct costs of an audit, steering their business away from aggressive advisers and promoters, would improve compliance. There are limitations to the strategy. The best tax planning is specifically designed for a HWI and will not be noticed as a problem.

A credible litigation strategy is an imperative to show HWIs that it is not an option to bankroll the government out of enforcement action and that the ATO keeps its promises, even if this requires high litigation expense. Using test cases to develop a strategic case law around Part IVA seems particularly important.

Raising the Bar and Lowering the Costs

For the critics, the expanded return at the heart of the HWI Taskforce risk assessment strategy amounts to saying: 'Give us the haystack and we'll find the needle'. Some advisers argue that what the taskforce should be doing is 'getting their rifle out, not their shotgun'. Advisers generally do not realise that a systematic risk assessment is completed on the information in the expanded return, and a team leader and manager check this assessment with sign-off.

One adviser made the point that the ATO could not do the job of targeting audits for HWIs in a sensible way before the expanded returns were introduced. Audits, as a result, were 'a lottery'. He therefore saw a rationale for continuing the expanded returns on an even wider front than their current coverage:

> The average innocent Australian would have less chance of being audited for the wrong reason.
>
> The questions in the HWI returns are pretty compelling. If everyone, other than PAYE returns, had to declare these things, there would be more compliance.

He illustrated the point with being forced to declare offshore income. He said it was one thing to be in a situation where you can defend a failure to declare something as an oversight. It was another to answer 'No' to that expanded return question on overseas trusts from which you might benefit, when it can be shown later that you knew the answer to be 'Yes'.

> Theoretically, that's go to jail stuff and people want to sleep at night.

Some other advisers made similar points: 'If you have been doing the wrong thing, some of those questions must be difficult to answer'. On this view, the genius of the expanded return is that it puts HWIs in the position where they have to lie outright rather than 'overlook' something. It forces into black and white what had previously been grey. Both conscience and fear of deterrence work better in the realm of black and white than in the realm of grey. This point applies to both HWIs themselves and to their advisers.

The expanded returns also have preventive value. Completing an expanded return reduces the degrees of freedom for redefining income and deductions for the purposes of a subsequent return or audit. We agree with the adviser who argued that this has preventive value in itself. Because HWIs do see the personal and financial costs of being on the expanded return program as something they want to avoid, there is also an opportunity for risk management by setting the standards the taxpayer has to meet to get off the program. One option would be to follow the risk assessment on an expanded return with an interview with the adviser. At that interview it could be common for the analyst to say to the adviser: 'On the basis of our risk assessment we are expecting your client to continue on the expanded return program next year unless her circumstances change so that these compliance risks no longer apply'. Each HWI risk assessment could include a judgment of which compliance risks would have to be removed for the risk assessment to be changed to 'low' (and therefore no expanded return). There could then be some strategic conversations with the HWI adviser about these risks that are keeping the HWI on expanded returns. In some cases agreement could be reached on a compliance management plan for getting off expanded returns.

Conclusion

The HWI Taskforce is tolerated as reasonable by many HWIs, resented by many, loved by none. It imposes considerable costs on taxpayers, which can be somewhat reduced. Overwhelmingly, in the view of advisers, it does its work in a way that complies with the Taxpayers' Charter. Its officers are mostly perceived as fair and professional, though lacking in tax technical skills compared to their opposite numbers.

The taskforce has a daunting job, because non-payment of tax occurs on a wide scale among HWIs and the Australian community and their political leaders are sensitive to this fact. A globalisation of tax hustling by aggressive promoters may unsettle a lot of the inertia that delivered voluntary compliance in the past. At the top of the market, their entrepreneurship with new financial products can be technically dazzling.

The fact of life is that if you are rich enough and aggressive enough, it is not necessary to pay much tax. Legal penalties are important and lower than they should be. But even if they were dramatically increased, legal penalties could never on their own make it rational to pay the level of tax that Parliament and the people expect the rich to pay. If revenue is escaping out of four open windows, closing three of them might simply see more flowing out the fourth, or a fifth window being prized open. This is not to say that it is impossible to achieve improved levels of taxpaying through a combination of measures. If the Commissioner works tirelessly at closing every window through which the revenue escapes as soon as he sees it, the returns to tax planning will fall because the high costs of developing shelters will pay returns for shorter periods. Combine this with inertia, the threat of expanded return oversight, audits, penalties, the desire of many for the quiet life free of governmental hassles, the desire of many others to pay their fair share, to eschew a self-image as a cheat, to sleep well at night, and the result can be an improvement of compliance, especially if all these levers are used in a way that is perceived as fair. Indeed, the taskforce does seem to have succeeded in incrementally improving compliance among those subject to its work, as evidenced by the jump in the tax paid by HWI-controlled private companies from substantially below to substantially above that of non-HWI private companies.

There is evidence from many areas of compliance with law of a tipping point phenomenon. Failure to meet the law's obligations becomes so widespread that enforcement authorities effectively give up, and have little choice but to do so, given the enormity of the task. Mark Kleiman (1993) calls it enforcement swamping, a phenomenon widely observed with drug-selling hot-spots in the US. Where the capacity for the police to enforce the law is fixed, a rise in crime in the neighbourhood reduces the punishment per offence. This lower level of punishment attracts new offenders. Enforcement swamping arises where enforcement capabilities fall too low to prevent this positive feedback cycle. Arguably the ATO had an enforcement swamping crisis with HWIs in the 1970s and early 1980s and is at some risk of descending into that situation today because of global pressures. Equally, there is encouraging evidence of the HWI Taskforce tipping the balance somewhat toward compliance. This perspective means that the nihilism of saying that the closing of three windows will simply see revenue rush out a fourth is quite misguided. The eternal vigilance of pushing windows shut as quickly as possible is critical to fending off enforcement swamping in an environment where this is an emergent risk.

The taskforce seems well designed to meet this formidable challenge. Purists might say enforcement should be targeted on individual and corporate taxpayers. I would say, in contrast, that enforcement should be focused on strategic foci of decision-making. HWIs that control many entities, the tax managers of large corporations, influential advisers and promoters are all examples of priority foci of enforcement effort. In establishing the HWI Taskforce, Australia has sensibly abandoned a simplistic purism in favour of targeting nodes of control over decisions of major import for tax compliance. It would be a policy error to take this pressure off.

Viewing compliance through the eyes of the advisers has enabled us to see that the taskforce is applying the ATO Compliance Model in a sophisticated way. We have seen that the understanding taxpayer behaviour part of the Compliance Model does require more sophisticated micro-macro analysis based on the HWI system. Building community partnerships can be strengthened by various improved communication strategies with advisers. The whole idea of the taskforce is a paragon of flexibility in ATO operations to encourage and support compliance. And finally, we have sought to develop some ideas for more and escalating regulatory options to enforce compliance, though perhaps the most important suggestion here amounts to the de-escalation of getting off the expanded return program in exchange for compliance undertakings.

Notes

1 The ATO acknowledges the comments made in this chapter and notes that they relate to past practices employed by the HWI Taskforce. The processes employed by the HWI Taskforce have significantly changed and the taskforce has implemented recommendations outlined in the report.

2 My gratitude to the HWI advisers, officers of professional associations and ATO staff who contributed to this research. I must say I was impressed by their professionalism. I especially want to thank Alice Dobes who participated in almost all the interviews conducted for the research and was a constant source of sound advice as were Andrew Stout and Kevin Fitzpatrick.

3 The main area of contingency fee usage in the past seems to have been with firms that offer to apply for refunds of sales tax in return for a fee of, say, 20 per cent of the refund.

4 In any case, within the Australian market, an adviser 'looking at the ball from different angles, will often come up with an opportunity for one client. Then he applies it to a few more clients. Then the idea might get out and some financial planner or little accountant might market it widely'.

5 The 'credibility and respectability' of investment banks with HWIs, as one adviser put it in our interview.

References

Braithwaite, J. (Chapter 9, this volume), 'Large Business and the Compliance Model'.

Kleiman, M. (1993), 'Enforcement Swamping: A Positive-feedback Mechanism in Rates of Illicit Activity', *Mathematical Computer Modeling*, vol. 17, pp. 65-75.

Levi, M. (1988), *Of Rule and Revenue,* University of California Press, Berkeley.

Lind, A.E. and Tyler, T.R. (1998), *The Social Psychology of Procedural Justice*, Plenum Press, New York.

Makkai, T. and Braithwaite, J. (1996), 'Procedural Justice and Regulatory Compliance', *Law and Human Behaviour*, vol. 20, pp. 83-98.

Novack, J. and Saunders, L. (1998), 'The Hustling of X Rated Shelters', *Forbes*, 14 December, pp. 2-3.

Picotto, S. (1996), *International Business Taxation*, Weidenfeld and Nicolson, London.

Ralph Report (1999), *A Tax System Redesigned: More Certain, Equitable and Durable*. Report of the Review of Business Taxation, Commonwealth of Australia, Canberra.

Revenue Canada (1996), *RC4024 The Audit Protocol*, Revenue Canada, Ottawa.

Slemrod, J. (1996), 'Tax Cacophony and the Benefits of Free Trade', in J. Bhagwati and R.E. Hudec (eds), *Fair Trade and Harmonization: Prerequisites for Free Trade?* (Vol. I), MIT Press, Cambridge, pp. 283-309.

Tomasic, R. and Pentony, B. (1990), 'Defining Acceptable Tax Conduct: The Role of Professional Advisers in Tax Compliance', Progress Report to the Criminology Research Council, Australian Institute of Criminology, Canberra.

Tyler, T.R. (1990), *Why People Obey Law*, Yale University Press, New Haven.

Tyler, T.R. (1998), 'Trust and Democratic Governance', in V. Braithwaite and M. Levi, (eds), *Trust and Governance*, Russell Sage Foundation, New York, pp. 269-94.

Tyler, T.R. and Dawes, R.M. (1993), 'Fairness in Groups: Comparing the Self-interest and Social Identity Perspectives', in B.A. Mellers and J. Baron (eds), *Psychological Perspectives on Justice: Theory and Applications*, Cambridge University Press, Cambridge, pp. 87-108.

Chapter 13

Tax System Integrity and Compliance: The Democratic Management of the Tax System

Valerie Braithwaite[1]

This book analyses taxpaying and tax collecting from a relational perspective. Together the chapters provide insight into how each side in this relationship perceives the other, what each expects and what each gives at a time when the tax authority is moving from a command and control mode of operation to one that is more responsive to the environment in which it must operate. The focus has been on compliance, that is, the extent to which taxpayers do what is expected of them and are prepared to cooperate with the authority. But if taxpayers offer compliance, what does the tax authority offer in return?

The usual answer to this question is government services. While not underestimating their importance, this representation of the obligations on the other side of the contractual arrangement risks narrowing our sensibilities to things that we can buy, in theory, in the market place. Governments supply much more than this:

> Somewhat ironically, the continued ability of citizens to act collectively in pursuing their common social and economic goals through democratically elected governments might rest with the ability of tax departments to meet the challenges to tax compliance posed by the disappearing taxpayer. That is to say, what is at stake in the challenge of tax compliance is not just tax revenues, it is democracy itself (Brooks, 1998, p. 33).

Governments are the guardians of democracy, the repository of collective conscience and wisdom for how the democracy should grow, and the decision makers on how the democracy will adapt to the rapid social and technological change accompanying globalisation. In return for taxes, taxpayers should not only receive goods and services, but also sound governance that is respectful and protective of democratic principles and processes.

The capacity of a government to deliver this outcome is referred to here as integrity. If taxpayers offer compliance, the tax office, as part of government, should reciprocate with integrity. This concluding chapter examines the interplay of compliance and integrity in the taxation context. In the first two sections, working definitions of integrity and compliance are developed. Next, the relationship between compliance and integrity is explored under conditions where efforts are made to take on board the perspective of citizens and under conditions where such considerations are marginalised. The argument developed is that integrity and compliance are most likely to be optimised when a tax authority pursues a citizen-inclusive approach to compliance through policies that encourage dialogue and persuasion, combined with an effective mix of incentives and sanctions. Integrity and compliance are most at risk of parting ways when a tax authority seeks to improve compliance solely through making changes to the administrative or legal infrastructure without regard to the sensibilities of citizens. Finally, the chapter offers some preliminary principles to guide the process of tax reform in a way that puts compliance and integrity at minimal risk. In so doing, recognition is given to the need to take account of the views of experts as well as citizens. In other words, a process of tax re-design must recognize the importance of engagement with the community's perspective,[2] as well as with expert advice from those who know the intricacies of tax law and legal proceedings, of data bases and storage systems, of auditing and enforcement practices, and of taxation's impact on government policy and the well-being of the democracy.

Defining Tax System Integrity

In recent years, the concept of integrity has been extended from the individual to the collective level (Skidmore, 1995; Laufer, 1996). Organisations are said to display integrity when they demonstrate a capacity to engage in ethical decision-making. This capacity involves an awareness of the moral issues in play, an openness to grapple with their complexity, resolve to embed moral responsibilities within business plans, and the follow through to put morally responsible decisions into practice (see Petrick and Quinn, 2000). Nowhere is the tension between doing what is right and gaining the competitive edge more apparent than in the private sector where profits are the bottom line for success. A diminished capacity for integrity, however, is not unique to the private sector. Public sector organisations are not immune from the problem, although its expression takes a different form (Gregory, 1999; Denhardt and Denhardt, 2000).

A system operating within the public sector can be said to have integrity if it has unity and soundness of purpose, and if it has processes in place to reflect on and evolve that purpose in response to community needs. Unity infers neither singleness of purpose nor institutional simplicity. Instead, it conveys connectedness in that an organisation's many goals are pursued and its many processes are implemented with awareness of and responsiveness to each other. In sum, unity implies at least loose coordination among parts such that, through reasoning and reflectiveness, an operational story can be told as to how the parts combine to form a valuable and purposeful whole.

An absence of integrity on the unity criterion may occur when goals are pursued at lower levels of an organisation that are antithetical to the organisation's overarching goals. An example would be the introduction of a collection system for a specific kind of tax that jeopardised protection of the revenue overall. We might call this integrity strain of a vertical kind in that actions taken at lower levels of the organisation are contrary to those expected at higher levels if the organisation's overarching goals are to be met. At other times, different functional groups at the same level in an organisation may fail to share information and may act in ways that undermine the capacity of the other to meet its objectives. Oversights of this kind describe a shortfall in integrity of a horizontal kind.

While unity conveys some overall coordination of effort, soundness conveys the moral appropriateness of the direction of effort. Within a democracy, the ultimate judge of the soundness of purpose of an institution should be the people. Integrity, in the sense of standing by goals and processes supported by the people, involves not only commitment to the system in its current form, but also commitment to revision of the system so that it can continue to serve those it represents. Service entails responsiveness to government in relation to policy, as well as listening to the community and 'helping citizens articulate and meet their shared interests' (Denhardt and Denhardt, 2000, p. 549).

Unity, soundness of purpose and responsiveness do not in and of themselves satisfactorily denote institutional integrity. Calhoun (1995) has observed that, at the level of the individual, integrity involves more than developing coherent well-reasoned positions on issues and standing by these commitments. Integrity, so conceived, can be deemed self-indulgent. The extra element that needs to be considered to sharpen this analysis of integrity is a social dimension. Integrity requires a person not only 'to stand by' a position, but also 'to stand for' that position when faced with others whose deliberations may have led them to a different outcome (Calhoun, 1995).

When extrapolated to the level of the collective, high integrity involves institutional engagement. But institutions cannot engage: That task must fall to the leadership ranks of the organisation. In the public sector, those with leadership responsibilities demonstrate the integrity of their organisation through communicating to government and the community what they stand for and why it is important. The often-cited public service phrase, 'to give frank and fearless advice to government',[3] exemplifies this aspect of integrity. The institution will fall short on integrity when '[s]ocial circumstances...erect powerful deterrents to speaking and acting on one's own best judgment' and thereby 'undermine the possibilities for deliberating about what is worth doing' (Calhoun, 1995, p. 259). Calhoun hastens to add that while integrity involves having a proper regard for one's own judgment, it should not be conceived as 'just a matter of sticking to one's guns' (p. 259). 'Arrogance', 'bullying', 'defensiveness', 'incivility', 'close-mindedness', and 'deafness to criticism' are not qualities normally associated with integrity. Acknowledging that others 'must themselves abide by their best judgment seems part of, not exterior to, acting with integrity' (p. 260). Integrity, therefore, can pull members of the collective in different directions,[4] creating a diversity of positions and tensions when these differences surface. Consequently, integrity does not imply orderliness in thought and action. On the contrary, it is a concept that reflects capacity to navigate through messiness, showing leadership, while allowing diverse opinions to be expressed, frankly and fearlessly, under an umbrella of an overarching shared purpose, derived through deliberation with citizens.

When this concept of integrity is applied to a tax system, the question arises as to the level at which the analysis should proceed. Should integrity be applied in a more focused way as to how taxpaying records are compiled and used for high wealth individuals, or to the way in which the law is written in relation to business taxation, or to the enforcement practices used by tax office auditors? An analysis of integrity can be undertaken in any of these domains. For the purposes of this chapter, integrity will be discussed at a broader level with reference to the overarching objectives and principles that govern the operation of the tax office.

The purpose of the Australian Taxation Office (ATO) is 'to shape and manage systems which support and fund services for Australians, giving effect to social and economic policy' (Australian Taxation Office, 2000a, p. 2). Associated with this purpose are five guiding principles: (a) to act with integrity; (b) to anticipate, identify and manage issues in real-time; (c) to be open and accountable with each other and clients; (d) to offer solutions that are in the community interest, while matching the individual circumstances of clients; and (e) to meet internal and external obligations (Australian Taxation Office, 2000a, p. 2). To effect these principles, the ATO has 12 standards expressed in the Taxpayers' Charter to guide tax officers in their dealings with taxpayers in the course of administering the tax system (Australian Taxation Office, 1997): Taxpayers are to be treated fairly and reasonably, to have their privacy respected, to be treated as honest in their tax affairs unless the taxpayer acts otherwise, to have decisions explained to them, to be offered assistance, advice, and information in a professional way, and to be helped to minimize their costs in complying with tax law.

Even at the level of general principles and codes of conduct, tensions arise. For example, is maximizing revenue collected 'to support and fund services for Australians' compatible with abiding by the Charter so as to 'be open and accountable'? In theory, the answer is yes, but field staff sometimes appear to be less sure (see Job and Honaker, Chapter 6, this volume). The tension can be illustrated through the following questions: Are authoritarian tactics justified in cases where tax officers are chasing down taxpayers who are evading their tax? Or to put it another way: Are Charter consistent tactics costly for a tax office and the public when dealing with unscrupulous tax evaders?

In order to ease these challenges to system integrity, the ATO adopted their Compliance Model (see Braithwaite, Chapter 1, this volume for a full description). Persuasion and education are the preferred methods for eliciting compliance and are assumed to be the most appropriate starting point for dealing with non-compliance in the absence of information that the wrongdoing is deliberate and likely to be repeated. In this way, the intentions behind the Taxpayers' Charter are put into practice. While education and persuasion denote the preferred starting point, tax officers and taxpayers know of a range of sanctioning options that can be and will be brought into play should taxpayers fail to cooperate. Consistent with the Charter and in keeping with the ATO's obligation to protect the revenue, the Compliance Model puts taxpayers on notice that tax officers will systematically increase the costs of non-compliance, while always holding the door open for a more responsive and cooperative relationship. In this way, the Compliance Model guides the ATO toward using its full enforcement capacity only when taxpayers have clearly or repeatedly signalled unwillingness to cooperate.

At the level of principles and codes of practice, the integrity story within the ATO is quite impressive. But action does not flow directly from these principles and codes. There is another plank that is necessary to define the way in which tax officers and taxpayers should interact in pursuit of the ultimate goal of supporting the Australian democracy, tax law. Tax law provides the rules that determine taxpayer obligations and the enforcement capabilities of tax officers. In most areas of this large body of law, it is difficult to find principles or guidelines that provide a meaningful template for making sense of these rules, and linking them to the other components of the system (Braithwaite, 2002). Furthermore, there is no evidence of a shared understanding between citizens and their elected representatives about how and why these rules evolve as they do (Ralph Report, 1999). In addition to the rules derived from tax law and ATO rulings, there are rules entrenched in the administrative system that define the work roles of staff, the reward structures of the organisation, record keeping and data storage capacities, and the reasons for and methods of communicating with taxpayers. Communication revolves around an elaborate system of automatically generated letters to taxpayers to inform them of their obligations, to query their actions, to deliver refunds and payments, to communicate failure to comply, and to impose penalties, all of which have an institutional history of their own.

These legal and administrative rules, some formal and some informal, are the centrepiece of operations for the Australian Taxation Office, and for the most part predate overarching objectives, the Taxpayers' Charter and the ATO Compliance Model. One might postulate that in a large bureaucracy, such as a tax authority, practices are more likely to flow from the institutionalised formal and informal rules, and less likely to flow from semi-detached blue prints introduced relatively recently in the history of the organisation to give it greater legitimacy in the eyes of the public. This means that the main challenge for a tax authority seeking institutional integrity is to convert democratically responsive principles of action into concrete operations and routines in the day-to-day practices of tax officers. This is the same challenge faced by corporations seeking regulatory integrity through turning their regulatory blueprints into meaningful practices (Parker, 2002). One of the central propositions of this chapter is that just as regulators look for substantive compliance in the actions of those they regulate, citizens look for substantive integrity in the authorities that seek to direct their actions.

The integrity that taxpayers observe in the tax system and its administration may not be the same as the integrity that tax officers see from within. When integrity is perceived to exist in the system by tax officials and those who are experts in its operation, it may be claimed that the system has passed the test of internal integrity. In the eyes of those who know the system well, the components are connected in such a way that high performance in one part enhances, or at least does not detract from performance in other parts, the overall purpose is sound, and the organisation is responsive, able to evolve to meet community needs. A system that is supported by a democracy, however, has to be accountable to the electorate. External integrity is, therefore, equally important and involves an additional level of scrutiny. Citizens must be able to observe integrity in the way in which the tax system is designed and operates, and in the way in which the tax authority deals with citizens and other branches of government.

Whether the perspective is internal or external, finding holes in the integrity of a complex system is always going to be relatively easy. Furthermore, to conceive of social systems without a good proportion of messiness is unrealistic and undesirable if any kind of innovation or social change is to occur. Thus, integrity should not be reduced to a score out of 10 on a checklist. The key to assessing the integrity of an organisation does not lie in how problem free the organisation claims to be; but rather it lies in the organisation's capacity to acknowledge difficulties. Where integrity is present, the organisation should be able to demonstrate awareness of and deliberation about departures from the standard, and how the actions taken to improve the situation were in the interests of sound democratic governance.

With this in mind, the focal point for analysis in the remainder of this chapter will be one particular kind of strain on integrity in tax offices worldwide; that which occurs when overall integrity is pitted against compliance. This problem is likely to be particularly acute for all regulatory agencies where short-term gains threaten long-term interests. The pursuit of short-term gains puts citizens and authorities at loggerheads. For citizens, integrity is what is expected of an authority at all times. For tax authorities, on the other hand, the day-to-day business is ensuring citizen compliance. At the organisational coalface, as performance targets are being set for a workforce, compliance is more tightly bound to the tax authority's short-term interests than integrity. Integrity comes into focus when there is time to stand back and consider long-term interest. Integrity also increases in salience, relative to compliance, when a tax office's accountability is called into question, or when legitimacy is called into play to deal with change or failure in the system.

What Does it Mean to Comply?

When direct requests are made of individuals, they may behave in accordance with the requests or not. In the first instance, we witness compliance, in the second, non-compliance (Deaux and Wrightsman, 1988). While the concept is an easy one to understand, it is not as easy to assess. Whether or not a person does what is asked of him or her is not always visible. Furthermore, whether or not a person interprets the request in accordance with its intent is sometimes far from certain.

These problems escalate when the requests for compliance are backed by law, or are made by authorities with the power to sanction compliance and non-compliance. Under such circumstances, non-compliance is far from being as uncomplicated as just saying 'no'. The line between compliance and coercion for an individual faced with a request from an authority with enforcement capacity becomes blurred. In such circumstances, individuals may have no choice but to meet the request, and if they do have choice, they are likely to have a vested interest in keeping their non-compliance out of the view of the authority. Whether or not they acknowledge non-compliance to others or even themselves will depend on contextual and individual factors. The social process of finding justifications for non-compliance through searching for legal loopholes or proclaiming ignorance complicates the picture even further (see McBarnet, Chapter 11, this volume). Assessing, even defining compliance, slips further from reach.

Difficulties of this kind are common to all compliance research. In the domain of taxation, a third problem warrants serious consideration: Are individuals aware that a direct request to follow tax law has been made to them, and do they have sufficient legal literacy to understand the request? As the law becomes more and more complicated, and as taxpayers turn to tax agents to do their tax for them (77% of Australians use a tax agent (Australian Taxation Office, 2002)), questions can be raised justifiably as to whether or not individuals are aware of their tax obligations (Coleman and Freeman, 1997; Inglis, 2002). Thus, in the area of the payment of income tax by the ordinary taxpayer, we might ask, are the requests received by the taxpayer, is attention paid to such requests, and if so, are the requests understood and remembered for future reference?

This complexity in defining and assessing compliance is represented diagrammatically below. For the moment, let us put to one side the fact that an authority does not issue one request but many, and that there may be third parties such as tax agents who moderate the relationship. In spite of the fact that the elements of compliance that remain in Figure 13.1 represent a simplified regulator-regulatee exchange, the diagram serves the purpose of uncovering the changing face of compliance across a complex set of enmeshed institutions that comprise a tax authority. In the process, insight can be gained into how the pursuit of compliance outcomes in different parts of the organisation can instigate responses within the tax authority and within government that may erode the integrity of the tax system overall.

Figure 13.1 represents compliance outcomes from the perspective of the regulator and the perspective of the regulatee. Behind each perspective is a culture relating to tax collection and taxpaying. The degree to which these cultures are compatible reflects the quality of the dialogue that has taken place between government, tax authorities and citizens. These cultures can comfortably coexist, or they can be sites of serious conflict, depending on circumstances. Periods of social change and tax reform define occasions when dialogue about the tax system needs to take place in a way that is inclusive of all interest groups, not just those elites who appreciate the finer details of tax law and tax administration. At intervals, tax systems must be taken to the polity for discussion in accordance with the best practices of democratic deliberation.

At the coalface, however, issues of shared understanding about the purposes of the tax system are not at the forefront of anyone's thinking; the issue at stake is compliance – will she or will she not, is she or is she not complying with the law? From the perspective of the regulator or tax officer in Figure 13.1, a direct request for an action to be undertaken must be made to the regulatee or the

Shared understanding of taxation in the democracy ⟷ Taxpayer culture

Tax office culture

		Request received as intended		Request acted on as intended	
		yes	no	yes	no
Compliance requested	yes	on track	compliance failure	on track	compliance failure
	no	bonus	system failure	bonus	system failure
Compliance visible	yes	on track	compliance/ system failure	compliance	compliance/ system failure
	no	blackhole with hope	blackhole without hope	blackhole with hope	blackhole without hope

Figure 13.1 Possible outcomes when tax office capacities are matched with taxpayer capacities

taxpayer. Reasons for the non-occurrence of the request might be that the regulator did not make it clear what action was required (the request was too vague or complex) or the request did not reach the target (e.g., a letter was sent to the wrong address, or was not sent at all). The regulator, having made the request, then has an interest in knowing if the regulatee has complied. The required response, therefore, may be one that is visible to the regulator (the regulator can confirm that the correct amount of tax has been paid or that a return has been lodged) or not visible (the regulator cannot routinely check on whether action has been taken, as in declaring cash income).

From the perspective of the regulatee or the taxpayer, the compliance question can be subdivided into two components: (a) receiving the request and processing it cognitively as the regulator expects, and (b) acting upon the request in the way the regulator expects. Failure to receive the request as intended might occur if the taxpayer has inadvertently misinterpreted the request (e.g., misunderstanding the difference between franked and unfranked dividends), or if the regulatee gives the request meaning that undermines the intent of the regulator (e.g., playing for the grey in tax law). Similarly, a failure to act upon the request, as when a tax return is filled out incorrectly, may be due to misunderstanding or carelessness, or it may be a case of just 'saying no'.

As we focus on each of the 16 cells in Figure 13.1, the many faces of compliance from an administrative perspective become apparent. If we look for the cells in which compliance is 'on track' or 'achieved', we find only four of the 16 possible outcomes meeting the criteria of success. The majority of the possible outcomes deviate from the classic case of compliance.

Taking the 'on track' or 'achieved' compliance outcomes first, it is helpful to ground the discussion by considering the types of tasks undertaken by a tax authority that come closest to meeting the specified criteria of a request being made and received as intended, and being visibly acted on as intended. One such example would be declaring bank interest on an income tax return. Data matching with bank records makes it possible for tax officers to keep a close eye on interest declaration for tax purposes. For the tax officer responsible for monitoring compliance of this kind, attention is likely to focus on detail, such as the integrity of the data bases used to match records and tweaking the system to catch those few who are slipping through the net. Compliance questions are likely to take the following form: Can detection rates be improved? Can data on non-compliance be matched with data of other kinds of non-compliance? Should the taxpayer be relied upon to self-report on tax matters and self-assess his/her tax contribution? It is equally valid to ask how reliable is the official data on non-compliance that is stored by the tax authority? What kind of auditing is necessary to ensure that the standards of compliance are maintained at high levels and that the community's standards match those expected by the tax authority? An equally relevant, but less often asked question for tax officers working with 'on track' or 'achieved' compliance, is how can the public be recognized for their cooperation?

Turning to the system failure cells, compliance now has less to do with assessment and more to do with engaging with the taxpayer. System failure occurs when the tax office has not made a direct request to the taxpayer concerning her obligations. In these cases, compliance means getting people to do something that they have not been doing 'naturally' either because it never entered their heads or because they chose not to do it. In addressing system failure, the focus of attention is likely to be on communication of the message. The clarity of the request, the educational apparatus supporting the request, and the political intent behind the message are important issues for consideration. Whenever questions are raised about system effectiveness, reasonable doubt also is raised over the extent to which a regulatee should be held responsible for non-compliance.

Compliance failure, on the other hand, is likely to be addressed in different ways from system failure. If the system appears to be working well from a communication perspective, non-compliance can be dealt with in either of two ways. One option is to listen to the community and understand the grounds of resistance so that changes can be made to policy and practice. As a result, compliance may be made easier for taxpayers, or the costs of non-compliance may be increased through greater surveillance and penalties. Another option is to change tack altogether. This option would not require taxpayers to understand the message. Technology may be used to engineer compliance that has not been forthcoming previously, and is represented in Figure 13.1 as 'bonus' compliance.

The 'bonus' cells are those in which an authority has its messages received and acted upon by a target without the authority having to make a direct request. Architectural strategies (Shearing and Stenning, 1985; Coglianese and Lazer, 2001) may be used by an authority to ensure compliance through making it not only the act of least resistance, but also the act that no longer requires a decision. For example, the provision of software that leads a taxpayer through a series of questions to estimate tax owing creates 'bonus' compliance for an authority in that various options for non-compliance are removed from consideration. This is not to deny the possibility of creative compliance while using the software package, but rather to recognize the non-compliance that is avoided through a process that generates compliance among taxpayers prepared to engage with a tax authority on 'automatic pilot'. The key compliance questions in these circumstances are big picture questions concerning legitimacy: Will segments of the population take exception to the technological imposition of compliance and challenge the authority of the tax office as a result? Or is architecturally guided compliance seen as a time saving and security oriented device that serves everyone's interests well?

Increasingly, tax officials are searching for ways of combining architectural regulatory strategies with 'natural systems' for 'best practice'. For instance, computer software that has the primary purpose of helping a small business owner manage the business better may also produce information for tax purposes, together with instructions on how to compile these data to meet tax reporting requirements. Key questions emerging from this perspective include how 'best practice' is learnt, how requests from regulators can be re-phrased to reflect 'best practice', and how compliance costs can be reduced for both regulatees and regulators.

'Bonus' compliance is an outcome that in itself has many facets. Other strategies that can be used by a tax authority to cultivate the growth of 'bonus' compliance involve reliance on principle versus rule based law (Braithwaite, 2002), or support for professional codes of practice for tax agents and tax lawyers (National Review of Standards for the Tax Profession, 1994). In these circumstances, the application of principles and codes can frame cognitive processing, steering taxpayers and their agents away from risky schemes that are on the border of avoidance and evasion.

The remaining cells in Figure 13.1 are called 'black holes' because regulators cannot see what becomes of their requests for compliance. In these circumstances, what it means to comply is the single most important question asked by the regulator. Tax officers search for imperfect indicators that will cast light on whether or not a response has been made to the request, and the options must be evaluated in terms of their relative merits. These are the circumstances where tax officials rely on informants or third parties to report wrongdoing that comes to their attention, and scan data bases in their search for inconsistent patterns that may flag cases of concealed tax evasion.

Among the options to be considered by administrators who oversee compliance problems of this kind is transferring responsibility for monitoring compliance to another party, possibly even the regulatee. Under these circumstances, regulatees would be accountable to the regulator through having procedures in place to regulate their own compliance, in other words, demonstrable self-regulation. In many complex areas of regulation, regulators require regulatees to outline their in-house strategies for managing risk instead of searching for compliance with externally imposed standards (Grabosky, 1995; Gunningham and Grabosky, 1998; Braithwaite and Williams, 2001).

Different facets of compliance – assessing compliance outcomes for accuracy, defining at least partially relevant outcomes where none are visible, evaluating the delivery of the request, understanding the 'no' response, and capitalising on 'bonus' compliance – are of interest across the tax office, but differ in their importance and relevance, depending on the nature of the request and the required response. Those with responsibility for the cash economy are likely to focus on 'black holes' and be drawn toward the re-design of the tax system to introduce greater transparency and accountability, and the co-option of other regulatory agencies to assist in monitoring and containment (Cash Economy Task Force, 1998). Tax officers dealing with large business might see playing for the grey as their major problem, an example of compliance failure that might be dealt with through developing better intelligence systems, targeting audits more effectively, and building capacity to elicit cooperative taxpaying behaviour (Braithwaite, Chapter 9, this volume). Wage and salary earners who invest in mass marketed tax avoidance schemes present another kind of challenge to a tax authority. Tax officers struggle with system and compliance failure tangled together so tightly that the way forward is uncertain (Senate Economics References Committee, 2001). The priorities are likely to involve tightening laws, building alliances with professional bodies, educating the public, and amending tax returns. Penalties in such circumstances become a regulatory tool that can have mixed results: A penalty indicates seriousness of an offence to the community, but in such circumstances penalties can create a backlash of cries of unfairness that might slow the process of reform (Hobson, 2002; Murphy, 2002a, 2002b). Ordinary taxpayers, on the other hand, who lodge their tax returns late, fail to declare income and over-claim deductions present the most straightforward compliance problem for tax administrators. It is not surprising that tax officers regard compliance in this context as a question of the taxpayer not showing due care; a problem that is most times dealt with through the application of appropriate penalties to impress upon taxpayers the need to give tax matters their most serious attention in the future.

The above discussion illustrates how understanding and improving compliance requires a tax authority to entertain multiple conceptions of compliance and to be able to change the frame of analysis for a compliance problem as attention moves from one area to another, that is, from personal income tax, to large corporate tax, to small business, to the cash economy, for example. For this reason, the question of finding strategies to improve compliance is one that, in the first instance, is best answered at the local level. Field operatives have the intelligence to analyse compliance problems in terms of the request and action framework provided in Figure 13.1; and furthermore, they have the experiential base for compiling a rich array of creative and workable interventions to deal with the problems they have observed. For tax administrations that are risk averse and that traditionally operate within hierarchical structures, devolving problem solving to local areas is a radical proposal (Job and Honaker, Chapter 6, this volume). Yet, as Sparrow (2000) has pointed out, tax administrations have started to grapple with this challenge and have produced evidence that institutional change is possible. Through setting up special purpose task forces that draw on the local knowledge of field staff and bring together an effective skill mix from different sources, strategies for improving compliance in relation to specific problems have been found.

Improvements in compliance are among the major yardsticks used by tax authorities and their governments to assess their performance. Commonly, compliance gains are considered against compliance costs, which refer to the financial and opportunity costs of compliance borne by taxpayers and tax officers. But there also may be a cost to the integrity of the tax system. Compliance gains may mean integrity loss, at least in the view of the public.

To understand the compliance integrity trade-off, consider the following example, one that is currently eating away at the hearts and minds of ordinary Australians (see Braithwaite, Reinhart, Mearns and Graham, 2001). While tax officers dealing with personal income tax scrutinize data sets to identify irregularities in self-assessed tax returns, tax officers dealing with large corporates and high wealth individuals work to establish cooperative relationships with their clientele in order to collect at least some tax from those who have the capacity to avoid paying any tax at all (Australian Taxation Office, 2000b). From a local compliance perspective, both components of the system, that is the personal tax and large business lines, work well in achieving their goals. For personal tax, data matching software increases the revenue collected at minimal cost to the tax office. A letter is issued informing the taxpayer that their tax assessment has been amended, in all likelihood with an invoice for tax owing plus interest and a penalty. The taxpayer can contest the assessment, but in all likelihood the taxpayer will defer to tax office authority. In the large business line, however, the interaction between taxpayer and tax officer is likely to take a different course. For large corporations, negotiation and regulatory conversation triggered by lawyers' letters will often be necessary to ensure that at least some tax is collected at regular intervals.

The important point to note here is that there is soundness in operations within each of these functional lines in the tax office: There is a consistent compliance goal operating in each part, that is, to maximize the revenue collected as efficiently as possible, given the context. The contexts, of course, differ substantially. Different types of tax are collected, different laws are applicable, and the resources available to take advantage of legal complexity and ambiguity are far greater among corporates than among ordinary taxpayers. At the local level, the compliance activities of tax officers working in personal tax and those in corporate tax seem defensible and reasonable. But there may be an unseen cost to the tax office overall, that is, a perceived loss of institutional integrity.[5]

The Compliance Integrity Dilemma

Compliance is a localized problem: Integrity involves the whole organisation. How then can a bridge be built between compliance and integrity? Some insight into the barriers to building such a bridge is gleaned when we look at Figure 13.1 as a blueprint for change. Let us assume that a change is made to the administrative and legal system represented in the left hand column of the diagram: A decision is made to improve compliance through making the request clearer to taxpayers. For instance, a new taxpayers' contract is introduced that lists, in painstaking detail, the actions that a taxpayer must take to demonstrate compliance with the tax office and the actions that taxpayers may expect from tax officers as they seek compliance from citizens. In Figure 13.1, this initiative would increase the proportion of citizens who are receiving a direct request to comply from the tax authority, and the dotted line would be expected to move down, indicating an increase in the proportion of people who are 'on track' for compliance (in the top row of Figure 13.1). But the outcome that is likely to be expected by the tax authority is a little different. The rationale for such a change is likely to be that once instructions about what everyone does are clearly articulated, compliance will improve overall. Figure 13.1 can be used to illustrate that tax office expectations need not necessarily become a reality.

The increase in direct requests that elicits 'on track' compliance brings with it a reduction in the 'bonus' compliance cells. What does this mean for a tax authority? Much depends on how taxpayers respond. For instance, a segment of the population may come to realize that their compliance has been engineered by the design of the tax system. They recognize their own 'bonus'compliance, absorb the new ground rules for engaging with the tax office, and decide that their past compliance is a gift that they would rather not give. Other unexpected changes may ensue. Taxpayers generally may not respond cooperatively to the new contract. They may not interpret the message as intended and instead adopt a literalist interpretation that results in challenges to the legitimacy of the tax office's actions in a range of areas. Or taxpayers simply may take exception to the terms of the new contract, and refuse to comply in the future.

Similar risks come into play when changes to the administrative and legal system result in compliance becoming more visible to tax officers (the bottom two rows of Figure 13.1). Greater visibility improves 'on track' compliance. An example of such a change was the introduction of a Goods and Services Tax (GST) in Australia in July 2001 which was implemented with the intention of improving the Australian Taxation Office's capacity to track business transactions. Administrative and legal tax reform of this kind can, in theory, contain growth in some parts of the cash economy. But with increased visibility, the magnitude of 'on track' compliance, system failure and compliance failure all increase. In order to obtain the expected compliance outcome, a tax office needs organisational capacity to follow through on all three issues. If there are impediments to enforcing the law when evasion is exposed, the supposed effectiveness of the change to the administrative and legal system leaves much to be desired.

None of this is to suggest that changes to the administrative and legal system should not occur. Change of this kind is necessary if the tax system is to evolve in response to the environment in which it operates. Such changes and their impacts dominate analyses of how well tax systems are functioning, not least of all because after-effects are often unexpected and complex. But as Figure 13.1 demonstrates, the unexpected and complex outcomes, while difficult to manage, are not a complete mystery. In large part, they lie in a failure to understand the second system shaping the compliance encounter, the human system or more specifically, the taxpayers' culture.

If the vertical dotted lines in Figure 13.1 are moved to the right, the compliance cells increase in size, and the system failure and compliance failure cells are reduced in size. This means an increase in those who understand the request from the tax office and in those willing to act on that request in a cooperative manner. Many of the papers in this volume are supportive of the proposition that outcomes of this kind are achieved through direct intervention in the human system, that is, going further than changing law and administrative procedures to improving the quality of the relationship between the tax office and the taxpayer. Actions might include the tax authority being reasonable and clear in its day-to-day communication with taxpayers, listening to taxpayers, treating them with respect, responding to concerns, and following through purposefully to elicit compliance. Those who engage with the human dimension of compliance in this relational way are likely to reap a double reward. As tax officers listen to taxpayers to better understand the reasons that underlie resistance to compliance, it is unlikely that the feedback they receive is solely related to their localized compliance problem. The functional lines of a tax office are meaningful within the organisation to those familiar with its operations, but are relatively meaningless to most outsiders who are likely to see the tax office and the tax system as one entity. Thus, while listening to the taxpaying community, taxpayers are faced with a reality that is not bounded by a localized compliance problem, and in the process find a bridge to engage with the broader issue of institutional integrity. They learn, through the eyes of those outside, how a localized compliance problem sits alongside compliance problems elsewhere in the organisation to create a picture of institutional integrity overall.

In summary, from a tax office perspective, administrative and legal system management (as represented in the left column of Figure 13.1), involving changes to the way messages are given and responses are monitored, create a complex mix of compliance outcomes for the organisation, as well as various challenges to the integrity of the tax system. In contrast, interventions in human management to improve taxpayers' readiness to cooperate with the tax office (as represented in the top row of Figure 13.1) are more uniform in their effects. Through building more cooperative relationships with taxpayers, tax officials can reasonably hope for improved compliance, as well as improvements in how the tax system is perceived from outside, that is, in its external integrity. Winning approval of this kind in the community may be particularly helpful when a tax system is forced to change through external pressures such as globalisation. Arguably, a community will be more forgiving of a high integrity system struggling to adapt to change than of a low integrity system placed under pressure from outside.

Compliance and integrity may be more likely to be mutually supportive when tax design deliberations are inclusive of the human system, but it should not be assumed that regulatory conversations of this kind are conflict free. There is an assumption, however, that out of this conflict will emerge acceptance, if not consensus, about how the tax system should evolve. Survey research in Australia during the period of the introduction of a Goods and Services Tax (GST) is supportive of this analysis (Braithwaite et al., 2001). Taxation, while not popular, is generally accepted as a social benefit. Resistance was a common enough response to the tax system in the Australian population (55%), but cynicism in the form of disengagement from the system was contained to a small proportion of the population (7%) (see Braithwaite, Chapter 2, this volume). These findings would lead us to expect some conflict in deliberations about taxation with a significant proportion placing themselves publicly in opposition to the tax office. But because most people are committed to a tax system in general, a process of genuine deliberation will build legitimacy in the long run as the authority demonstrates integrity and citizens accept their obligations to pay tax.

Hostility from taxpayers because the relationship with the tax authority is poor provides one reason why tax authorities need to be ever vigilant that their actions consistently convey soundness of purpose. Failure to communicate and critically analyse soundness of purpose occurs most dramatically in the public view when compliance is prioritized by the organisation above overall integrity. Admittedly, setting priorities for compliance management is not left to chance by any tax authority and remains the subject of much deliberation and debate at the senior levels of the organisation and of government. The question, however, remains: How should trade-offs be made that maximize revenue gained from compliance activities while protecting the integrity of the tax system?

Conclusion

The above analysis reveals why finding the optimal mix of compliance and integrity is no easy task. At the end of the day, the quality of the solution to a compliance integrity dilemma rests on the experience and wisdom of senior bureaucrats. What the above analysis can offer, however, are three principles that may be useful in understanding how good decisions come to be made by senior tax managers when a compliance integrity dilemma arises.

First and foremost, both compliance and integrity can be boosted by investing in the human dimension of taxpayer management. Fundamentally, this means making a concerted effort to build a shared understanding with the community about what a tax system does and how it is best designed. Taxpayer management extends from the general to the specific. At the general level is the task of educating the community about the importance of a tax system and persuading them of its value. Outlining the principles for and methods of tax collection for the public and committing the organisation to the effective monitoring of compliance are further steps that a tax authority can take in an effort to win public support and establish a cooperative and responsive relationship with the community at large. At a more specific level, taxpayer management involves not only the pronouncement of how tax law is being interpreted, but also accessible explanations for these decisions, along with discussions of penalties and settlement options.

In all these ventures, responsiveness to community concerns is a key feature of effective taxpayer management. Responsiveness means listening, and publicly acknowledging and resolving identified problems. Taxpayer concerns should be taken seriously and engaged with openly, inclusively and thoughtfully against the backdrop of basic system goals and principles. Sometimes, the result may be a change in tax office policy and practice. Other times, it may be insistence that the tax authority's actions are consistent with principles that the community has and continues to endorse. In no circumstances should responsiveness be interpreted to mean appeasing special interest groups at the expense of system integrity.

Investment in the human management dimension in the long term should give rise to a mutually reinforcing relationship between compliance and integrity. Increased compliance should boost the external integrity of the tax system, and the external integrity of the tax system should encourage compliance. Investment in the human management system or taxpayer culture offers a further bonus to a tax authority facing changes to the administrative and legal system. The coordination of taxpayer management strategies is not only desirable, but also practicable and relatively uncomplicated. Just as it can build cohesion in the community, it can provide a basis for unity in a tax authority as difficult trade-offs are made re-designing the legal and administrative system.

The second principle to emerge is that administrative and legal adaptability is a necessary part of building internal tax system integrity, although the immediate effects on compliance can be uncertain, as can the immediate effects on both internal and external integrity. In such circumstances, tax authorities need to be strategic, taking a long-term view, and putting the infrastructure in place so as to manage unexpected outcomes. Part of being maximally responsive to the environment is having a finely tuned intelligence system and a rich network of support that can be part of the process of testing and redirecting change until an appropriate balance between needs for compliance and integrity are met.

While senior managers must take responsibility for making critical decisions about balancing compliance and integrity, knowledge and understanding of how compliance might be best improved lies in the stories of field staff. It is only through drawing on these stories and opening and acting on communications from the coalface, that senior managers are able to pre-empt the trade-off costs for their organisation. Without bottom-up feedback, top-down management of administrative and legal change is likely to be fraught with difficulties and setbacks. Thus, the third principle emerges, one that involves an integration of compliance and integrity action plans. Through adopting a bottom-up approach that carries tales from the field, tax authorities can develop a range of plans of an administrative and legal nature for improving compliance. From a review of compliance management plans, senior managers can choose a preferred sub-set that will improve compliance outcomes and build tax system integrity. To choose poorly (the top-down process) or to have poor options from which to choose (the bottom-up process) risks long-term damage. Failure to administer the tax system in a way that demonstrates basic respect for the democratic principles of participation and accountability is a dangerous game. A tax authority that de-legitimizes itself in the eyes of citizens limits its effectiveness and short-changes citizens in terms of what they can expect from democracy.

Notes

1 An earlier version of this paper was presented at the 'Compliance Workshop: What Does it Mean to Comply?', organised by the Regulatory Institutions Network, 17 June 2002, Australian National University. My thanks to Barbara Nunn for broadening my perspective on integrity, and to my colleagues, Clifford Shearing, John Braithwaite and Greg Rawlings, for their insightful and constructive criticisms.

2 A distinction is drawn between the community's perspective, within a context where consultation is genuine and inclusive, and the community's reaction, within a context where a change is imposed. Community reaction provides a distorted view of the community perspective because resentment at being excluded from the decision-making process can be mixed with genuine deliberation about the substantive issue.

3 The importance placed on giving frank and fearless advice is reflected in the public service code of conduct (see Australian Public Service Commission, 2000).

4 Integrity can also pull individuals in different directions internally (see Calhoun (1995) and Dobel (1999) for discussions of why integrity is not necessarily at odds with ambivalence, inconsistent actions over time, or value conflicts).

5 *The Community Hopes, Fears and Actions Survey* revealed much less community confidence in the Tax Office's capacity to respond effectively to taxpaying defiance from high wealth individuals and large corporates than to ordinary taxpayers and small business (Braithwaite et al., 2001).

References

Australian Public Service Commission (2000), *Australian Public Service Values*, http://www.apsc.gov.au/publications02/values.htm.

Australian Taxation Office (1997), *Taxpayers' Charter*, Australian Taxation Office, Canberra.

_____ (2000a), *Strategic Statement 2000-2003*, Australian Taxation Office, Canberra.

_____ (2000b), *Cooperative Compliance: Working with Large Business in the New Tax System*, Australian Taxation Office, Canberra.

_____ (2002), *Taxation Statistics 1999-2000*, Commonwealth of Australia, Canberra.

Braithwaite, J. (2002), 'Rules and Principles: A Theory of Legal Certainty', *Australian Journal of Legal Philosophy*, vol. 27, pp. 47-82.

_____ (Chapter 9, this volume), 'Large Business and the Compliance Model'.

Braithwaite, J. and Williams, R. (2001), 'Meta Risk Management and Task System Integrity', *Centre for Tax System Integrity Working Paper No. 23*, The Australian National University, Canberra.

Braithwaite, V. (Chapter 1, this volume), 'A New Approach to Tax Compliance'.

Braithwaite, V. (Chapter 2, this volume), 'Dancing with Tax Authorities: Motivational Postures and Non-compliant Actions'.

Braithwaite, V., Reinhart, M., Mearns, M. and Graham, R. (2001), 'Preliminary Findings from the Community Hopes, Fears and Actions Survey', *Centre for Tax System Integrity Working Paper No. 3*, The Australian National University, Canberra.

Brooks, N. (1998), 'The Challenge of Tax Compliance', in C. Evans and A. Greenbaum (eds), *Tax Administration: Facing the Challenge of the Future*, Prospect Media, St Leonards, pp. 7-33.

Calhoun, C. (1995), 'Standing for Something', *Journal of Philosophy*, vol. XCII(5), pp. 235-60.

Cash Economy Task Force (1998), *Improving Tax Compliance in the Cash Economy*, Australian Taxation Office, Canberra.

Coglianese, C. and Lazer, D. (2001), 'Management-based Regulatory Strategies', Regulatory Policy Program Working Paper RPP-2001-09, Centre for Business and Government, John F. Kennedy School of Government, Harvard University, Cambridge.

Coleman, C. and Freeman, L. (1997), 'Cultural Foundations of Taxpayer Attitudes to Voluntary Compliance', *Australian Tax Forum*, vol. 13, pp. 311-36.

Deaux, K. and Wrightsman, L.S. (1988), *Social Psychology* (5th ed.), Brooks/Cole, Pacific Grove.

Denhardt, R.B. and Denhardt, J.V. (2000), 'The New Public Service: Serving rather than Steering', *Public Administration Review*, vol. 60(6), pp. 549-59.

Dobel, P. (1999) *Public Integrity*, Johns Hopkins University Press, Baltimore.

Grabosky, P. (1995), 'Using Non-governmental Resources to Foster Regulatory Compliance', *Governance: An International Journal of Policy and Administration*, vol. 8(4), pp. 527-50.

Gregory, R.J. (1999), 'Social Capital Theory and Administrative Reform: Maintaining Ethical Probity in Public Service', *Public Administration Review*, vol. 59(1), pp. 63-75.

Gunningham, N. and Grabosky, P. (1998), *Smart Regulation: Designing Environmental Policy*, Clarendon Press, Oxford.

Hobson, K. (2002), 'Say No to the ATO: The Cultural Politics of Protest against the Australian Taxation Office', *Centre for Tax System Integrity Working Paper No.37*, The Australian National University, Canberra.

Inglis, M. (2002), 'Is Self-assessment Working?: The Decline and Fall of the Australian Income Tax System', Paper presented at the 5th International Conference on Tax Administration, ATAX, University of New South Wales, 4-5 April, Sydney.

Job, J. and Honaker, D. (Chapter 6, this volume), 'Short-term Experience with Responsive Regulation in the Australian Taxation Office'.

Laufer, W.S. (1996), 'Integrity, Diligence, and the Limits of Good Corporate Citizenship', *American Business Law Journal*, vol. 34(2), pp. 157- 81.

Murphy, K. (2002a), 'Procedural Justice and the Australian Taxation Office: A Study of Tax Scheme Investors', *Centre for Tax System Integrity Working Paper No. 35*, The Australian National University, Canberra.

_____ (2002b), 'Trust Me, I'm the Taxman: The Role of Trust in Nurturing Compliance', *Centre for Tax System Integrity Working Paper No. 43*, The Australian National University, Canberra.

National Review of Standards for the Tax Profession (1994), *Tax Services for the Public*, Australian Government Publishing Service, Canberra.

Parker, C. (2002), *The Open Corporation: Effective Self-regulation and Democracy*, Cambridge University Press, Cambridge.

Petrick, J.A. and Quinn, J.F. (2000), 'The Integrity Capacity Construct and Moral Progress in Business', *Journal of Business Ethics*, vol. 23(1), pp. 3-18.

Ralph Report (1999), *A Tax System Redesigned: More Certain, Equitable and Durable*. Report of the Review of Business Taxation, Commonwealth of Australia, Canberra.

Senate Economics References Committee (2001), *Inquiry into Mass Marketed Tax Effective Schemes and Investor Protection: Interim Report*, Parliament of the Commonwealth of Australia, Canberra.

Shearing, C.D. and Stenning, P.C. (1985), 'From the Panopticon to Disney World: The Development of Discipline', in A.N. Doob and E.L. Greenspan (eds), *Perspectives in Criminal Law: Essays in Honour of John Ll.J. Edwards*, Canada Law Book, Aurora, pp. 335-49.

Skidmore, M.J. (1995), 'Ethics and Public Service', *The Annals of the American Academy of Political and Social Science*, vol. 537, pp. 25-36.

Sparrow, M. (2000), *The Regulatory Craft*, Brookings Institution Press, Washington D.C.

Index